Managing Uncertainties in Networks

A network approach to problem solving and decision making

D1713722

Public and private sector organizations in our contemporary network society are increasingly faced with controversies over the way the problems they encounter should be handled. Problem solving takes place in complex games and networks in which stakeholders behave strategically, guided by diverging or conflicting perceptions and rules. As a result, problem solving and decision making are dominated by substantive, strategic and institutional uncertainties. Neither scientific research, command and control nor project management strategies provide an adequate response to these uncertainties. Instead they require sophisticated forms of network analysis and network management.

Managing Uncertainties in Networks is a new text that examines developments in the area of network strategy. It provides a conceptual framework to analyse and understand the nature of uncertainties involved in problem solving and decision making in networks. The book presents strategies and management recommendations for public and private sector organizations operating in networks, as well as analytical tools required by practitioners seeking to support their own strategy formulation.

Building on the important and ever-growing literature on uncertainty, decision making and networks, this is a vital and long-awaited staple written by two leading authors in the field. It is key reading for students, scholars and practitioners in business and government, seeking to understand the dynamics of problem solving in network settings.

Joop Koppenjan is Associate Professor at the Faculty of Technology, Policy and Management at Delft University of Technology.

Erik-Hans Klijn is Associate Professor at the Department of Public Administration at Erasmus University of Rotterdam.

Managing Uncertainties in Networks

A network approach to problem solving and decision making

**Joop Koppenjan and
Erik-Hans Klijn**

 Routledge
Taylor & Francis Group

LONDON AND NEW YORK

First published 2004
by Routledge
11 New Fetter Lane, London EC4P 4EE

Simultaneously published in the USA and Canada
by Routledge
29 West 35th Street, New York, NY 10001

Routledge is an imprint of the Taylor & Francis Group

© 2004 Joop Koppenjan and Erik-Hans Klijn

Typeset in Baskerville and Gill Sans by
Florence Production Ltd, Stoodleigh, Devon
Printed and bound in Great Britain by
The Cromwell Press Ltd, Trowbridge, Wiltshire

British Library Cataloguing in Publication Data
A catalogue record for this book is available from the British Library

Library of Congress Cataloging in Publication Data
Koppenjan, Johannes Franciscus Maria, 1955–
   Managing uncertainties in networks: a network approach to
   problem solving and decision making/J.F.M. Koppenjan and E.H. Klijn.
      p. cm.
      Includes bibliographical references and index.
   1. Uncertainty – Social aspects. 2. Complexity (Philosophy)
   3. Social networks. 4. Decision making. I. Klijn, Erik-Hans. II. Title.
   HM291.K666 2004
   301'.01'156–dc22   2003022394

ISBN 0–415–36940–1 (hbk)
ISBN 0–415–36941–X (pbk)

Contents

Illustrations

Figures

Tables

Boxes

Preface

In contemporary network society public and private organizations are challenged by increasingly complex tasks and problems. They are expected to take the lead in solving societal problems (public organizations) or to conduct their business in a socially responsible manner (private organizations) and have to do this in a context that has become substantially more complex in the past several decades. To achieve their objectives and to fulfil their tasks, they are dependent upon a range of other organizations. Firms function as part of larger and sometimes international chains and networks, where they must balance between cooperation and competition when determining their position vis-à-vis other companies. Governments are part of a complex network of organizations and organizational units, within which they must seek to fulfil their tasks. Companies must confer with governments that attempt to regulate their behaviour and have little respect for the pursuit of profit and continuity. In their attempts to regulate society, public parties notice that they are dependent upon companies who have considerable resources at their disposal, follow their own goals and are not just subject to regulation, but try to influence society themselves.

Public and private actors find that dealing with the issues confronting them requires expert knowledge, while at the same time a wide range of stakeholders will wish to participate in the problem solving process. Citizens and clients have become self-aware, make demands and will not take no for an answer. And, always, there is the risk of issues catching the eye of the mass media that enlarges every mistake and publicly calls public or private actors to account for their actions. Nowadays, governments are even being blamed in the media for the rising number of deaths due to high summer temperatures.

The environment is becoming more and more important to organizations. At the same time this ever-present, unavoidable and obstructive environment means that public and private organizations, trying to deal with problems, are increasingly confronted with uncertainty. They are part of wider networks, in which they are dependent upon other actors, whom they cannot control and whose behaviour they don't fully understand and can't predict.

This book is about the implications of uncertainty in our network society for complex problem solving. More specifically: it identifies the kinds of uncertainties governments, private firms and representatives of civil society encounter in their attempts to address the problems they face. What is the nature of these uncertainties? Where do they come from? And how should they be dealt with? The central premise of this book is that conventional methods of addressing uncertainties are far from effective. In fact, they are often counter-productive and lead to controversies, impasses and sub-optimal solutions. Inspired by network theory and ideas of network management we present a framework for an alternative way to look at uncertainties and to address them in a more effective way.

In a previous publication (Kickert, Klijn and Koppenjan, 1997), we wrote that networks can no longer be disregarded in contemporary society and that network theorists must consider it their duty to develop ideas for their management. This attention to the management opportunities of networks was relatively new at that time and contributed to the theoretical and practical value of that study. Seven years later, we can see that the attention to networks and network management has only increased. The same can be said about the relevance of this approach, given the complexity of issues that confront government and private organizations in the network society. At the same time, thinking about and research into network management has developed further.

This book strives to provide a comprehensive overview of these developments. We hope to contribute to the improvement of the ways in which private and public parties approach their environment and to the quality of the processes in which complex problems are dealt with in our society. Thus, we also hope that our book will reach policy makers, managers and advisers in government, business and civil society. Naturally, we also hope that this book will inspire our fellow scientists or at least contribute to further intellectual debate. Above all, this book is meant for students, who are, after all, the future generation of practitioners, advisers and scholars.

Writing a book like this also takes place in an environment. Just as a doctor cannot be trusted to look after his own health, and a teacher should not teach his own child, we probably will not always have managed the uncertainties that arose from our environment properly. Conversely, we are quite certain to have been sources of uncertainty for our environment. We thus wish to express our gratitude to the people surrounding us who, nevertheless, supported the realization of this book.

First, we wish to thank Francesca Poynter and Rachel Crookes of Routledge for the enthusiasm with which they encouraged us to write this book and for the patience and trust they showed when the writing took more time than initially expected.

We thank Julie Raadschelders for translating our texts. Her flexibility in always making time for us when, during our erratic writing process, we unexpectedly finished yet another chapter, has greatly helped the completion of this book.

We wish to express our gratitude to the scientific community in which we have worked during the past several years. We are intellectually in debt to our colleagues. The Department of Policy, Organization and Management in the Faculty of Technology, Policy and Management at the Delft University of Technology, and the Centre for Public Management of the Department of Public Administration at the Erasmus University in Rotterdam offered us the means and the time to write this book. Last, but not least, we would like to thank Nelleke van der Well-Janssen, Caroline van Doorn and Marlene Klompenhouwer for their administrative support during the production of the book.

Joop Koppenjan and Erik-Hans Klijn
Delft/Rotterdam, September 2003

Chapter 1

Uncertainties in dealing with complex problems in the network society

1.1 Introduction: dealing with complex problems

Government, business and civil society in our contemporary network society are increasingly faced with long-standing controversies over complex societal problems. Decisions on the use of biotechnology, the location of airports or the restructuring of public sector services such as health care, can become the subject of intensive conflict and debate. These problems are characterized by a high degree of wickedness (Radford, 1977; Mason and Mitroff, 1981). This first manifests itself in the fact that the involved parties disagree not only about the solution, but even about the nature of the problem. Research and scholarship are brought in to establish clarity, but these often only increase confusion. Frequently, these attempts result in knowledge conflicts where parties attack each other's positions with scientific reports containing contradictory findings.

But the wicked nature of these problems cannot only be linked to the complexity or, perhaps, the technologically advanced nature of the issue. A further feature of these issues is that they cut across the traditional jurisdictions of organizations and cross the traditional boundaries between the private and public sector. Governments, businesses and civil society are unable to tackle these issues by themselves. The complexity of these issues gives rise to arenas of interaction: actors are forced to operate in the context of strategic games and networks that are new to them and in which their standard operating procedures are no longer adequate (Marin and Mayntz, 1991; Thompson *et al.*, 1991; Marsh and Rhodes, 1992; Kickert *et al.*, 1997). In the case of *Brent Spar*, where Greenpeace challenged the decision of Shell to sink an obsolete oil rig into the ocean, Shell found itself suddenly exposed in the world's media and had to defend itself vigorously against attacks – which had an immediate effect on their sales figures of gasoline in Europe (Rice and Owen, 1999). In addition to substantive uncertainty, there are strategic and institutional uncertainties.

As a consequence, traditional methods of dealing with problems, which often hold complex issues to be an intellectual design question and approach them by giving research and science a central role, no longer suffice. The wicked problems that confront governments, private companies and societal interest groups in a complex society require a different, new approach.

Box 1.1 Example of wicked problems: the greenhouse effect

The difficulties surrounding the reduction of CO_2 and the implementation of the Kyoto Accords are a good example of a wicked problem where both substantive uncertainties and strategic and institutional uncertainties play a role.

The problem of CO_2 concentrations in the air has been one of the most important environmental issues for some time. CO_2 concentrations increase as a result of burning fossil fuels and other human activities. As a consequence, the gradual warming of the earth may have far-reaching consequences for life on earth. While a reasonable consensus has emerged at present about the fact that there is a problem, we know very little about the causal effects of increased CO_2 concentrations, and there is still much uncertainty about the potential environmental effects of increased CO_2 (higher temperature, changes in precipitation and aridness etc.). Furthermore, various actors have different assessments of these effects. So it is not surprising that a lot of discussion is still going on.

But the problem is not only one of information or perception. There are huge decision making and organizational problems because of the large number of actors involved and the absence of strongly developed institutional frameworks for cooperation at an international level. To do something about this problem, agreements must be made at government level about the reduction of CO_2 emissions. This is a difficult process since every state has its own opinions and interests. The Kyoto Accords constituted a first attempt to make international agreements between states in this field.

The decision of President Bush not to ratify the Kyoto Accords has had major consequences for the behaviour of other actors. It not only increases the uncertainty already existing, it also means a major setback in attempts to develop an institutional framework meant to overcome strategic and institutional uncertainties.

The aims of this book are both to argue that uncertainty is an inherent characteristic of modern society which is not simply caused by a shortage of knowledge or information, but also by the strategic and institutional features of the network settings in which these wicked problems are articulated and processed, and also to develop a conceptual framework to help understanding of the nature of these uncertainties and to adequately deal with them.

Therefore, we first discuss the background and the nature of the uncertainties that play a role in complex problems. We will argue that traditional approaches are no longer adequate and suggest the network approach as a source of inspiration for dealing with uncertainties in a more satisfactory manner. Next, we outline the structure of the book, which presents our ideas about how to deal with these uncertainties.

1.2 Problem solving and decision making in the network society

In recent decades the environment in which organizations must operate has become more and more complex. The environment for private companies consists of consumers/buyers and competitors, and also supply companies, support companies, organizations that represent their interests, governments who impose rules, monitors and judges, consumer organizations, and societal interest groups. These all make demands upon products and methods of production (Brandenburger and Nalebuff, 1996; Grabher, 1993). Government organizations not only deal with political officials, but also with citizens, target groups, interest organizations, advisory bodies, experts and judicial bodies.

A high density and a variety of organizational networks characterize society. In doing their work and in solving problems, organizations of various different natures meet. These meetings are rarely non-committal. The organizations 'want something from each other'. They can no longer fulfil their task alone, whether they like to or not. Problems cannot be solved by organizations on their own. Hence, hierarchy as an organization principle has lost much of its meaning. The model of the 'lonely organization' that determines its policy in isolation is obsolete (Miles and Snow, 1986; Alter and Hage, 1993). Equally obsolete is the image of government at the apex of the societal pyramid. The opportunities for steering society from one centre are diminishing (Rhodes, 1997; Hanf and Scharpf, 1978; Van Heffen *et al.*, 2000).

Horizontal networks replace hierarchies. Thus, a double development can be seen. Through processes of specialization, professionalization, decentralization, individualization and informatization, there are increasing numbers of places in society where people, groups, and organizations make important decisions (Castells, 2000). As a result, there is increasing fragmentation. Simultaneously, these local decision makers control limited resources and are influenced by the decisions of others. The mutual dependency between local and central parties increases. Horizontal relationships are formed: networks. These dependencies and novel societal forms are not limited to public and private domains but cross territorial boundaries as well. As a consequence of this paradoxical development of increasing fragmentation on the one hand and growing dependency on the other, society increasingly consists of a web of networks. We live in a network society (Castells, 2000).

Network society and wicked problems: the inevitability of the environment

The wickedness of many societal problems can be connected to a number of characteristics of this network society. Without presuming to be complete, and sketched with very broad strokes, we believe that the following developments are specifically important:

*   *Increasing intertwinement.* Through increased specialization and dynamics in knowledge and product development, greater dependencies are created between organizations. In part because of globalization of the economy and the high-quality knowledge demanded for production and services, the costs for production and service delivery have increased while the period for realizing gains has decreased. Hence, companies may increasingly engage in

strategic alliances in order to share costs and knowledge and to spread risks (Faulkner, 1995; Nooteboom, 1997). Governments are also increasingly dependent upon the knowledge, authority and resources of other parties – inside and outside government – for the achievement of their policy goals (Hanf and Scharpf, 1978; Marin and Mayntz, 1991; Rhodes, 1997). Thus, in the public realm there is also an intensification of relations between (levels of) governments and between governments and private companies.

- *Deterritorialization and globalization.* Private companies increasingly operate in a worldwide theatre. Economic activities are less bound to geographical places or limited to nations. Economic investments (and financial transactions) span the globe and seek places where profit is highest. Companies, consequently, engage in international cooperation (Faulkner, 1995; Nooteboom, 1997). This also means that economic investments and developments can be less influenced by nation states (Faulkner, 1995; Castells, 2000).

- *Turbulent environments.* The environment does not leave organizations at rest: organizations cannot ignore their environment. The idea that companies are only focused on profit maximization is less frequently accepted. It is the environment that calls increasing attention to the notion of including the external effects of production as a standard element of company management. By means of private law suits (e.g. court cases against weapons producers in the US where families of victims of violence sue companies) but also through societal pressure (e.g. the opposition to Shell's decision to sink the oil rig *Brent Spar* into the ocean), companies are forced to consider externalities. Among private companies, an increasing tendency can be perceived where consideration of these dependencies is pursued through the introduction of corporate governance. As far as governments are concerned, they have always been a focus of societal attempts at influencing. The strategies of interest organizations, the leaking of policy memos, and the ever-present eye of the television camera make it impossible for governments to withdraw from these societal influences by appealing to the general interest or the primacy of politics.

- *Value pluralism.* Our complex society lacks a simple hierarchy of values. Collective associations lose at least some of their importance. The relationships of individuals and organizations with larger communities and common value patterns are not as self-evident as in the past (for reflections about the disappearance of social capital, see Putnam, 1993). Society has several organizational networks and subcultures, each with its own value system. Furthermore, individuals are more able to choose where they put their support and tend to follow their own value judgements rather than adhere to given value judgements (Castells, 1997; Sociaal Cultureel Planbureau, 2000). Visions of what the general interest is are less commonly shared than they used to be. So it is too simple to say that government represents the general interest: value pluralism in society has become too great for that and government itself is internally fragmented and variable. For public and private organizations, this means that the demands placed upon them vary and change over the course of time: there are diverging and competing values that also change over time.

- *Horizontal relations.* Ideas about how organizations interact with groups and individuals have changed. Government can no longer automatically rely on the support of companies, citizens or other (levels of) governments for their policies. Relations become more business-like. Citizens and administrators increasingly base their behaviour on cost-benefit calculations. Companies are also confronted with this increasingly business-like nature of interaction in the production chain and in their contacts with shareholders and competitors (Alter and Hage, 1993; Graeber, 1993; Nooteboom, 1997, 2000). Horizontal relations replace loyalties and authoritative relations: there is a transformation from an authoritative to a negotiating society. This translates into new styles of management and the use of other steering instruments (Rhodes, 1997; Denters *et al.*, 2003). Thus, government increasingly involves companies and target groups in making and implementing policy. Concomitantly, there is a shift in the use of instruments. There is less emphasis on unilateral legal instruments such as legislation and regulation. More frequently, instruments that leave room for consultation and cooperation, such as subsidies, covenants and contracts, are chosen (Richardson, 1982; Kooiman, 1993; Brandenburger and Nalebuff, 1996; Kickert *et al.*, 1997).
- *Development of knowledge and technology: new uncertainties and risks.* The progress of technology and scientific research has not resulted in a reduction of technological uncertainties. The application of new scientific findings and new technologies not only opens new avenues for problem solving and the pursuit of prosperity, but also creates new problems, new risks and new uncertainties (Beck, 1992). The debate on genetically manipulated food between the US and the European Union is a manifestation of the controversies to which the awareness of these new dangers may lead.

  As knowledge grows, we become more aware of the complexities that surround us and new questions are raised. Specialization has also resulted in a high degree of fragmentation of knowledge and methods (Nooteboom, 2000). Furthermore, an awareness is growing that answers provided through scientific research are determined to a large degree by the questions asked and the assumptions used. In applied research, it appears that various research organizations hired by different problem owners also present different research results. Scientific research no longer provides unequivocal and authoritative solutions for dealing with problems (Gibbons *et al.*, 1994; Nowotny *et al.*, 2001).

These developments have important consequences for approaching the complex issues that confront individuals, companies, governments and societal interest groups. Growing individualization, fragmentation and value pluralism mean that consensus about the nature of the problems, the relevant criteria to judge these by, and the desired solutions will not emerge automatically. Growing specialization and network formation also means that complex problems are increasingly resolved in a setting of mutual dependencies. This requires more from the interactions and management efforts aimed at the solution of social problems.

Furthermore, the network society is characterized by a high degree of dynamics and boundary-crossing activities so that the existing institutional frameworks are unable to handle societal problems that arise from this. They may even hinder effective problem solving. In addition to the nature and solutions of problems becoming more difficult to determine, the complexity of how problems are handled is also a result of the inevitable involvement of other parties and the complexity of the involved institutional arrangements. Complex societal issues thus develop into wicked problems that are characterized by substantive, strategic and institutional uncertainty.

1.3 Uncertainties: wicked societal problems

Uncertainty arises when parties are confronted with societal problems and do not know what the effects of their efforts to resolve them will be. This uncertainty about the effects of behaviours may come from a lack of knowledge and information. Uncertainty, though, also stems from the fact that the behaviour of individuals is not predetermined but based on both conscious and unexpected choices (March and Olsen, 1976; Crozier and Friedberg, 1980). This results in a high degree of indeterminacy of issues and generates uncertainty about both the development of those issues in the future and the effects of efforts to resolve the issues. Furthermore, uncertainty concerns the complex institutional context of societal problems.

Uncertainty involved in complex societal problems in a network setting, thus, has three manifestations: substantive, strategic and institutional uncertainty. In this section we briefly address these three.

Substantive uncertainty

First, there is uncertainty about the nature of complex problems. *Substantive uncertainty* concerns the availability of information. Often the necessary information is unavailable or not available on time. We thus assume that the increase of CO_2 in the atmosphere causes the rise of temperature on earth (the greenhouse effect) but as long as we do not know what concentrations have what effect, we cannot assess all of the effects of this increase. For many complex infrastructural projects (construction of roads, railways, airports, etc.) extensive studies about the effects of various investments become known too late in the decision process to be part of the discussion (Klijn, 2003).

Substantive uncertainty not only involves available information and knowledge though; both of these are frequently contested. Since actors have different perceptions of problems and view them from different frames of reference, they also interpret the available information differently. Thus, simply collecting information and tapping into knowledge cannot solve the substantive uncertainty of wicked problems. The interpretation of the meaning of information is an additional source of substantive uncertainty. More information, therefore, does not necessarily lead to less uncertainty – in fact, it might lead to more uncertainty.

Strategic uncertainty

In addition to substantive uncertainty, there is the *strategic uncertainty* surrounding wicked problems. This springs from the strategic choices actors make with regard to articulating complex problems (Allison, 1971; Crozier and Friedberg, 1980; Kingdon, 1984 and 1995; Ostrom, 1990). Since actors involved ground their actions in unique perceptions, which other actors often do not acknowledge or are unaware of, a large variety of strategies may develop around a complex issue. Furthermore, actors respond to and anticipate each other's strategic moves. Because of these mechanisms, it is difficult to predict what strategies actors will choose and how the 'interaction' of these strategies will influence the problem situation and problem solving process. Complex and highly undetermined types of interactions characterize wicked problems. This strategic uncertainty is not easy to reduce and can never be completely eliminated. In a complex society characterized by network formation and horizontalization, actors have discretion to make their own choices. Unexpected strategic turns are an intrinsic characteristic of interaction processes surrounding wicked problems.

Institutional uncertainty

Finally, wicked problems are characterized by *institutional uncertainty*. Not only do wicked problems involve many actors, but also these actors often work from different institutional backgrounds (Burns and Flam, 1987; March and Olsen, 1989). Wicked problems often cut across the existing demarcations between organizations, administrative levels and networks. As a consequence, participants not only have different perceptions, objectives and interests, but they also come from different organizations, administrative levels and networks. Interactions between actors are difficult since each will have their behaviour guided by the tasks, opinions, rules and language of their own organization, their own administrative level and their own network. Thus, interaction in wicked problems is characterized by clashes between divergent institutional regimes. For all actors at the beginning of the process, this results in a high degree of uncertainty about how the process will be handled and how the interaction with other actors will develop. This institutional uncertainty is another feature of wicked problems that cannot simply be 'solved'. It is rarely possible to directly influence the existing institutional frameworks since they develop gradually as part of a historical process and are anchored in formal legal frames, deeply-rooted informal institutions or long-term societal transition processes.

1.4 Dealing with uncertainties: the inadequacy of standard responses

Substantive, strategic and institutional uncertainty make it very difficult for societal actors to act with regard to complex societal problems. At the same time, the threat from the problem, or the pressure to do something exerted by their own organization, or the societal, administrative or political environment, will prevent the understandable inclination to postpone or even to exclude action. This raises the question of how societal actors will handle these types of uncertainties in practice.

A number of standard responses can be distinguished. In addition to avoidance or delay mentioned above, other responses include information collection (research or involving experts) or top-down measures aimed at the simplification of the social context in which the problem is handled (reducing the number of actors, centralization of authority, simplification of procedures) (Arentsen *et al.*, 1999).

Information collection as a standard response

Information collection as a standard response, i.e. initiating (scientific) research or involving experts, is especially focused on substantive uncertainty. This response is based on the idea that substantive uncertainty is a result of a lack of information and knowledge. Making these available would result in creating substantive certainty about the nature of the problem and the measures necessary. In so far as it is acknowledged that parties have differing perceptions of the problem situation and the (effects of the) solution and judge information differently on that basis, the expectation is that the quality and objectivity of research can reduce or remove differences in interpretation.

In practice, however, research seldom ends the uncertainty involved in wicked problems. Research cannot resolve the issue that different opinions exist about the problem. Furthermore, the assumption that research is objective and therefore authoritative is problematic. Quite frequently, vehement discussions emerge about the validity of research or about the assumptions used in the research. The discussions on the greenhouse effect are, of course, a clear example of this. Differences of opinion are, in such cases, transformed into a debate about the design, execution and interpretation of research. As a result, different actors will try to initiate their own research.

Top-down measures as a standard response

Unilateral and top-down measures as a standard response are especially focused on tackling strategic and institutional uncertainty. This response strongly focuses on top-down steering to reduce or eliminate freedom of action for other participants.

When attempts are made to exclude actors from participation in the problem solving process, however, resistance is created since the interests of these actors are ignored. Given the complexity that characterizes contemporary network societies, actors seldom have the knowledge and resources to resolve problems on their own. In so far as they believe that they can, this mostly stems from an underestimation of their external dependencies and a limited view of the nature of the problem situation and the interests involved. To the extent that they succeed in pushing through their favourite solution, the result is often a sub-optimal solution.

More frequently, attempts at top-down steering will get bogged down by strong resistance from the uninvolved but interested actors during decision making or implementation processes.

When measures are aimed at simplifying the institutional context, there is a risk that the sub-optimal solutions will be institutionalized and have long-term consequences. Frequently, attempts at institutional simplification essentially add new institutional arrangements to those already in existence (e.g. by adopting a new law or creating a new, coordinating body), thus enhancing institutional complexity and uncertainty instead of decreasing it.

Searching for more adequate responses to uncertainty

Because of the nature of uncertainty that characterizes wicked problems, the chances for success of information gathering or central steering are not very high. The information gathering strategy cannot cope with differences in problem perceptions nor with the strategic nature of wicked problems. The strategy of unilateral central steering is unable to control the strategic freedom of autonomous actors or the institutional dimension of uncertainty. This conclusion raises the question of what, then, constitutes a satisfactory response to the uncertainties of wicked problems.

1.5 Managing uncertainties in complex networks: a network perspective

We need other ways to deal with the uncertainties of complex societal issues. Solving wicked problems is, given the substantive, strategic and institutional uncertainties, not only an intellectual design activity but also a strategic and institutional challenge. Given the mutual dependencies that make it impossible for each of the involved actors to solve complex problems in isolation, the process of problem solving is, first, an issue of interaction where the actors with a stake in the problem must manage to coordinate their perceptions, activities and institutional arrangements. In searching for ways to map and manage substantive, strategic and institutional uncertainties, in this book we use the recent ideas of network theory. The mutual dependency of actors in dealing with wicked societal problems is a central notion in the network approach (see Kickert et al., 1997; Klijn and Koppenjan, 2000). The network approach provides theoretical concepts and normative starting points for analysing and assessing complex processes of problem solving in network settings and the roles that perceptions, interactions and institutions play in this. Furthermore, it provides prescriptions for improving the interactions between parties as well as management strategies for initiating and supporting interactions. Below, we briefly discuss the main components of the network perspective.

The policy network approach as a theoretical and normative starting point

The starting point in the network approach is that actors are mutually dependent for their goal achievement. Actors cannot achieve their goals without the means possessed by other actors. As a result of such dependencies, interaction patterns around policy problems and clusters of means emerge between actors. Over the course of time, these interaction patterns acquire some robustness. Rules develop that regulate the behaviour of actors and resource distributions emerge. These condition the interaction within the networks without completely determining them. We call this process of building and solidifying networks, network formation.

The networks that are established provide a context in which actors behave strategically and where they meet with other strategically behaving actors. Within these networks, pushing and pulling takes place regarding the prioritization and formulation of problems and the way they should be solved. We speak of policy games: a series of interactions between actors concerning certain policy issues. Not all actors of the network are involved in these policy games. Only those whose interests are directly affected will participate. The actors' positions in the individual policy games are determined by their place in the network and their strategic behaviour in the game. The outcome of the policy game is the result of the way the participants' strategies come together (Klijn and Koppenjan, 2000).

Actors do not select strategies at random. They are led by their perceptions of the game, of their own stakes and of the strategies of the other participants. Perceptions are the images that actors have about their game situation, and they use them to give meaning to and evaluate their actions and the actions of others. On the basis of these perceptions, actors select strategies and evaluate the (possible) outcomes of policy processes. Substantial differences in perception may cause blockages in policy processes or lead to stagnation. In this sense, perceptions are vital for the course of and outcomes of policy processes.

Managing uncertainty from a network perspective: the importance of joint action

A central question in the network approach is how joint action can be achieved. To achieve mutually satisfactory outcomes, actors must cooperate. After all, problem solving and decision making occur in the tension between dependency and a variety of objectives and interests. Given the substantive, strategic and institutional uncertainties at stake in dealing with wicked problems, these cooperation processes can be regarded as learning processes. Interaction processes are considered to be searches wherein public and private parties from different organizations, (levels of) government and networks jointly learn about the nature of the problem, look at the possibility of doing something about it, and identify the characteristics of the strategic and institutional context within which the problem solving develops. Hence, cooperation presupposes learning between actors, crossing the boundaries of organizations, networks and coalitions. This is referred to in the literature as 'cross-frame reflection' and learning between 'advocacy coalitions' (Rein and Schön, 1992; Sabatier and Jenkins-Smith, 1993) and can be viewed as the sustainable development of shared insights, methods of working and institutions. Substantive, strategic and institutional uncertainty has to be met with cognitive, strategic and institutional learning processes.

Since cooperation and learning behaviour do not emerge spontaneously, it is necessary to support interaction around complex issues in network settings. We refer to strategies which are meant to further these interaction processes as network management (Kickert *et al.*, 1997; O'Toole, 1997; Agranoff and McGuire, 2003). The literature on the network approach suggests network management is labour intensive and certainly not easy. It requires numerous skills, tacit knowledge of the network and negotiation skills since the adopted strategies are implemented in a situation where singular hierarchical relations are lacking. The role of the network manager is one of mediator and stimulator of interaction and not one of central director. This role is not given a priori to one actor. In principle, this role can be fulfilled by several actors, sometimes by even more than one actor at the same time, both public and private. In addressing the central question of this book, namely, how uncertainties can be handled in dealing with complex societal issues, a great deal of attention is focused on identifying, analysing and elaborating network management strategies used to initiate and support interaction and learning processes between the involved actors.

The policy network perspective distinguishes itself from other, more rational, approaches to problem solving and uncertainty by using the multi-actor nature of problem situations and the presence of diverging and sometimes conflicting perceptions, objectives and institutions as the starting point for the analysis. It investigates what the consequences of this insight are for the way problem solving processes evolve and for the way these processes can be designed and managed.

Thus, the policy network approach links theory building and analysis closely to a management perspective. The objective of this book is not only to provide concepts for the analysis of problem solving under the condition of uncertainty, but also to develop recommendations about how that uncertainty can be dealt with.

Contributions to network theory: linking substantive, strategic and institutional perspectives

With this book we also aim to contribute to the further development of network theory. Within the tradition of network theory, over time, two schools have emerged that have developed relatively independently from one another. On the one hand, there are network theoreticians focused on the institutional aspects of the networks and the process of network formation. A strong focus on mapping the morphological characteristics of networks and the processes that create them are characteristic for at least part of this school (Blau, 1982; Laumann and Knoke, 1987). There is also a strong focus on analysing interdependencies (Aldrich, 1979; Rhodes 1981) and closedness of networks (Rhodes, 1988). At the same time, this school has kept its distance from the development and outcomes of concrete problem solving processes and policy making. This is reflected by the absence of an action perspective and management recommendations (compare Blom-Hansen, 1997).

On the other hand, there are approaches where the strategic interaction process (also referred to as the policy game), and the management of it, play a central role. Although the mutual dependencies between parties – the core of the network concept – is the starting point for the analysis and recommendations in this second approach, there is less attention to the institutional characteristics of networks. This interactionist variant of the network approach, therefore, might also be labelled as a qualitative game approach. Qualitative in order to distinguish it from quantitative game theory (Allison, 1971; Crozier and Friedberg, 1980; Agranoff, 1986; O'Toole, 1986 and 1988; Mandell, 1990; Kickert *et al.*, 1997).

In this book, we link these institutional and interactionist traditions of the network approach. We do so by distinguishing between strategic and institutional uncertainty, which enables us to look at both factors in our analysis and prescriptions and specify their relation.

We will also address one element of the criticism of the network approach, namely, that it is focused on processes and institutions but neglects the substantive aspects of problems and discussions. The fact that it may be impossible to arrive at an objective problem definition and a knowledge of reality does not necessarily mean that substance does not matter. We do, however, acknowledge that in the network approach attention on the role of substance and knowledge has been limited and relatively underdeveloped so far. We try to remove this imbalance by placing substantive uncertainty, in addition to strategic and institutional uncertainty, central to our analysis. In doing so, we attempt to link network theory with approaches where – usually from a multi-actor perspective – attention is given to the cognitive aspects of problem solving and policy processes. This specifically includes approaches that focus on mapping problem perceptions, learning processes and the structure of argumentations and discourses (Rein and Schön, 1986 and 1992; Sabatier, 1988; Fischer and Forester, 1993; Sabatier and Jenkins-Smith, 1993; Roe, 1994; Hajer, 1995). To sum up: in trying to connect substantive, interactionist and institutional approaches to complex problem solving processes in our analysis and recommendations we focus on the roles of three forms of uncertainty and the way they are linked.

A running case: the zinc debate in the Netherlands

We illustrate our argument with various examples taken from different sectors and countries. One example will serve as a 'running case study' in the following chapters. This provides us with the opportunity to develop an in-depth and coherent analysis of the various aspects of uncertainty within wicked problems and their management. This example concerns an environmental issue in the field of water management: the ongoing discussion about the extent and harmfulness of zinc emissions from building materials. This case is introduced in Box 1.2.

1.6 Objectives, research question and structure of this book

This book is inspired by the observation that many contemporary societal problems are wicked. We have seen in this chapter that wickedness has been closely

Box 1.2 The zinc debate: solving the problem of zinc emissions from building materials

The Dutch government is confronted with the environmental and health risks of zinc which, together with rainwater from gutters, guard rails and other zinc or zinc-containing products, ends up in drains and sewerage systems and ultimately in the surface water and sedimentation on the bottoms of streams, canals etc.

The National Institute for Public Health and Environment (in Dutch: RIVM), a government associated research institute, on the authority of the Ministry of Housing, Spatial Planning and Environment (in Dutch: VROM) determined the maximum allowable quantities of zinc. The National Institute for Integral Fresh Water and Waste Water Management (in Dutch: RIZA) on the authority of the Ministry of Transport, Public Works and Water Management (in Dutch: V&W) translated these general norms into more specific norms for surface water. Water managers have to achieve these norms in their water purification efforts. So far, this case appeared straightforward and hardly an example of a wicked problem. In reality, though, this was just the beginning of the problem.

Water managers, confronted with the costs of this problem, had to pass them on to the citizens. This provided a reason for water managers to attempt to reduce the use of zinc in building materials. Although they did not have the formal instruments to do so, they tried to convince local governments to engage in covenants with project developers who had agreed not to use zinc. As a result, the zinc industry, fearing its market share, now had reason to dispute the norms of national government as well as fend off the efforts of local and regional governments to reduce the use of zinc.

And thus began an ongoing strategic game between a large number of actors: government departments, research institutions, private actors, municipalities and water managers at the regional level. In fulfilling their roles and their core business, these actors clashed and engaged in a conflict that touched upon their vital interests. Private companies feared for their market share. Water managers were confronted with the costs of purification. National government was held accountable for the interests of the environment and of public health.

Hence, the reason why these parties became actively engaged. The zinc industry initiated research that contradicted the norm methods used by RIVM, which, in turn, responded with a report criticizing the industry's research. The latter responded with yet another report. When zinc was placed on a list of products that must be avoided in the context of sustainable building, the industry conducted its own product evaluations (Life Cycle Analysis). Thus developed an ever more complex policy process where not only the norms themselves were subject to debate but also the distribution of roles between participants. The existence and nature of the problems, the quality of scientific methods and research findings, the performance of actors and the complexity of decision making resulted in many actors losing sight of the bigger picture. Interactions occurred at various levels (national government, regional government, municipality), in various policy sectors (environmental and product policy, water policy and management, public housing) and in various spheres (public and private). Mutual perceptions strengthened distrust and conflicting strategies while policy implementation stagnated. In short,

contd

what at first sight appeared to be a simple societal problem became a problem with all the features of a wicked problem: diverging problem definitions, contested knowledge, complex decision making and complex institutional context.

These conflicting strategies did not bring the parties closer together. Even worse, the issue escalated, and the parties became entrenched and refused to listen to each other. Each was convinced that the others approached the issue from cynical self-interest; that the other parties did not listen and only provided information with the aim of bolstering their own positions. Research by the industry was immediately viewed as partisan and unscientific, intended to trivialize the environmental effects. The industry considered RIVM's defence of its norm method the result of cynical scientific policy by a monopolistic research institute, and the pursuit of emission reduction was seen as a bureaucratic interest. Additionally, the activities of local and regional government trying to discourage the use of zinc were viewed as semi-illegal. In this spiral of mutual distrust, each party felt it was banging its head against a wall in trying to convince the others. The only way out appeared to be to continue fighting, seeking support with possible third parties and hoping that the tide would turn.

Clearly, such a conflict is destructive for all those involved. Norms are still being set. Water managers have to purify water and face the costs. In the meantime, the pursuit of emission reductions is far from effective and the image of zinc as a product and the zinc industry as a branch of industry has been damaged.

Sources: Klijn *et al.*, 2000; van Bueren *et al.*, 2003.

related to changes in society over the past decades. This development can be summarized as the emergence of a network society that influences the nature of issues in society and the ways of dealing with them. In this network society, hierarchical relations lose relevance because authority, knowledge and means are distributed across a large number of actors. Activities in the network society go beyond the institutional boundaries of organizations, public and private sectors, and administrative units. Complex issues and the contexts in which they are articulated and managed also transcend particular boundaries, giving issues their wicked nature: they are characterized by substantive, strategic and institutional uncertainty. An effective approach to wicked problems requires societal parties to learn to deal with these types of uncertainty in a satisfactory manner. The standard responses that actors generally tend to use in dealing with uncertainty are not only sub-optimal but are also often counter-productive. Instead of reducing uncertainty, they strengthen it.

The objective of this book

In order to develop a more satisfactory response to the uncertainty that characterizes wicked problems in network settings, and inspired by and building upon a network perspective, we pursue five objectives within this book:

1   We argue that uncertainty is an inherent characteristic of modern society that is not simply caused by a shortage of knowledge or information, but also by

the strategic and institutional features of the context in which these issues are articulated and dealt with.

2   We develop a conceptual framework for understanding the nature of this uncertainty. The framework connects ideas on the role of knowledge and rationality in decision making processes with network theory. Central concepts are content, strategic interaction games, networks, and cognitive, strategic and institutional learning.

3   We offer analytical tools that can be used to analyse games and networks where issues of uncertainty are at stake.

4   We offer a theoretically based approach to management strategies aimed at dealing with issues of uncertainty in strategic games and networks.

5   We contribute to network theory by connecting substantive, strategic and institutional perspectives on complex problem solving and decision making in network settings.

Research question

The central question of this book is therefore: how can the substantive, strategic and institutional uncertainties that are so characteristic of complex societal issues be analysed and managed in a way that is appropriate, given the features of these uncertainties and the sources from which they stem?

Structure of this book

The answer to this question is organized as follows. On the one hand, we distinguish between analysis and management; on the other hand, we use the triad of substantive, strategic and institutional uncertainty. This results in the following structure.

Part 1: Analysis of uncertainties in dealing with complex problems in networks

In the first part of this book, we discuss the analytical framework used to analyse the complex processes by which wicked problems in a network context are solved.

Chapter 2 deals with the manifestations and sources of uncertainty about the content of complex problems and their solutions. Among other things we discuss the contribution of research, science and experts to the management of substantive uncertainties in processes of problem solving.

In Chapter 3 we address the nature and sources of strategic uncertainty in problem solving. We demonstrate that the involvement of multiple actors, interests and strategies results in a complex and unpredictable strategic game, where this uncertainty is strengthened by the fragmented nature of the policy game and the dynamics of developments in the environment.

Chapter 4 deals with the institutional uncertainty around wicked problems. We discuss networks as institutions with their own patterns of interactions and rules. We also present central concepts such as rules for analysing the institutional context of networks and problems. We show how these wicked problems can be played out in multiple networks and what the consequences of that will be.

In Chapter 5, complementing the discussion of the nature and sources of the three types of uncertainty, we analyse the most important (governmental) standard responses used in practice to deal with uncertainty.

Chapter 6 connects the previous chapters and culminates with the presentation of the conceptual framework for the analysis and assessment of processes of problem solving in complex network settings. The ideas we develop in the second part of this book to arrive at a more effective management of uncertainty are built on this framework.

Part 2: Management of uncertainties in dealing with complex problems in networks

In Part 2, we elaborate our suggestions for managing uncertainties. The first step towards a more satisfactory handling of uncertainties is acknowledging that these uncertainties play a role and that acquiring insight into the nature of uncertainties in concrete processes of problem solving and decision making is crucial.

Therefore, in Chapter 7, we present tools for mapping uncertainties. Applying these analysis tools helps us to recognize and better understand uncertainty.

Next, we propose strategies for handling recognized uncertainty. In Chapter 8, we discuss the opportunities for managing substantive uncertainty through the creation of substantive variety and improving and supporting mutual learning behaviour. We also address how research and science are embedded in these processes.

Chapter 9 presents opportunities for managing strategic uncertainty through the initiation, design and facilitation of policy games.

In Chapter 10, we address opportunities for influencing institutional factors and the empirical and normative limitations involved.

We conclude the book with Chapter 11, in which we present an overview of the findings, resulting from the analysis in this book. In addition to this we reflect on the conditions which influence the opportunities for management of uncertainties and we also look at the normative assumptions and implications involved in the choice of a network approach in attempting to manage uncertainties in modern society.

Part I

Analysis of uncertainties in dealing with complex problems in networks

Chapter 2

Uncertainty about content

Knowledge conflicts and asymmetrical debates

2.1 Uncertainty about content: an introduction

In dealing with complex problems actors are confronted with uncertainty. A major source of uncertainty has to do with the difficulty they experience in determining the nature of the problem. Often crucial information or knowledge is lacking or not instantly available. But this is not the only source of uncertainty about content of the problem. Often the problem is not so much the lack of information and knowledge, but its status. The interpretation of information and the establishment of meaning may be problematic and become the subject of conflict. The development of the knowledge conflict about the environmental impacts of zinc in the Netherlands, described in Box 2.1, provides an illustration of this.

What does the zinc case illustrate?

The Dutch debate on zinc can be seen as typical for a lot of attempts within the public and private sector to deal with uncertainties involved in complex societal problems. Despite a lot of research efforts and intensive debate about zinc corrosion from construction materials into water since 1989, there was great uncertainty about the nature and size of the problem. Opinions continued to differ regarding eco-toxicity. The methods for establishing norms used by government and industry had both been rejected, but there was no apparent alternative. There was little development in the debate with regard to the size of emissions and the opportunity to realize product innovations. The initial problem definition by government was challenged by industry which perceived the problem in a different way. The confrontation focused on the seriousness and content of the problem, the manner of measurement, and the contribution of construction materials. In this technical discussion, each party had scientific research done in the hope of convincing the other. Advocacy research turned out a plethora of reports, but these failed to lead to a substantive dialogue – instead they served to strengthen each party's commitment to their own position. There was 'closedness' and entrenchment. This 'dialogue of the deaf' also had an asymmetric structure: parties talked past each other. While industry believed it could convince by fighting the scientific basis of the method for establishing norms, government believed from the outset that regardless of the precise method for establishing norms, emissions should be

Box 2.1 Uncertainty about content illustrated: the knowledge conflict about zinc

The background. In the 1970s and 1980s, environmental policy aimed at reducing the pollution of Dutch waterways by focusing on large polluters. While this policy proved effective, water managers noticed that the maximum values of polluting substances were frequently exceeded in a variety of places. Researchers and policy makers attributed this to diffuse sources: emissions caused by use of these products spread over an area. In the 1989 National Environmental Policy Plan, the Ministry of Housing, Spatial Planning and Environment (VROM) presented a list of prioritized substances that deserved special attention since they could be found in high concentrations in the water. One of these elements was zinc. It was decided that a research report would be prepared by RIVM, a scientific institution affiliated with the ministry. This report would provide the scientific foundation for policy and define the maximum allowable values and desired values for zinc.

The charge. The zinc report, published in 1992, provided technical information about the danger to the environment and health resulting from large concentrations of zinc. There was simply too much zinc in the water and the waterbeds: some 85 per cent of the biological species were safe, but a protection rate of 95 per cent was desired. Besides agriculture, the most significant source of zinc emissions is the corrosion of zinc and zinc products used in construction. This source was estimated at 4,124 tons of zinc for 1989 alone. While the extent to which this source of zinc contributed to pollution was not quite clear, norms had been drafted prior to the research report. Within RIVM, an extrapolation method was developed using eco-toxicity data, and this method was applied to all important metals. Based on this method, the Ministry formulated maximum and desired values for inland waters, including those for zinc, in its 1991 Memo 'Environmental Quality Targets for Ground and Water'.

In 1993 the Institute for Experimental Housing (IEH) – a private institute with public funding – distributed its 'Guidelines for Sustainable Building' to municipalities across the country. These guidelines advised architects, construction companies and municipalities to avoid the use of zinc in view of the negative environmental effects.

The defence. The procedure for drafting research reports allows private industry and environmental interest groups to write an Addendum. Finally, the Health Council, an authoritative advisory body of the government, will provide the cabinet with a recommendation concerning the research report and the addenda. In 1994, industry requested Van Tilborg Business Consultancy, Inc. to draft an Addendum. Published in 1995, it presented an alternative model for determining norms called the Deficiency-Toxicity/Optimal Concentration Area for Essential Elements (DT/OCEE model). Unlike the RIVM model (known as the Aldenberg-Slob method), this model considered the concentration of zinc naturally present in the environment as well as the adaptive ability of flora and fauna to changing circumstances. Van Tilborg also pointed to shortcomings in the RIVM research report: the number of measurements was too limited and included species such as the American sponge that does not appear in the Netherlands. Furthermore, it was argued that the contribution of corroded construction materials to the zinc concentration in inland waterways was negligible.

On the basis of this Addendum, industry filed a claim against the IEH and demanded that the qualification of 'avoiding' be deleted from IEH's guidelines. The IEH had the Addendum studied by TNO, which – on the basis of a literature review – concluded that the Addendum lacked a solid eco-toxological foundation. As a result, the court rejected the industry's demand and suggested that Van Tilborg could not be regarded as an independent party.

Next, the IEH worked to improve the factual basis of the guidelines. To do so it used the Life Cycle Analysis (LCA) – a method for determining the environmental effects of materials – of rain gutters. The LCA on gutters was conducted by Tauw Inc. (an engineering company) commissioned by the RIZA, a research institute of the Ministry of Traffic and Water Management (Tauw 1). The zinc industry claimed that this study was insufficient because it did not consider the re-use of materials. They commissioned Tauw to conduct another investigation that would take recycling into account (Tauw 2). In 1996, as a sequel to the IEH guidelines, the first National Package for Sustainable Construction – developed by organizations in the building and housing sector – was published. It provided, among other things, recommendations about which materials to use based on existing reports (such as Tauw 1) and existing government policy. The advice was, again, to avoid the use of zinc for gutters, drainpipes and roofs.

Response and counter response. In early 1996, RIVM and the RIZA published a report entitled 'A Further Look at Zinc', which reviewed the most important data in view of criticism from the zinc industry. This report provided no reason to reject or alter the Aldenberg-Slob method or change the norms in the research report. RIVM believed that the industry critique had been refuted. The zinc industry responded with their own report entitled 'A Further Look at Zinc Refuted', in which they defended the DT/OCEE model.

The judgement. Parties eagerly awaited the advice of the Health Council, in the belief that it would provide a conclusion to the discussion. The advice was published in 1998. The Council questioned the existing methods of determining zinc concentrations. None sufficiently considered the fact that zinc is an essential element in nature and occurs in varying concentrations. The development of a new method would take a substantial amount of time. Meanwhile, the Council advised a pragmatic approach that would take high and low concentrations for ecosystems in water and ground into account, and to differentiate measures by area depending upon background concentrations. The Council also stated that cabinet policy for reducing emissions should continue.

Interpretations of the judgement. In view of the recommendation, the cabinet concluded that measures for limiting diffuse emissions of zinc and other metals were legitimate and that it would debate this with industry. At the same time, industry concluded that the Council agreed with their critique of the method used for arriving at norms and anticipated their own involvement in the further development of the new method. The consultation that followed was difficult. Government held to the water quality norms and emission estimates while industry disputed them.

In the meantime, the discussion about eco-toxicity of zinc moved to the European level. The Netherlands served as rapporteur in a risk analysis for the EU. In this procedure, data are collected and tested on the basis of peer reviews. Then the results are discussed between the member states and may result in policy measures. The Ministry of Housing, Spatial Planning and Environment contracted RIVM to fulfil this rapporteur's role and RIVM thus got the lead in the analysis. The Aldenberg-Slob method was initially used to determine the eco-toxicity of zinc, and the RIZA method was used to determine the origin of zinc emissions. This generated criticism from industry. External experts updated the data in the eco-toxicity database and evaluated these on the basis of criteria developed between the parties involved. However, industry claimed that in the final report to the EU at the end of 1999, the 'old' criteria from RIVM reports were used.

Is uncertainty reduced? In early 1999, the debate seemed to be getting somewhere. First, the zinc industry indicated that they were thinking about product innovations. Developers worked on coatings for gutters, roofs and facades. Zinc companies developed a programme for the use of duplex systems for controlling corrosion, the development of a compound with decreased corrosion and layer thickness optimization. The zinc industry sought a governmental guarantee that these products would be given a chance even though they were more expensive than the existing products. Furthermore, they wanted national government to ask local and provincial governments to limit their policy of discouraging the use of zinc in construction projects. Government, however, did not want to provide these guarantees.

In the debate on the volume of zinc emissions from building materials, parties hoped to overcome their differences by means of 'fact sheets' that provided an overview of the points of agreements. While the fact sheets were incomplete, they did serve to bring parties closer together. Thus, the ministries became convinced that more research into the corrosion speed of zinc was necessary. The RIZA and the zinc industry together requested TNO to investigate this. A much lower emission of zinc corrosion emerged from this research than in the previous governmental reports. Also, TNO concluded that the total zinc emission could no longer be explained from the known sources and its estimated size. This was because of the reliability interval of the estimates and the presence of alternative sources of zinc (for instance, zinc emissions from plant leaves and trees). Furthermore, the parties agreed that it was not the corrosion speed, but the discharge speed that was an important parameter for estimating zinc emissions in the environment.

Sources: Klijn et al., 2000; van Bueren et al., 2003.

reduced. Although the contesting parties became more and more convinced of their own point of view, for other parties involved, such as municipalities, water authorities and construction companies, the overall substantive uncertainty of this problem increased.

A familiar pattern in dealing with uncertainty: other examples

The pattern that emerged from the handling of substantive uncertainty in the zinc case is far from unique. In a variety of policy issues in divergent areas

and in different countries, differences of opinion exist about the nature of problems and their solutions while efforts to find the truth result in knowledge conflicts,
report wars and 'dialogues of the deaf' (see Wildavksy and Tenenbaum, 1981;
DeLeon, 1988; Van Eeten, 1999). Some examples include:

- Highly charged discussions between biologists, policy makers and the fisheries
  sector within the EU regarding fish stocks in the North Sea and the necessity
  of measures such as the establishment of catching quotas.
- The issue of climate change, where scientists disagree about whether there
  is global warming, whether CO_2 emissions are its cause, and whether this
  will give rise to catastrophes. There is disagreement about facts as well
  as about methods of measurement and data interpretation (Labohm and
  Toenes, 2001).
- The clash between the tobacco industry and governments in Europe and
  the US where the fact of tobacco being harmful is no longer controversial,
  but where the discussion has moved to the question of whether smoking is
  addictive, whether addictive substances are added and at what point in time
  the tobacco industry knew that smoking was harmful to health. The tobacco
  industry has rejected the report 'Tobacco Explained' from the British Action
  on Smoking and Health as a 'subjective selection of facts for industry documents', while European governments regard this report as authoritative.

Comparable discussions occur on the expected positive and negative effects of, for
instance, the construction of airports, nuclear facilities, disposable waste facilities,
highways, railroad connections, the effects of biotechnology on food safety, etc.
(Wynne, 1982, 1989a/b; see Wildavsky, 1991, 1995; Jasanoff, 1994; Hisschemöller
and Hoppe, 1996; Pauly, 2001). And these discussions are certainly not limited to
issues with highly technological components and physical risks, because the same
type of discussion has taken place regarding, for instance, the effectiveness of
smaller class sizes in school. In the research on the correlation between class size
and performance, the latter is very difficult to measure. Researchers argue
about which performance must be evaluated and for how long it should be measured. Frequently, a limited number of cognitive skills are investigated in the short
term. There is also a difference of opinion about the correlation: are there intervening variables such as the expectations of the instructor regarding the learning
performance of their pupils?
　Many societal problems for which governments seek solutions through
regulation are hard to grasp: at closer analysis, there is often uncertainty about
the content, the causes, the effects and the solutions. Investment in data collection and analysis appears to have a counter-intuitive effect: instead of reducing
uncertainty, it enhances it. Certainties that appeared to exist at the start of the
problem solving process evaporate when even the most basic facts cannot be
agreed upon. Thus, Jasanoff (1996) observed that in the debate about deforesta-
tion in the Himalayan mountain range, researchers could not even agree about
basic data such as per capita fuel wood consumption.

Box 2.2 Uncertainty about the problem: estimates of zinc emissions from construction materials

The facts fail to speak for themselves. Thus, the estimates of zinc emissions from construction materials varied from 490 to 4,120 tons per annum, variations that were influenced by the choice of reference years and the applied research methodology. See Table 2.1 (Klijn et al., 2000).

Table 2.1 Estimated zinc emission as result of corrosion of zinc and zinced steel in the Netherlands (in tons per year)

Document	Year of reference	Zinc emission	Estimation in % of original basis document
RIVM, Basis document zinc (1992)	1989	4,125	100
RIZA/RIVM, SPEED document (1993)	1985	2,700	65
Central Bureau for Statistics (1994)	1990	1,340	32
Addendum Industry (1995)	'Present'	490	12
RIZA, WSV report (1996)	1993	1,691	41
VTBC (1996)	1995	562	14

And then, when agreement is finally reached about the facts, that agreement appears to become irrelevant because of emerging differences of opinion about the *meaning* of these facts. Even the methods used to find the truth are subject to disagreement. In this way, accomplishing the objective of policy analysis, defined by Wildavsky as 'speaking truth to power', becomes highly uncertain (Wildavsky, 1987; Hoppe, 1999). How can we pursue rationalization or scientific support of policy when the efforts at finding the truth result in information overload and conflict? This raises questions concerning the mechanisms in the efforts of parties to control these uncertainties and their implications given the nature of substantive uncertainty in complex policy processes. The question is, specifically, what do experts and knowledge contribute in efforts to reduce substantive uncertainties? In the next section, responses to substantive uncertainty and its implications are further characterized. In Section 2.3, we discuss the sources of substantive uncertainty: namely, the lack of certainty about scientific knowledge and the lack of consensus about the nature of the problem. In Section 2.4, we suggest ways for handling these sources of uncertainty in a more satisfactory manner.

2.2 Two responses to substantive uncertainty and their implications

Reaction Type I: information gathering, use of expert knowledge and (scientific) research

The standard response to substantive uncertainty is data collection, the use of experts and research. Uncertainty is thus regarded as a lack of knowledge about the facts. The problem is perceived to be technical. The objective of traditional policy analysis fits this approach (see Hoppe, 1999). This includes providing policy makers in government and industry with scientifically grounded problem analysis and solutions. The aim is to rationalize the process of problem solving. This response to uncertainty not only operates upon an assumption about the nature of the problem, but also about the contribution that knowledge and science can provide. We define science as fundamental and applied research by experts inside and outside universities and the knowledge to which this leads. The assumption behind the Type I reaction to uncertainty – information gathering – is that of neo-positivism: that scientific research into causal relations on the basis of empirical-analytical research will lead to objective knowledge about the nature of the problem, the background causes, the possible interventions and their consequences. Neo-positivism assumes a clear demarcation between objective knowledge production and the political choices of policy makers in government and business on the basis of these neutral findings. At the same time, it is assumed that experts and science produce conclusive and authoritative answers. Thus, Rosenau argues that uncertainty about environmental problems arises both from the mystery of nature as well as from the variation in human behaviour. While politicians may arrive at conflicting interpretations of research because of vague results, they remain dependent upon science: criteria of proof lie at the heart of environmental policy. Research outcomes that are found are based on proofs that are dictated by nature. 'At some point the data become too telling to ignore.' It may take a while before research results in conclusive evidence, but sooner or later, the 'knowledge of the facts' will be decisive (Rosenau, 1993: 248).

This notion about the role of knowledge and science is sometimes characterized as 'Mode I science in a Mode I society'. Under the influence of specialization and differentiation, society is divided into subsystems. The subsystem of science is organized by disciplines and produces specialized knowledge that other subsystems can use as a basis for their actions. Science derives its authority from its autonomy and epistemological nature, where criteria of reliability, objectivity and truth are central. This framework is guarded by the scientific epistemological community. In this *neo-positivist, modernist vision*, science is separate from other societal domains such as government and the market, and is presumed to produce true, objective and universal knowledge. This notion finds support especially among the technical and natural sciences disciplines (hard core betas) that defend the superiority of scientific knowledge vis-à-vis other knowledge sources (Gibbons *et al.*, 1994). However, this notion is also well represented in economics and traditional policy analysis.

Much of the development of government policy in technical areas such as health care, the environment, and traffic and water management is based on this notion. Large research institutes financed by government provide 'objective' information which is accepted as an authoritative starting point for problem analysis and government intervention. A notion of science as an autonomous producer of objective knowledge is thus – paradoxically – linked to an instrumental view of the use of scientific knowledge and the malleability of society: science provides the knowledge that can be directly used for societal interventions (see Weiss, 1977).

Response Type II: counter-expertise

Can information gathering, expert knowledge and science support this claim of uncertainty reduction? It appears that expert knowledge and research outcomes embraced by the parties actively involved often meet with a lack of authoritativeness in wider circles. This leads to initiatives where other stakeholders initiate research that supports *their* problem definition and assumptions. This second type of response to uncertainty consists therefore of initiatives for counter-expertise resulting in a debate in which the various parties provide support for their own claims of truth. Research and policy analysis then acquire the function of policy advocacy. Research questions and strategies may be commissioned by one of the stakeholders and the resultant findings then used strategically in the process of problem solution.

The motives of the parties in this battle for the truth can be both instrumental as well as political–strategic (see Weiss, 1977). Parties may hold the expectation that their research will lead to objective, universal answers. Their efforts are then aimed at convincing other parties of the conclusiveness of their research. The shortcomings perceived in the research of others may provide a motive for parties to try to do better themselves. But it may also be the case that while experts and contractors are aware of the limitations of their own research, this does not inhibit them from using that research as legitimation for their arguments. All the more so since others are using research in the same way. Thus, Wildavsky (1995) points to a frequently found pattern in environmental and security issues: coalitions of pressure groups and government organizations spread alarming stories on the basis of scientific research that are then broadly discussed in the media, but which prove ultimately to be untenable. The background of this pattern is the interest that organizations have in this information: that is to stay in business.

On the basis of empirical research into the strategic use of risk information, Weterings (1992) claims that private companies and governments are inclined to underestimate the risk of certain activities. Private companies do so because they have an economic interest in this as, indeed, do governments (economic development, tax income). But governments also do not wish to increase feelings of uncertainty among citizens and other interested parties living in the vicinity of industry. The pattern in the response of companies and governments regarding risk information is one of initial denial or downplaying, followed by reluctant acknowledgement that something is wrong in order not to lose their credibility. The inclination of societal organizations and of people living nearby to provide scare-stories is, according to Weterings a consequence of their position as being at risk. They are subjected to these risks and thus estimate their impact to be higher. Furthermore, they occupy a weaker position in the policy game, which they compensate for by using information strategies and manipulating the media.

Outcomes of Type I and Type II responses: report rains and 'dialogues of the deaf'

From a democratic point of view, Type II responses to uncertainty are not necessarily negative. The various knowledge contributions to the debate enrich the substantive arguments. In a discursive democracy, it is fitting that claims to truth are not grounded solely in the knowledge monopoly of, for instance, research institutions funded by government but, instead, are challenged by countervailing forces in a dialectical process that can result in informed decisions. Science and democracy, then, go hand in hand (Habermas, 1981; Dryzek, 1990; Fischer and Forester, 1993).

In practice though, parties are often not focused on dialogue and truth finding, but on winning. They use research and its findings as ammunition in the struggle for power. They 'shop around' to find experts who will support their standpoints, engage in cherry picking by presenting only those research findings that fit their position and use research to discredit undesirable solutions. Consequently, the argumentation struggle escalates: in response to counter-expertise, the commissioner of the initial research may decide to undertake more research in the hope of refuting the critique of its earlier findings. Also, other actors may decide to get involved in this struggle for knowledge and truth. The result is knowledge conflicts in which parties fire reports at each other and which, in turn, result in information overload, making it increasingly difficult to determine what is true. Coalitions of policy makers, experts and interest groups create 'contradictory certainties' (Hoppe, 1999).

The conflicting research results do not lead to substantive debate or synthesis. There is no knowledge accumulation, no learning in a cognitive sense. Uncertainty and confusion only increase. On the basis of this pattern, one can conclude that critical policy analysis has failed to accomplish its mission. Disappointed over the non-use of the findings of analytical research, advocates of this approach argued for lessening the distance between researcher and users. Keywords used were 'utilization focused evaluation' and 'usable knowledge' (Lindblom and Cohen, 1979; Patton, 1987; Wildavsky, 1987). On the basis of the patterns distinguished above we can conclude that research commissioned by one of the stakeholders is not authoritative for all parties and often increases rather than reduces substantive uncertainty.

Since it is no easy task to determine what is true, the process of problem solving acquires the nature of an argumentation game or discourse. In this discourse, parties attempt to establish a consistent storyline or structured argument in order to convince or force other parties to adapt their problem perception. Researchers provide ammunition to parties for their moves in this discourse where those parties try to arrive at shared meanings or try to impose their own interpretations on others (Hajer, 1995; Hoppe, 1999).

The risk of this development is that not all parties in the argumentation game have equal opportunity. Not everyone can follow the discussions, and experts, policy makers, institutionalized interest groups and the media will be the most influential. Politicians and citizens are flooded and outmanoeuvred by information overload and an array of interpretations. Weakly organized interest groups are not heard. From a substantive point of view, there is a risk that substantive stagnation will make problem solving more difficult or may even result in a 'flight from rationalism': i.e. making decisions without solid substantive foundations or developing compromises that cannot hold in the light of available scientific knowledge – the production of 'negotiated nonsense' (De Bruijn *et al.*, 2002).

2.3 Sources of substantive uncertainty: problem frames and ambiguity

Thus, Types I and II responses to substantive uncertainty do not lead to its reduction, but to its proliferation. Problems where these patterns occur are referred to in the literature as 'unstructured', 'untamed', 'intractable' and 'wicked' (Radford, 1977; Mason and Mitroff, 1981; Hisschemöller and Hoppe, 1996).

Uncertainty on knowledge and disagreement on values: wicked problems

A characteristic of this type of problem is that, in addition to a lack of knowledge and information, there are two more sources of uncertainty:

1   uncertainty or conflict about knowledge: there is not a lack of knowledge, but the status or interpretation of that knowledge is unclear;
2   uncertainty or conflict about the yardsticks used to determine the nature and degree of seriousness of the problem and also the effectiveness of the proposed solutions: parties can look at a problem from various frames of reference.

Distinguishing between these two sources of uncertainty, we can see four types of problems (see Table 2.2):

1   Technical problems: about which there is no societal conflict and where knowledge and technique are not problematic. For these problems a Type I response is adequate: solutions are possible by engaging experts and conducting research.
2   Untamed technical problems: where everyone agrees they must be solved, but for which there are no agreed upon technical solutions. For instance, there is a worldwide consensus that HIV/Aids needs to be addressed, but a medical–technical solution is still lacking. In the pursuit of this, experts may compete with each other and knowledge conflicts may emerge.
3   Untamed political problems: where technical solutions are available but where their application meets with societal conflict. Consider, for example, the technical capability to manipulate the gender of a human embryo. The application of this technique is controversial.
4   Finally, there are problems where both knowledge uncertainty and societal disagreement are present. This type of problem is the focus of attention in this book.

Problem solution strategies are aimed at manipulating Type 2, 3, or 4 problems in such a way that they will become a Type 1 problem; taming untamed problems. As indicated earlier, Type I and II responses are insufficient for this.

Table 2.2 Four types of problems

	Certainty on (scientific) knowledge	
	Large	Little
(Societal) agreement on problem formulation		
Large	Technical problems	Untamed technical problems
Little	Political problems	Wicked problems

Source: Hoppe, 1989.

It is necessary to improve the certainty about scientific knowledge and the consensus about measurement and problem definitions. This assumes a proper insight into the nature of both sources of uncertainty. We will address these issues below. First, we outline how parties define problems and their consequences. Then, we discuss the nature of uncertainty in the case of scientific knowledge.

Source of uncertainty 1: the presence of different problem frames

An important source of substantive uncertainty comes from the fact that problems are not 'things'. They are not objective circumstances or artefacts out there, waiting to be discovered and resolved by policy makers. A situation is only a problem when we perceive and experience it as such: there must be a gap between an existing or expected situation, and a desired situation. Often we are only aware of this gap once we are confronted with a new solution or comparing the problem situation with other situations (for instance, by comparing what we have or can do with that what others have or can do). Kingdon stated: 'If you have only four fingers on one hand, that's not a problem, that is a condition' (Kingdon, 1984: 115).

Also, our knowledge of the existing situation is limited and subjective by definition: our perception of the world around us is selective. What we see and what we do not see are highly influenced by our expectations and by what we find to be relevant: our *frame of reference*.

Frames of reference

The frame of reference encompasses the ideas about facts, interests, norms and values regarding reality, and our position within it, that we have internalized on the basis of previous experiences and perceptions. We use these ideas as orientation points and filters when looking at reality: we use them to organize, select, and attribute meaning to the vast amount of disorganized information we receive (Allison, 1971; Weicke, 1979; Rein and Schön, 1986, Sabatier, 1988). This is largely an unconscious process. Our frame of reference is thus highly determinant of our identity. Although each individual has his own unique frame of reference, there will also be important similarities with those of other individuals in the same social groups (White, 1992).

Each individual has a frame of reference, and it will, in various important situations, be comparable to that of other individuals in the same social groups. Through socialization (rearing, education, friendships, work experience), frames of reference are formed and influenced. Groups, organizations and entire societies share important norms, values and reality definitions, although overlap is never complete. Boundaries can be drawn where the differences are greater than the similarities.

The social construction of problems

With this frame of reference, we arrive at perceptions of reality and the situations in those perceptions which we regard as problematic; that is to say, unsatisfactory circumstances to which we wish to devote our attention, energy and resources in order to decrease or eliminate the gap between the current and the desired situation. A problem, thus, is not objectively perceived. It is not a fact, but a perceived gap: a social construction based on perceptions of existing situations, their causes and consequences, their future developments and potential solutions. Problem formulation is, therefore, highly subjective (Cobb and Elder, 1983; Dery, 1984).

The importance of problem perceptions

Problem perceptions may be social constructions, but they are not without consequences: 'if men define situations as real, they are real in their consequences' (Thomas, 1966). Parties base their behaviours on their perceptions of the environment and the problems they perceive in that environment. These problem perceptions determine the direction in which a solution is sought. Problem

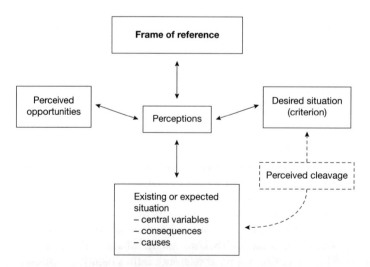

Figure 2.1 Problems as social constructs

Box 2.3 Conflicting problem perceptions in the case of the *Brent Spar*

Shell, for instance, had based its decision to sink the *Brent Spar* in the Atlantic Ocean on scientific risk analysis. The conclusion was that sinking the obsolete oil drill platform was the best solution from an economic and ecological point of view, a conclusion that also proved convincing to the British government. However, environmental groups – and Greenpeace especially – did not perceive the *Brent Spar* as an isolated issue. Although the scientific analysis of Shell was contested – unjustly in retrospect – the core of the disagreement was that Greenpeace perceived the problem differently from Shell: sinking the *Brent Spar* was not a once-only event, but it set a precedent for a new practice where the ocean could legitimately be used as a rubbish bin for a range of dumping. The cost-benefit analysis fitting their problem definition was quite different from that reached by Shell. The direction in which solutions were sought was very different too: sinking was not an option. Instead, the solution selected in the end, namely dismantling and recycling the platform, was more costly in an economic sense, (Scientific Group on Decommissioning Offshore Structures, 1998; Rice and Owen, 1999). Whether this was the better solution is, however, impossible to determine objectively even in retrospect. This depends on the perspective from which we view the problem.

---

formulations include some solutions while excluding others. That's why the definition of a problem often becomes the subject of conflict. Determining the nature of the problem allocates power.

Diverging and conflicting problem perceptions

From the above we can conclude that parties may have different perceptions of the same situation. Perceptions may vary about:

- the existing or expected problem situation (the core variables that are part of the problem, the consequences, the causes and the demarcation of the problem);
- the possible situation (possible changes and the availability of means or solutions);
- the desired situation and the yardsticks to evaluate the existing situation.

In situations where problem solving requires cooperation, we often silently assume that our partners in debate share our problem definition, while in reality they might hold a very different understanding of the situation: perceptions and yardsticks differ so that the gaps that actors wish to bridge may be very different (Dery, 1984). This may be a cause for misunderstanding and conflict, especially when parties are unaware of these diverging gaps. In the literature, situations in which parties talk past each other are called 'dialogues of the deaf', i.e. prolonged

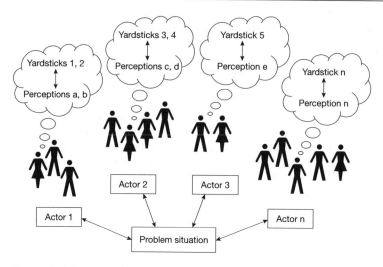

Figure 2.2 Different problem perceptions of a solution

impasses about substantive standpoints, all plausible by themselves, but mutually exclusive (Deleon, 1988; Van Eeten, 1999).

The formulation of the problem can also be the target of conscious attempts at influencing: whoever is in a position to determine the problem formulation in the process of problem solving, also determines the scope within which solutions are sought (Schattschneider, 1960). Rein and Schön call this the 'framing of the problem'. By mobilizing support, where acquiring media attention is very important, initiators (problem owners) can place their problem definition on the societal or political agenda. This process of influencing agendas and problem framing is known as agenda setting (Cobb and Elder, 1983). In this process of agenda setting, not all problems and proposed perceptions are accepted. The exclusion of problems and their formulations is known as the process of *non-decision making* (Bachrach and Baratz, 1962; Van Eijk and Kok, 1975).

Closedness and dynamics

Perceptions are hard to change since they are based on the frame of reference of the individual, organization or group involved. Thus, there is a high degree of closedness with regard to information that would challenge the correctness of a problem definition or preferred solution. Furthermore, a problem definition provides guidance for the direction a solution can take; a direction which is in line with the interests of the party involved. Hence, a strong immunity exists to different perceptions or counter-voices. Sabatier (1988), for instance, suggests that exchange of information and learning between parties with different frames of reference is very difficult (Sabatier uses the term 'policy core'). Not to mention the adaptation of the frame of reference itself. When actors close themselves from a substantive debate with others and do not wish to reflect upon their own

Box 2.4 Diverging and conflicting frames: asymmetrical argumentations

The *Brent Spar* example shows that for a long time, the conflict between Shell and Greenpeace was one of a 'dialogue of the deaf': there was an asymmetrical argumentation structure since the parties debated from different problem definitions making it impossible for them to reach a consensus. In the end, Shell's problem definition failed to survive in the public arena and the solution that ultimately won was the one in the policy frame of Greenpeace.

The zinc discussion also resulted in an asymmetrical argumentation structure. The zinc industry believed the eco-toxicity of zinc to be exaggerated by the government. They attempted to prove that the method by which RIVM determined norms for zinc was scientifically unsound. The problem definition of government did not concern the exact eco-toxicity of zinc, however, but the degree of emissions, which was considered to be too high. When the Health Council criticized the Aldenberg-Slob method used by RIVM, this was a Pyrrhic victory for the zinc industry. Governmental measures towards emission reductions were regarded as legitimate and industry appeared to have backed the wrong horse. Nevertheless, the knowledge conflict about norms and methods used to set them continued to be an important element in the discussion.

In both cases conflict and misunderstanding go hand in hand. There is a struggle about framing the problem. Some parties are aware of this; others less so. As a consequence, they talk past each other and fail to move any closer. It is also striking that they never arrive at a joint problem definition. Either one party succeeds in getting its problem frame to dominate the (public) debate (Greenpeace in the case of the *Brent Spar*), or both parties continue to operate from their own frame of reference (as in the zinc case).

problem perception, we can speak of substantive or cognitive fixation (in 't Veld *et al.*, 1991; Termeer, 1993).

That problem perceptions are difficult to influence, does not mean they cannot be changed. Under the influence of new information about an existing situation, such as possible (new) solutions or (unintended) consequences of used yardsticks, it is conceivable that judgements about the nature and seriousness of the problem can change. This will, however, not occur as a simple stimulus–response reaction. The frame of reference operates as a filter for judgement and it makes the changes of perceptions relatively unpredictable to outsiders.

Cognitive impasses: blockades and stagnations

When actors in a policy debate do not wish to reflect upon their own problem definition, or when their varying problem definitions entangle them in an asymmetrical argumentation structure, a 'dialogue of the deaf' emerges. Such a substantive stalemate or impasse can be characterized as a cognitive blockade or stagnation. A cognitive blockade emerges when perceptions clash and parties become engaged in a knowledge conflict. Cognitive stagnation occurs when parties, unintentionally, talk past one another as a consequence of asymmetrical argumentation structures. Frequently, both phenomena occur simultaneously.

Source of uncertainty 2: divergence and frames in knowledge production

Where neo-positivism (Mode I science) acknowledges uncertainty about knowledge, it provides a number of possible explanations and responses:

1   Uncertainty springs from the state of science: when research efforts are in their early stages, knowledge about the problem situation will be limited. Future research will bring less uncertainty.
2   Uncertainty springs from the complexity of problems: the number of variables involved and their mutual relations. The aim of, for instance, operations research is to split problems into elements and calculate the values of the variables and their relations and the possible fluctuations therein in the hope of acquiring a hold on complexity and determining the uncertainty margins.
3   Uncertainty results from a lack of knowledge about the future. Extrapolations are difficult because of possible interruptions in the trends. The alternative is to design future scenarios in order to see whether problem formulations and solutions are robust. Although the increasing capability of computers enables us to increase the number of possible futures and their consequences, this approach is also subject to criticism. After all, the potential number of futures is unlimited and there is little chance of arriving at robust solutions. By way of solution, adaptive policy development embraces an incremental strategy, which policy must also include provisions for learning. Through monitoring during implementation new information becomes available on the basis of which the design can continuously be adapted to the new situation (Walker, 2000).

Characteristic of these explanations of uncertainty is that they emerge from a lack of information and knowledge. The remedies are found in searching for knowledge. When it is recognized that this knowledge is, in principle, uncertain, then an attempt is made to use approximations in order to approach reality as much as possible or to make provisions that will make this information available in the future. This approach bypasses the other two sources of uncertainty: namely, uncertainty about the status or interpretation of knowledge, and the lack of consensus about problem framing. Characteristic of this approach to uncertainty is that the frame from which the problem is approached is not questioned and that uncertainty reduction is primarily an intellectual and not a social activity: stakeholders are not involved (Arentsen *et al.*, 1999; Hoppe, 1999).

Divergence and frames in knowledge production

The expectation that scientific research leads to clear outcomes and decreased uncertainty (i.e. leads to conclusiveness) is often not justified in practice. Instead of convergence, we find divergence: an 'indefinite proliferation of diverse issues, findings and hypotheses rather than convergence' (Lindblom and Cohen, 1979: 47). Possibly, some questions can be answered and knowledge becomes available which was hitherto unavailable, but the overall result is that new questions arise and that the problem proves to be even more complex than initially believed, etc.

This divergence is strengthened because the amount of research increases under the influence of policy advocacy. Obviously, each research project is limited in its design and execution. Choices are made with regard to delineating the subject, the research question, the theoretical starting points, concept definitions, indicators, measurement and analytical methods, and interpretations of data. No matter how solid the arguments for these choices may be, they are always arbitrary to some degree. Frequently, scientists disagree about matters of delineation, assumptions about indicators, methods or interpretations. They also may question the scientific quality of someone else's work and his or her qualifications.

The background for the struggle over method and these knowledge conflicts within the academic domain is that research decisions are not value free, but are influenced by hierarchical relations, financial considerations, and ideologically inspired beliefs. Here, relations between scientific communities and between scientists and contractors play a role. The scientific domain is not an autonomous and coherent subsystem within society, as assumed in Mode I science, but is fragmented and entwined with societal sectors. Thus, societal conflict and problem definitions enter the scientific domain. Knowledge production then becomes a two-level game: not only does scientific research aim to influence policy, but, at the same time, the policy practice influences science (in 't Veld, 2000).

The implication of the insight that knowledge production involves social aspects is that research is not value free. Research questions are prompted by perceptions about what is relevant. Knowledge is developed within a specific framing of the problem.

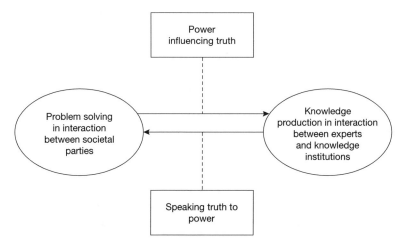

Figure 2.3 The relations between knowledge production and problem solution as a two-level game

> ## Box 2.5 Frame-bounded analysis in the *Brent Spar* case
>
> In the *Brent Spar* case, the scientific foundation of the decision to sink the plat-
> form was given within the issue delineation of Shell: it was really not the case that
> economic criteria were given central consideration and that the ecological argu-
> ments were not considered. The difficulty, however, was that Shell's definition of
> the problem was not shared by others. Therefore, research did not become
> authoritative in the debate. In the problem frame of other parties, sinking was not
> a once-only event but seen as the beginning of a new practice where the North
> Sea would become a rubbish disposal area. This then required that entirely
> different questions be addressed, and that the cost-benefit analysis be conducted
> in a substantially different manner. No matter how well Shell had conducted its
> research, in the perception of those opposing it, it simply was not relevant.

To illustrate this frame-boundedness of research, Wynne (1998) points to the phenomenon of reductionism. Risk analysis often aims at determining an objec-tively allowable risk, for instance the probability of fatalities for individuals or groups in the vicinity of an industrial compound in the case of an accident. Risk is reduced to one dimension that does not fit the perception of risk of, for instance, those living nearby or of the emergency services. The problem definition used determines the manner in which the problem is analysed – and consequently, the

Table 2.3 The two modes of science

	Mode I science	Mode II science
Vision of society	Mode I society: subsystems with task differentiation	Mode II society: intertwinement and mutual dependencies
Organization of science	Disciplinary and sectoral	Interdisciplinary and integral
Nature of relations between science and society	Knowledge production is independent	Knowledge production is influenced by society
Vision of knowledge production	The knowledge production process is neutral and objective	Knowledge is socially constructed
Nature of scientific knowledge	Objective, universal and conclusive	Tentative, frame-bound and divergent
Knowledge use	Instrumental use	Strategic and conceptual use
Source of authoritativeness	Internal accountability on basis of criteria of reliability, truth and objectivity	External accountability with regard to choices at all phases of research process
	Scientific, disciplinary and sectorally organized forum	Societal, interdisciplinary and intersectoral forum
Contribution to uncertainty reduction	Conclusiveness; facts speak for themselves	(Inter-subjective) meaning provision

research findings. And the problem frames of stakeholders and scientists involved may differ.

The neo-positivist (Mode I) type of science ignores the social aspects of knowledge production and thus the fact that research departs from a certain definition of the problem. This insight is characteristic of a post-positivist look at science and society: Mode II science in a Mode II society (Gibbon *et al.*, 1994; Nowotny *et al.*, 2001). Knowledge is developed in an interaction process between knowledge producers who make subjective decisions partially inspired by societal influences. Research is not separate from other societal subsystems, it is entwined with them. Authoritativeness is not derived from independence and internal scientific procedures. Acknowledging that research is frame-bound leads to more external accountability of choices. This, however, does not mean that the expectations placed upon research results, in terms of uncertainty reduction and the provision of reliable and true knowledge, decrease. Rather, the criteria to determine whether knowledge meets these requirements are different. Ideally, this would lead to a situation of mutual inter-subjective interpretations of preliminary, tentative research findings.

2.4 Conclusion: dealing with substantive uncertainty

In this chapter, we have seen that substantive uncertainty does not only emerge from a lack of information and knowledge about causal relations. An important source of uncertainty is simply the amount of information and number of interpretations that confront problem solvers. There is not so much a shortage of knowledge, but an excess of ambiguity (March and Olsen, 1976, 1989; Noordergraaf, 2000). This ambiguity results from the fact that within a problem situation, various actors are involved. These actors have diverging and sometimes conflicting perceptions of the problem. On the basis of these perceptions, they will judge knowledge and information differently.

When parties insufficiently consider the fact that they have different problem frames, knowledge conflicts and asymmetrical debates are the result. Information

Table 2.4 Lack of knowledge and ambiguity as sources of uncertainty

	Substantive uncertainty	
	Lack of knowledge	Ambiguity
Characteristics of uncertainty	Lack of information and knowledge for grounding action	Information overload, confusion and knowledge conflicts
Nature of uncertainty	Lack of information and knowledge about causal relations in a problem situation	Presence of diverging frames from where problems and solutions are judged
Adequate response	Information gathering, use of experts, conducting research	Joint production of meaning

gathering, the use of experts, and conducting research will then prove to be counter-productive: the variety of interpretations and the impasse between parties is strengthened rather than reduced. Ambiguity assumes a different response. It requires reflection on individual frames of reference, taking into account varying problem perceptions of relevant parties (Rein and Schön, 1986, 1992; Roe, 1994). It requires the search for cross-frame discourse or learning across the boundaries of policy advocacy coalitions (Sabatier, 1988; Sabatier and Jenkins-Smith, 1993; Van Eeten, 1999). Only when parties are aware that different frames of reference are involved, will it be possible to discover the real substantive questions that need to be addressed. It then becomes conceivable that a joint frame of reference is developed from which a shared meaning is given to facts and research results. The question is thus how information gathering, use of experts and (scientific) research in ambiguous situations can be used in such a manner that they – despite the limitation to research in terms of conclusiveness – result in authoritative outcomes that are meaningful in the sense that they can serve as a basis for action. This question will be addressed in the next chapters, and especially in Part 2 of this book.

Chapter 3

Uncertainty and process

Problem solving as a strategic game

3.1 Strategic uncertainty in problem solving: introduction

Uncertainty is not only a knowledge problem, as was discussed in the previous chapter, but it also results from the presence of various parties – each with their own perceptions, objectives and strategies. The behaviour of these actors with regard to problems and solutions results in complex and unpredictable games. Uncertainty in dealing with wicked problems not only has a substantive dimension, but also a strategic one. In this chapter we analyse the nature and sources of strategic uncertainty. We start by looking at the zinc case by way of illustration (see Box 3.1).

This sketch of actors, strategies and interactions reveals the strategic complexity of the zinc game. Not only are there differences of opinion, but equally striking is the lack of interaction. Parties send each other written documents, but there is rarely face-to-face contact. When there is, it fails to result in a substantive exchange of ideas, but merely remains an exchange of points of view and procedural agreements. Coordination is further inhibited by the fact that actors make decisions in various settings, often inaccessible to others. Still these decisions have consequences for other parties and for the progress of the problem solving process as a whole. As a result of this the game does not develop in a linear fashion, but has a zigzag and erratic nature. There are conflicts and stagnation, the outcome is uncertain and, above all, parties are unable to coordinate their strategies.

What does the zinc case illustrate?

Despite the complexities sketched above, we must also state that the zinc case is a relatively simple issue: there are other problems that are technically far more complex. The process regarding the zinc problem evolves in an almost de-politicized manner and – given the limited size of the group that will experience the negative consequences of government policy – the potential for mobilization and politicization is limited. Mediation efforts by employer associations were motivated by the fear that the conflict would damage the image of the private sector. What is an interesting observation is that, apparently, the process of problem solving of such a de-politicized problem – at the subsystem level with a

Box 3.1 The zinc game: four rounds of strategic moves by actors

Round 1. In 1989, the Ministry of VROM compiled a list of substances, from diffuse sources, for which the concentration in the Dutch waters were too high. The objective was to take steps to reduce the emissions of these substances. One of these substances was zinc. The research institute RIVM, which is linked to the Ministry of VROM (Housing, Spatial Planning and Environment), was asked to develop a scientifically grounded norm. To this end, RIVM drafted a so-called 'Basic Document'. In the meantime, VROM determined tentative norms in 1991. The Basic Document on zinc appeared in 1992. VROM also developed a policy on sustainable building in this same period. The building sector was asked to monitor the environmental effects of their activities. At the local level, municipalities adopted this policy as well. They made certain demands with regard to the materials used in local building projects based on preference lists. The 'Guide to Sustainable Building of the Society for Experiments in Public Housing', which was published in 1993 and advised against the use of zinc, was authoritative in its decision. This policy of municipalities was also encouraged by water managers who have to implement water quality norms and were confronted with high water purification costs.

Round 2. While the zinc industry did not initially consider the Basic Document on zinc a threat, the municipal policy of discouraging the use of zinc roused them. In 1993, the industry fought the Guide to Sustainable Building in court, but to no avail. They then turned to the Ministry of VROM, which claimed to have no influence over the content of the Guide to Sustainable Building and also pointed to the autonomy of local governments: VROM only determines environmental quality norms, not the policy to implement them. The industry decided to draft a response to the Basic Document and hired a consultant. In this response, the method and findings of RIVM were attacked. It now became clear that parties had a serious disagreement and that the content of the Basic Document was questionable. In 1995, VROM requested the Health Council to prepare a formal recommendation on the matter. Actors expected this recommendation to bring the matter to a close.

Round 3. The discussion intensified while the parties awaited the recommendation. In 1996, the industry organized itself into the Association for Zinc and the Environment. They engaged the Ministries of VROM and Traffic and Water Management in discussion, and fundamental differences of opinion emerged. The Ministry of Transport, Public Works and Water Management believed that zinc emissions should be further reduced, especially through the pursuit of alternative building materials. Meanwhile, the National Programme for Sustainable Building was published; this was a new list of preferred building materials compiled by the building industry itself, but without the participation of the zinc industry. This list also discouraged the use of zinc. Water boards and municipalities joined forces and urged more vigorously for reducing the use of zinc. At the provincial level, 'regional teams' were created to develop action programmes to reduce emissions from diffuse sources. At the national level, they brought together their activities in the Coordinating Body for Integral Water Management – the body in which

ministries, sub-national governments and water managers coordinate the implementation of water management policy.

Round 4. In 1998, the Health Council's recommendation was published. It criticized the methods to set norms of both RIVM and the zinc industry, but suggested
there were grounds for government policy aimed at reducing zinc emissions. Based
on this, the Cabinet proposed to take measures in consultation with the private
sector. In the meantime, the Association for Zinc and the Environment had
become part of the Association of Sustainable Building Materials, which also
included participation by the copper and the lead industries. This association
proposed a covenant with agreements on a mutual policy for reducing zinc
emissions. In 1999, the ministries rejected a covenant claiming that it lacked solid
commitments with obligations for specific results and clear specifications which
would make monitoring credible.

Instead, the parties settled for an exchange of letters. The Association of
Sustainable Building Materials sent a letter with various proposals for product development and in exchange requested a minimum guarantee from the government that
these products would be given a serious chance, especially when they would prove
to be more expensive than the existing products. All in all, parties found it hard to
commit themselves to joint actions and to achieve binding agreements about reduction. They did get closer, however, especially regarding their perceptions of the
quantity of emissions. Research they had commissioned jointly, suggested that these
were considerably lower than previous government data indicated.

Local governments and water managers viewed the Health Council report as
support for their attempts to reduce the use of zinc. The Association of
Sustainable Building Materials reacted to their continuing efforts by organizing
seminars in late 1998 for architects and civil servants of municipalities, provinces
and water boards. A first meeting between the Association and representatives
of the North-Holland regional team resulted in an exchange of points of view,
without the parties coming any closer to agreement.

During this period, at the European level, a comparable discussion emerged
about the eco-toxicity of zinc. The Netherlands served as the rapporteur and
drafted a risk assessment for the European Union. The Ministry of VROM charged
RIVM with this task and, in turn, RIVM worked with the zinc industry. But here,
too, parties were unable to agree.

Sources: Klijn *et al.*, 2000; van Bueren *et al.*, 2003.

strong technical nature – acquires the features of a strategic game and becomes
engulfed in uncertainties springing from unpredictable behaviour and the
complexity of the game setting. So, problems which we would view at first sight
as 'low politics' and relatively technical, are subject to the same strategic mechanisms with which we associate issues in the field of 'high politics'.

A classic case of the latter is offered by Allison's study of how White House
decision makers responded in October 1962 to the Soviet installation of nuclear
arms in Cuba (Allison, 1971; Allison and Zelikow, 1999). Allison characterized
crisis decision making at the White House as: (a) a rational decision by the

President supported by discussion in the crisis team; (b) a decision upon limited information and options presented on the basis of the routines of the organizations involved; and (c) as a compromise between the proposals that had been suggested in a negotiation game by parties involved in the crisis team.

Over the course of time, this game character of complex decision making and problem solving has been documented in a rich variety of theoretical and empirical studies. These studies examine relatively technical as well as non-technical subjects; high and low political issues; large- and small-scale problems, crisis type decision making and routine decision making, economic and post-materialistic or ideological conflicts (some examples, although this is not a comprehensive overview, include March and Olsen, 1976, 1983; Nelkin, 1977; Hanf and Scharpf, 1978; Richardson and Jordan, 1979; Rhodes, 1981, 1988; Wynne, 1982; Kingdon, 1984; Nelson, 1984; Lovenduski and Outshoorn, 1986; Rosenthal *et al.*, 1991; Wildavsky, 1995).

Uncertainty as a consequence of strategic behaviour: problem solving as a game

The process described above provides a number of interesting viewpoints for a discussion about uncertainty. It shows that interactions between public, private and semi-private actors take place in a complicated game of strategies. Thus, dealing with societal problems occurs in a context of strategic uncertainty; there is uncertainty about the strategies actors will select and about the circumstances that will influence the course of the game.

In this chapter, we analyse this strategic complexity as a cause of uncertainty. In Section 3.2 we provide an overview of the development of theory about problem solving processes as a game. In Section 3.3 we discuss the elements of the game. Section 3.4 provides a theoretical interlude about the meaning of the fragmented context in which policy games are played. In Section 3.5 we show what this fragmentation means for the conceptualization of policy games. The evolution and the outcomes of policy games are discussed in Sections 3.6 and 3.7 respectively. Section 3.8 provides a summary to this chapter.

3.2 Theories of problem solving: from rational model to game approach

As outlined above, the evolution of complex processes of societal problem solving does not appear to be at all rational. Rational choice models, also referred to as policy phase models, suggest a completely different course of the problem solving process. Simon (1957) described the policy phase model concisely in three phases: 'intelligence' (what is the problem?), 'design' (what solution/alternatives are there?), and 'choice' (which alternative is the best?). Others provided a more detailed model, distinguishing generally the following phases. During the agenda formation phase, a problem arises on the agenda. Next, the problem is further investigated. Alternatives are then developed and their effects explored. Also, objectives and criteria are determined. An assessment of criteria and effects leads

Table 3.1 A phase model of problem solving

1	Formulate the problem
2	Analyse the problem situation
3	Identify solution alternatives
4	Set goals and priorities
5	Compare costs and benefits of alternatives
6	Make a selection from the alternatives
7	Implement solution
8	Monitor and control implementation of solution
9	Evaluate

to the choice of the best alternative, which must then be implemented. This is followed by evaluation: assessing the process and outcomes. This phase model can be found throughout the literature on policy and policy making (Jenkins 1978; Dunn, 1981; Anderson 1984; Hogwood and Gunn, 1984; Quade, 1989). Table 3.1 presents an example of a phase or stage model.

These phases are 'logical', not 'chronological' steps: the process is viewed as a cycle with several possible iterations. One could speak of a 'policy life cycle' (Parsons, 1995). Figure 3.1 provides a representation of the policy life cycle.

One primary characteristic of the rational phase model is that the process of problem solving is regarded as an intellectual design process. The model places the individual decision maker and his decisions at the centre. Problems in terms of a gap between an existing or an expected situation and a norm are solved by first specifying the nature of the problem situation and its consequences and causes. Then the means that might be used to tackle these problems and objectives are defined. Alternatives are selected, implemented and evaluated. Successful problem solving depends on the degree to which objectives are achieved or, better still, upon the degree that the gap is narrowed. Problem solving can fail as a result of insufficient information about the nature of the problem situation and the effects of solutions, the lack of clear goals and specifications, not considering all options

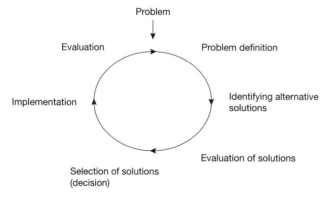

Figure 3.1 The policy life cycle

Source: Parsons, 1995: 77.

Table 3.2 Approaches to decision making

Level	Nature of decision making	Central insights	Approaches/actors
Individual	The individual (central) decision maker assesses alternatives on the basis of his own objectives and as complete information as possible	Limitation of information-processing capacity: 'bounded rationality'	Rational synoptic decision making and the 'classic' critiques and amendments (incrementalism, Lindblom, 1959; satisficing-model, Simon, 1957; mixed scanning, Etzioni, 1968)
Group	Decisions are made in groups, where the group process influences course and outcome	Group processes influence information provisions, value judgements and interpretations	Social-psychological decision making approaches such as 'group-think' and 'entrapment' (Janis, 1982; 't Hart, 1990)
Organization	In modern societies organizations make decisions in relative autonomy. The type of organization matters: rational bureaucracies versus professional 'organized anarchies'	Organizational filters, intra-organizational contradictions and attention structures influence information processes and the decisions based upon them	Organizational process-model; bureau-political model (Allison, 1970); 'garbage can' model (Cohen et al., 1972)
Inter-organizational	Decisions between mutually dependent organizations are taken in horizontal settings with a highly 'disjointed' nature	Subjective perceptions, power relations, dynamics and coincidence influence information and decision making	Lindblom's 'disjointed incrementalism' (1959, 1979); game approach (Allison, 1970; Crozier and Friedberg, 1980); stream model (Kingdon, 1984)

and making assessments in a non-transparent way. In short, because phases are skipped or not properly applied.

Since the formulation of the central premises of the rational phase model in the 1950s, several alternative approaches to decision making and problem solving have been published. In the 1950s and 1960s, the critique was focused on the limitations of the rationality of the individual decision maker (Simon, 1957; Lindblom, 1959). There is 'bounded rationality': the decision maker does not have all of the information and his capability to process information is limited. In the policy sciences, the initial emphasis on policy making as a rational design activity of an individual (central) actor is being replaced by policy making as a social interaction process between various parties (individuals, groups, organizations) in a certain context. This includes focusing on conflict, power, irrationality and institutions (Allison, 1971; Edelman, 1971 and 1977; March and Olsen, 1976; Lindblom, 1979; Crozier and Friedberg, 1980; Janis, 1982; Cobb and Elder, 1983; Hoppe and Edwards, 1985; Parsons, 1995). Table 3.2 provides an overview of these developments by comparing the characteristic ideas and insights about decision making at the various decision making levels and by naming the most important models and their authors.

Complex societal problems are not solved in a social vacuum by the autonomous cognitive-analytical exercise of a central actor. Problem solving takes place in an arena in which mutually dependent actors mould and shape problem definitions and solutions. It is not only an intellectual design activity aimed at taming substantive uncertainties, but also a strategic game in a multi-actor and multi-purpose setting. In addition to substantive uncertainty, involved parties also experience strategic uncertainty. These arise from the unpredictability and uncontrollability of the strategic 'moves' of other parties. Within these games, processes of problem solving develop which are fundamentally different from what the policy phase model presumes. Table 3.3 contrasts both approaches and shows that each leads to different descriptions, explanations, judgements and recommendations.

3.3 The basic elements of the policy game

What are the elements of a policy game? In this section, we discuss the actors, their strategies, the arena where the game is played and the game type that develops within it.

Actors, resources and dependencies

Complex societal problems usually involve a variety of parties: individuals, groups and organizations from both the public and the private domains. Individuals include citizens or clients of companies, but also individuals who are members of a group or work in an organization. Groups include interest groups such as residential associations and ecological and environmental groups, but also more small-scale cooperation types ('teams', 'project groups') within and between organizations. Organizations include a wide diversity of public organizations from various levels of government or from various sectors, but also for-profit organizations and societal organizations (sector organizations, not-for-profit organizations and the like).

Table 3.3 Problem solving as an analytical activity versus a strategic game

	Problem solving as intellectual design	Problem solving as strategic game
Policy making	An intellectual design process that is sometimes interrupted by political considerations	A political power game that is dominated by strategic considerations
Perspective	Central actor who solves problems in relative autonomy and whose problem perception is taken as the starting point for analysis and design	Mutually dependent actors who pursue a solution through negotiation and strife
Processes	Sequential processes that can be subdivided into phases or steps with a clear beginning and end	Zigzag and erratic processes in which information, means, and objectives are exchanged and a collective outcome is achieved in an incremental manner
Decision	A scientifically grounded answer to a well defined problem, in which appropriate means are sought on the basis of a given objective	A political compromise where problems are sometimes found to fit existing solutions and the available means co-determine the choice of objectives
Uncertainties	Arise from a lack of knowledge and information about the nature of the problem and solutions	Come from the behaviour of actors as grounded in their interests, positions and preferences
Information	Emphasis on scientific knowledge gathering; knowledge use leads to better problem solving	Selectively used to support partisan arguments
Criterion for success	Decreasing the gap between the problem situation and criterion; achievement of *ex ante* formulated objectives	Improving the position of those involved when compared to the existing situation
Fail factors	Lack of information about causal relations; lack of a clear framework for appraisal; inadequate planning, lack of means; too many actors involved	Inadequate processes of interaction and information exchange so that mutual solutions are not developed
Prescriptions	More information and research; clarification and prioritization of objectives; tighter planning and centralization; limiting and structuring participation	Improvement of conditions for cooperation and joint image building through facilitation, mediation and arbitration

What links this diverse field of actors is that they depend upon one another. This dependency springs from the fact that in order to solve a problem, resources or means are required that are not possessed by any one actor, but rather are divided among actors. Resources include the whole range of formal and informal means parties possess in order to achieve their objectives. This may include formal competencies and decision making powers (authority), clearly identifiable resources such as money, organization, human resources, but also less tangible

Table 3.4 Typology of dependency relations between actors

	Substitutability of the resource	
	High	*Low*
Importance of the resource		
Large	Low dependency	High dependency
Small	Independence	Low dependency

resources such as authority, legitimacy, strategic capability, mobilization power and the like. Scharpf (1978) argues that an actor's degree of dependence is determined by the importance this actor attaches to resources 'owned' by others and by the possibility of substituting these resources or acquiring them through other actors. The importance and the substitutability of these resources determine dependency relations (see Table 3.4).

Complex problems require a combination of various resources owned by different actors. In these situations, there are mutual dependencies that are not equally divided across parties, i.e. there may be a case of asymmetric dependencies where party A is more dependent upon party B than vice versa.

We also need to realize that parties are not always aware of their dependency, and they sometimes overestimate their own potential or power. They will not always behave according to their dependency upon others. This is one of the important causes why they are unable to achieve their objectives.

It is also important to distinguish between 'realization power' and 'hindrance power'. When parties control an important and irreplaceable resource, they can block the creation of a solution strived for by others. They can do this when their interests threaten to be harmed by a certain solution or because they think that they will acquire a better negotiating position by creating barriers. When parties want to realize a solution, they must possess realization power: this is rarely concentrated within one party but usually requires the willingness of various parties to invest their resources in a joint process of problem solving.

When the interests and perceptions of parties involved in a game are convergent, then realizing a solution is not that difficult. In such a situation, the policy game can develop according to the phases of the rational model. But such a situation can hardly occur with complex problems engulfed in uncertainty. In this situation, a strategic game will develop where parties, on the basis of diverging or conflicting interests and perceptions, find themselves in a complex negotiation game that has a quite different dynamic.

Interests, perceptions and strategies

Policy games are created when actors recognize that they depend upon other parties for the realization of their objectives. As a result, they develop strategies: actions or intentions for actions aimed at influencing (the behaviour of) other parties, the content of problem formulations and/or the solutions considered, or the development of the problem solving process.

Actors base these strategies on perceptions: the images they have of their environment and of the problems and opportunities within it. In the previous chapter, we addressed problem perceptions, but perceptions can concern different topics. Perceptions are images of:

- *Problems*: actors have different ideas about the nature of the problem but also about the urgency and meaning of the problem. Thus, water boards view the problem of zinc in surface water as more important than municipalities do.
- *Solutions*: different actors often propose different solutions. In most cases this has to do with the perception they have of the advantages and disadvantages that are linked to their solutions.
- *Other actors*: actors can hold different perceptions about other actors in their environment. These differences may relate to the objectives they pursue, the resources they control, the strategies they intend to use, etc.
- *Developments in the environment*: actors can also have very different perceptions about the nature and meaning of developments in the environment. For instance perceptions may vary on the prospects of the national economy and the impacts of that on the problem situation.

Perceptions possess a certain stability since they are generally formed gradually on the basis of experiences that actors have had over the course of time. Furthermore, they are closely related to how actors define themselves, their environment and their interests. Nevertheless, perceptions may change abruptly, for instance under the influence of invasive or threatening events in the environment (Cobb and Elder, 1983; Kingdon, 1984).

Both the objectives of actors as well as their strategies are derived from and inspired by their perceptions. Objectives are concrete translations of (parts of) perceptions. Actors can make choices here. Not all the values, criteria and yard-sticks that underlie their perceptions have to be translated into objectives. Thus, while water boards may have perceptions about clean water, they have to formulate the objectives that target certain priorities and from which they expect the best effects. Their perceptions about the importance of certain problems can, therefore, influence them to make different choices than their perceptions would indicate. Water boards may choose to give increased priority to measures aimed against pesticides and herbicides instead of measures against the pollution of surface water by heavy metals, despite the fact that both can be considered environmental problems. Hence, objectives are more concrete than perceptions, they imply choices and they are formulated in more operational terms. Figure 3.2 defines strategies as goal–means combinations based on perceptions, aimed at influencing the content of problems and solutions, the process evolution and the strategies of other parties.

Since actors depend upon other actors, they will use their strategies to try to influence – or at least anticipate – the behaviour of other actors. They will attempt to make sure that the objectives and goal–means combinations that they pursue correspond with their assessment of the strategies of other actors and the content of the policy game wherein these strategies are played. There is a 'bounded rationality': the guiding motive for strategic action is the realization of one's own

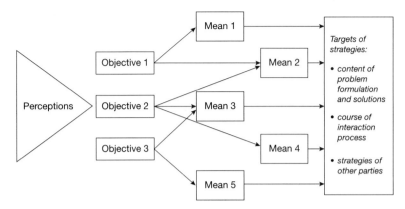

Figure 3.2 Strategies as goal–means combinations based on perceptions

objective, although the definition of this objective is shaped by perceptions, limited information and non-rational elements such as sympathies and antipathies, loyalties, rules, etc. (Crozier and Friedberg, 1980; March and Olsen, 1989; Ostrom, 1990).

Strategies are not necessarily cooperative. It may be attractive for actors to slow down or block the progress of the policy game, for instance, when the process appears to be moving towards a policy measure that could harm the actor's interests. Some actors are simply not interested and do not participate in a certain interaction process. When other parties are dependent upon an actor's resources, they have to convince that actor to participate.

Several different types of strategies can be distinguished:

1   Go-alone strategies. These are strategies where the involved actor has formulated a substantive solution to a problem and attempts to realize this more or less despite his strategic dependencies. This type of strategy may result in the selection of this solution – with all of its (dis)advantages. It is, however, also conceivable that this strategy will evoke the resistance of other parties and will result in blockages.
2   Conflictual strategies. These are strategies aimed at preventing or blocking solutions or policy measures considered desirable by one actor.
3   Avoidance strategies. These are strategies where parties do not really resist a particular solution, but adopt a passive attitude or avoid conflict. For instance, because they are not really interested or because they want to avoid the costs that accompany policy measures or conflicts.
4   Cooperative strategies. These are strategies where the actors acknowledge their external dependencies, do everything to interest other parties in their plans and then try to achieve a favourable result in the negotiation process.
5   Facilitating strategies. These are strategies inspired by the fact that cooperation is necessary to achieve a mutually beneficial solution. They are aimed at bringing parties together, mediating in conflicts, and so forth. These strategies

may arise from an actor's substantive interest but may also come from an actor's desire to limit transaction costs or from a sense of responsibility for the course of action in a certain area.

Arenas and game types

The game of problem solving takes place in an *arena* where actors present their strategies. The arena is the place or field where actors meet and play their game. It is the place where a specific group of actors make choices on the basis of their perceptions of problems, solutions and each others' strategies (Cohen *et al.*, 1976: 25; Ostrom, 1986; Ostrom *et al.*, 1994).

The evolution and outcome of decision making processes is determined to a large degree by the mix of strategies brought into the arena. We call this mix of strategies 'game types' (Godfroy, 1981). These are characteristic combinations of strategies that have a stimulating or limiting influence on the evolution of the problem solving process as it develops in various arenas. Game types can lead to blockades or stagnation, for instance, because a go-alone strategy triggers conflictual strategies or because a cooperative strategy ends up being an avoidance strategy. Strategies, however, are not static: under the influence of strategies of other parties, new insights or external development strategies may be adopted. As a consequence the game type changes. This may result in the ending of the blockades or stagnation, and the beginning of a more cooperative strategy (compare Ostrom, 1990). The reverse is also possible: initial cooperation can revert to conflict which, in turn, strengthens conflictual strategies. Figure 3.3 presents the policy game as a mix of actors' strategies in an arena that form a game type at a given moment (t_1). Over the course of time, the game type may change: after a while (t_2) actors may have coordinated their strategies. And then later (t_3), changed strategies may again result in a new game type.

Because of actors' dependencies, problem solving in policy games is essentially am exercise in cooperation. Parties are dependent upon one another for tackling problems. They must interact with each other. At the start of the policy game, there is uncertainty and perhaps also conflict about the content of, and approach to, the problem. By means of mutual cooperation, these uncertainties and disagreements may be reduced and problem solving becomes possible. For this, it is necessary that a game type develops in which at least a substantive group of the involved actors coordinate their strategies. At the very least, this may result in an

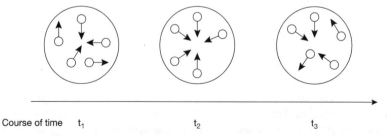

Course of time t_1 t_2 t_3

Figure 3.3 The policy game as a mix of strategies (game types) that actors bring to the arena

acceptable practice (a 'negotiated environment' or an 'agreement to disagree') that enables parties to continue their own practices in such a way that others are not harmed. When ambitions are higher, it becomes necessary to achieve a compromise between the desired solutions or to develop a joint image of the problem situation in order to create a basis for joint action.

Strategic uncertainty: the unpredictability of strategic action

The problem with achieving this coordination is that actors' interests, perceptions and strategies diverge and conflict. But what makes playing the game even more difficult is that the strategic behaviour of actors is highly unpredictable and subject to change. This is the case especially when parties respond to and anticipate each other's behaviour. While actors can assess the strategies of other parties, they cannot be certain that their assessment will prove to be correct. As a result, a complicated game of action and counter-action emerges that cannot be predicted.

Hence, the zinc industry's decision to attack RIVM's method for setting norms came as a surprise to the public parties involved. They reacted by rejecting the data provided by the industry. Thus a dynamic was created in which one party's standpoint was strengthened and the other party's standpoint was rejected.

A significant barrier to achieving common action is the risk of opportunistic behaviour: actors do not invest in solutions themselves but, instead, leave it to others to find solutions ('free rider behaviour': Olson, 1965; Ostrom, 1990; Williamson, 1996), actors cooperate until they have achieved their goals ('hit and run'), and actors delay their investment in solutions until it is certain that they can actually be realized ('wait and see'). The risk of opportunistic or strategic behaviour discourages parties from investing in problem solving and this makes the creation of joint solutions more difficult.

This strategic uncertainty causes a situation where solving complex problems is more than a simple game of negotiation in which a number of players with diverging interests and objectives arrive at a compromise through an exchange of objectives and means. There is also another source of uncertainty that makes it even more difficult to satisfactorily conclude policy games: the fragmented nature of the policy game itself. We will address this next.

3.4 Theoretical interlude: the fragmented nature of policy games as a source of uncertainty

In practice, problem solving processes do not evolve chronologically nor do they have an established logic. They are highly erratic by nature. Cohen *et al.* (1972) have characterized this erratic nature most radically in their 'garbage can model of decision making'.

Problem solving according to the 'garbage can' model

This model applies to complex situations where there is no set hierarchy of objectives and values, where routine procedures are absent and where participation in the processes is not guaranteed. Cohen *et al.* call these situations *organized anarchies*. While their model initially referred to professional organizations such as hospitals

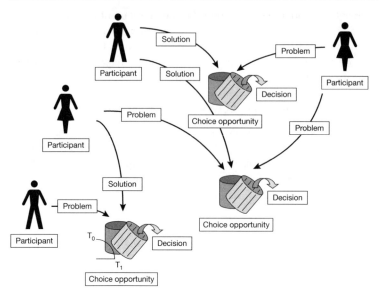

Figure 3.4 The 'garbage can' model

and universities, they have also applied it to network type situations: decision making in the public sector where various different actors are involved. In organized anarchies, activities such as problem formulation, design of solutions, participation and decision making develop independently from one another. Cohen *et al.* speak of *streams* of problems, solutions, participants and 'choice moments' that independently flow through the organization. A choice moment is a 'garbage can', in which participants drop their problems and solutions. According to our conceptualization of the policy game in the previous sections, a 'garbage can' can be regarded as an arena. An arena may be a formal setting, for instance the official gatherings of representative bodies or management teams, but it may also have the nature of an informal setting (e.g. decision making during informal dinners, lobby activities, before or after official meetings, etc.).

The composition of the content of the 'garbage can' depends upon the production of waste (problems, solutions, participants), the availability of other 'garbage cans' and the speed with which they are emptied. The outcome of decision making depends to a high degree upon what is 'accidentally' in the 'garbage can' in terms of problems, solutions and participants at the moment of decision. Figure 3.4 presents the evolution of decision making on problems and their solutions according to the 'garbage can' model.

Kingdon's streams model: problem solving as coupling of streams

Kingdon (1984) has applied the stream model of Cohen, March and Olsen to public decision making processes. He adapts it in a number of ways. He distinguishes between three streams: *problems, solutions* and *political events*. With the latter stream, Kingdon pulls important political factors into his model. These include such events as cabinet change, but also changes in the political climate as certain problems and solutions in the political system become less urgent and others gain priority. Participants are not in one stream, but within and between *all* streams. After all, problems are not separate from people (or groups or organizations). Problems are articulated by people. The same can be said for solutions: people are required to develop solutions and to bring them to the attention of others in order to get them accepted and implemented. For the coming together of participants, problems and solutions into 'garbage cans', Kingdon introduces a new metaphor: *the policy window*. He borrows this concept from space travel. When a satellite is launched towards a celestial body, it must be done in a particular time frame. Only then is the constellation of celestial bodies such that the objective can be reached. If the rocket is launched too early or too late it will miss its target. Kingdon argues that the same holds for policy. When the streams between problems, solutions and political events are linked, the possibility of realizing policy emerges: to make a decision about the solution of a problem. Even though a problem may be urgent or a design promising, without this linking of streams, decision makers will make no decision. Policy windows can be regarded as policy opportunities where the problem owners, proponents of solutions and decision makers, are in touch with each other (linked) and work towards achieving a solution. In addition to policy windows, there are problem and political windows: these partial couplings may provide a stepping-stone for a problem solution, but are, by themselves, insufficient.

Couplings mostly do not emerge of their own accord. They are realized by *policy entrepreneurs*: actors in search of solutions to their problems or support for their solutions. Some couplings are structured and predictable. A well-known policy window in the Netherlands, for instance, is the formation of a new cabinet after an election, when the main outline for government policy over the next four years is defined. The cabinet formation becomes a target for problem owners and solution providers.

It is also important to note that these couplings are temporary. New developments in the streams (for instance, the rise of new issues, the occurrence of focusing events such as crises or incidents, the fall of a cabinet, changes in economic or political fortunes) can lead to the decoupling of streams, which brings an end to the policy opportunity. Figure 3.5 presents the streams of problems, solutions and political events, and their couplings and decouplings, as described by Kingdon in his stream model.

The fragmented nature of policy games as source of uncertainty

The stream models of Cohen *et al.* and Kingdon turn the rational model of problem solving more or less upside down. In the phase model, agenda setting and problem analysis are followed by development and selection of the solution on the basis of unambiguous and explicit criteria. In the stream model, problem formulations and solutions develop independently from one another and separately from the relevant actors and arenas where decisions are made. In addition

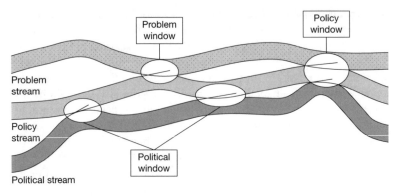

Figure 3.5 Kingdon's stream model

Source: Pauly, 2001: 25.

to problems in search of a solution, there are solutions that search for problems, participants who search for problems and/or solutions and choice moments in search of participants.

Also, the stream model differs from negotiation models where parties arrive at compromises through exchange on the basis of clear and stable goals. It emphasizes the fragmented context in which policy games develop.

As a result, parties rarely meet, important decisions are made in various places that are not linked to each other and participation in decisions in arenas fluctuate ('people move in and out constantly' (Heclo, 1978)). Furthermore, the process of problem solving is disturbed by developments in the societal context such as 'swings' in the political–administrative climate and the changing of the political guard by which both preferences and key decision makers may be replaced. So, uncertainty is not only produced by the strategic behaviour of parties, but also by the asynchronous nature of developments and the chances that these are coupled and decoupled.

Not only does this add an extra dimension to strategic uncertainty but it also strengthens the inclination and opportunities for strategic behaviour. First, because problem solving occurs in a context in which institutions are weakly developed: in arenas where representatives of various organizations participate, rules and shared perceptions that make the behaviour of actors predictable are often not present or only weakly developed. Many inter-organizational arenas reveal the characteristics of organized anarchy. This is certainly the case when parties have not interacted before, when there are unique and complex strategic issues on the agenda, or when there is a crisis type situation characterized by an 'institutional melt-down'. The second reason why these conditions are favourable for strategic behaviour, is that parties will try to anticipate the erratic characteristics of the process (for instance, by resorting to delaying tactics in the hope that a policy window will close), so that their behaviour becomes even more unpredictable.

The question can be raised, however, whether the authors of the 'garbage can' model are not going too far with their notion of organized anarchy. However important the infuence of fragmentation, capriciousness and chance may be, the perception of problem solving in the situation of an institutional vacuum is too simple a presentation of reality. We believe that even in a situation of extreme fragmentation, there are institutional factors that influence actors' behaviour. We discuss this at length in the next chapter. March and Olsen have acknowledged this: in their later work they have given explicit attention to the rediscovering of institutions in complex decision making processes (March and Olsen, 1989).

Although the stream model may appear extreme at first sight, upon closer inspection, there are several points of recognition. For instance, the criticism of decision making about the construction of the Betuwe rail line in the Netherlands is, essentially, that national government started the process with a solution – a rail connection between Rotterdam and the German border – without a discussion about its usefulness and necessity. The Betuwe line was a solution in search of problems. Over the course of time, various problems have been coupled to the Betuwe line (the weak competitive position of Rotterdam harbour, delayed growth of the Dutch economy, environmental issues), but these have not resulted in changing the solution. An adequate problem formulation would not have placed the *solution* at central stage, but would have placed the question of 'how the link between Rotterdam and its hinterland can be improved?' there instead. Such a problem formulation would have left room for other solutions such as water transport.

The decision making on the Betuwe line is not an exception. It is quite normal that the process of problem solving begins with the availability of a solution instead of acknowledging and defining the problem. Apparently the design of solutions to complex societal issues develops relatively independently from the societal problems which they are intended to solve. The television was introduced in the Netherlands by the 'solution owner' Philips. What societal values were served and what problems were solved had yet to be discovered. The same can be said at the moment about the introduction of new ICT technology.

3.5 Fragmented policy games: problem solving at the crossroads of arenas and games

The 'garbage can' model and the stream model show that societal problem solving takes place in a fragmented context, where decisions about problems and solutions are often made in different locations. Problem solving consists of a large number of smaller decisions made by various parties in various streams and in various locations with regard to aspects of the problem formulation and possible solutions. When these partial decisions meet – i.e. are linked because problem owners, solution owners and decision makers meet and agree upon a problem solution combination – the possibility emerges that they are integrated and can result in problem solving.

To be sure, we believe that the fragmented policy game keeps not just problem owners, solution owners and decision makers separate. Besides the three streams there are other lines of division that keep actors apart and problem solving fragmented. In complex societal problems, different government levels, sectors (public and private) domains, and alliances are involved so that the lines of division also run through various clusters of problem owners, solution owners and decision makers. In other words, complex policy games are played in various different arenas at the same time and most actors will participate in only some of these arenas, and possibly certain parties (or interests) will not be represented in any arena.

Policy games as a series of decisions in various arenas

Thus, policy games are complex not only because there are many players making unpredictable strategic choices, but also because they are often simultaneously involved in more than one *arena*. This is because most problems have different dimensions and thus touch upon different types of policies and actors. For instance, in decision making on airport expansion, issues such as transport, economy, employment, planning and zoning, noise, safety, and so forth, play a

---

Box 3.2 The fragmented nature of the zinc game

Thus in the zinc case, the zinc industry made a concerted effort to attack the scientific method used to determine norms for zinc. Completely unexpectedly, they were confronted with a list of sustainable building materials by the SEV, that labelled zinc as a material to be avoided. On the list later compiled in the context of the National Programme on Sustainable Building, zinc did not come out well either. An important reason for this was that the zinc industry was not represented in that arena. Decisions that influenced the content and course of the game, were made in various arenas. We can distinguish:

- the 'norm arena' where VROM, RIVM, the zinc industry and Health Council made decisions about norms for zinc;
- the 'emissions arena' where VROM, V&W, the RIZA (the research institute related to V&W) and private companies discussed zinc emissions and zinc products;
- the 'sustainable building arena', where representatives from the construction business compiled lists that rank products according to their environmental effects;
- the 'diffuse sources arena', where national government, municipalities and water authorities made decisions about and discussed the implementation of water quality policy;
- the 'international arena', where RIVM, together with other parties, conducted a European risk analysis.

In these arenas, limited clusters of actors, partially in the context of parallel games such as that of sustainable building, made decisions that had consequences for others and for the evolution of the problem solving process as a whole. As a result, the policy game for the zinc industry became a multi-front war where it was impossible to arrive at a coherent strategy for playing in all of these arenas in a coordinated manner. Such a comprehensive strategy was beyond the capacity of the zinc industry. Furthermore, in many arenas, they simply had no access.

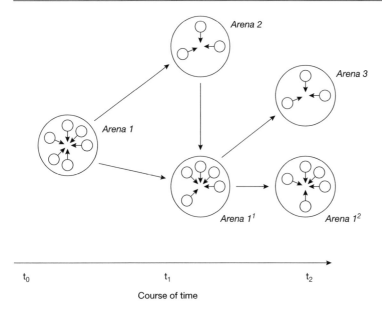

Figure 3.6 Policy games as a series of decisions in various arenas

role. As a consequence, decisions about the future of the airport are made in the context of various types of policies in various arenas and at various government levels. As a result, the policy game acquires a highly fragmented character. Course and content of the game are, after all, determined by decisions that are made by actors in various locations based on very different rationalities. There is a fragmented and 'loosely coupled' decision making system (Weick, 1979). This fragmentation makes opportunities for influencing and steering decision making processes very difficult. Actors can be confronted with unexpected decisions made in other arenas in which they do not participate, which nevertheless have major consequences for them.

Figure 3.6 visualizes policy games as a series of decisions in various arenas.

Policy games and their relation to other games

The complexity of policy games is also enhanced because games are not played in a vacuum, but amid other games. Within an arena, actors can play more than one game. As a consequence, these games influence one another. A loss in one game can be compensated by a gain in another, or vice versa.

Policy games influence each other. Through couplings, new trade-offs can be realized between games. Because of this, it is conceivable that in the one game, support for unpopular measures is created because there is compensation in another game. Furthermore, the coupling of games may have a mitigating effect upon the conflicts and strategies that actors use. The bill for strategic misbehaviour in one game will become due in another (Axelrod, 1984; Taylor, 1987). Box 3.4 provides an example of such a conscious coupling.

Box 3.3 Decision making on a tunnel under the Green Heart as a result of another game

In the Netherlands, the discussion about whether the high-speed train from Paris to Amsterdam should run through the Green Heart of the country was greatly influenced by the conclusion of the discussion about allowing night flights at Beek Airport in South Limburg. The Social Democratic Minister of the Environment, De Boer, had strongly opposed these night flights but had lost. Now the decision on the construction of the high-speed train through the Green Heart threatened to make the environment the loser once again. The Green Heart is the rural centre between large cities in the most densely populated western region of the Netherlands, and it is under constant pressure. The area also has a large symbolic meaning: the struggle to protect the Green Heart is the focus of the Dutch nature and environmental movements and the touchstone of nature and environmental policy of the Dutch government. Once it was proposed to construct the high-speed train through a part of the Green Heart, the credibility of the Minister of the Environment and the intentions of the Social Democratic party in the area of the environment were at stake. This was the umpteenth time that the Social Democrats had exchanged nature and the environment for the economy. As a result, this conflict was played up dramatically by the Environment Minister, party members and Members of Parliament who profiled themselves on nature and environmental issues. The result was a decision to build a 9-kilometre-long tunnel for the sum of 0.4 billion euro under the pastures; an investment which will be hard to understand for people who have not been actively participating in the decision making process.

Box 3.4 Road pricing in the Netherlands: the conscious coupling of games

In many countries, there is debate about how to solve the traffic jam problem. In the Netherlands, this resulted in a proposal in the 1990s to introduce road pricing during rush hours. Through tolls on the access roads to large cities during the rush hour, the use of road capacity would be spread across the day. Quickly, a strong lobby of automobile interest groups, private companies and big cities opposed these plans. The governments of the large cities, in particular, regarded these plans as a modern version of city walls with a stifling effect upon the local economy. Furthermore, increased traffic was feared on the local byroads as drivers attempted to circumvent the tolls. The plan for road pricing appeared to suffer an early death, until the Minister of Transport, Public Works and Water Management linked it to several other projects in the area of traffic and transport. She started negotiations with each of the large cities to arrive at a package deal where contributions to large infrastructural projects were linked to cooperation for the introduction of toll-gates on the highways around the city. One by one, the large cities agreed and made cooperation agreements with the ministry.

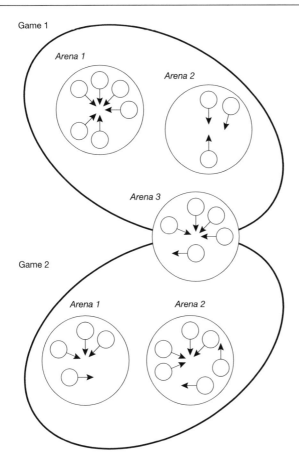

Figure 3.7 Coupling of games

Although in the case of road pricing in the Netherlands (see Box 3.4) the minister ultimately decided against introducing toll-gates and opted instead for a more innovative and flexible system of electronic kilometre charges, this example shows that coupling games and linking issues may lead to new opportunities for exchange and negotiation. Thus, support can be found for a measure that is, at the start, unpopular. Anticipating these mechanisms, the strategies of actors can be focused on coupling games or – when they believe that such coupling will jeopardize the option they desire – to decouple. Figure 3.7 visualizes the relation between arenas and games and between the games themselves.

3.6 The evolution of the policy game: rounds, impasses and breakthroughs

Policy games develop through a series of successive decisions about the nature and content of a problem, about solutions and about how these matters are being decided. Just as there is no central decision maker, there is no central decision. There are a number of explanations for this:

- Often, parties only have the opportunity to make decisions about aspects of the decision. They only have control over limited resources and are dependent upon decisions by other parties in other places.
- Since actors often interact in organizational arenas with a limited mandate, they have to regularly consult with their parent organization, or, in the case of public organizations, with political superiors and representative bodies, in order to secure the legitimacy of agreements. As a result, they can only proceed one step at the time.
- Furthermore, the development of ideas at the start of the problem solving process has not yet concluded: it has often only just started at that point. This means that parties still have to choose positions and select objectives. This is done incrementally. Through a series of interactions and partial decisions, a better understanding gradually emerges about the nature of the problem situation, the actors and interests involved, possible objectives, problem perceptions and solution directions, and relevant arenas and coupling opportunities.

The evolution of policy games is not that of a linear process where a problem is solved on the basis of authoritative *ex ante* problem formulations or objectives. The policy game looks more like a sports match played in a number of rounds (Radford, 1977; Crozier and Friedberg, 1980; Teisman, 1992). A round opens with an initiative or policy intention of one of the parties that serves as 'trigger' to the others. What follows is that in an initially unclear or conflictual situation, parties discuss with each other and negotiate about what is to be done (March and Olsen, 1976). Then, through a series of steps, parties will search for mutual adjustment or joint solutions. This process is not without problems. *Impasses* are in the way of achieving satisfactory solutions for all parties. Impasses may emerge because actors are unwilling to invest in the process (*stagnation*) or because there is a conflict where some use their veto or blocking power (*blockage*). Impasses may eventually lead to terminating the policy discussion, but may also result in a *breakthrough*. Breakthroughs come about by crucial decisions that reformulate the problem, conciliate opposing solutions or change the group of those involved.

Each round ends with a *crucial decision*, a decision that offers a solution for the question that is central in the particular policy round. The content of such a solution is often quite unexpected: it is frequently based on a redefinition of the original problem and a transposition of earlier positions and objectives, so that the scope for solution is changed or enlarged. The game then assumes an unexpected direction.

A crucial decision heralds a *new round*, where it guides the subsequent policy game. If a round resulted in a clear outcome and offers perspectives about what needs to be done, this will have a motivating and centripetal impact upon the parties. The players for the next round join when they see new chances. Thus, a 'whole new ball game' emerges with new stakes, new perceptions and new strategies.

The turns the game takes as a result of these successions of rounds are reinforced by changes in the environment. Since policy games stretch out over long
periods of time, the conditions under which the parties meet change continuously.
Under the influence of societal, economic or political changes in the environment (swings in the political climate, cabinet change, change of the economic
tide, availability of new technology, or emergence of focusing events such as
authoritative reports, societal mobilization, or the occurrence of incidents,
accidents or disasters), the group of those involved and the nature of problem
perceptions, objectives and strategic positions may alter significantly. Because
of this, earlier decisions can be repealed and the process of problem solving
broken or taken in a new direction. It is in this sequence that parties who lost in
earlier rounds may have new opportunities to compensate for their loss or even
score a victory in a new round. This shifting back and forth between impasses and
breakthrough under changed circumstances gives the policy game an erratic and
zigzag appearance. Figure 3.8 visualizes a policy game moving through different
rounds. The vertical axis provides the development of the content of plans, the
horizontal axis the development over time. The direction of the arrows indicates
the degree to which the process zigzags (substantively) and evolves by fits and starts
(in terms of time).

3.7 Outcomes of the policy game: impacts on content, process and institutions

The outcomes of the problem solving process do not reflect the goals of parties
at the outset of the process. Solutions develop under the influence of various
strategies and events that manifest themselves in assorted rounds and arenas.

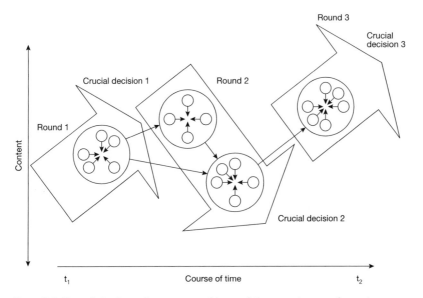

Figure 3.8 Rounds in the policy game: problem solving as a zigzag and erratic process

---

Box 3.5 Rounds in the zinc game

In the zinc game four rounds can be distinguished:

1   The interaction until 1993 in which scientific policy development dominated without parties protesting against it. This round ended with a decision by the zinc industry to do something about the declining returns on zinc products.
2   The 1993–1995 period, during which the zinc industry entered the policy game and challenged existing policy. This ended in a request for a formal recommendation from the Health Council that was intended to bridge the differences.
3   The 1995–1998 period, during which – awaiting the recommendation of the Health Council – parties took their positions and tried to convince others that they were right. This round was concluded by the recommendation of the Health Council.
4   The period after 1998, when it appeared that the Health Council was unable to bring parties together, and when none of the parties scored a definite victory. Parties occupied new positions, while no attempt was made to arrive at mutual problem solving. In the European arena, the old contradictions appeared to be replicated. This round is not yet concluded.

Often, the outcomes consist of a series of intermediate products and temporary solutions that influence the problem situation prior to a future solution. In the zinc case, there was continuous work on developing new standards systems and policy measures based upon them, while the existing norms and existing policy measures remained in force. Sometimes old solutions coexist together with new ones. Problem solving can develop out of a variety of barely coordinated measures that are simultaneously selected and implemented by several actors. These measures work alongside each other, sometimes strengthening and at other times opposing one another. As a result, new solutions, when not coordinated properly, will have a limited impact.

But solutions are not the only outcomes of a policy game. Outcomes can be categorized into three groups: in addition to the creation (or not) of substantive decisions, outcomes may emerge at the level of the process or on the institutional level. Below, we address these three types of outcomes. We need to keep in mind that outcomes do not only result at the end of the process, but also during the process, as intermediate products of previous rounds.

Substantive outcomes

Substantive outcomes may take different forms:

*   First, it is possible that solutions are not achieved and the problem is not resolved. This is known as 'non-decision making' (Bachrach and Baratz, 1962; Van der Eijk and Kok, 1975).

- It is also conceivable that the desire for solid action results in taking unilateral measures that, by necessity, are based upon limited information and only satisfy a small number of involved interests: 'blunt' solutions or 'adverse selection' (Jensen and Meckling, 1976). It is highly likely that these decisions will, in turn, generate unilateral measures from other parties as a form of counter-steering. As a consequence, solutions remain uncoordinated and chaotic, the realization of objectives is uncertain, while unintended and un-desired effects emerge.
- Third, types of mutual action are conceivable where actors coordinate or integrate their solutions. This type of outcome can take different forms. It may involve compromises where parties settle for – in their perspective – a sub-optimal solution that does not optimize their objectives, but still constitutes a gain in comparison to the existing situation. Also conceivable are *package deals* where a loss in the one area is compensated by a gain in another. This *compensation* can also take place across space and time: parties accept losses since they create rights in future or parallel arenas, rounds or games. Finally, *goal intertwinement* is possible: finding a solution that does not necessitate the exchange of objectives, but that manages to simultaneously achieve the vary-ing objectives of parties. Often, innovative solutions that can only be achieved by expanding the scope for solutions or redefining the problem situation are necessary. Thus, solutions are realized that are richer than those the parties initially had in mind with their go-alone strategies (Teisman, 1992; Klijn and Koppenjan, 2000).

Outcomes at the process level

In addition to substantive outcomes, the policy game also results in outcomes at the process level. This concerns the effect upon the *relations* between involved organizations that can shift between the extremes of cooperation and hostility under the influence of interaction and idea exchange. The course of events in a policy round may cause a deterioration in conditions for future collaboration, but it may also result in a situation where parties build credit with each other. The starting position for further interaction and cooperation can thus be influenced in a favourable or unfavourable direction.

Institutional outcomes

Third, policy games have *institutional outcomes*: they may lead to the creation or modification of relations, mutual orientations and perceptions and a shared language. These impacts occur at the level of institutions: the enduring relations between actors. These enduring relations make up the networks that actors are part of. Under the influence of policy games, these relations are further shaped or modified. Previously unrelated actors or networks may gradually become connected. In such cases, we speak of a network formation or network change. The relation between network and policy games and the significance of it for solving complex policy problems is the topic of the next chapter.

Box 3.6 Solving the Venice water problem: an example of goal entwinement

The way the Venice water problem is dealt with provides an example of goal entwinement. The objective to safeguard Venice and its lagoon from high water events, as we frequently may witness in television accounts, is complicated by the complexity of the natural and socio-economic system of which Venice is a part. Interventions in the system interfere with the variety of functions and character-istics of this system. In developing solutions a vast number of interests and objectives has to be taken into account. Besides safeguarding the city and its cultural heritage, there is the problem of the environmental, ecological and morphological deterioration of the lagoon, due to both natural developments (changing water highs, tides and hydrodynamics) and human activities (erosion and pollution caused by the construction of jetties, dredging sea routes, fishing, indus-trial activities, tourism). There are also socio-economic interests at stake: industrial and shipping activities require an open access to the sea. Furthermore, measures may not compromise or alter the appearance of the city and the lagoon, nor the city's architecture, monuments and landscape.

Since functions and interests are closely interwoven, the Italian government chose, at an early stage, an integral problem solving approach, by developing a package of measures. The design of the water protecting barriers (MOSE: Module Sperimentale Elettromeccanico or Electromechanical Experimental Module) itself reflects this. The dam, costing 2.3 billion euro, has no above-water structure between its gates. The barriers of the dam are mobile and will only be closed in the case of high water (average five times a year). When not used they will be invisible. The design is adapted to morphological measures taken at the lagoon entrances. But MOSE is also part of a broader package of measures (brought together in the General Plan of Interventions) aimed at the restoration of the hydro-geological balance and the morphological structure of the lagoon, the reduc-tion of pollution and protection of flora and fauna, additional measures for coast protection, and local defences that protect the lower lying parts of built-up areas. The latter reduce the number of times MOSE will have to close its barriers. So, as the mobile barriers are closed only in the event of high waters, the environ-mental impact and interference with port activities caused by the barrier between sea and lagoon are minimized.

However, this integrated solution, entwining so many interests and objectives, was not realized in a straightforward manner, nor without effort and conflict. In 1973 a special law was adopted that declared the safeguarding of Venice a matter of 'priority national interest'. In 1984 objectives were formulated and institutional arrangements established. Scientific research and initial design activities started. The conceptual design for MOSE was completed in 1989; the preliminary design in 1992. The Environmental Impact assessment resulted in a negative judgement in 1998 by the Ministry of the Environment regarding the environmental compat-ibility of the design. Additional research activities were started, based on improved models and scenarios and improvements and innovations were introduced in the design. In 2001 another research and design round was necessary to address remaining uncertainties and objections. In December 2001 the go-ahead for the final design was given, followed by the decision in April 2003 to start with the real-ization of the MOSE-system. So, we see a gradual development of the solution in a number of design and decision rounds, supported by parallel research activities. During these activities, knowledge and insights regarding the system, the problem and the impacts of a solution increase. Also, parties involved develop a concept of the consequences of the project for their environment and specify their demands. New objectives are formulated and new doubts and questions arise, as a result of which new research questions and requirements emerge and the solution has to be adapted to incorporate new insights and demands. Despite these prolonged rounds of consultation, research and design, progress is made: scientific consent grows, uncertainties are addressed and countered and, due to continuous adapta-tions of the design, goals become increasingly intertwined, eventually allowing final decision making to take place (www.salve.it/banchedati/Domande/uk/Domande. asp; www.save.it/uk/sezioni/itermose/mosenews/mosenews.html; www.salve.it/ uk/news/news.htm).

3.8 Conclusion: dealing with strategic uncertainty

We conclude here by remarking that the solution of complex problems not only involves coming to grips with substantive uncertainty, but also with strategic un-certainty. Strategic uncertainty comes from the unpredictability of the strategic behaviours of other parties as well as from the fragmented nature of policy games. Prior to the game, information about perceptions, goals and strategies is not available – if only because parties will not position themselves until the process has begun and, furthermore, because unexpected events may occur that cause parties to alter their strategies and which take the game in unexpected directions. There is little in these games that displays the phase model or policy life cycle of the rational approaches to problem solving and decision making. Thus, it will not be strange when we suggest that approaching problem solving as a policy game results in different recommendations for handling uncertainty. Only by engaging in interaction, will parties gain information and will positions and stand-points become clear. A 'negotiated environment' gradually emerges where certainties are created, through mutual perceptions and binding decisions and agreements, that enable common action and joint solutions. At the same time, this chapter demonstrates the vulnerability of these processes: interaction may derail and initial cooperation may end in the opposite: sudden changes in the environment may obliterate long-running investments in mutual problem solving in no time. Also, the environment of problems can be so complex and the hostility and distrust between other parties so deeply rooted that it is a question of whether the actors have sufficient resources and 'gamesmanship' (Lynn, 1993) to coordi-nate their actions.

In Part 2 of this book, we address the question of which methods are available for actors involved in policy games to confront strategic uncertainty and to arrive at coordinated efforts to deal with wicked problems.

Chapter 4

Uncertainty and institutions

Patterns, rules and trust

4.1 Networks as the institutional context for interaction and games

Games and strategic actions of actors do not occur in a vacuum. Actors, issues and games have a history. Actors have met in previous games, must adhere to certain rules – some formal and codified, others shaped informally in the past. Some players trust each other, so they are more inclined to share information and they have no need to formulate everything in detailed contracts. This can significantly reduce uncertainty within or between networks. Other players may experience substantial distrust. This makes interactions more difficult and increases uncertainty about the behaviour of other actors and of the outcomes of policy processes.

This 'solidified history', expressed especially in rules but also in more or less stable patterns of interactions and perceptions and relationships of trust among actors, represents what we call the *institutional characteristics* of networks. These characteristics are very important for a proper understanding of the actions of actors and the process of games taking place in networks. The institutional context in a policy issue of some size manifests itself in various ways during decision making. By way of an introduction, we will discuss two of these: the institutional complexity of decision making and the closedness of decision making.

Institutional complexity and fragmentation in the zinc case

According to one of the actors involved in the debate on zinc emissions, 'There are no direct contacts with RIVM, which is a scientific institute, and you must not bypass another ministry'. In making this statement, he emphasizes a striking characteristic of the case, i.e. there was apparently little contact between the actors from different networks even though the game was played in different networks. This has to do with the institutional complexity of decision making concerning zinc emissions and the closedness and different institutional regimes of the networks involved.

When looking at the debate on zinc emissions, we see enormous institutional complexity and fragmentation. In Chapter 3, we discussed this complexity at the level of arenas. Decision making often takes place in different arenas, but that is not the only area where complexity resides. The different arenas are also embedded in different networks.

In the zinc debate, we found at least three networks (sustainable contact patterns between participants) in which the five arenas that we distinguished can be found:

- First, the *water network* includes all participants concerned with water quality such as the Ministry of Traffic and Water Management, the RIZA, water boards, and the water departments of provinces and municipalities. These actors meet frequently in various platforms, such as the CIW. They also share several convictions about water quality and how it has to be improved. Decisions and policy about diffuse sources are almost exclusively made in this network.
- There is, however, also a *public housing network* with different actors, such as VROM (its public housing unit), builders and project developers, architects and provincial and municipal departments involved in building and housing. These actors also have their own contact patterns and convictions. Decisions about sustainable building are made entirely in this network (i.e. in the sustainable building, Dubo arena).
- Finally, there is an *environmental/products network.* Here we find actors such as the environmental units of the Ministry of VROM, RIVM and private industry. In this network, decisions about norms are made, product policy is set and, hence, decisions made about the legal standards applied to products. The emissions arena is largely situated in this network, although the Ministry of Traffic and Water Management also participates in this network. As far as the national Dutch network is concerned, the international arena is almost entirely situated in this network. The emissions arena is the only arena which contains actors of all three networks.

Figure 4.1 provides an overview of the networks and arenas and displays the enormous institutional complexity and fragmentation of the zinc game.

This figure clarifies the fact that some actors are in different networks. These are actors who have relatively little contact with each other. But the figure also shows why parties in the debate often believe they have been confronted with decisions they did not see coming, or they do not know where to turn to in order to attempt to influence decisions. The institutional complexity mentioned earlier has much to do with this uncertainty and confusion among actors in complex decision making. Institutional complexity and fragmentation makes it difficult for actors to be present in the relevant arenas. In addition, actors often don't have the overall picture of the various arenas, so they don't know where decisions are made – and even if they do, they are not always able to be present in that arena.

Thus, the sustainable building lists are made in the Dubo arena. While some actors from the public housing network participate in this arena, actors from the water network (Traffic and Water Management, the RIZA, provinces and municipalities) rarely do. Environmental quality norms are determined in the objective setting arena which is dominated by participants from the environmental network. Diffuse sources policy is especially an issue for the water network in which, for instance, the zinc industry participates only minimally. Thus,

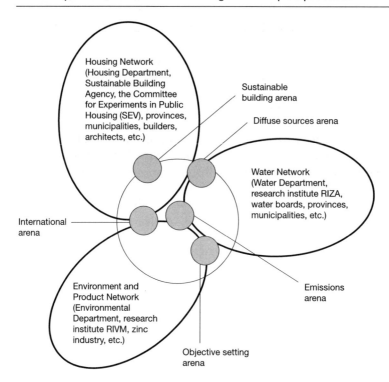

Figure 4.1 Arenas and networks in the zinc game

institutional fragmentation creates a situation where actors are frequently surprised by decisions made in arenas where they do not participate.

Institutional regimes and compartmentalization: examples of the zinc debate

The institutional context of the zinc game is not only complex and fragmented because the game is played in multiple networks and arenas; the game must also deal with the different institutional regimes of the identified networks. As the quote above about contacts with RIVM suggests, these institutional regimes can limit the access of actors to networks and arenas. As a consequence of (unwritten) rules about departmental autonomy, it is unusual for one department to make contact with another. A comparable phenomenon occurred in the contact between water boards, which are part of the water network and the overall water management. Actors from other departments simply did not establish contact with the water boards. In order to do so, they would have had to make contact with actors from that network at the level of the head of the department of Traffic and Water Management who, in turn, would bring them in touch with the water boards. This type of unwritten domain rule makes sectors and networks relatively closed for outsiders which, in turn, inhibits contact between networks.

Also, there are several important rules within networks that prescribe behaviour in games. In the water network, for example, there are explicit rules for the valuation of information. Actors in the water network are, first and foremost, technically oriented. They also work with highly aggregated data about water quality, pollution and the quantity of undesirable materials in water that are acquired through measurements and models. Furthermore, they place high value on the source of the data. Data from the RIZA and the ministry are regarded as authoritative, while data from other sources are deemed less authoritative. In short, within the water network, there are recognizable rules for determining the quality and reliability of data. When the zinc industry started its own campaign and provided information about the harmfulness of zinc, this information was regarded as unreliable and discounted by the water network in a partisan fashion. Hence, the zinc industry failed to access the network because of rules about positions and information considered valid within the network.

Institutional characteristics of networks

This example shows the importance of institutional characteristics in explaining behaviour, process and outcomes in decision making processes – especially in complex decision making processes central to this study where knowledge and value differences play an important role. Institutional characteristics of networks are an important cause of uncertainties in problem solving in decision making. They can, however, also contribute to good decision making. Furthermore, institutional characteristics are often related to one another. Thus, decision making in the zinc debate was characterized by relatively closed networks, comparatively substantial mutual distrust – especially between public actors and the zinc industry, and by patterns of perception far removed from one another. In short, the decision making game was characterized by, at first sight, an unfavourable institutional context.

Thus, there is every reason to consider these characteristics. First, we outline the contours of networks as institutions. We discuss the institutional characteristics as patterns of interactions, rules and their mutual relations as well as their relation to concepts discussed in Chapter 3. Next, in an aside, we briefly discuss how institutions are considered in public administration literature (as well as other literature). This provides us with the basis for a more in-depth discussion of an important element of networks as institutions, i.e. rules (Section 4.4). This also provides us with the opportunity to compare the institutional network perspective presented here with other perspectives. In Section 4.5, we discuss trust and the meaning of trust for cooperation and interactions. We conclude this chapter with an account of institutional complexity and fragmentation and the way in which institutional aspects of networks change.

4.2 Towards an institutional network theory

Following the ideas presented in Chapter 1 we can define networks as 'more or less stable patterns of social relations between mutually dependent actors, which form around policy problems and/or clusters of means and which are formed, maintained and changed through a series of games'. From this definition it is clear that networks provide a context for games, the interactions, in which the ultimate outcomes of policy processes are realized. Below we discuss the patterns of social relations and introduce the concept of rules since they play an important role in the analysis of networks as institutions.

Patterns as characteristics of networks

Networks gradually emerge because actors begin interacting. As indicated in the previous chapter, this occurs because actors are mutually dependent. If actors want to achieve goals which are interesting and valuable to them, this dependency forces them into interaction. This interdependency establishes patterns of interaction and actor perceptions emerge.

Interaction patterns: stability in contacts

Through interdependency and repetitiveness of interaction, stable interaction patterns are created in networks. These patterns are often quite logical in the sense that actors who interact frequently with each other must also deal with each other when the goals and organizational identity are taken into consideration. Thus, it is not surprising that many networks are sectoral by nature as they are studied and discussed in the literature (Wamsley, 1985; Laumann and Knoke, 1987; Rhodes, 1988; Hufen and Ringeling, 1990; Marsh and Rhodes, 1992). In various policy sectors, such as health care, public housing, justice, traffic and transport, etc., many actors are linked since they are part of a chain of policy plans leading towards concrete products or services. Also, these actors all share an interest in the financial means made available for the realization of sectoral policy and the services and products linked to it.

In the zinc case, various water boards interact with the RIZA and the provinces. Provinces have tasks in the area of water management. They need the water boards in order to achieve certain water quality standards and environmental objectives, and the water boards need the provinces since the provinces make decisions which are important to them. For both parties, frequent interaction is an important condition for keeping informed about new developments, for influencing the behaviour of others, and for achieving objectives.

Interaction patterns can be considered in different ways. It is possible to consider the intensity of interactions and to determine which actors have the most contact with each other. Looking at the variety of interactions will provide a better understanding of how many different actors maintain contact with one another. The intensity and variety of interactions provide information about which actors are central and which are peripheral to the network (see Aldrich and Whetten, 1981; Scott, 1991). They also show how easy it is for actors to communicate with other actors.

Interaction patterns and closedness: the negative side of networks?

Interaction patterns are often specific to an individual network and may sometimes remain unchanged for years. In related literature on iron triangles, subsystems and policy communities, the negative side of networks is often emphasized. Because of fixed interaction patterns, largely shared perceptions and all sorts of implicit rules, networks become inaccessible to other actors (see Freeman, 1965; Freeman and Parrish Stevens, 1987; Laumann and Knoke, 1987; Ripley and Franklin, 1987; Jordan, 1990). In this view, fixed interaction patterns occur together with shared opinions (patterns of perceptions) and rules about access, but also, for instance, about what are and are not legitimate problem formulations. In the power research of the 1960s and 1970s and the related study of agenda formation, this closedness of networks vis-à-vis outsiders is particularly emphasized. In their 1962 article 'Two Faces of Power', Bachrach and Baratz pointed to this when they stressed that decision making is often focused on safe elements while other aspects remain outside consideration (Schattschneider, 1960; Bachrach and Baratz, 1962, 1970). This invisible side of power, in which certain groups hold power on the basis of social and political values or institutional agreements, is thus highly institutional by nature and only visible through an institutional analysis of networks.

As long as there are no major tensions in networks and actors outside the network do not attempt to interfere with actors and decisions in the network, stability and tranquillity can be sustained. It becomes different when actors outside the network try to get involved in network issues (see, for instance, literature about subsystems and iron triangles: Freeman and Parrish Stevens, 1987; Ripley and Franklin, 1987; Jordan, 1990).

Patterns in perceptions: content and trust

Networks may also be characterized by certain perception patterns. As indicated in the previous chapter, actors act on their perceptions, which contain different understandings of the content (nature of the problem, desired solutions, etc.) and the other actors (for instance, the power and competence of actors). These

---

Box 4.1 Shaking up the fisheries network

When the European Union began intervening with national fisheries policies starting in the early 1980s, the interaction patterns in many European countries were affected. The relations in the Dutch fisheries network were particularly shaken. Quota regulations and other EU measures not only disturbed the equilibrium and created conflict, but they also generated different interaction patterns between actors (van Buuren, 2002; van Buuren and Klijn, 2004). For instance, environmental groups attempted to increase their involvement in fisheries policy, the departments desired greater distance from the fisheries sector, and the fisheries associations assumed a more independent position in relation to the product board that serves as their umbrella association.

understandings are created through the experiences and interactions of actors with each other. It is therefore logical that as a result of intensive interaction, actors come to share certain perceptions or that their perceptions converge. Various theories emphasize this phenomenon of shared perceptions and converging perceptions (Termeer, 1993; Termeer and Koppenjan, 1997), of policy belief systems (Sabatier, 1988), and of 'reframing of frames' (Rein and Schön, 1986). Networks can thus be distinguished from each other in terms of the degree to which actors more or less share certain perceptions. It is, however, also possible that groups of actors in a network share similar perceptions. In this case, there are separate groups of actors within networks whose perceptions are comparable (see Termeer, 1993; Klijn, 2001).

The more similar that actors' perceptions are – they will never be completely homogeneous – the easier it generally will be to reach consensus in complex games. At the same time, it will be harder for other, possibly new, actors with different opinions to access the network. Furthermore, if there is an increasing convergence of perceptions, the danger exists that actors will fail to recognize new problems and solutions. In short, the increasing convergence of perceptions in a network of actors has advantages (possible acceleration of policy games in networks) and disadvantages (certain closedness and the risk of not being open to new ideas).

One of the most important patterns in the perceptions of actors is the *trust* that actors have in other actors. We regard trust as a (stable) perception about the intentions of other actors. The trust of an actor concerns the expectation that other actors will refrain from opportunistic behaviour even when there is occasion for such behaviour. When that trust is mutual, network patterns of actors with strong or weak trust relations may emerge. This not only distinguishes networks from each other, but it also means that in their concrete policy games actors can begin the game based on other expectations. The meaning of trust as an institutional characteristic of networks will be discussed in Section 4.6.

The structure of the network: rules

Because of their sustainable interactions, actors create patterns of interactions and perceptions as well as network structures, i.e. rules and resources. Rules emerge during interactions and may be formal (consciously created) or informal (produced together during the course of the interaction). Rules, as fixed and generalizable procedures, can provide actors with an anchor in relation to questions such as who belongs in the network, what is the position of certain actors, what is the identity of different actors, and also what is regarded as a qualitatively good product.

While network rules constitute interactions and meanings in networks, in a longer-term perspective, they are also formed and sustained by, and changed through, these interactions. The English sociologist Giddens labelled this the *duality of structures* (Giddens, 1979, 1984). Structures – understood as sets of rules – are a necessary condition for action but are simultaneously changed during action.

The example of the development of languages clarifies what this duality of structures entails. We use grammar to realize language games: speaking and writing. Without these rules communication would be impossible. If words changed meaning constantly, and if we changed our sentence structures all the time, we would no longer understand what someone else was saying. In short, rules can create a necessary stability and predictability. They also create conditions for patterns visible in language: certain common ways of speaking, frequently or infrequently used words. At the same time, the formation of these patterns is a consequence of choices made during the use of language. Hence, the rules of language prescribe what is correct and what is incorrect language ('this is grammatically incorrect') but not whether certain sentences or specific use of language, all within the rules of grammar, are widely used or not.

At the same time, the rules of grammar change during daily use. New words and meanings emerge and certain ways of formulating are used less and lose their meaning. This is because in the daily use of speech and writing, the rules of grammar are applied and reinterpreted. This process of application generates a gradual change of rules. The institutionalization process, where rules are made and changed, never ends (Berger and Luckman, 1966; Zijderveld, 1974; March and Olsen, 1989; Scott, 1995). Thus, the word 'cool' is not proper Dutch, but when many Dutch people start using it, it becomes common and the language rules are adapted. 'Codification' of this process occurs when the 'wrong word' is incorporated in an official dictionary. It then becomes accepted language.

Returning to networks and interactions: rules, formalized or not, regulate the behaviour of actors in the game without determining it completely. Outcomes of games, after all, are determined through the interaction of the strategies of participating actors and the choices that they make. The statement that rules regulate the game behaviour of actors, thus, certainly requires closer inspection. This will be pursued in Section 4.4. By way of concluding this section, we outline the various elements of networks.

Changeability and dynamics in networks

We have now looked at the various elements of networks: actors, strategies, perceptions, interaction patterns, perception patterns and rules. As an intermediate step, it is useful to connect these. Actors, games, perceptions and strategies are elements of the process while patterns (of interactions and perceptions) and rules are institutional characteristics. Obviously, the institutional characteristics of networks change less rapidly than the process characteristics. This is because institutional changes only become manifest when multiple actors make different choices. Table 4.1 provides an overview of the elements, the dynamics of these elements, and how they are established and changed.

We now acquire the impression of a network in which the games and strategies of actors are highly dynamic while the institutional level is less dynamic. The dynamic of, and developments in, games have to be sustained for some time by multiple actors in order to translate into institutional characteristics and ultimately, into network rules. In principle, rules provide stability in this dynamic and change

Table 4.1 Institutional and process characteristics of networks

	Dynamics	When/how
Institutional characteristics		
Rules	Small, changes normally take a lot of time	Actors commonly share generalizable procedures, codes, etc. Rules only change slowly over time since multiple actors must accept the changes. Rules are, in principle, the most stable element of the network. They only change rapidly in situations of crisis or major turbulence in the networks
Interaction patterns	Gradual	Emerge through regularity of contacts between actors in games (accumulation of all games in network between actors), changes gradually with the interaction choices of actors in games
Perception patterns	Gradual	Result of individual actor perceptions, but can develop through interactions between actors (convergence or divergence of perceptions)
Process characteristics		
Game	Relatively dynamic	Confrontation of different strategies of actors in arenas. Games are highly dynamic because confrontations or strategies may have many consequences as do the strategic reactions of actors to confrontation. Thus, there is a continuous dynamic of events, actor responses, outcomes, etc.
Actor perception	Gradual change and adaptation	Perceptions of actors are shaped and changed through their experiences. They display a fair degree of stability but change as a consequence of the learning experience of actors (dissatisfied with the process, contact with other ideas, etc.)
Actor strategy	Very dynamic	Actors quickly adapt their strategies, because of the behaviour of other actors, dissatisfaction with results or changed goals or perceptions. The most dynamic element of networks in the game

only gradually through reinterpretation. We discuss this in Section 4.4. First, we address different institutional theories as a stepping-stone for the section about rules.

4.3 Institutional theories and the network theory: an interlude

A variety of institutional explanations exists (see Scott, 1995). What they have in common is that they provide a supra-individual explanation for the behaviour of actors. This is not to say that individual behaviour is irrelevant, but that this behaviour is influenced by the institutional conditions in which it occurs.

Table 4.2 Two logics of action

	Logic of consequences	Logic of appropriateness
Need for knowledge	What are my alternatives? (strategic analysis)	What kind of a situation is this? (situational analysis)
Values	What are my values? (goals)	Who am I? (identity)
Considerations	What are the consequences of alternatives to my values? (means–ends analysis)	How appropriate are different actions for me in this situation?
Choices	Choose the alternative that has the best consequences (utility maximization)	Do what is most appropriate

Source: adapted from March and Olsen, 1989: 23.

Institutions provide organizing principles in a complex reality. In this sense, institutional theories clearly differ from rational theories of decision making (see March and Olsen, 1989), which explain outcomes of decision making processes in terms of the rational behaviour of actors and in the interaction of behaviour alone.

Institutional perspectives: rules that regulate behaviour

March and Olsen clarify this by distinguishing between a logic of appropriateness and a logic of consequences. Institutional theories depart from a logic of appropriateness while (rational) choice theories operate more on a logic of consequence. Table 4.2 displays the most important differences between the logic of appropriateness and the logic of consequences.

As is clear from the table, rational choice approaches to action focus on the rational goal behaviour of actors while institutional theories focus on how institutions regulate behaviour. The concept of institutions is frequently defined in a broad stroke. According to Scott, 'Institutions consist of cognitive, normative and regulative structures that provide stability and meaning to social behaviour. Institutions are transported by various carriers – cultures, structures and routines – and they operate at multiple levels of jurisdiction' (Scott, 1995: 33).

March and Olsen define institutions as follows, 'Institutions are constructed around clusters of appropriate activities, around procedures for assuring their maintenance in the face of threads from turnover and from self-interest, and around procedures for modifying them' (March and Olsen, 1989: 24).

The concept of rules is common to many definitions of institutions. Institutions and institutional arrangements can be regarded as sets of (formal and informal) rules (see also Ostrom, 1986; Klijn, 1996; Scharpf, 1997; Steunenberg, 2001). Scharpf (1997: 38) defines institutions as, 'systems of rules that structure the courses of actions that a set of actors may choose'. Hence, he regards institutions as rules that structure the behaviour of actors (Scharpf, 1997: 39). It is characteristic for institutional theories that, 'rules and systems of rules in any historically given society not only organize and regulate social behaviour but make it understandable – and in a limited conditional sense – predictable for those sharing in rule knowledge' (Burns *et al.* 1985: 256, in Scharpf, 1997: 40). Rules structure the behaviour of actors but, in interaction, are also formed by these same actors (Scott, 1995).

Different institutional approaches

Several institutional theories have a different outlook on the nature of these rules, where they come from, how they operate, etc. With Scott (1995) we distinguish between three groups of institutional theories: regulative, normative and cognitive. Table 4.3 provides the most important differences between these three.

In addition to these three types of institutional theories, a distinction is generally made between theories with a more economic orientation and those with a more sociological orientation. In economically oriented institutional theories, the regulative understanding of rules and institutions dominates. In this view, as is clear from the table, rules bound behaviour and are maintained by all sorts of sanctions. Rules are also primarily regarded as formal rules, and there is a strong inclination to consider the emergence of rules as more or less a rational choice process. This approach can be found in public choice theory and neo-institutional theory in economics (see Kiser and Ostrom, 1982; Ostrom, 1986; Williamson, 1996; also Steunenberg, 2001). Here, rules operate as a protection against the opportunistic behaviour of other actors (see the neo-institutional approach, Williamson, 1996).

The sociological based approach to institutions departs from the social embeddedness of rules. Rules are formed and shaped in social interactions. In a way, they are solidified procedures for actions which are, over a longer period of time, also changed by actions (Berger and Luckman, 1966; Scott, 1995; Klijn, 1996). Hence, at a particular moment, institutions are given and they are structuring – but not determining – actions. In the longer run, however, institutions change

Table 4.3 Types of institutional theory

	Regulative theories	*Normative theories*	*Cognitive theories*
Basis for compliance	Expedience	Social obligation	Taken for granted
Mechanisms for creation and maintenance	Coercive	Normative	Mimetic
Action logic	Instrumentality	Appropriateness	Orthodoxy (generally accepted)
Indicators	Laws, sanctions	Certification, accreditation	Prevalence, isomorphism
Basis of legitimacy	Legally sanctioned	Morally governed	Culturally supported, conceptually correct

Source: adapted from Scott, 1995: 35.

gradually through reinterpretation, adaptation or rejection of certain rules in daily behaviour (see March and Olsen, 1989; Klijn, 1996). This 'duality of structures' (see Giddens, 1984), also clarifies how change processes occur in institutions. We will elaborate on this later. It must be observed though, that this approach is sometimes stereotyped. Steunenberg, for instance, uses the example of a jogger subjected to the law of gravity (Steunenberg, 2001: 19). But since social laws are not natural laws, this is not a good example, as he admits elsewhere. The example and the wrong presentation of institutions as both dependent and independent variables (pp. 21–22) in which the element of time is insufficiently acknowledged, appear to serve mainly to reject the sociological approach.

Theories that fit into a more sociological approach of institutions either emphasize the normative influence of rules (see, for instance, March and Olsen, 1989) or the cognitive influence of rules (Powell and DiMaggio, 1991). The first group of theories emphasizes normative expectations that go along with rules (March and Olsen, 1989: 22–24). Actors know which behaviour is appropriate and what they can and cannot do. Rules especially come from social obligations and derive their legitimacy from the fact that they are regarded as morally just. The second group of theories places more emphasis on the fact that rules create meanings and establish a meaningful context for actors. Rules determine what topics are important, what categories are significant, etc. In a way, rules are self-evident and provide a socially constructed framework for action (Scott, 1995: 42).

Towards an institutional network perspective

The institutional perspective used in this book, the network perspective, is closest to the cognitive and sociological approach to institutions (see Klijn, 1996) but cannot be entirely derived from it. As a starting point, we take the view that actors form rules in earlier interactions (sometimes deliberately and rationally in common decision making, but more often as a by-product of their interactions) and that these rules serve as the context for bounded rational action. However, we emphasize that the development and existence of rules have rational components. After all, the transaction costs of interactions would be huge if every interaction or transaction also required negotiation about the rules. In this sense, the theory applied in this book also contains elements of a more economic approach to institutions.

4.4 Rules in networks: a social infrastructure

Networks are characterized by rules that actors have formed in earlier interactions. Given each network's history, each network has its own characteristic rules. These rules regulate the behaviour of actors in the network in the sense that they prescribe what actions are permitted, which actors can participate in which games, but they also regulate the network's opinion about the quality of products or services that are produced in the network.

That rules regulate behaviour, however, is a statement that requires elaboration (as promised earlier). Social rules such as network rules are not natural laws and actors can deviate from them. In order to determine what we mean when we state that rules regulate behaviour in networks, we first need to look at the characteristics of rules and how they operate. After this, and in order to get a handle on the issue of *what* they actually regulate, we distinguish between the types of rules that can be found in networks.

Characteristics of rule-guided behaviour

Rules are learned during participation in policy games in the network. However, whether they are formal or informal by nature, they are never completely unambiguous, they are never entirely clear to everyone, and they never possess the same meaning for everyone. Rules are only partially codified. But what does it mean to say that actors follow rules? This question can also be formulated in the following way: what are the characteristics of rule guided behaviour if we look at the literature on rules (Duintjer, 1977; Giddens, 1984; Burns and Flam, 1987; Cohen, 1989; Klijn, 1996).

Rules constitute social practices

Without rules, i.e. generalized procedures that regulate behaviour, policy games in networks would be impossible since the players do not have the shared meanings that allow them to interact. The earlier example of language demonstrated this notion. Rules provide a framework within which concrete interactions can take place and can be interpreted. Hence, rules constitute social practices. Rules make a meaningful discussion about water quality possible, they create a forum where communication on that subject is possible, and they help determine which actors have something sensible to say about it. In short, just as language rules enable speaking, network rules enable interaction between actors by providing meaning to action.

This does not mean that certain social practices can be guided by one rule only (Giddens, 1984). Social practices are generally supported by a series of overlapping rules. This also has the consequence that action situations are somewhat ambiguous. It is not always clear which rules are applicable, whether rules are aligned with each other, and whether they are clear to actors. This is also related to the various characteristics of rule-guided behaviour as discussed below.

Rules must be followed

Rules presume regularity but not a strict pattern. The difference between the two is important and concerns the fundamental difference between social and physical rules. It points to the fact that rules must be followed, and can only be sustained because actors choose to do so. As such, rules are thus open to critique and change. They will only continue to exist when they are continuously confirmed by actors (in a spoken or silent manner). Actors develop interpretations of the situation in which they find themselves, and they translate these into actions from the adequate rules available. The application of rules to specific situations is usually uncertain and requires interpretation. This interpretation is an important source of conflict

about, and change of, rules (Weick, 1979; March and Olsen, 1989). This interpretation clash can be compared to the actions of a judge. A judge interprets
cases he is presented with and tries to apply the existing rules of adjudication.
New interpretations are included in jurisprudence and the meaning of existing
rules can change. Adhering to rules and the continued existence of rules is a
consequence of the actions of actors who use rules as a framework of interpretation for these actions. This example shows that comparing social rules with
the rules of chess, for instance, is not quite right. Rules regulate the meaning of
game actions in chess, but cannot be changed during the game. Rules in a network,
on the other hand, can change during the game, even though these changes are
gradual and occur during a series of games. Hence, the concept of a game as used
here cannot be considered similar to the concept of a game when used to refer
to chess or soccer.

Rules deal with the competency of actors

Rule-guided behaviour means that actors know how they are expected to act in
certain situations. This knowledge is often implicitly stored in memory. It is, as
Duintjer argues (1977: 27), a practical knowledge; the art of understanding which
rules are to be followed in a particular situation. Here too, the example of language
is enlightening. While few individuals would be able to explicate the grammar
rules they use, most implicitly know which grammar rules apply, and when they
make mistakes there is usually someone to correct them. Actors learn this during
socialization processes (Burns and Flam, 1987).

Hence, the regularity in interactions between actors is often crucial for the
development and sustainment of rules. After all, it is during interactions that rules
are tested and taught to 'novices'. Without frequent interactions, rules will slowly
lose meaning. They will remain in the memory of the actors, but when they are
no longer used and have no function, they will slowly erode in importance. For
example, rules are very important for routine actions in networks. Explication of
rules usually only occurs when routines become controversial or they no longer
provide the desired result for actors.

Rules are trans-situational and not actor-bound

Rules concern the relations between actors. They regulate the interactions between
actors and are, by definition, not actor-bound or specific to one situation. Cohen
(1989: 43) writes:

> Rules of conduct are trans-situational, in the sense that they are involved in
> forms of conduct that are (I) reproduced and recognized many times over
> during the routine activities undertaken by members of a collectivity, and
> (II) reproduced and recognized for a considerable period in the history of
> that group, [. . .] rules of conduct may be conceived as trans-situational prop-
> erties of a collectivity that enter into the reproduction of institutionalized
> conduct.

Rule-guided behaviour concerns mutual social practices (Duintjer, 1977). If rules are considered relevant only by one actor in the network we refer to it as an individual decision rule but not as a network rule.

Rules and action: a complex relation

Since social practices within networks, as stated, are almost always regulated by overlapping sets of rules and since rules are abstract and ambiguous, players must constantly apply the rules as they know and understand them to each concrete situation. It is not always clear which rules are applicable to a specific situation and how they must be applied. Thus, application and interpretation of rules can generate shifts and changes in the set of network rules. Furthermore, rules can be consciously broken. The fact that rules must be followed means, after all, that they are considered acceptable by the actors in the network.

In this way there is a continuous interaction between the rules, the structure of the network, and the games in which these rules are applied. In this interaction, patterns of interactions and perceptions are maintained or changed. Clearly, in a 'normal routine situation', only a small portion of the rule pattern of the network is subject to discussion. The transaction costs would be too high if rules that have been formed earlier must be confirmed or even created anew in each subsequent game. A large part of the rule structure must be self-evident and subject to minimal debate.

Since rules are trans-situational and not actor-bound, they are shared by multiple actors. This, too, means it is highly unlikely that rules will change from one day to the next. Furthermore, rules are often embedded in an entire set of interconnected rules, which makes them less vulnerable to rapid change.

Thus, rules assure a certain *stability* in the behaviour of actors without determining that behaviour or its outcomes. One could say that it enables actors to assume certain behaviour by others, without having to confirm it in concrete situations. Rules reduce uncertainty in policy games but, at the same time, that reduction cannot be complete since actors are not factors.

Types of rules in networks

Now that we have clarified network rules and how they operate, it is time to see what they regulate. In other words, what type of rules can be found in networks. A variety of typologies can be found in the literature (see, for instance, Ostrom, 1986; Burns and Flam, 1987). Ostrom (1986; see also Kiser and Ostrom, 1982) distinguishes:

- position rules: these specify positions of actors;
- boundary rules: these concern how actors gain access and can exit a position;
- scope rules: these concern the kinds of issues and set of outcomes that are addressed in a network;
- authority rules: these clarify what is allowed in a particular position;

- aggregation rules: these regulate the distribution of decision functions and indicate how partial decisions can be grouped together;
- information rules: these specify channels of communication but also the language and type of message transmitted through these information channels;
- pay-off rules: these regulate the benefits of actors.

Although Ostrom's distinction is valuable and used as inspiration in this book, we do not apply it in its entirety. An important reason is that this categorization excludes an important category, namely rules that establish the identity of actors and their professional standards, etc. Ostrom fails to acknowledge these because she departs from an economic perspective upon rules where these are explicitly formulated in games between actors. In order to connect our typology to a well-known distinction between constituting and regulating rules (see Searle, 1971; Duintjer, 1977), we distinguish between arena rules and interaction rules.

Arena rules are rules that provide a yardstick to actors in determining the nature of the network and arena in which they operate. They specify positions, realities and rewards. They are rules that define social reality. As such, they are sometimes hardly recognized as rules and can have an almost tautological nature. These rules have the nature of what Searle, the English analytical philosopher, calls constituting rules (Searle, 1971; van Eemeren and Koning, 1981). For instance, a constituting rule is one that defines when someone is checkmated in a game of chess, a situation where he can no longer move without being under check. These are the rules that define the nature of the game.

Interaction rules have a more procedural character and inform actors what is and what is not allowed in a network. They modify, so to speak, action within the context of arena rules. An overview of these two types of rules, and examples of them, can be found in Table 4.4.

Table 4.4 Types of rules in networks

Description	Aspects	Examples
Interaction rules		
Rules that regulate game interactions	Access to policy games	• Exclusiveness • Selection • Exit opportunities
(Rules that specify what is and what is not allowed in games between actors)	Interaction in policy games	• (Non) intervention • Information provision • Conflict
Arena rules		
Rules that regulate the setting of the game	Reality	• Identity of actors • Product rules
(Rules that define the social practices and distinguish important matters from unimportant ones)	Reward	• Status • Evaluation criteria
	Positions	• Competencies

Source: Klijn, 1996.

Interaction rules may concern access to the network or arena or the interactions in the game. Access rules define how exclusive games are, how actors are selected for certain games, and what exit opportunities they have. A non-intervention rule is a clear example of an interaction rule, as are rules about what information is made available and what rules apply in cases of conflict. At the beginning of the chapter, we noted how a non-intervention rule between departments prevented departments other than Traffic and Water Management from seeking contact with water boards or research institutions.

Within the category of arena rules, we recognize three sub-sets of rules: reality rules, reward rules, and position rules. Reality rules define good and bad argumentation, information and standards for actors. Professional codes of behaviour (e.g. medical doctors) or products (e.g. housing) play an important role here. At the beginning of the chapter, we identified the rules that guide the water network with regard to reliability and credibility of information. Also, arena rules determine which *reward rules* (financial but also intangible) and which *position rules* are important to the network.

Finally: rules as a unit of analysis

Network rules provide insight into the institutional structure of the network and provide important information about the opportunities and limitations of action in specific networks. Many outcomes of policy games could not be explained without knowledge of the rules relevant to the network. The problem, however, is that analysing rules isn't always so easy. This is especially true for informal rules. Formal rules are relatively easy to identify since they are codified in legal texts or jurisprudence. Informal rules must be reconstructed from remarks and interviews of those involved. This requires time and effort, but the result is certainly worthwhile as the example of the zinc case shows.

4.5 Trust as a help against uncertainty

As indicated in Chapter 3, there is substantial uncertainty in networks about the strategic behaviour of other actors. At the same time, actors need each other since knowledge is dispersed and the means to achieve interesting (innovative) products, services or policies may not be available to one actor alone. This dependency means that organizations in public as well as in private networks often engage in long-term relations with other actors where knowledge and expertise is exchanged to make innovative products and services a reality.

The specificity, uniqueness and difficult marketability of knowledge make it difficult to regulate interactions through contracts (see Ring and van der Ven, 1992, 1994; Nooteboom *et al.*, 1997; Lane and Bachman, 1998; Nooteboom, 2000). After all, contracts cannot foresee every unexpected circumstance, and we have seen that unexpected circumstances often occur in networks because of:

- changing actor strategies;
- strategic complexity of interactions in networks;

- the fact that frequently, products or policy must be realized that can only be developed during the process.

For this reason, more authors are emphasizing the importance of trust between actors in order to achieve successful cooperation. Trust is not only expected to have a positive effect on cooperation, but it is also an important condition for realizing innovation (see, for instance, Lundvall, 1993; Lane and Bachman, 1998). In this section, we discuss this feature of networks, but we first address what trust actually is. Next, we discuss some important advantages of trust for cooperation in networks. We conclude with some factors that might influence the creation and maintenance of trust.

What is trust?

Trust is regarded as perceptions of the good intentions of other actors. The intentions of another actor are central here. Rousseau, Sitkin, Burt and Camerer define trust as 'a psychological state comprising the intention to accept vulnerability based upon positive expectations of the intentions or behaviour of another' (Rousseau et al., 1998: 395). This is related to most observations made in contract theory where trust is defined as a situation where an actor believes that another actor will refrain from opportunistic behaviour even when the opportunity for that occurs (see Lyons and Metha, 1997; Nooteboom, 2000). In both instances, it concerns an expectation about the intention of another actor and that intention concerns the expectation that the other actor will respect the interests of the 'trusting' actor. Trust, therefore, includes (Nooteboom, 2002; Klijn, 2002):

- *Stable perception* of an actor A about the *intentions* of another actor B; trust is the perception of an actor and not an action or choice by an actor. Actions and choices of an actor can, of course, be a consequence of trust or a lack thereof. Better still, the concept of trust is exactly relevant given the assumed relationship between trust and action and making choices. Trust as a stable perception does not have to be reciprocal. It is, however, unlikely that non-reciprocal expectations and the resulting behaviour patterns can be sustained for long. In a network, stable perceptions may exist among all actors. In this case, the network is characterized by a high degree of trust.
- The expectation of an actor A that another actor B will *abstain from opportunistic behaviour* when an opportunity for that emerges. This concerns the expectation of actor A that the other actor B will take the interests of actor A into account. Essential to trust is not that an actor will abstain from opportunistic behaviour, but that he will do so in situations where there is an opportunity for such behaviour (see, for instance, Rousseau et al., 1998; Nooteboom, 2002).
- Trust is related to *uncertainty*: in the case of trust, there must be some uncertainty about the behaviour of a partner in future situations and advantages/benefits concerning how a problem will be resolved. If such uncertainty does not exist, trust is not necessary (Gambetta, 1988a).

In general, one can say that trust must have both a rational and an altruistic basis (see Zucker, 1986; Fukuyama, 1995; Lyons and Metha, 1997; Lane and Bachman, 1998). Without a rational basis trust cannot continue to exist. If this were the case, trust would truly be blind, as Williamson suggests (1996). Also, trust must be confirmed and result in a mutual advantage for its partners. Trust is given to partners within certain limits. When expectations are repeatedly violated, the trust in another actor must be reviewed or may even disappear entirely. On the other hand, trust cannot only be calculating. If so, it would hardly be resistant to uncertainty and unexpected developments. The essence of trust is that an actor is vulnerable to other actors and presumes shared expectations with other actors. When actions do not fit expectations or agreements are not lived up to, the other actor is given the benefit of the doubt on grounds of previous experience. In short, trust means that in the case of failing performance, partners do not immediately search for the cause in malcontent or self-interest but in external factors, temporary competency problems or other reasonable explanations. It is this attitude that encourages the forgiving strategies that enhance cooperation and prevent actors from ending up in a prisoner's dilemma (for more on the relation between strategies and game outcomes, see Axelrod, 1984).

The meaning of trust in networks

Trust is an important factor in the creation of desired interactions and cooperation. Furthermore, it reduces uncertainties about the behaviour of other actors. Several advantages of trust for cooperation are mentioned in the literature.

Reducing transaction costs

First, trust may result in reducing transaction costs. On the one hand, trust reduces the risk involved in transactions and cooperation since it enhances predictability. In situations where actors have strong faith in the positive intentions of the other actors' behaviour, the possibility of unexpected interactions as a consequence of opportunistic behaviour is reduced. On the other hand, trust also operates as an alternative to contracts and certainly as a welcome supplement. Drawing up contracts involves transaction costs (Williamson, 1996; Sako, 1998; Ring and van der Ven, 1992; Nooteboom, 2002). Trust may reduce the necessity of including elaborate contractual clauses and regulations in order to defend against future uncertainties.

Improving investments and stability in relations

Uncertainty in network games is also a consequence of instability in the relations between actors. Actors do not know to what degree cooperation with other actors might be useful and are inclined, under this uncertainty, to focus on costs (such as production costs, cooperation costs and costs of opportunistic behaviour of others). There is too little attention to the aspect of benefits and to long-term dynamics in relations and investments (Ring and Van der Ven, 1992; Nooteboom *et al.*, 1997). Frequently, in order to achieve new and interesting solutions, invest-ments – in the broad sense – must be made by partners, the benefits of which are uncertain. An economic perspective focused on costs quickly emphasizes the risk of such investments and the problem of opportunistic behaviour. In this situation, an actor may refrain from such investment.

If there is a substantial amount of trust, actors are more likely to make such investments despite the risks and uncertainties involved. This offers an explana-tion of why actors engage in risky investments that cannot be explained exclusively from an economic perspective. It can also explain why certain types of coopera-tion in networks result in synergistic advantages and why other networks fail to achieve such advantages.

Stimulating learning and the exchange of knowledge

As indicated in the previous chapter, a part of the uncertainty in network games concerns the fact that the outcomes and products are difficult to specify before-hand, so it is necessary to learn from interactions during decision making. But learning requires knowledge exchange. Intensive interaction is necessary when parts of that knowledge are tacit and therefore difficult to trade.

Nooteboom (2000) mentions the example of small companies that maintain a large network of contacts with other organizations in order to get the specific information they do not have themselves. These types of knowledge exchanges require a minimum amount of trust since drawing up contracts in such a network of organizations is much too expensive, especially given the limited means of these companies (for more on networks of relations between companies see: Miles and Snow, 1986; Graeber, 1993; Parker and Vaidya, 2001). Hence, trust in networks improves knowledge exchange and learning.

Stimulating innovation

The innovation challenge is closely related to a number of the previous issues. We have already pointed out the importance of innovative solutions in the decision making process for wicked problems. Problems often have a comprehensive char-acter and require a knowledge input from many actors. To resolve new problems and to get the necessary actors interested, innovative ideas and solutions are frequently necessary.

From the perspective of economic transaction costs, the uncertainty of inno-vation is great. Actors do not know the outcome beforehand, they must share information with other parties and it is virtually impossible to have built-in guarantees against opportunistic behaviour since no one knows beforehand what type of opportunistic behaviour can be expected (see, for instance, Lundvall, 1993; Parker and Vaidya, 2001).

Trust can facilitate innovation since it reduces uncertainty about opportun-istic behaviour. The usual alternative in the case of substantial uncertainty, i.e. vertical integration (integrating parts of other actors within an organization) (see Williamson, 1996), is not always that attractive for various reasons. Vertical integration results in high internal transaction costs (strong bureaucratization through centralization and greater economies of scale). Furthermore, and this is a frequently overlooked factor, innovation exists by the grace of diversity of knowledge, ideas, etc. Vertical integration, that unifies parts of an organization, reduces that diversity (see Nooteboom, 1998). Trust is, then, a viable alternative that protects diversity yet provides a way to reduce the risks of innovation.

Emergence of trust

The value of trust appears to be that it offers a possible coordination mechanism for complex decision making in networks and supports the need of innovative solutions in decision making. A high degree of trust decreases transaction costs between cooperating actors, enhances the probability that actors will exchange information even when the results are uncertain, and encourages learning and innovation. Where cooperation in networks is intensive and uncertainty is high, this becomes an important factor. It is also clear that trust develops over time and it is sustained because it is continuously confirmed and not repeatedly violated. In this sense, the distinction between a calculative and an altruistic orientation appears more analytical. In practice, both types will simultaneously occur but perhaps to different degrees. Much of the literature suggests that calculated trust is particularly important at the beginning of a relationship. Especially when partners share no prior history and are working together for the first time, trust must be created upon the expectation that cooperation will be beneficial to both parties. When this cooperation continues and is strengthened, altruistic trust becomes more important (see Lyons and Metha, 1997; Sako, 1998; Rousseau et al., 1998).

That trust develops and can increase or decrease also implies that trust can be regarded as both an independent and a dependent variable in public administration research. Trust as an independent variable can enhance cooperation, and as a dependent variable it is enhanced by other factors. Factors mentioned in the literature that are considered to influence the emergence and growth of trust are (see Putnam, 1995; Deakin and Wilkinson, 1998; Lane and Bachman, 1998; Rousseau et al., 1998):

- Interactions in the past, both theories about social capital and business administration and economic theories emphasize that more interaction and social contacts will improve the creation of trust. The implication is that in networks with intensive interaction – not considering other factors – there will be more trust between parties.
- The reputation of other actors: experience in the past and hearsay about the professionalism of a partner can enhance the development of trust between parties.
- The expectation of future benefits: the knowledge that continued interaction between actors in networks will be mutually beneficial which, in turn, provides a favourable condition for the development of trust.
- The nature of binding network rules: network rules can have different effects on the creation and growth of trust, so network rules that result in strong

domain demarcations will not be conducive to the creation and development of trust. Also, when accepted by actors, the conflict regulation rules are likely to create and sustain trust (see Klijn, 1996, 2001).

Thus, links can be made between the different institutional characteristics of networks. This also makes clear that these characteristics are logically linked to one another. Networks in which the trust between actors is low are often characterized by rules that emphasize conflict and domain. This is why it is frequently so difficult to change these institutional characteristics.

4.6 Conclusion: closedness, complexity and change

As indicated earlier, networks are not static. The same can be said for institutional characteristics: they gradually change. Previous interactions, reinterpretations and adaptations of rules may in turn modify rules, interactions and patterns of perception. Generally this takes time.

Institutional characteristics in networks can be studied in two ways. First, as given features at a given time. In this case, one looks at characteristics that influence game situations, actions and perceptions of actors and, thus, the outcomes of policy games. In other words: the institutional characteristics become the independent variables and the evolution of the game and the game outcomes become the dependent variables. Second, one can study the changes of institutional characteristics over a longer period of time. Here, the focus is on changes in interaction patterns, perception patterns and rules as a consequence of the dynamics in strategies or external developments. In this case, the institutional characteristics are the dependent variable and factors such as external developments, developments in the strategies of actors, and so forth, form the independent variable.

In this concluding section, we discuss briefly both approaches. We first discuss closedness and institutional complexity, which are important features with institutional characteristics as factors in games and interactions. After that we briefly discuss the process of institutional change.

Closedness of networks

As we have seen in the introduction to this chapter, existing networks can facilitate interaction because the actors in networks have common organizational arrangements and shared rules to make these interactions easier. But networks can also inhibit interactions. The literature on iron triangles and subsystems points to this (Freeman and Parrish Stevens, 1987; Jordan, 1990). Barriers to interaction concern actors outside the network but can also refer to interactions between actors inside the network (see also Ripley and Franklin, 1987; Schaap and van Twist, 1997). It is evident that closedness of networks has consequences for interactions in the networks and the games between them. When actors cannot gain access, their interests are not represented. The course of interaction and the outcomes will be different from a situation where excluded actors have access to the arena.

Networks can be closed to actors outside the network. This can be done consciously in the sense that actors in the networks try to exclude other actors from the interactions. Actors do this by using the means or rules available to them to keep other actors out of their network, for instance, by calling upon rules of exclusivity (whether formalized or not) but, for instance, also by ignoring requests for access. Closedness can also be unconscious because actors use certain self-evident but unspoken access rules, or because certain rules with regard to content are self-evident. This makes it very difficult for actors outside the network to conform to the construction of reality as it exists in the network (see Klijn, 1996; Schaap and van Twist, 1997).

Frequently, closedness is a combination of deliberate as well as unintended closedness. It was more or less the former that occurred when the zinc industry wanted to access the water network through its public relations campaign on the harmfulness of zinc. The zinc industry failed to gain substantial access to the water network because the network ignored the industry, and the network did not view the information produced by the zinc industry as objective information. Actors in the water network clung to information and information provisions that enhanced closedness while, at the same time, they deliberately ignored the zinc industry.

Different arenas and networks: clashing rules?

Institutional characteristics can also result in substantial institutional complexity, as we saw at the opening of this chapter. Decision making occurs in arenas, and it can be particularly complicated when the game occurs in different arenas – even more so when these arenas are in different networks. Actors are not only confronted with other actors who hold very different perceptions, but also with actors who are likely to consider different rules as correct and valid. Figure 4.2 visualizes a policy game where two policy networks are involved.

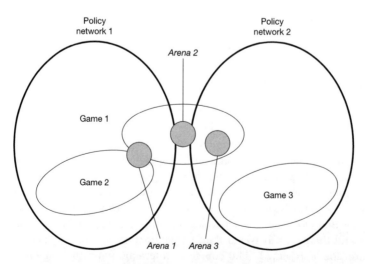

Figure 4.2 Policy games in different arenas and in different networks

Institutional fragmentation can create uncertainty in attempts to solve complex problems when actors do not know precisely where the important decisions are being made, but it can also create uncertainty because common rules are not available to facilitate the interactions.

Process of institutional change

As indicated earlier, rules change when actors no longer confirm them or when they openly break or ignore them. The basis for change in institutional characteristics lies, in short, in the sustainable changes in strategies of actors in the network. Actors may have different reasons for changing their strategies. Two causes appear to be important: actors evaluate their own strategies and behaviour in the past and reach the conclusion that they must change their strategies in order to more effectively achieve their goals. This might be because they regard the outcomes of an earlier period as insufficient or ineffective. But it might also be because they witness other strategies that are better than the ones used previously. Actors perceive external events, that is events outside the network, as important and change their strategies in response to these external developments.

While the precise reasons for these changes in strategy can vary, both changes occur through the perception of actors. Actors develop notions about their environment, about other actors, and about the nature of the problem and respond to these by changing their strategic choices. It is clear that little will change if only one actor changes his strategy patterns. This will result in a minor change in interaction and perception patterns and will probably not have any influence on changing rules. It is different when multiple actors change their strategies. In this case, after some time, the network visibly changes through different interaction and perception patterns. And after a longer period of time, actors change their strategy and begin interpreting the available network rules differently, and as a result changes in the set of rules will occur as well.

These kinds of institutional changes usually take quite some time. Rapid changes as a consequence of an imminent crisis or substantial external pressure are an exception. These kinds of changes cannot be managed easily, but it is not impossible to establish change in the characteristics of networks. The question of how change can be directed, which we call institutional design, will be dealt with in Part 2 (Chapter 10).

Chapter 5

Uncertainties and governments
Old and new responses

5.1 Introduction: government responses to uncertainty

Most policy processes and interactions about solving societal problems in a network society are characterized by substantial uncertainty. In previous chapters, we demonstrated how this uncertainty has substantive, strategic and institutional aspects. These uncertainties result in risks for organizations. It is difficult to respond adequately to uncertainty since the effects of the response are unpredictable – precisely as a result of the uncertainty itself. Over the course of time, public organizations have developed a number of standard responses, which we review in this chapter.

In Section 5.3, we discuss centralization and consultation as two of the 'classic' government responses which continue to maintain their value at present. An important background for these responses, especially centralization, is a strong belief in the primacy of politics. This assumes that governments will play a central role in dealing with wicked problems. For this reason we start the chapter with a section that discusses the fact that governments rarely play this central role in practice and that they are, in fact, not equipped to do so (Section 5.2). When these two 'classic' responses are unsatisfactory, the question of what alternative responses are available to governments emerges. We introduce New Public Management (NPM) and co-governance as two more recently developed methods for addressing uncertainty. Both alternatives are discussed in more detail in Sections 5.4 and 5.5.

We conclude by arguing that NPM is especially useful for known problems in relatively stable environments. Wicked problems require intensive cooperation between governments and also between governments and the societal environment, crossing the boundaries of the policy networks that have developed over time – including non-institutionalized interests and citizens. Co-governance appears to be a useful approach for wicked problems. The fact still remains, however, that efforts to establish cooperation between public and private parties from different networks are difficult and methods for encouraging such cooperation are not well developed. There is a need to manage the efforts of parties in a way that confronts wicked problems and achieves cooperation in a network-type setting. We call this network management: the subject of Part 2 of this book.

5.2 The primacy of politics: a problematic doctrine

How do public organizations respond to the uncertainties they encounter in complex decision making processes? The doctrine of the primacy of politics is an important consideration when looking at the responses of public organizations, so we will first discuss this doctrine.

The primacy of politics

The primacy of politics is an old doctrine which plays a dominant role in thinking about steering and problem solving in almost all Western countries. A precise and universal formulation of this doctrine, i.e. one that is relevant to all countries, does not exist but, *grosso modo*, the most important characteristics include (Schumpeter, 1943; Kuijpers, 1980; Klijn, 1996):

- elected political office holders are responsible for making policy and for expressing the vision concerning choices about societal problems (substantive initiators and priority);
- elected representatives are the first to weigh interests and conflicting values in decision making about societal questions (politics as an arena of weighing interests);
- their judgements prevail over substantive judgements of others and especially over sectoral, interest-bound, judgements of societal associations (value hierarchy);
- elected political office holders are accountable for the activities of the entire subordinate bureaucratic apparatus (political–administrative relations).

The primacy of politics has both an empirical and normative meaning. Empirical in the sense that many (especially in the media) believe that decision making proceeds according to the primacy of politics doctrine, holding that politicians in political bodies outline the objectives and civil servants faithfully execute policy which conforms to these political priorities. This belief exists in spite of substantial research about the complexity of decision making, the intertwinement of strategies of public and private actors and the complexity of problems and solutions. In the normative view, the primacy doctrine has an even stronger meaning in the sense that both in political institutions and the media, and among the citizenry, the idea that elected office holders determine, and have to determine, the course of societal developments to a large degree remains strong.

Displacement of politics: the difficult reality of the doctrine

When we set these elements of the primacy of politics against the empirical reality of complex decision making, we can see a lot of tensions. These tensions result from the fact that decision making takes place in various places and has become very complex. Decision making has moved to international arenas (e.g. the European Union), to all sorts of organizations in the societal arena, to sectoral organizations, and to private organizations as the result of an emphasis in recent decades on markets as a method of governance (privatization, agentification, etc.).

Tension with the evolution of policy processes

The tensions are clearly visible when we analyse political institutions using the rule typology for institutional analysis (introduced in Chapter 4) and compare that analysis with the empirical characteristics of complex decision making, which have been detailed in previous chapters. An overview is given in Table 5.1.

The table shows that there is a large gap between formal and informal rules of political institutions – as they are perceived by those involved – and the empirical reality of complex decision making. In the formal and normative model of political institutions, political office holders are not only above other actors, but they have the opportunity to enter and intervene in processes at any time. These rules are only mitigated by possible informal agreements between political institutions regarding these rules. These more or less formal rules, and the expectations that they create within the public, citizens and media, however, contrast sharply with the *actual* role and potential of political institutions. Time and again, these tensions are subject to lengthy discussion in the media when politicians are held accountable by the media or the public about implementation issues, about the behaviour of more or less independent government services and, even, of independent bodies, or about the mismanagement of public goods such as long-term care waiting lists, public safety or the progress of large infrastructural projects.

Political logic in solving wicked problems

Another significant area of tension exists between the reward rules of political institutions and the empirical reality of complex decision making processes in which wicked problems are tackled. Political reward rules are governed by the opportunity of 'scoring' by achieving interesting policy proposals and projects but also by preventing political damage. Negative publicity and media attention can be extremely harmful for a politician's position and future. Many politicians have experienced this first hand in complex system changes in, for instance, health care policy (think of Hillary Clinton at the beginning of the Clinton administration) or in adapting existing relations in policy areas in response to European legislation on fisheries (quota limitations) or on the environment.

In practice, decision making procedures are lengthy, the outcomes are often uncertain, and the results are difficult to attribute. The reward rules of political institutions promote a certain reluctance and little commitment to long uncertain policy processes, but protracted and complex decision making processes often require strong political commitment and drive in order to maintain momentum and overcome possible stagnation. In short, not only do the high expectations about status and access opportunities that are linked to political institutions clash with the empirical reality of complex decision making processes, but the political reward rules fail to stimulate strong political commitment and drive.

Table 5.1 Rules of political institutions and empirical characteristics of complex decision making

Political institutions	Empirical characteristics of complex decision making	Problems
Position/authority rules		
Primacy of politics (status of superiority)	Empirically political bodies only incidentally involved	Assumed dominant position based on rules of parliamentary democracy in sharp contrast with empirical reality
Identity and product rules		
Representatives of political ideology, political statements. Good products are those in which political ideology and ideas are recognizable	Search processes for content, binding and combining of values instead of optimization. A good product is one that is able to muster the support of various groups and is achievable	Politicians cannot identify and profile themselves with complex decision making; consequences: lack of commitment
Pay-off rules		
Dominant pay-off rules: • media attention/ prevention of damage through the media • successful policy proposals (scoring) • growth of voting share	Long-term process, outcomes uncertain and difficult to attribute	Pay-off rules enhance reluctance (political risks in the media, slow results)
Entry rules		
In principle, access to decision making is always possible every-where (right of intervention). Politics determines agenda	Practical opportunities limited (lack of knowledge, time, political will, etc.)	Broad access opportunities create a notion among those that are involved that does not correspond with empirical opportunities
Interaction rules		
Need for clear information for judgement formation. Relatively simple interaction rules (also highly formalized or informal but well known)	Information limited because of complexity, different perceptions, etc. Interaction rules are ambiguous especially when multiple networks are involved	Tension between strong need for clarity in interaction within political institutions versus complexity and uncertainty of information, methods of interaction, etc. in practice

Limited representation: even more problems

There are more problematic assumptions in the relationship between political bodies and governance. In the traditional view the idea is assumed that political institutions have the ability to represent the preferences of citizens and implement these. But, as we have seen in Chapter 1, individualization has proceeded in the network society and the relation between political institutions and citizens has weakened. This is expressed in highly variable voting behaviour, decreasing membership of political parties and also in the increased 'activism' of citizens with regard to the plans of public actors. This trend becomes clear when we look at the decreased membership of political parties in European countries (see Table 5.2).

As we argued in Chapter 1, citizens no longer accept government measures without thought. But this also means that elected representatives must seek citizens' support and gather information about what citizens in this evolving society want. By testing and adopting alternative types of decision making, public actors all over the world seek to involve citizens and societal groups in the decision making process. The aim is not only to decrease the use of veto power, but also to enhance the spread of knowledge among actors. Experiments such as interactive decision making, citizen panels and interactive planning procedures have developed in the

Table 5.2 Membership of political parties in European countries

Country	Year	Total number of members	Change in comparison to 1980 (%)	Members as % of electorate	Change in comparison to 1980 (%)
Western Europe					
Belgium	1999	480,804	−22.1	6.6	−2.4
Germany	1999	1,780,173	−9.0	2.9	−1.6
France	1999	615,219	−64.6	1.6	−3.5
Ireland	1998	86,000	−24.5	3.1	−1.9
The Netherlands	2000	294,469	−31.7	2.5	−1.8
Austria	1999	1,031,052	−30.2	17.7	−10.8
United Kingdom	1998	840,000	−50.4	1.9	−2.2
Switzerland	1997	293,000	−28.9	6.4	−4.3
Northern Europe					
Denmark	1998	205,382	−25.5	5.1	−2.2
Finland	1998	400,615	−34.0	9.7	−6.1
Norway	1997	242,022	−47.5	7.3	−8.0
Sweden	1998	365,588	−28.1	5.5	−2.9
Southern Europe					
Greece	1998	600,000	+166.7	6.8	+3.6
Italy	1998	1,974,040	−51.5	4.1	−5.6
Portugal	2000	346,504	+17.0	4.0	−0.3
Spain	2000	1,125,731	+249.0	3.4	+2.2

Source: Sociaal Cultureel Planbureau, 2000: 131.

search for the 'unknown' citizens, but classic citizen participation methods, such as consultation, have also increased in importance (see also Klijn and Koppenjan, 2000a; Lowndes *et al.*, 2001; McLaverty, 2002; Denters *et al.*, 2003). These ideas fit well with the governance response to uncertainty, as we will see below.

5.3 Standard response to uncertainty: central norms and consultation

The zinc case discussed earlier actually gives a good example of the standard response of public organizations to problems of complexity and uncertainty. Public actors in general, and government departments in particular, responded to a deterioration of water quality resulting from zinc emissions with a strong emphasis on prohibitions. They attempted to manage the problem through norms and guidelines that, subsequently, had to be adopted by lower public bodies. The (normative) justification of such a response is generally found in the primacy of politics. Public actors can respond unilaterally and in a top-down manner precisely because they represent the common interest.

Central norms and 'mandated science' as a standard response

In concrete terms, the standard response consists of a number of elements:

- *Steering: top-down.* The standard response assumes that decision making can be organized and managed from a central location. This assumption is both empirical (this is how we do it) as well as normative (this is how it should be done). Normatively, the standard response is usually justified by referring to the primacy of politics. While the actual role of politics was limited in the zinc case – as it is with so many other decision making processes, there was a high degree of top-down decision making with a strong emphasis on uniform norms. Thus, an attempt was made to overcome uncertainty. Attempts to avoid strategic uncertainty are made through centralization or by placing implementation outside the organization.
- *Environment analysis: ignoring the surrounding environment and excluding potential veto players.* The standard reaction is a go-alone strategy, even though it is not always pursued consciously. Actors try to come to grips with the content of a problem and discover its meaning for their own group or organization. Such a response is highly internal and the question of how others view the problem does not arise. However, this internal focus can also be part of a more conscious response. By involving fewer actors in decision making, an actor hopes to generate results and to reduce the uncertainties generated by the strategic behaviour of others.
- *Knowledge interest: research for reducing (knowledge) uncertainty.* In addition to a strong emphasis on centralization, the standard response to reduce uncertainty is by doing research. In the standard response, there is little room for ambiguity, competing researchers or disagreement over the meaning of results. In public

Box 5.1 Standard reaction in the zinc case

The political primacy for the environment rests with the Ministry of VROM. VROM develops a programme that deals with various types of pollution. This manner of doing things is highly bureaucratized and professionalized. Thus, at a given moment, zinc is addressed in a decision making environment that is de-politicized and shielded from the environment and not highly transparent. Strategic uncertainty is limited under these circumstances: the issue is highly de-politicized and societal stakeholders are uninvolved. Substantive uncertainty is central: they seek scientific foundations for policy through a scientific research institution created for that purpose (RIVM). Characteristically for this policy, the government essentially addressed the zinc issue by proposing norms to defend the general public interest, and these norms were subsequently defended scientifically. While political decision making formally rests with the representative bodies, and civil servants prepare the substance of the policies, there is actually a high degree of delegation to scientific research when dealing with uncertainty. There is a distinction between norms and implementation. The methods designed for achieving norms are the responsibility of sub-national governments. In the zinc case, the national government explicitly refused to direct the implementation.

What is striking in the zinc case is that the involvement of science in policy preparation led to a high degree of closedness against the outside world. When stakeholders began protesting and demanding substantive discussions with the government, they were faced with a social asymmetry: they spoke with civil servants who were unable to address the substantive aspects of the issue since that expertise rested with scientists at RIVM, and the scientists at RIVM were not accessible to stakeholders. This social asymmetry explains the cognitive closedness (absence of cognitive reflection) that was characteristic of a large part of the process.

It is also worth noting that when the Ministry of VROM became the international rapporteur for zinc, it again opted for a delegation of this responsibility and role to RIVM. Partially this was a reflex: substantive uncertainty can be reduced by hiring scientists. Partially this response was an institutional necessity because of previous responses. VROM did not have the expertise to fulfil this role adequately in its administrative ranks.

organizations, this response is reinforced since actors can base their views on the research results of institutes that are linked to the department.

- *Risk management: excluding risks.* There is a strong tendency to avoid risks and to place possible risks and their consequences outside the organization. Thus, the department responds with stiff norms to avoid being accused later of not taking the problem seriously. In short, a 'strong top-down' response is motivated in part by a fear of future accusations of not having responded strongly enough.

Although the appearance of the standard response is not always exactly the same, a combination of the characteristics discussed above is usually visible. In many cases the standard response is that of a classic bureaucracy. Through standard-ization and control, it attempts to reduce complexity and remove uncertainty. The problem of this response, however, is that it ignores the basic characteristics of most decision making processes which include a dynamic process, a variety of perceptions and problem definitions, and institutional fragmentation. It also ignores the fact that implementation of policy initiatives often requires the coop-eration of others.

Furthermore, delegating substantive policy questions to scientists strengthens asymmetric relations and thus increases the closedness of the policy debate. A substantive discussion is made impossible when politicians and civil servants refer to scientific insights instead of accounting to stakeholders about their policy choices. In fact, this disqualifies the quality of the contribution that stakeholders may provide to the discussion. They are laymen and, furthermore, partisan.

Consultation as a variant to the standard response: neo-corporatism and network formation

A variant of governments' standard response to uncertainty is consulting with a limited number of dominant interest groups and/or implementers. In the context of social-economic questions, one can think of the well-known neo-corporatist policy style (see Schmitter and Lehmbruch, 1979; Lehmbruch and Schmitter, 1982). This response pattern is not limited to social-economic issues; it can be found in a variety of areas such as social security, health care, agriculture and education (Richardson and Jordan, 1979; Rhodes, 1988). The basic elements of this reaction are:

- *Steering: top-down with central consultation*; decision making takes place in arenas in which (central) public organizations interact with parent organizations of dominant interest groups in certain sectors. Public actors make top-down decisions, but only after agreement between the most important actors in the policy area.
- *Analysis of the surrounding environment: only dominant interest groups involved*; the environment is not entirely ignored, as is it is in the standard response, but it is selectively included in decision making. Only well-organized, dominant interest groups are approached.
- *Knowledge interest: emphasis on achievability of policy proposals*; knowledge uncertainty is reduced by limiting information collection to include only information which is directed at an achievable solution and using information provided by dominant actors.
- *Risk management: avoiding risk by including veto-players*; risks are made manageable by including important veto players in decision making and implementation.

The neo-corporatist response is actually an amendment to the standard response. With respect to substantive uncertainty, this response has the advantage that societal knowledge is used in achieving solutions. Furthermore, in this approach, the government no longer has sole responsibility for policy content; it can refer to other societal organizations that are involved.

This response reduces strategic uncertainty: by involving the most important societal parties in decision making, a 'negotiated environment' is created. This consultation provides the opportunity to generate support for measures. Even if one is not successful in generating support, the consultation helps to decrease the unpredictability of the response of other parties. The interest that these parties have in maintaining the response will mitigate their resistance to the policy measures.

This response to uncertainty is also the foundation for the development of networks. By institutionalizing the consulting relations, a variety of cooperative networks between governments and societal organizations have emerged in various policy areas. The more or less durable coalitions of politicians, administrators and 'established' societal organizations formed around specific subjects or types of policy are referred to as 'iron triangles', 'sub-governments', policy communities and policy networks (Cawson, 1986; Ripley and Franklin, 1987; Jordan, 1990; Rhodes, 1990, 1997; Marin and Mayntz, 1991; Marsh and Rhodes, 1992; Klijn, 1997).

The assumption that forms the foundation for this response is that, in involved policy areas, there is a limited number of societal parties that can authoritatively represent the interests in that specific area. One needs to keep in mind that in the hey-day of neo-corporatism, institutionalized societal organizations actually fulfilled that function more or less. Under the influence of trends like more horizontal interaction, fragmentation and the individualization of modern network society, this function has become more problematic. And, thus, neo-corporatist structures and policy networks have been subject to more criticism. The critique levelled against corporatist institutionalized societal organizations includes (see e.g. Ripley and Franklin, 1987; Marin and Mayntz, 1991; Marsh and Rhodes, 1992):

- partial interests organize themselves at the cost of the common interest;
- they protect the established interests and thus limit innovative policy;
- they lead to non-transparent decision making so that responsibilities are hidden and participation by outsiders is limited;
- they result in limited democratic legitimation since it is difficult to influence and control such organizations through democratically elected bodies.

Since the institutionalized interest organizations have lost their disciplined and passive base of support, they are less able to represent the variety of interests at central consultation levels. They are also less capable of mobilizing relevant policy knowledge. If one expects the substantive and strategic uncertainty of societal issues to be reduced along these lines, one is likely to be disappointed.

A closer look at two standard responses

Although the standard response and the neo-corporatist variant differ substantially in a number of ways, certain similarities also exist. In both responses, there is the tendency to reduce, ignore or limit uncertainties. In the standard response, public organizations specifically focus on substantive uncertainty by placing a strong emphasis on a uniform norm, ignoring environmental actors and relying on objective scientific research. In the neo-corporatist response, public actors focus on reducing strategic uncertainty by consulting societal actors and generating support for policy proposals. This substantive actor input also reduces substantive uncertainty. Both responses are similar in that they share a tendency towards centralization: in the first response, scientific research contributes to the establishment of a national, uniform norm; in the second response, governments and societal organizations consult at the central level. Neither response fits well with initiatives to achieve decentralized solutions which are differentiated according to local and regional variations. At the local level, this may lead to sub-optimal solutions; for example, when the preventive care principle is taken as a guideline for national policy, it can lead to high societal costs in dealing with concrete problems.

Another shared characteristic is the relative closedness of decision making processes. In the standard response, this closedness is expressed in the limited opportunities for societal organizations to operate outside the formal consultation and appeal procedures and to participate in the problem solving process. This is reinforced by the highly scientific or technical nature of the process of problem solving. In the neo-corporatist response, the arena is open to tightly organized interest groups, but one drawback is that interests that are less organized or not organized are excluded. The characteristics of both standard responses are summarized in Table 5.3

The standard responses of public actors in decision making processes for difficult problems are thus circumscribed by serious limitations. As methods for dealing with the uncertainties of wicked problems in a complex network society, the standard responses are increasingly dysfunctional. Governments, obviously, noticed this in policy practice. In response, they have developed new ways for dealing with uncertainties. In the remainder of this chapter, we discuss two important alternative approaches to complex problems: New Public Management and governance.

Two new responses to uncertainty: division and linking

In addition to the standard responses to uncertainty in solving difficult problems, two other responses have been developed in recent decades. These are:

- a separation of responsibilities and authority with regard to policy and implementation and with regard to political decisions and their ultimate realization;
- a response that seeks to make complex interdependencies manageable by acknowledging the complex interactions in difficult problems and linking these interactions.

The response focused on separation is characterized by the pursuit of a more limited and effective public sector that concentrates on management strategies derived from the private sector for achieving objectives. This response is known as New Public Management (NPM), and it focuses on the use of market mechanisms in the public sector (Hood, 1991; Kickert, 1997).

The second response to uncertainty, governance, concentrates more on linking the complex interactions between actors in solving difficult problems. This

Table 5.3 Two standard responses to uncertainty

	Central norm and mandated science	*Structured consultation*
Steering	Top-down, emphasis on legal steering (norms, prohibitions and commands)	Central consultation with dominant actors resulting in central norms and measures
Analysis of the surrounding environment	Limited, environment ignored and actors excluded as much as possible	Limited to most important players in terms of veto power and organization power
Knowledge interest	Emphasis on objective knowledge collection – often by research institutes linked to government	Input of information and knowledge from societal actors
Nature of the solution	Emphasis on knowledge collection for optimal problem solution (from a public actor perspective)	Emphasis on solutions that have societal support
Risk management	Risk avoidance by norms, preventive care principle and scientific legitimation of solutions	Risk avoidance by assuring cooperation of dominant, well organized actors
Disadvantages	Lack of opportunities to integrate various interests and knowledge stocks. Sub-optimal solutions at the level of concrete problems and projects. Strengthening strategic uncertainties and risks. Limited democratic legitimation	Dominant interests of limited group of actors at the cost of participation by actors with interests that are less, or not at all, organized. Sub-optimal solutions at the level of concrete problems and projects. Lack of scientific support. Lack of democratic legitimation

response is based on recognizing the importance of links between interactions, bringing actors together and realizing policy proposals by using the knowledge and support of involved actors.

Both responses are also linked to other ideas about the role of public actors and their relation to their environment. This supports the rationale of either separation or linking. In NPM, there is a strong emphasis on separating policy making and implementation; reducing uncertainty by separating responsibilities and emphasizing efficient market coordination and an objective-setting role for public actors. In the governance response, the emphasis is on the links between policy and implementation, on the complexity of governance challenges and on dealing with uncertainty and developing a more process-type role for political actors. Table 5.4 summarizes these two alternative responses to solving uncertainties in complex decision making.

Table 5.4 Two new responses of public actors to uncertainty

Focus	Objective	Vision of public actors and public sector
NPM response		
Organizational and institutional adaptation and arrangement within public sector	Improving the effectiveness and efficiency of public service delivery and public sector organization (doing more with less)	• Central idea of separation • Public actors must focus on core business aims (developing policy and providing guidance, the primacy of politics) • Complexity and uncertainty are reduced by separating and delegating implementation to separate organizations
Governance response		
Dealing with uncertainties through adaptation of inter-organizational steering structure	Dealing with and improving inter-organizational decision making	• Central idea of linkages. • Public actors depend upon other actors, leading to complexity of decision making • Complexity and uncertainty are managed through process guidance

5.4 New Public Management response: markets and contracts as an answer to uncertainty

The NPM solution consists of a number of elements. Of central importance is the notion that when policy making is separated from execution, uncertainties are made more manageable – this includes the separation of responsibilities. In this section, we look more closely at the NPM solution. First, we address the ideas behind NPM, next we address ideas about steering in NPM. We discuss the Private Finance Initiative in Great Britain as an example of NPM reform. We end with some conclusions about the assumptions and problems of NPM steering.

The New Public Management response as inspiration: market-like mechanisms

Although there is no definitive image of the NPM solution, in general one can say that NPM can be characterized by a number of features which are connected to each other but do not necessarily have to be present at the same time (see Pollitt, 1990; Hood, 1991; Kickert, 1997; Ketll, 2000; Lane, 2000):

• a strong focus on improving the effectiveness and efficiency of government performance;

Box 5.2 Private Finance Initiative as an example of New Public Management: road service in the UK

The first ideas for using the Private Finance Initiatives (PFI) for road service in the UK date back to the early 1990s. In 1992, the Private Finance Initiative was launched to encourage the private sector to become involved in government projects. At the end of 1992, the Department of Transport in the UK announced that private parties might be able to provide the design, construction (build), finance and operation (DBFO) of roads under long-term contracts.

The idea of contracting

Some ideas about these DBFO contracts were established in a policy document entitled 'Paying for Better Motorways' which was published in May 1993. Two main benefits of contracting out the obligation to build and operate road services to the private sector were outlined. The first was that private partners could absorb risks at each stage of a project, and, because of the long period of the contract, they could experiment with new ways to build and operate roads. A second aim of the PFI initiative was to promote a private sector road maintenance industry which barely existed at the time, according to the Department of Transport.

The nature of the contract

In general, the contract between the Highways Agency and the contractor is specified according to the desires of the agency and some fundamental requirements for design, construction, operation and maintenance of the project road. To ensure that the DBFO company (the contractor) operates within and fulfils the obligations of the contract, the Highways Agency monitors its activities. It does so by appointing representatives who monitor the construction, operation and maintenance activities. The contract contains a penalty point mechanism which awards points for failures in the performance of the contract. If the number of points exceeds specified values, the monitoring activities are increased. If the number of penalty points reaches a certain maximum, the Agency has the right to terminate the contract.

- a strong focus on ideas and techniques which have established their value in the private sector;
- a strong focus on the use of privatization and contracting out of governmental services, or (parts of) governmental bodies to improve effectiveness and efficiency;
- a strong focus on the creation or use of market or semi-market mechanisms, or at least on increasing competition in service provision and realizing public policy;
- a strong interest in the use of performance indicators or other mechanisms to specify the desired output of the privatized or autonomized part of the governmental body or the service that has been contracted out.

NPM ideas such as contracting out and privatization have played an important role in public management reforms in countries such as the UK, New Zealand and Australia. But traces of the NPM approach are also visible in countries such as the US, Sweden, the Netherlands and Canada (see Pollitt and Bouckaert, 2000: 80). Using privatization, contracting out and separate controlling agencies (see Pollitt *et al.*, 2001), New Public Management reforms seek different demarcations in the relations between private and public spheres. Through instruments such as contracting out and privatization, not only do we acquire a different relationship between the public and private sectors, but we also disentangle the complex responsibilities that were created during the evolution of the welfare state.

Effective steering governments: lean and efficient, with clear separate responsibilities

The aim of most of the New Public Management reforms was to transform governments into leaner but more effective steering organizations. Or to do 'more with less' in the words of Osborne and Gaebler, two of the proponents of these governments reforms. Governments should be steering, i.e. setting goals and trying to achieve them, instead of rowing, i.e. doing all of the service provisions themselves. Or in their own words:

> Governments that focus on steering activity shape their communities, and nations. They make more policy decisions. They put more social and economic institutions in motion. Some even do more regulating. Rather than hiring more public employees, they make sure other institutions are delivering services and meeting the community's need.
>
> (Osborne and Gaebler, 1992: 32)

Osborne and Gaebler's plea for an entrepreneurial government is essentially one for a clear specification of both the desired products or services and the outputs that have to be achieved in relation to these services. But it also implies a clear separation of responsibilities between decision making and delivery, and between political actors and providers. Osborne and Gaebler state that:

> Entrepreneurial governments have begun to shift to systems that separate policy decisions (steering) from service delivery (rowing) . . . It allows them to use competition between service providers. It preserves maximum flexibility to respond to changing circumstances. And it helps them insist on accountability for quality performance: contractors know they can be let go if their quality sags; civil servants know they can not.
>
> (Osborne and Gaebler, 1992: 35)

With these ideas, new substance is given to the doctrine of the primacy of politics because politically responsible actors only need to focus on formulating objectives and starting points.

Box 5.3 PFI contract procedures: the process of achieving a PFI contract in road service

Before a contract is signed and implemented in a PFI procedure, a multitude of activities have to be organized. The table below specifies the various steps of the procedure in which DBFO contracts are tendered in the case of road provision.

Table 5.5 Procedure for DBFO contracts

Steps in the procedure	Actor(s)	Activities
Public pre-phase	Highway Agency	Identification of projects, available money, cost benefit analysis
OJEC announcement	Highway Agency	Advertisement in the Official Journal of the EC describing the project and inviting interested parties to submit applications
Pre-qualification	Highway Agency and interested consortia	Reducing the number of interested consortia (preferably to four)
Invitation to tender	Highway Agency	Agency issues document with project specifications
Analysis of the offer	Highway Agency and chosen consortia	Obtaining clarification of the bid (reviewing technical solutions, examining financial model, insuring that core requirements are met, etc.)
Invitation to negotiate	Highway Agency and chosen consortia	Negotiations between agency and bidders are initially oriented on risk allocation (value for money), and later on details of the contract
BAFO and selection of PPB	Highway Agency	Drafting best and final offer (BAFO) of consortia and selection by Highway Agency of Provisional Preferred Bidder (PPB)
Negotiations with PPB	Highway Agency and chosen consortium	Finalizing the contract with the preferred bidder incorporating very detailed negotiations
Signing the contract	Highway Agency and chosen consortium	Formalizing the agreement

After an announcement in the Official Journal of the EC, consortia are invited to submit applications. For each project, the agency had an average of eight interested responses in projects that were tendered in the past ten years. To reduce the number of consortia, a pre-qualification takes place. The agency selects a limited number (the desired number is four) of bidders with whom it analyses the bidding offer and negotiates on the proposals. The negotiation focuses on the financial elements of the bid and the contractual details. The agency then chooses a preferred bidder with whom it negotiates further, up to the moment that a definitive contract is signed. If the negotiations with the preferred bidder do not match the original proposal or other problems arise, the agency can turn to the second best bidder.

Conditions that make NPM ideas work

In this view, governments operate as skilful buyers who decide what they want, specify outputs and then decide which organizations – public but autonomous, non-profit or private – can best deliver the services the government requires. Political steering and responsibility is guaranteed by a clear specification at the beginning of the process and by separating policy formation from policy implementation (Osborne and Gaebler, 1992; Lane, 2000; Pollitt *et al.*, 2001). Thus interdependencies and responsibilities are separated. Political actors are no longer involved in complicated implementation processes because they have been outsourced. Furthermore, the process can be tested with clear output performance indicators. The political actors are responsible for setting the goals while the implementing actors are responsible for the realization of these goals. But to make this idea of governance work, two very important conditions have to be met: clear goal specification and good monitoring procedures.

The need for clear product specification

Product specification is essential in order to know precisely what is being contracted out. It is also important because it provides the principal with a basis for evaluating the performance of the contractor. However, one of the main characteristics of the complex problem solving processes we have examined so far is that such a clear specification of policy goals or products is hard to make because of institutional fragmentation and strategic and knowledge uncertainty. Often, we simply do not know what the problem is, how much we know about the problem or how to tackle it. But it is also very hard to make the desired distinction between policy formation and implementation because of the various decisions that are being made by a wide variety of actors in different arenas. So, mostly, there is not one agent with whom the principal has to deal, but many agents.

Even in the case of what appears, at first glance, to be simple service delivery such as health care, road contracting, housing provision, the goals and products that have to be specified are often far more complex in nature. As a result, it is difficult to specify the product clearly in unambiguous terms.

This makes the contracting out arrangement – which can be seen at the heart of NPM reform proposals for improving government steering capacity – as a solution that is suitable mainly for certain types of cases, i.e. situations in which consensus has been reached on the type of solution and knowledge uncertainty has been reduced by mutual, consensual, validated knowledge. For this to be the case, the wicked problem must be 'tamed' – and some wicked problems can never be tamed. If these conditions have not been met – and this will be the case quite often, as we have shown in earlier chapters – then contracting out will be difficult as a governance mechanism. Or to phrase it differently: contracting out and NPM ideas for governance seem more appropriate for situations in which the wicked problem has been tamed to some degree and actors can agree upon at least part of the implementation process.

The need for monitoring

Because the quality of the output in a contract relation depends upon the effort that the contractor puts into the production process, monitoring is important. After all, the contractor might have an incentive to exert less effort (Williamson, 1996; Deakin and Mitchie, 1997). Thus, monitoring is used to protect against the potentially opportunistic behaviour of the contractor.

This potential for opportunistic behaviour becomes more important as actors become more dependent on each other as a result of specific investments (Williamson, 1996). Safeguards in the contract are often used to protect one's self against the opportunistic behaviour of other actors. But monitoring and including safeguards in the contracts assume that interactions *can be* monitored and that behaviour can be predicted.

However, as we have already seen, interactions in decision making in societal problem solving processes are highly complex and frequently unpredictable. This makes the possibility of monitoring interactions and/or providing safeguards, difficult. As the number of interactions involved in realizing a product or service, or in realizing policy outputs, increases, the number of arenas also increases – as does the difficulty in monitoring them. Thus, tightly structured contracts which require a substantial amount of monitoring are probably not well suited to complex situations where monitoring is costly.

One additional observation is that if governing services or policy frequently requires a whole network of organizations, the performance of these networks is enhanced by a certain amount of trust and learning, as we saw in Chapter 4 (Graeber, 1993; Lane and Bachman, 1998; Klijn and Koppenjan, 2000). But the tendering process stimulates competition and self-oriented opportunistic behaviour among organizations (at least during the phase before the actual tendering takes place). Milward and Provan find a tension between the need to tender service provision in order to acquire and maintain incentives for cost efficient services, and the need to promote interaction and learning processes between organizations in order to encourage better service delivery. Contracting out tends to disrupt the network, after which new learning and interaction processes are needed (Milward and Provan, 2000). Some organizations are new to following the tendering process, and they have to learn to cooperate with the other actors. Thus, new ways of interacting and interaction rules have to be developed.

Conclusion: the persisting idea of central steering

If we look at the ideas of the New Public Management reform, one striking conclusion can be drawn. In many ways, it looks like the standard reaction to uncertainty. Just like the standard reaction, it attempts to exclude uncertainty and risk by using top-down control on the one hand (with a strong emphasis on specifying goals and output indicators), and by diminishing the risk of implementation on the other hand. While NPM uses different mechanisms to govern uncertainty, the idea of central steering is the same. This also holds for the idea of maintaining control by using specified regulation. The only difference is that in the standard reaction, the specified regulation is primarily aimed at the lower levels of the bureaucracy (implementation divisions of central government or lower level governments) while in the case of NPM, the regulation is aimed at private actors or autonomous parts of the bureaucracy.

If one thing is clear, it is that the idea of contracting out, which is seen in the private sphere (where the idea originated) as a relationship between more or less equal parties in bargaining relations, changes when applied to the public sector in a notion of central steering. The idea of setting the stage and then contracting out looks very much like central steering revisited. The difference is that in contracting out, the government doesn't want to do it all by itself but instead wants to determine how others do it by using contracts, performance outputs and other incentives.

To be successful as a governance strategy, opportunities for specifying products and/or policy aims and the ability to monitor procedures and create clear incentives and mechanisms against opportunistic behaviour are needed. These requirements are not always realistic when dealing with complex problem solving processes.

5.5 Governance: horizontal steering and cooperation as an answer to uncertainty

The governance response to complexity and uncertainty is very different from that of NPM. The former takes complexity, dependency and the involvement of many actors as a given and attempts to develop steering mechanisms that can handle the complexity and uncertainty which are the consequences of dependencies. The ideas behind these new types of steering are closely related to those discussed in earlier chapters. On the one hand, they are inspired by the theories discussed above. On the other hand, the governance response is inspired by experiences in policy initiatives ranging over numerous sectors and experiences with disappointing results in steering large projects.

Governance: the ideas behind horizontal types of steering

A clear example of a governance response, at least verbally, is the emphasis the Labour Government of Tony Blair placed upon joined-up government and partnerships when he assumed office. From the beginning, the Labour Government emphasized the fact that policy initiatives had to be taken together with societal and private actors instead of being imposed from above. The emphasis on partnerships and joined-up government provided the Labour Government with a new identity and legitimacy for its actions. It connected the efficiency of the market with the involvement of society (see e.g. Falconer and McLaughlin, 2000; Newman, 2003; Pollitt, 2003).

These ideas are reflected in the ambitious plans of the Labour Government for the modernization of local government. The document that formulated these plans, 'Modern Local Government: In Touch with the People', even stated:

'The government wishes to see consultation and participation embedded into the culture of all councils and undertaken across a wide range of each council's responsibilities' (DETR, 1998; see also: Lowndes *et al.*, 2001).

In short, modern government does not govern *above* the citizens, societal groups and private actors, but *with* them through horizontal types of coordination. It is a trend visible in several Western European countries, referred to under various labels, and manifest in various ways at the central or local level, such as open or integral planning procedures, interactive decision making or community governance (for an overview, also see McLaverty, 2002). It is also evident in the increasing focus on public–private partnerships for the realization of large projects or public services (see Osborne, 2000; van Ham and Koppenjan, 2002). The most important elements of the governance response to uncertainty are:

- An emphasis on horizontal types of steering, assumed to be better able to gain cooperation from societal actors. These horizontal types of steering supposedly ensure that actors will use their veto power less frequently (*enhance support*).
- An emphasis on a better use of the knowledge gained from societal actors in order to improve the quality of policy and public services (*quality improvement*). Private actors will often have knowledge of the market whereas societal organizations have knowledge of preferences (among users of services, or citizens in large projects), of societal trends or of sectoral knowledge (consider, for example, knowledge in the development of demand in medical care, opportunities for coordination, etc.).
- An emphasis on the early involvement of societal actors so that the legitimacy of decisions is enhanced (*enhancing legitimacy*). Frequently, governance reform proposals aim to improve or innovate the democratic process or at least try to re-establish the link between politics and citizenry.
- Strategic and knowledge uncertainties in decision making processes can be dealt with by involving actors early in the decision making procedure and by tapping into the different knowledge sources of actors in order to arrive at a shared vision (*enhancing quality and innovative capability*).

Just as with the NPM response, the governance response is often linked to ambitious plans for improving the functioning and organization of the public sector. Emphasis is placed on strengthening inter-organizational cooperation, the increased involvement of citizens and the private sector in decision making, and strengthening the integral character of decision making. The assumption is that better results can be achieved as a consequence. The governance response often includes methods for increasing citizens' involvement in decision making or assessing public services and large projects as well as other policy initiatives by methods such as citizen panels, types of interactive decision making and citizen consultations (Klijn and Koppenjan, 2000a; Lowndes *et al.*, 2001; McLaverty, 2002; Denters *et al.*, 2003).

Box 5.4 Expansion of the Rotterdam harbour: an example of governance by interactive policy making

The Rotterdam harbour is one of the most important ports in Europe and is also very important to the Netherlands' economy. Since the early 1990s the municipality of Rotterdam, in cooperation with other municipalities in the region, the national government and businesses, has been planning the improvement and expansion of the harbour area. One project concerns the construction of a second large industrial area near the harbour (the Second Meuse Plain). This expansion of the port area should solve the shortage of space experienced in Rotterdam. Since the project was (and is) of national interest the cabinet decided in April 1996 to submit the decision regarding the perceived shortage of space to an exploration phase, an interactive decision making process that should result in a so-called project decision. In its letter the cabinet formulated a double objective: improvement and expansion of the harbour should be coupled with improvement of the living environment in the region.

Design and outcomes of the interactive process
For the organization of the interactive decision making process, a project group consisting of civil servants from four ministries was established. The project was called the VERM project. VERM stands for the Exploration phase of the Spatial Development of the Main Port Rotterdam. The interaction process took place between April 1996 and July 1997 when the cabinet formulated its project decision on the basis of the outcomes of the exploration phase. All sorts of organizational arrangements such as workshops, focus groups, etc. were used to elicit a wide range of views. At the end of the interactive process the project group prepared an advisory report to the cabinet. The cabinet proposal itself, i.e. the project decision, was prepared within the usual administrative framework in the ministries. In principle, three alternatives were central to discussions during the interactive process:

- the zero option: no expansion, economic utility has not been convincingly demonstrated;
- expansion of the harbour's area within the existing terrain (intensive development) and supplementary functions outside the harbour area;
- expansion of harbour activities by expanding the harbour area (by constructing the Second Meuse Plain).

Preparation for the project decision that the cabinet would again take place in the ministries.

The role of politicians in the interactive process
The ministries, various national political figures and Parliament did not really participate in the open planning process. But at various times there was contact between the VERM project group and high-level staff of the ministries (especially the Ministry of Transport, Public Works and Water Management). Already, in the preliminary phase, the project group was told that the ministers and Members of Parliament were not participating in the discussions since they had, so it was said, their own responsibilities. Based on this, the top officials at the ministry retained

the right to determine the project decision, a position that was repeated in later discussions.

In the discussion concerning the expansion of the Rotterdam harbour, politicians seemed to recognize only two roles: that of a distant, non-involved actor or that of a proponent of a specific interest. The first role was reflected in the position of the Second Chamber of Parliament and of national political authorities. Based on the idea that representative institutions have their own explicit area of sub-stantive responsibility, these actors did not want to commit themselves and, there-fore, also did not want to take part in the interactive decision making process. It is striking that Parliament, in the discussion surrounding the cabinet's project pro-posal, argued for more attention to be given to environmental objectives, while the discussion in the interactive decision making process was rather dominated by the already developed option of the Second Meuse Plain. A more intensive involvement of politicians perhaps could have led to a more serious elaboration of alternatives that could have expanded the range of choices of the Second Chamber. The distant role assumed by national politicians clashed with the assumptions of interactive decision making, which aim not only at the creation of a certain degree of variety but also presume a shared commitment during the process.

Source: Klijn and Koppenjan, 2000a.

Effective steering: linking interactions and developing integral solutions

The intent of governance reform is not only to make the public sector more effec-tive, but also to generate solutions that better fit the complex problems of society and break through the separation in policy sectors. The emerging image of public actors is not one of a government that has to do more with less, as in NPM, but a government that must achieve policy and public services together with citizens and provide solutions that are innovative and can transcend sectors. Whether these services should be provided by public or private organizations is immaterial in this approach, as long as policy products and services are effective, efficient and serve societal and citizens' needs.

Yet, there is some tension between the rhetoric of governance reforms and the practice. Thus, on the one hand, the importance of added value and an integrated approach is applauded, as is the trust between actors, but, on the other hand, there is an emphasis on the steering capacity of public actors for managing this complex process through horizontal steering. This becomes clear in the joined-up government and local reform effort since they advocate cooperation yet are initiated in a top-down manner (see Newman, 2003).

Managing and linking the interaction of involved actors is usually the crucial factor for success. In many reports and research on Public Private Cooperation (PPP) (see Osborne, 2000; van Ham and Koppenjan, 2002; Klijn and Teisman, 2003), interactive decision making (see Klijn and Koppenjan, 2000a; Edelenbos and Monnikhof, 2001; Denters *et al.*, 2003) and citizen participation at the local level (McLaverty, 2002), it appears to be difficult to activate the necessary horizontal types of steering and actors, to generate added value, and then to place all of this in the existing departmental/administrative and politically customary types of decision making that are characterized more by a certain degree of centralism, risk separation and risk exclusion. In fact, the development of management strategies for horizontal steering is still in its infancy and there is much more experience with classical types of vertical steering.

Conclusion: management as conditions for successful steering through governance

Just like the NPM responses, the governance responses to uncertainty have a number of conditions for success. Success requires linking different perceptions and strategies and overcoming different institutional regimes from different networks or institutional regimes that limit cooperation. When we view the governance strategy as the entirety of horizontal strategies and the cooperation of different actors then, clearly, it is difficult to link all of these strategies. It is clear that as horizontal types of steering, governance strategies require management actions which are different from classical central intra-organizational management strategies. Coordinating interaction between actors in networks is not automatic and the organizational provisions for establishing such interactions are usually missing. Furthermore, it is very intensive, requiring other management capacities, and the question of whether governments have these capacities remains. References to disappointing experiences with new governance types indicate that steering is not easy.

Hence, an important role exists for organizing, arranging and consciously influencing these governance strategies. We call these conscious attempts 'network management'. This is the subject of Part 2 of this book, where we address the various strategies of management and their capacities and limitations.

5.6 Conclusion: governance and the need for network management

In this chapter, we looked at public actors' responses to uncertainty in complex decision making processes for difficult problems. In addition to the standard response, which is largely top-down and seeks to reduce uncertainty by excluding actors and certain solution directions, we looked at neo-corporatist responses. Both responses have a high degree of closedness in common.

An important foundation for this closedness is the doctrine of the primacy of politics which assumes a strong steering role for political actors who dominate other actors in decision making. This doctrine, as well as the underlying institutional rules of the game, provides a stark contrast with the daily practice of decision making processes. The doctrine of the primacy of politics often creates tension in decision making methods that predominantly include the input of citizens and other societal groups.

As alternative types of steering, we looked at two responses to uncertainty that have emerged recently: NPM and governance. The first response departs from a separation of policy making and execution. Implementation is conducted by independent administrative entities or private or semi-private actors, and coordinated through more market-type mechanisms (output steering and performance demands, market competition and contract formation). The primacy of politics doctrine can be shaped anew in these types of steering by emphasizing clear steering objectives and guidelines established by political bodies. Implementation then occurs at a greater distance from political bodies. These types of steering are useful for situations in which objectives and products are clearly defined and monitoring can be arranged properly. One can think of relatively simple products and services (e.g. rubbish collection, harbour pilot services, weather monitoring systems, and also various judicial services such as prisons), or of other parts of complex decision making that are no longer disputed and are thus ripe for implementation.

Next, we looked at the governance response to uncertainty which attempts to manage it by accepting the dependencies of actors and linking the interactions of actors. While these types of responses are concerned more with the complexity we discussed in previous chapters, experiences with public–private partnerships, interactive decision making and other types of governance responses have shown that concluding the processes in a satisfactory manner is not an easy task. Adequate management strategies necessary for conducting complex steering methods are scarce, despite the fact that linking interactions in these new types of management strategies is important. In the second part of this book, we discuss possible management strategies for dealing with complex decision making processes applied to difficult problems.

Chapter 6

Summing up
Dealing with uncertainties in networks

6.1 Introduction: building blocks for a theoretical framework

In this chapter we summarize the central ideas presented thus far and combine them in a theoretical framework. This framework is meant for the analysis, evaluation and explanation of, and prescriptions for, the way we deal with the uncertainties involved in wicked problems that occur in fragmented policy games within complex policy networks.

We first discuss the theoretical and normative assumptions that underlie our approach for dealing with uncertainty. We will do this by summarizing the line of reasoning in the previous chapters with regard to the main dimensions of the setting in which complex problems are dealt with, namely: content, process, institutions and management (Section 6.2).

In Section 6.3, we provide an overview of the most important causes of uncertainty. These have been discussed in previous chapters as an explanation for problem solving processes and their outcomes. They provide the 'handles' for developing a better way to deal with uncertainty in problem solving processes – the subject of the second part of this book. In this paragraph we combine these building blocks into a theoretical model.

In Section 6.4, we address a question that we have not yet dealt with, i.e. how we can evaluate the outcomes of complex problem solving processes. We present a number of criteria which form the basis for making such an assessment.

This chapter concludes with a preview of Part 2 of this book in which we discuss numerous ways of dealing with the various uncertainties that play a role in solving complex problems in policy networks.

6.2 A network approach to problem solving and decision making

Complex and difficult problems are surrounded by uncertainty. Besides the substantive complexity of these problems, there are other sources of uncertainty as well. Many actors are involved and their interests are at stake. They will use different strategies in various arenas based on their own perceptions, interests and objectives in order to influence the problem situation and the problem solving process. In addition to strategic uncertainty, there is usually institutional complexity: problems and policy games frequently cut across different networks which means that there are no unambiguous institutions that support interactions (sustainable relations, comparable perceptions, a common language, shared rules and mutual trusts). A large degree of institutional uncertainty is generated from the incompatibility of the institutions involved.

The theoretical and normative assumption that underlies the network approach we use, is that handling these types of uncertainty in dealing with difficult societal problems is essentially a matter of *mutual adjustment and cooperation*. This, given the fact that:

- in the problem situation and the problem solving process, the interests of multiple, mutually dependent actors are involved;
- answering the question of whether a problem exists is not an objective, scientific activity but, instead, it is based on the values, norms and perceptions of these actors which leads to different answers;
- an adequate handling of problem situations requires mutual effort where a careful combination of resources, activities and ideas must be established.

Mutual adjustment and cooperation lead to better results than go-alone strategies by (public) actors because:

- As a result of resource dependency, various actors will have veto opportunities which they will use if they do not like the go-alone strategy. Go-alone strategies will thus lead to blockades and stagnation and hence to inefficient and ineffective decision making.
- Knowledge is dispersed across many actors, go-alone strategies lead to poor solutions since the knowledge available in other places is not utilized. Hence, go-alone strategies result in solutions that fall substantively short for tackling complex problems.
- Go-alone strategies lead to sub-optimal solutions since they generally depart from an optimization of certain values. However, multiple values are often involved in decision making and solutions must reflect these. Go-alone strategies tend to optimize certain values at the expense of others in the decision making process and outcome.

Thus, go-alone strategies generally lead to sub-optimal, substantively poor and ineffective problem solving. But cooperation comes at a cost. The transaction costs of cooperation can be high. This means that problem solving always involves weighing the potential added value of cooperation (in terms of effectiveness and substantive quality, but also in terms of other benefits such as democratic legitimacy) against the limitations and costs of such cooperation.

The network approach outlined in this book also offers the opportunity for analysing where and how cooperation stagnates. Thus, this approach can help us determine whether cooperation should continue or not. Actors might not have any other choice but to continue cooperating since the problem requires a solution, and there are too many dependencies for go-alone strategies. On the other hand, decision making may not proceed any further because actors become diametrically opposed, lose interest in an issue or because the costs of possible solutions and cooperation are too high. An important element of the network approach is that joint decision making has to result in a relative improvement of problem solving in comparison to the outcomes that can be realized based on go-alone strategies. Another possible outcome is that a satisfactory solution of decision making is simply not possible at a particular moment in time. This is not always bad. There are many hasty decisions that actors later regret. Policy proposals can lack qualities to convince the involved actors to overcome resistance. A non-decision as an outcome can even be a good outcome. Closer analysis must establish whether non-decisions are the result of the veto power of parties with interests, of incomplete, barely thought-out policy proposals, or of badly managed interactions. The theoretical and normative assumptions of the network approach are summarized in Table 6.1.

6.3 Explanations for the evolution and outcome of policy games in networks

In previous chapters we have provided concepts for analysing problem solving processes in networks. We implicitly suggested the mechanisms that influence the evolution and outcome of these processes. In this section, we outline these concepts and relations in more detail. We do so by asking what explanations can be put forward, and to what degree and in what manner difficult societal problems are successfully handled. Thus, the dependent variable is the evolution and outcome of the problem solving process. In this type of research, we characterize these processes by examining the deadlocks and breakthroughs that occur and the (intermediate) outcomes that are generated. In other words, the central question is: how can stagnation and blockades on the one hand, and breakthroughs and resultant outcomes on the other, be explained? We distinguish between five categories of explanations or independent variables: cognitive causes, social causes, institutional causes, network management and external factors.

Cognitive causes: 'dialogues of the deaf' versus cross-frame learning

Cognitive causes for stagnation can originate from the varying perceptions about the nature, causes and effects of problems and their solutions (Termeer, 1993). These concern differences of opinion about the nature of the problem and the quality of the available knowledge and solutions. Characteristic of this kind of discussion is that the parties talk past each other and are, in reality, discussing different things. There is a 'dialogue of the deaf'. Since each party outlines its own research, the differences of opinion and the cognitive reticence that causes it are strengthened. Decision making on large projects, complex system changes and complex technical issues often results in a war of reports. Instead of decreasing knowledge conflicts and substantive uncertainty, scientific knowledge serves to enhance them.

Table 6.1 Theoretical and normative assumptions of the network approach

---

Assumptions

Content
- Problems are not objectively identifiable situations, but the perceptions of actors
- In a problem situation, the problem perceptions of actors can strongly diverge
- Substantive uncertainty is not only caused by the nature and complexity of the problem, but also by the diverging perceptions of actors involved
- Research into the nature and size of problems is not objective, but is based on a particular 'framing' of the problem
- Unilateral attempts to convince other actors of one's own perceptions of the problem – using information strategies – frequently result in knowledge conflicts that enhance the substantive uncertainty
- When actors reason from very different problem perceptions and are unwilling to reflect, this increases the likelihood that any interaction will lead to a 'dialogue of the deaf'
- Problem solving requires joint image building
- For joint image building, frame reflection and cross-frame discussion are necessary

Game
- Actors depend upon each others' resources to achieve their objectives, i.e. for handling a problem situation
- Dependencies provide actors with hindrance or even veto power which will delay or block the realization of objectives, i.e. the solution of problems
- Dependencies between actors can be asymmetric (power differences) and are related to the (perceived) possession of resources
- Actors do not always assess their own dependencies correctly; there is a tendency to overestimate one's own problem solving capabilities
- Actors use strategies to achieve their objectives, i.e. problem solutions. They base these strategies on their perceptions. Strategies are aimed at formulating the problem and/or solutions, the process of problem solving and the strategies of others
- Outcomes in the game are the result of interaction of actors' strategies
- Strategic uncertainty is generated by the (sum of) unpredictability and changeability of strategies
- Problem solving is not a linear process from problem formulation to solution, but it zigzags and proceeds in fits and starts
- Strategic uncertainty is strengthened because decisions are made in different arenas
- Problem solving requires coordinating the different strategies used by various actors

Network
- Dependencies between actors lead to more or less durable interaction patterns
- Interaction patterns result in network characteristic perceptions, a shared language, shared rules and mutual trust
- These institutional factors constitute the behaviour of actors and influence cooperation in the network
- These institutional characteristics result in a certain closedness of the network in relation to the outside world
- When problem situations cut across networks, interaction and cooperation is inhibited because actors operate from differing institutional backgrounds which are not compatible
- Under the influence of interactions, institutional factors are shaped, sustained and adapted

Management
- Given the variety of interests and objectives and the resulting conflicts about the distribution of costs and benefits of problems and solutions, cooperation does not emerge on its own nor does it proceed without problems
- In order to improve cooperation, it is necessary to monitor interactions (network management)
- Mutual action can be improved by stimulating cross-frame discussions, bringing actors together, monitoring interaction, and improving the institutional facilities that support this interaction

A *substantive breakthrough* requires joint image building: i.e. cognitive learning is possible and substantive uncertainty is reduced through a convergence of ideas and perceptions, and a mutual understanding of the meaning of situations and events. This requires frame reflection and cross-frame debate where problems and solutions are formulated anew (Rein and Schön, 1986, 1992). The availability of new substantive ideas or the decision to include these ideas in the discussion play an important role in this debate and reflection. Another important factor is the degree to which actors are able to organize research so that instead of fulfilling the advocacy role of one party, it supports the process of joint image building.

Social causes: the problem of coordination and cooperation

Social causes of deadlocks emerge when the strategies of actors – whose resources for dealing with the problem are indispensable – are uncoordinated, in conflict or when there is no interaction between actors. Conflicting strategies are usually a consequence of the differing perceptions and objectives of actors. Limited coordination may be caused by the fact that parties are insufficiently aware of their mutual dependency or they have failed to discover a mutual interest. It might also be caused by the uncertainty of how to approach the problem, who will play what role in the problem solving process, and how much it will cost. If the risks of joint action are substantial, actors might decide not to pursue it. As a consequence, parties may be unwilling to invest their resources.

A breakthrough can emerge when parties are able to coordinate their strategies, so that their individual actions are no longer in conflict and joint action becomes a possibility. For this to occur, the reduction of strategic uncertainties is crucial. This can be done by engaging in interaction, by linking arenas, and by mitigating the risk of strategic behaviour through, for instance, process agreements (van Bueren *et al.*, 2003). Actors have to formulate a solution that makes it possible to link their objectives and, when there are unequal costs for some actors, that offers opportunities for compensation (Allison, 1971; Teisman, 1992).

Institutional causes: building a Tower of Babel

Institutional causes of stagnation include, in the first instance, the absence of mutual institutions (relations, rules, shared orientations and a shared language). These institutions help to reduce the risks of participating in policy games, often have a mitigating effect upon conflicts, and provide procedures for creating interaction and managing conflict.

A weakly developed mutual institutional structure might explain why stagnation occurs. It is not that there are *no* institutions: they are there, but they are not tuned in to each other. Instead of supporting interaction, they prevent or hinder interaction: i.e. the incompatibility of orientations, rules and languages that guide the parties' behaviour makes the problem solving process something like building the Tower of Babel (March and Olsen, 1989). Institutional causes can also result from the nature of institutional characteristics. Cooperation is more difficult in networks with strong autonomy rules than in networks where rules are less rigid (Klijn, 2001). Networks with strong patterns of distrust will also have difficulty cooperating.

In short, a strong institutional structure, such as recognizable rules and relatively strong trust relations between actors, may result in low transaction costs since provisions furthering cooperation do not need to be developed from scratch, and parties can rely on existing arrangements. Such a structure, however, can also have negative effects if it contains elements that are unfavourable to cooperation. Furthermore, the strong institutional structures of different networks can clash when decision making takes place in arenas situated in more than one network.

Institutional breakthroughs occur when blocking institutions are adapted or abolished. Also, the creation of new organizational structures and formal rules can support the interaction between parties that are involved in long-term processes of problem solving and thus result in a breakthrough. The creation of the most important supporting institutions, however, is not something that can be accomplished in the short run. They are more typically the consequence, rather than the cause of interaction processes. At issue are the ad hoc rules, perceptions and expressions which parties only gradually come to share during a long-term process. In the end, they may become part of the institutional structure.

Management as cause

An important explanation for the occurrence of deadlocks, breakthroughs and the emergence of policy outcomes can be the presence or absence of attempts to manage policy games and the quality of these management efforts. Interaction between parties in complex policy games is difficult to achieve because of different interests, uncertainties and the risks and costs involved with that interaction. This is especially the case when policy games cut through different policy networks since actors have different perceptions, operate upon different rules, speak different languages, and thus do not know what to expect of other actors. In this case, the shared institutions which can regulate behaviour are absent. When one or more actors operate as broker, facilitator, conflict manager or arbiter, there are increased chances for preventing or at least limiting the destructive influence of deadlocks, realizing breakthroughs and making decisions (Agranoff, 1986; Susskind and Cruikshank, 1987; Forester, 1989; Mandell, 1990; Kickert et al., 1997; Meier and O'Toole, 2001).

External developments

Deadlocks and breakthroughs may relate to developments in the environment of a network which lead to changing perceptions, changing power relations, or changing institutional structures (Kingdon, 1984; Sabatier, 1988). These developments may make problem formulations outdated or may bring new solutions within reach. The support for certain problem frameworks or solutions, achieved after substantial effort, may dissolve in one stroke. Conversely, a long lasting blockade or stagnation may be dissolved and new policy windows may open.

Table 6.2 Factors that explain the evolution and outcomes of policy games

	Deadlocks	Breakthroughs and outcomes
Cognitive causes	• Unilateral information search behaviour and cognitive fixation • Asymmetric argumentation structures • Advocative research	• Increased cognitive reflection and substantive variety • Joint image building through cross-frame discussion • Joint research efforts
Social causes	• Lack of interaction because dependencies and fragmented arenas are not acknowledged • Game types with conflicting strategies • Risks of strategic behaviour • Proposals that do not match the perceptions and interests of parties	• Interaction and the coupling of arenas and games • Mutual adjustment of strategies • Agreements to avoid strategic behaviour • Goal intertwinement
Institutional causes	• Lack of shared institutions (perceptions, rules, language, trust) that enhance and support interaction • Incompatible institutions • Institutional characteristics that limit cooperation	• Adaptation or elimination of blocking institutions • Creation of shared institutions
Management causes	• Lack of systematic management efforts • Wrong or badly executed management efforts	• Presence of management aimed at enhancing a cross-frame discussion, goal intertwinement, interaction, coordination of strategies and institutional support
External developments	• Environmental developments which may eliminate the support for mutual solutions and enhance deadlocks	• Developments in the environment that help break through blockades or stagnation and provide new opportunities for mutual solutions and cooperation

External developments do not always directly influence policy games. This depends, in part, on the degree to which actors view these developments as opportunities and use them to influence the policy and/or the content of proposals. Examples of external developments are changes in the market/economic situation, changes in the societal climate, changes in political priorities and the political composition of the cabinet, the availability of new technology, etc.

Relations and interactions between factors

It is clear that we cannot view the various explanatory factors separately because they influence one another: *cognitive fixations* can be strengthened by the *strategies* that actors use, just as the content of the policy discussion will influence the parties' positions. *Institutional factors* do not directly influence the policy game, but they operate through the actors' strategies and their perceptions of the risks and opportunities related to go-alone strategies or cooperation. Also, *network management* influences the content of the process and the actors' strategies. The influence of management on outcomes is indirect: through actors' strategies and game interactions. Conversely, management is subject to parties' efforts to influence it and is, thus, influenced by the policy discussions that take place. Furthermore, management efforts are influenced by existing institutions. *External developments* operate through actors' perceptions and actions at the institutional level, through cognitive and social factors and in network management.

Finally, we must point to the relation between the dependent and the independent variables. In long-term processes, where many factors and actors influence each other, and actors consciously respond to events in their environment, causal relations are highly complex, dynamic and reciprocal. They can hardly be captured in causal schemes that create a static idea of the relation between dependent and independent variables. In reality, the relations are constantly in flux, and we can see a continuous interchange between factors and process where, for instance, actors' perceptions and choices are established under the influence of earlier events in the process. Thus, the problem solving process can be regarded in part as 'its own cause': the dynamic of the process influences cognitive and social factors and network management – and, in the longer run, the institutions which are involved and therefore its own evolution. In the causal model below, we visualize the evolution of policy games in networks. The interaction between factors is indicated by causal lines between the policy game and factors in both directions or through feedback loops between factors.

This does not mean, however, that everything is related to everything else and that causality is relative. As Figure 6.1 shows, some relations are more direct than others. Also, causal relations work at varying speeds: influences at the institutional level will operate more slowly than influences at the process level. What this means for parties in the policy game is that if they want to make decisions at a certain moment, then they must do so within a specific constellation of actors and factors which explains the strategic options that are available and the consequences that the options will generate. But this constellation is only a snapshot. Further along in the policy process, for instance in the next policy round, parts of this constellation may have changed, partially under the influence of actor behaviour, process outcome, or external circumstances, and other factors will then play a role.

Multi-causality and multi-level explanations

The multi-causal character of complex processes of problem solving make it very difficult to isolate the effect of one factor. A deadlock in the policy game is usually the result of a number of factors at different levels (content, game, network) that exert simultaneous influence. Conflicting actor strategies may explain the deadlock, but at the same time, the lack of institutions that can support the process may also be influential. Neither explanation can be reduced to the

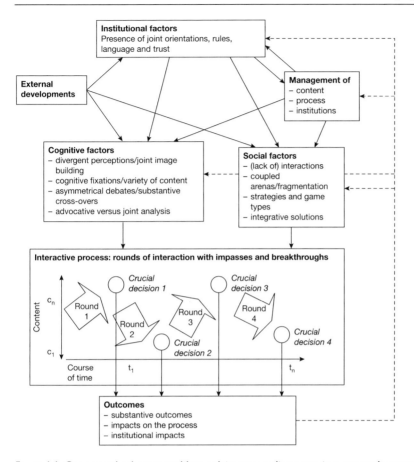

Institutional factors
Presence of joint orientations, rules,
language and trust

External
developments

Management of
– content
– process
– institutions

Cognitive factors
– divergent perceptions/joint image
  building
– cognitive fixations/variety of content
– asymmetrical debates/substantive
  cross-overs
– advocative versus joint analysis

Social factors
– (lack of) interactions
– coupled
  arenas/fragmentation
– strategies and game
  types
– integrative solutions

Interactive process: rounds of interaction with impasses and breakthroughs

Content

c_n

c_1

Round
1

Round
2

Crucial
decision 1

Round
3

Crucial
decision 2

Round
4

Crucial
decision 3

Crucial
decision 4

Course
of time

t_1

t_n

Outcomes
– substantive outcomes
– impacts on the process
– institutional impacts

Figure 6.1 Conceptual scheme: problem solving as a policy game in a network context

other (stagnation is possible even if there are institutions; the lack of institutions does not always lead to stagnation). Conflicting strategies, for instance, only partially explain stagnation. If we were to limit ourselves to conflicting strategies alone, background factors and other more deeply embedded causes would remain out of our purview. In short, explanations of policy game processes and outcomes can rarely be reduced to one or a few factors because they are the consequence of the interplay between different factors at varying levels – each of which is also subjected to a certain dynamic.

Other possible questions

Finally, while this study is specifically focused on problem solving in situations of uncertainty, the network approach can also be a source of inspiration for a variety of different questions. An important angle, for instance, is the question of how institutions are created and how they change under the influence of a series

---

Box 6.1 Explanations for the evolution and outcome of the zinc game

Ten years of discussion about the zinc problem reveal a slow process with substantial deadlocks and few breakthroughs. There was little substantive progress. Conflicts persisted concerning the degree to which zinc products are harmful, the contribution of construction materials to zinc emissions and the necessity and impacts of policy measures. No cooperation was established during the process and go-alone strategies dominated. Institutional fragmentation limited interaction; the zinc industry organized itself, but was unable to gain sufficient access to arenas in other networks. There were no real breakthroughs in the policy game, even though in some way the differences between parties diminished: by suggesting the zinc industry formulated a new agenda that made further meetings meaningful, the parties slowly came closer on the amount of zinc emissions from building products, interaction between the zinc industry and governmental departments increased. In Table 6.3 the factors that influenced the evolution and outcomes of the zinc game process are summarized.

---

of policy games. While this question leads to a different framing of the dependent variable, it does not necessarily lead to a different conceptual model: the causal mechanisms and interplays do not change because we ask a different question; only the focus of research attention changes. For this question, attention is aimed at rules and changes in rules (dependent variable) over time as a consequence of actors' changing strategies and game patterns. These, in turn, can be inspired by how actors perceive external developments. Thus, in the Netherlands, fishing organizations respond to EU regulations on quotas and professionalization, increasingly by attempting to arrange their own affairs and professionalize rapidly. As a result, their product board has a less prominent role to play. In other words, authority rules are altered when the fishing organizations gain a stronger position at the expense of the product board. All of this happens because in daily interaction, fishing organizations no longer acknowledge the rules of authority and even explicitly put them up for discussion.

6.4 Assessing the evolution and outcomes of policy games

In this section, we indicate which criteria will be used to assess the evolution and outcome of processes aimed at solving wicked problems.

Evaluation problems in complex decision making processes

In rational approaches to problem solving, a scientifically grounded problem formulation or an *ex ante* formulated objective of one central actor is usually the point of reference for the evaluation. In a network approach of the process of problem solving, this point of reference is problematic for a number of reasons.

Table 6.3 Explanations for the evolution and outcome of the zinc game

	Deadlocks	Breakthroughs and outcomes
Cognitive factors	• Diverging problem perceptions lead to cognitive fixation, knowledge conflicts and asymmetric debates • Research results in a war of reports	• With the promise of product innovations, the zinc industry enlarges the scope for problem solving and creates new opportunities for exchange • Joint research efforts lead to increased agreement on amounts of emissions
Social factors	• Parties use unilateral strategies that infringe upon each other's core values (zinc industry products have negative effects; the deterrence policy of local governments damages the sales of the zinc industry; substantive critique of the norm method threatens RIVM) • Mutual distrust increases under the influence of strategies • The fragmentation of policy game makes it more difficult for the zinc industry to interact with all parties • The organization of the decision making process on the norms is untransparent	• The ineffectiveness of its strategies leads the zinc industry to search behaviour and adapt its strategy, i.e. from non-participation via conflictual strategies (fighting norms, policy measures and LCAs) to a more constructive approach (the proposal for a covenant and for product innovation)
Institutional factors	• Parties from different networks participate in the game: rules limit the opportunity of interaction and access to arenas. Thus, attempts by the zinc industry to support their standpoint with scientific research clash with the ideas and rules of other parties about impartial research	• During the course of the process, the monopoly of large research institutes on the provision of substantive knowledge is less self-evident and the zinc industry acquires more access • The zinc industry organizes itself and, thus enhances its strategic capability
Network management	• The ministries make no effort to bring the parties together. They point to the autonomy of local government and are hesitant in their talks with the zinc industry	• Some efforts to exert influence by the employers' association and the Ministry of Economic Affairs are aimed at mitigating the conflict: they encourage the zinc industry to adopt a more constructive strategy
External factors	• Developments in the Sustainable Building Policy game highly influence the zinc game	• The decrease in acid rain is viewed as the cause for the decrease in zinc emissions from building materials

1   *Lack of substantive yardstick.* There are no clear substantive yardsticks for comparing the outcomes of problem solving processes. In the case of difficult problems, there is no authoritative substantive problem formulation on the basis of which realized solutions can be measured and judged. Actors do not agree on the nature, content and demarcations of the problem in science nor in the policy practice.

2   *Lack of a central objective as yardstick.* Since many actors participate in the policy game, it makes no sense to use the goal attainment of one of the parties as the assessment criterion. Frequently, government claims that its objectives are of a different order than those of other parties and, as a result, they must be regarded as the central assessment criteria. They refer to the primacy of politics and the role that government plays as the representative of the general interest. There are, however, arguments upon which that claim can be contested. The claim of the primacy of politics is grounded in the notion that democratically elected governments who pursue certain objectives are expressing the will of the majority of the people (see Ripley and Franklin, 1987; Hirst, 1990; Marsh and Rhodes, 1992; Rhodes, 1996). But this totally disregards the problems of how individual preferences are represented at a collective level. The relation between election results and individual preferences with regard to specific issues is limited by definition (see Arrow, 1963). Furthermore, there can be a broad gap between the programmes that got political office holders elected and the concrete objectives targeted by specific government organizations. The problematic nature of the claim that government represents the general interest is also apparent when government organizations (e.g. different departments or levels of government) confront one another in concrete policy games. One governmental organization may support a project based on economic considerations while another creates blockades based on environmental notions. Who, then, represents the general interest? As a result, the general interest cannot be clearly defined and is of little use as a substantive benchmark. Policy games involve a range of objectives and values that are articulated and defended by different public and private parties. This range would be violated by considering the objectives of one party as the ultimate yardstick for assessments.

3   *Lack of ex ante yardsticks.* At the beginning of games dealing with wicked problems, the objectives and problem formulations are not fixed. Instead, they develop during the course of the process. Essentially, policy games are objective-seeking processes where parties work towards a common ground for collective problem solving by doing and learning. This includes adapting their perceptions, objectives and criteria. Thus, *ex ante* objectives or problem formulations are not criteria for assessing outcomes since they do not reflect the criteria that parties use further along and towards the end of the process; by which time, they are obsolete and irrelevant. When *ex ante* objectives are used to determine the success and failure of policy games, they are ultimately exposed as obsolete and irrelevant. Furthermore, they will result in a negative assessment of the learning behaviour that parties display during the policy game since learning implies a deviation from *ex ante* objectives and problem formulations.

Success and failure in policy: assessment criteria

When we view policy games in networks as search activities in which the initial uncertainties and conflicts are reduced through interaction, it seems obvious that the quality of problem solving processes can be measured by the degree to which learning has occurred.

Parties can learn in various ways. Given the necessity of coordination in order to deal with wicked problems in network settings, we are interested in certain types of learning. In terms of Sabatier, we are especially interested in the learning between advocacy coalitions (Sabatier, 1988). We define learning as the sustainable increase in shared knowledge, insights and methods of working between parties. We distinguish between learning processes in the areas of content (cognitive learning), process (strategic learning) and institutions (institutional learning). Thus, success and failure in policy games depend upon the degree to which parties have learned in these three areas. Clearly, these learning effects have to be reflected in the (intermediate) outcomes generated during policy games. These outcomes provide indications for determining learning. Below, we discuss these types of learning and elaborate on the evaluation criteria for success and failure in problem solving in complex policy games.

Substantive criteria: cognitive learning

We define cognitive learning as the increased knowledge and insight about the nature, causes and effects of the problem, the possible solutions, and their consequences. The amount of research done is not an indicator for this type of learning since research might not have resulted in enhanced knowledge or insight but, instead, in information overload, misinformation, increased substantive uncertainty or a knowledge gap between involved parties.

Cognitive learning effects are visible in the refinement of problem definitions and the solutions that actors agree upon as well as the degree to which these take the varying interests and objectives of share- and stakeholders into account. We distinguish between two types of cognitive learning effects: joint image building and goal intertwinement.

Joint image building has been accomplished when better insight into the nature of the problem and the consequence of solutions has emerged as a consequence of interaction and (scientific) research and parties have come to an agreement. When neither of these two criteria is met, ambiguity continues to exist: the problem is still untamed. When research efforts have been undertaken but parties cannot agree on their meaning and significance, we have a situation of superfluous knowledge. Knowledge has been generated, but does not help the process move forward; it enhances uncertainty (Van de Riet, 2003). When parties achieve a consensus that is not based on insights from (scientific) knowledge, we refer to negotiated nonsense; and when solutions are based upon such knowledge, they probably will be realized, but may not meet the desired expectations. What is necessary, in the end, is the realization of negotiated knowledge: consensus about insights that are supported by research findings and are

Table 6.4 Joint image building as evaluation criterion

	Consensus about problem formulation and solutions	
	Yes	No
Agreed scientific validity of problem formulations and solutions		
Yes	Negotiated knowledge	Superfluous knowledge
No	Negotiated nonsense	Ambiguity

scientifically defensible (de Bruijn *et al.*, 2002). Table 6.4 provides an overview of the degree to which policy games may generate negotiated knowledge.

In *goal intertwinement*, cognitive learning is expressed in enriched, innovative and agreed-upon solutions that intertwine actors' diverging objectives and/or reduce or compensate the costs and negative side-effects (Fisher and Ury, 1981; Teisman, 1992). Goal intertwinement is also regarded as a win–win solution; solutions that can realize the objectives of multiple parties simultaneously (Kickert *et al.*, 1997; see also Huxham on collaborative advantage: Huxham, 2000). Perhaps it is more accurate to speak of Pareto-optimal solutions: outcomes that constitute an improvement in the existing situation for all parties. When the objectives of one of the parties cannot be achieved, the solution may still be worthwhile. When parties are negatively influenced by a solution, they can be compensated (Dery, 1984; Klijn and Koppenjan, 2000).

In using this evaluation criterion, we not only take into account the fact that multiple perceptions of a problem situation and multiple objectives can exist, but we also consider the problem of the dynamic. We do this by taking the *ex post*, realized solutions as the starting point, and determining how these relate to the objectives that parties regard as relevant at that moment.

Goal intertwinement can be determined by actors during and after the policy game by asking to what degree they are content with the realized (intermediate) solutions. Teisman (1992) calls this the criterion of '*ex post* satisficing'. In making this assessment, actors will compare what they received in terms of outcome with the effort they expended in realizing it – based on what they found relevant at that particular moment. There is a danger of *ex post* rationalization, for example to hide loss in order to prevent loss of face. This is why the assessment must compare the achieved outcomes with the problem perceptions, interests and objectives parties expressed earlier in the process. Furthermore, it is important to determine what the total package looks like: how does the sum total of *ex post* judgements of parties play out? In addition to the sum total of actors' *ex post* judgements, we can determine the degree to which (intermediate) solutions have been *substantively enriched* in comparison to earlier proposals, as well as the degree to which they incorporate the interests and desires of interested 'third' parties (the so-called 'inclusiveness criterion') (Klijn and Koppenjan, 2000).

Using the criterion of goal intertwinement requires explicit attention to the danger that two or more parties manage to achieve a win–win situation by passing

Table 6.5 Goal intertwinement as evaluation criterion

	Enrichment and inclusiveness of solution	
	Yes	No
Ex post *satisficing with involved parties*		
Yes	Goal intertwinement	Compromise
No	There has been learning, but not enough or at far too high a cost	No cognitive learning; ineffective and inefficient process

the costs on to outsiders. So, in addition to the benefits, we must also look at the costs of a solution (which includes the option of doing nothing) in order to examine the intended and unintended effects and their distribution among all actors involved. Table 6.5 provides an overview of the degree to which (intermediate) outcomes of policy games meet the criterion of goal intertwinement.

Process criteria: strategic learning

We define *strategic learning* as the parties' growing consciousness of each others' involvement and their mutual dependencies. This learning is reflected in the increased capacity to deal with conflicts of interest in games wherein cooperation alternates with conflict. In the end, this means that parties have managed to satisfactorily participate in mutual negotiation processes in the search for problem formulations and solutions that take into account both their own objectives and interests as well as those of others. This becomes clear from the type of strategies that actors employ, the game types realized and the length of the processes. If blockades and stagnation emerge, then we can conclude that actors are unable to define a mutual interest as the basis for mutual action. Breakthroughs indicate that – from a process point of view – actors have progressed and have learned. However, the length of the processes must be related to the degree to which cognitive learning has occurred. Coordinating action, generating negotiated knowledge, and intertwining objectives takes time. By definition, blockades and stagnation are not always wrong since they do contribute to the articulation of interests and objectives. They are, in fact, necessary conditions for goal intertwinement. Only when deadlocks become dysfunctional, i.e. conflicts escalate and become destructive and stagnation results from feelings of powerlessness and cynicism, can matters get out of hand from a process point of view.

In addition to the occurrence of deadlocks and the length of the process, we could also look at the quality of the process to determine strategic learning. This concerns the degree to which parties want to limit interaction costs and risks of strategic behaviour, the degree to which they have come to know and trust each other, and have found a modus vivendi for dealing with each other – despite differences of interests, perceptions and objectives. To determine this, the following points of attention should be considered:

- How reliably do parties behave?
- How are interests of parties taken into account?
- How are decisions made?
- Have opportunities for appeal and objection been regulated?
- How are conflicts dealt with?
- Is there network management, mediation and/or arbitration?

Also, when assessing the quality of the policy game, it is important to determine to what degree parties interacted with interested third parties who are not (or not yet) represented in the game (Majone, 1986; Mayntz and Marin, 1992; Kickert *et al.*, 1997). When the attention of parties is focused on discovering each others' strategies and achieving what they regard as their common interest, groupthink type processes may develop that, in turn, result in negotiated nonsense and the transfer of costs and risks to parties whose interests are not represented (compare Janis, 1982). The demands on the process with regard to the degree that third party interests are considered, become especially important since the involved interests are not substantively determined a priori (refer to the comments above about the general interest). Also (scientific) research cannot provide objective, conclusive answers and is partially influenced by a circle of actors who actively participate in the policy game. So, (scientific) research is no guarantee that under- or non-represented interests are well taken care of. The attention to the interests of 'third' parties concerns issues such as accessibility to the policy game, transparency and accountability. Criteria for the evaluation are thus:

- the degree to which the game is accessible to third parties;
- the degree to which processes of problem solving are transparent;
- the way the involvement of democratic platforms in problem solving is organized.

Institutional learning

We define *institutional learning* as the degree to which parties in policy games are able to use or develop relations, rules, meanings, languages and trust that will support and make their interactions more predictable. At first, this will involve ad hoc agreements which go no further than the policy game or even the policy round in terms of purpose. However, when they acquire a more durable character, network formation or network change has occurred. In this case, institutional learning has emerged so that the nature of relations between parties in a policy game is changed for the long term. As a consequence, the institutional uncertainty in the policy game between parties from different networks decreases. Parties and networks become linked and the further evolution of the policy game(s) that develop around new problems or proposals for solutions develops in a relatively uncomplicated context. There are now provisions that facilitate and support the interaction between parties. Parties know where to find one another, know how to deal with one another, and can better shape their interaction (see Pauly,

Table 6.6 Assessment criteria for policy games in network settings

Criteria

Content

- Mutual acknowledgement of meaning and joint image building; the development of negotiated knowledge
- Goal intertwinement resulting in Pareto-optimal outcomes

Process

- Lack of non-functional blockades and stagnation; realization of breakthroughs; length of process matches the degree of cognitive learning
- The degree to which parties become acquainted, develop interaction rules and trust and choose cooperative and negotiation focused strategies
- Openness, transparency and democratic legitimation of the process for third parties

Network

- Network change, i.e. network formation: the development of durable provisions that support interaction: new relations, organizational arrangements, joint meanings, a common language and trust

2001). This policy game context is more robust, also in the sense that institutional provisions will neither collapse with the first conflict nor will they be changed as a result of the influence of one of the actor's strategies (Hood and Jackson, 1991). But, by definition, institutional learning implies a change in the existing relations within a network. This change can also mean the end of a relationship. Table 6.6 provides an overview of the assessment criteria for policy games in network settings.

6.5 A preview of Part 2

In Part 1 of this book we have dealt with the nature of the process for solving complex societal problems in network settings. We discussed types of uncertainties as they emerge and have shown how these influence the problem solving process. We have shown that attempts by parties to deal with these uncertainties often fall short, quite frequently because the nature of the uncertainties is not well thought out or the uncertainties are underestimated. At the same time, we have identified a number of points concerning a more adequate response to these uncertainties. With regard to substantive uncertainties, we posed the question: how can one arrive at joint image building and goal intertwinement? With regard to the policy game, the question is how the game should be organized so that coordination and cooperation are enhanced without transferring the costs of cooperation to third parties. And with regard to institutional uncertainties, there is the question of how to deal with the lack of – or conflict between – institutional provisions in the policy game. We address these questions in Part 2.

Part 2

Management of uncertainties in dealing with complex problems in networks

Chapter 7

Mapping uncertainties in games and networks

7.1 Introduction

In Part 1 of this book we argued that uncertainty is more than knowledge uncertainty. Uncertainty is also closely related to the strategic and institutional characteristics of the interactions: the presence of various actors, their perceptions and strategies, the game that develops among them and the characteristics of the network setting in which the game is played.

Analysing issues in strategic games and networks: actor, game and network analysis

A first step on the way to handling uncertainty in order to arrive at an approach to the problem, is to map its nature and causes. Knowledge about the strategic and institutional context of the problem situation is required for developing an adequate response that will avoid the disadvantages involved in a substantive course.

In short, 'tools' are needed in order to understand the strategic and institutional context of complex problems. In this chapter, we present a number of approaches to mapping uncertainties in the process of problem solving using the network approach. This can be done by conducting, sequentially, an *actor analysis*, a *game analysis* and a *network analysis*. Below, we discuss the main outlines of the analysis tools. We are aware that advanced techniques exist that can assist in implementing these phases (or stages) of analysis. In our discussion here, we limit ourselves to the main outline of the method. We are especially interested in providing an understanding of the nature and potential of the analyses and their meaning for the larger process of problem solving. We refer to relevant literature for suggestions on how these methods can be designed at the technical level.

The actors, game and network analysis must provide an overview of the conditions and circumstances under which complex decision making processes of wicked problems take place. This analysis will not completely remove uncertainties. Recall that in Part 1 we emphasized the inevitable and permanent character of uncertainty in complex processes of problem solving in a modern network society. Our analysis suggestions are, thus, not an attempt to eliminate that uncertainty through the back door. Instead, the analysis is intended to be helpful for mapping the nature of uncertainties. It will not make them disappear – but the knowledge generated through these analyses may provide a better understanding of the actors involved, the nature of the policy game being played and the institutional conditions under which it is played. While knowledge can contribute to a better insight into the nature of uncertainties, it does not remove them. Actors must still seek methods for dealing with the uncertainties. The opportunities they have for doing so will be discussed in subsequent chapters.

The tools presented here will result in the creation of a map of the environment that parties can use in their attempt to handle uncertainties in order to improve the problem situation. At the same time, the metaphor of a 'map of the environment' also suggests the limitations of the tools presented here. The question is, after all, how reliable is that map? Depending on the quality and boundaries of the analysis, the map may provide incomplete or incorrect directions. Still, the map does not have to be complete in order to point parties in the right direction. As a result, in this chapter we point to the fact that the depth of analyses may vary: sometimes there is time for in-depth analysis, at other times – in view of limitations of time and capacity – a quick scan is more appropriate.

A serious limitation of the map is that it quickly becomes obsolete. Given the dynamics that characterize problems, processes and networks, parties should realize that these analyses can only provide a snapshot of a dynamic whole. Thus, the map of the environment has limited usefulness. This means that these analyses have a short-term and limited nature and must be conducted and adapted frequently in order to provide the opportunity for changing and progressing insights, new developments and changes in actor composition and game type. When parties are not aware of these limitations, these analyses can even become counter-productive. Analysis supports observations and common sense, it is not a substitute for them.

The structure of this chapter

The methods of analysis presented in this chapter focus, sequentially, on mapping the actor field involved in a problem situation (actor analysis), the characteristics of the game situation (game analysis) and the characteristics of the network setting in which the game is played (network analysis). Within each of these methods, a number of analytical steps are taken that will be discussed in subsequent sections. In practice, the three methods and analysis steps will not have to be carried out simultaneously. Depending on the uncertainties that parties are grappling with and the knowledge requirements that they formulate, they may limit the number of methods or steps in the methods. But the fact still remains that the analyses build on each other. For instance, some steps in the actor analysis must be taken in order to execute a network analysis. In Section 7.2 we provide an overview of the steps that can be taken in the context of the three analysis methods. Section 7.3 includes a discussion of the steps taken in the context of an actor analysis. The content of game analysis is discussed in Section 7.4. Section 7.5 presents the working method of a network analysis. In the final section, we address the relation between the steps in the analysis and management strategies.

We demonstrate the management questions and actions that can be linked to the different analytical steps.

7.2 Actor, game and network analysis: an overview

The steps for executing actor, game and network analysis are built upon the central concepts and insights presented in Part 1. The idea is that the analysis is conducted by individual actors, for instance a policy administrator who must solve an urban innovation issue or a project developer who wants to develop a real estate plan. The tools, in other words, can support the stakeholders in designing or improving their strategic responses to certain problems or challenges. But the tools can also serve an actor who is prepared to take the role of network manager and wants to coax parties into cooperation and break through conflicts and stagnation. Conceivably, the tools could also be used in an interactive setting as part of an intervention track supervised by the network manager.

The steps proposed here serve as guidance to an environment analysis, not as a blueprint. In practice, one might choose to skip certain steps if they are less relevant. Also, each step can be conducted intensively or as a quick scan. Table 7.1 provides an overview of the three analysis tools by indicating the steps that can be taken in the context of each of these three tools, the objective of these steps and the knowledge questions that are at stake.

In the remainder of this chapter, we discuss the steps taken in the context of the three analysis methods.

7.3 Actor analysis: identifying actors, problems, perceptions and dependencies

The first steps of the analysis determine who the most important actors are, what problem perceptions they hold, and what their position is with respect to the problem situation. To do so, we discuss how to identify actors and how to characterize their mutual relations.

Step 1: Take a tentative problem formulation as starting point

Since a complex problem in a policy game that takes place in a network setting does not have an authoritative definition, a first difficulty in executing an analysis is the question of how to determine the boundaries of analysis. After all, there is no substantive starting point: different actors will have different views of the problem and may, in fact, be defining different problems. This also means that they will arrive at very different demarcations of the issue, the set of actors who are involved, the game, and the arenas and networks involved. As a result, it is important for the individual conducting the actor analysis to determine which perspective will be used to start the analysis. We envision two possibilities (for some guidelines see also Patton, 1997):

Table 7.1 Steps in actor, game and network analysis

Step	Intention	Important question
Actor analysis		
Take a provisional formulation of a problem or initiative as starting point	Mapping a problem situation or initiative as starting point for further analysis	• What does the current or expected situation look like? • What are the (undesirable) consequences that flow from that? • What are regarded as the causes for this situation? • What is the desired situation? • What goals and criteria underlie this? • Which solutions/policy alternatives are pursued?
Identify actors involved	Which actors need to be taken into account?	• Who can be distinguished as the acting units? • Which actors in the network are important to realizing one's own objectives or policy goals? • Which actors have an interest in finding a solution to the problem situation?
Reconstruct perceptions of actors	Mapping images of actors with regard to the problem, the solution and other actors	• What images do actors hold about aspects such as problem, causes, solutions and (competency) of each other? • To what degree do these perceptions differ, are there clear groups? • What obstacles could be caused by differences in perception?
Analyse actor positions and dependencies	What positions do actors take with regard to the problem situation and how much do actors depend upon each other?	• What means do different actors have at their disposal? • How important are these means and can they be acquired elsewhere? • Is there unilateral or mutual dependency? • Are actors critical, dedicated and/or comparable?

Game analysis

Determine the relevant arenas

Acknowledging coherent groups of actors and interaction situations around demarcated policy issues and/or initiatives that are meaningful to the initial initiative or policy game

- Where are the decisions made that are important to the initiative/policy game that is analysed?
- Which actors interact in which context (sector, policy content, ad hoc etc.)
- How coherent are these groups of actors?
- Do these groups of actors have relations with each other (linkages)?

Identify and analyse stagnation

Inventory stagnation in the game and determine the nature and structure of stagnation as a starting point for managing interventions

- Is there stagnation in the game?
- What is the nature and structure of the stagnation?
- Which players are involved in the stagnation?
- Are these blockades or stagnation?
- To what extent is the stagnation cognitive by nature?
- To what extent is the stagnation social by nature?

Network analysis

Inventory of interaction patterns of actors

Through mapping the frequency and diversity of interactions of actors, networks and the actors who belong to them can be determined

- Which actors interact frequently and which infrequently?
- Which actors have a varying contact pattern and which do not?
- Which actors are central and peripheral in the network given their contact pattern?

Inventory of patterns in actors' perceptions

By determining the relation in perceptions between actors, one can discover which networks actors belong to

- What perceptions do actors hold with regard to problems, solutions, and their environment?
- To what degree do these perceptions correspond to those of other actors?

Inventory of institutional provisions that connect parties

Make an inventory of and analyse the formal and informal rules and other organizational arrangements in the network relevant to the policy game

- What formal rules and juridical procedures apply?
- What informal rules can be distinguished (for instance, with regard to information provision, access opportunities, professional codes, etc.)?
- What meeting and consultation procedures or other organizational constructions exist in the network that structure the policy game?

1   The analyst selects the position of a specific stakeholder, who poses as the problem owner or initiator for a solution, as the starting point for analysis. He adopts his formulation of the problem situation and gives it the status of initial problem identity.

2   The analyst formulates his own idea of the problem on the basis of his own, initial substantive problem exploration and gives it the status of problem identity.

The initial problem identity is no more than a working hypothesis which the analyst will adapt – or possibly reject – under the influence of the data from the actor analysis. Its function is to help the analyst get an idea of the problem situation, to determine what it consists of, and which components are relevant, thereby starting the actor analysis. Questions that the analyst will answer in developing this initial problem identity include:

- What does the current or expected situation look like?
- What (undesirable) consequences result from it?
- What are considered the causes for this situation?
- What is the desired situation?
- What objectives and criteria serve as the foundation for this?
- What solutions/policy alternatives are pursued?

Step 2: Inventory of actors

The second step of the analysis starts by answering the question: which actors are important from the perspective of the initial problem identity? In order to trace actors, a number of questions can be answered:

- Which actors are actively involved in the problem?
- Which actors possess hindrance or realization power, in the sense that they have authority or other resources that play a role in the emergence or solution of the problem situation?
- Which actors have the knowledge, insights and ideas that can contribute to the enrichment of the problem formulation, i.e. that can be considered for the solutions?
- Which actors can be expected to be involved at any particular moment?
- Which actors are not likely to participate, but are affected in some way by the problem or the approach to it?

Clearly, differing emphasis in the selection criteria distinguished above will lead to different actor sets in the analysis (for stakeholders analysis see Bryson and Crosby, 1992). Thus, the emphasis may be on mapping the hindrance power (especially when pursuing support) but also on determining the opportunities for substantive enrichment (especially for generating (new) solutions).

Actors and the problem of 'compound' actors

An actor can be an individual, a group or an organization who takes action in view of a problem situation. A problem emerges when we deal with *compound actors* ('corporate actors') (Scharpf, 1997). For instance, the actor 'government' will, in practice, be represented by different departments (the Ministry of Traffic and Water Management, the Ministry of Housing and Environmental Affairs, etc.) and these, in turn, can be involved in the problem situation with more than one organizational unit. The question then becomes: which organizational unit can be labelled the actor?

When different units of an organization are involved – and each unit has their own perceptions – it makes sense to list each of these units as separate actors. When only one unit of a department is involved, the question is then: is the unit or the ministry the actor? The decision rule for this is to select an organizational level as high as possible, without losing information or including irrelevant objectives. Avoid analysing actors at the level of 'government' or 'private enterprise' at all costs. Such a high aggregation level will significantly reduce the information quality of the analysis.

Step 3: Inventory of the problem perceptions

Central to the third step is the reconstruction of perceptions. As indicated in Chapter 3, perceptions concern different aspects. For the sake of simplicity, we focus here especially on the problem perception of actors. While these include actors' ideas about solutions, we give these less attention here than the problem perceptions, but will discuss them at length in the next chapter. Through the perceptions, we can identify the actors' objectives and interests.

Making an inventory of problem perceptions

Actors have their own perceptions of the problem situation: their idea of what the problem is. The initial problem identification of the problem owner is only one of the possible formulations of the problem as it plays a role in the initial situation. The complexity of a problem situation consists of various problem perceptions existing next to one another. In Step 3, an inventory is made of the problem perceptions of the actors selected for the analysis. A problem formulation consists of a number of aspects: a standard by which to measure, an indication of the existing or expected situation, causes and possible starting points for improvement. The problem perceptions held by different actors can vary with regard to each of these aspects (see also Dery, 1984; Patton, 1996).

In this step of the analysis, we systematically map the problem perception of the different actors involved. Sometimes, documents exist where actors have systematically presented their perceptions. Often, however, actors' perceptions will not be explicitly documented. They exist only in the minds of those involved. In all cases, the problem perception can be incomplete and can even be inconsistent in parts. It then becomes the analyst's task to reconstruct the problem perceptions of the involved actors to the greatest extent possible. At the same time, he must be cautious not to fill in issues for the actor since it might be the case that an actor has not even thought about a certain aspect of a problem or simply has no opinion about it. The following questions can be addressed in order to map the actors' problem perceptions:

- What standard do actors use to assess the situation?
- What is their perception of the existing and/or expected situation? What is the crux of the problem? To what degree and in what sense are there gaps in the actors' perceptions? How do they determine this?
- What are the most important causes of the problem situation in their view?
- What influencing techniques/means do they distinguish with regard to the problem situation and its causes?

Perceptions can be mapped on the basis of both qualitative and quantitative approaches. A qualitative approach, for instance, is used when a description of each actor's opinions about the problems at hand and their possible solution directions is made on the basis of interviews and written documents (policy documents). It is important to systematically describe and compare the actors' perceptions. To do so, one can select central themes that can be determined by means of documents or interviews. The list of questions above can serve as an aid so that the inventory recorded for each actor includes the same issues.

A written survey would be used in a quantitative approach. This can be done by submitting a list of statements to the respondents who must then indicate (for instance on a five-point scale) whether they agree with the statements. The results can be presented in straightforward tables, but graphic presentations of actors' positions can also be presented, for instance with a multi-dimensional scaling technique (for more elaboration, see the tools for network analysis). Actors who are plotted close to one another on the graph have highly comparable perceptions while actors who are more removed from one another have less comparable perceptions.

Determining objectives and interests

Objectives indicate what actors desire to achieve in a certain situation; what changes they wish to realize (or what they desire to maintain). All actors involved

---

Box 7.1 Perceptions of actors in the zinc case

Table 7.2 provides conclusions about the differences in perceptions of actors. Clearly, the positions of actors in the zinc industry are quite different from those of other actors (see especially statements 1 and 3). They do not believe that replacing zinc with other materials will contribute to improving the environment while most other actors are convinced that it will.

Table 7.2 Average scores on zinc statements (1 = entirely disagree, 5 = entirely agree)

	All respondents	Departments/ministries	Provinces and municipalities	Water Boards	(Organization of the) zinc industry	Researchers/advisers	Building companies/developers
1 Replacing zinc and zinc products with other materials provides an important contribution to improving the environment	3.16	3.3	4.4	3.4	1.0	3.0	2.8
2 Zinc emissions are a problem for water managers	3.11	3.5	3.3	3.8	1.3	2.9	2.8
3 Discussion about zinc emissions cannot progress without clear measuring methods, results and calculation	3.7	3.5	3.1	3.9	5.0	2.4	4.8
4 Solutions to the zinc problem must be found in product innovations	3.7	3.7	3.6	3.5	3.3	3.7	3.8
5 The authority to ban zinc is the exclusive domain of national politics and cannot be the subject of policy at the regional level	3.52	2.0	2.7	3.6	5.0	3.9	5.0
6 Because zinc can be recycled, it is more durable than the alternatives	2.53	2.4	1.7	2.8	4.2	2.1	3.5
7 Decisions about the use of zinc as a building material have great economic consequences and must be approached with great care	3.35	3.6	2.6	3.1	4.8	3.9	2.8
8 The zinc discussion cannot be separated from other diffuse sources	3.41	2.9	3.2	3.9	3.3	3.19	4.0
9 The zinc discussion cannot be solved in the Netherlands	2.54	1.7	1.9	3.0	3.8	2.3	3.5
10 The zinc discussion must be the subject of European policy	3.85	3.7	3.7	3.1	4.7	3.9	4.3

in a problem have a more or less clear set of formulated objectives. Knowledge of these objectives will provide insight into the causes of the existence and persistence of a problem as well as into the solutions available for tackling the problem. Objectives spring forth from the actors' perceptions; objectives are a concretization of these perceptions. Not all perceptions are translated into objectives and actors can choose what they want to strive for at a given moment.

Although an actor usually pursues a series of objectives simultaneously – which often have nothing to do with the problem – with a problem analysis, we are primarily interested in the objectives that directly concern the problem situation. These objectives can be discovered by asking: What does the actor want to achieve with regard to the problem situation?

Interests are guiding values pursued by an actor. In contrast to objectives, these are not directly linked to a concrete problem situation. Interests are closely linked to the identity of an actor (which is highly regulated by the network rules) and the totality of the actors' perceptions. They are also more durable than objectives. For a company, profit maximization and endurance may be major interests. For the Directorate-General of the Environment of the Ministry of VROM, major interests include serving the environmental interest. Hence, a whole series of perceptions about problems, environment, domain rules and professional codes (the latter two are rooted in the network rules) come together to form an interest.

By determining the actor's interests, we can see the degree to which a change of objectives – necessary for reformulating a problem and creating a new approach to the problem – might be acceptable to the actor involved. Interests can be determined by answering: Why does this actor pursue this objective in view of the problem situation?

Interests and objectives can be determined through the content analysis of documents (statutes, reports, plans, brochures, internet sites). But not all goals and interests are listed explicitly. Furthermore, real objectives and interests may differ from the official ones. A critical attitude is required of the analyst. He must use extra sources such as articles, commentaries, studies and interviews. On the basis of these data, the analyst must reconstruct the interests and objectives of the actors involved. This can be done in two ways.

The 'quick and dirty' method

First, the analyst can determine interests and objectives by 'quick and dirty' guesswork on the basis of texts and interviews. This means that the analyst must argue why, in his view, an actor defends certain interests and pursues certain objectives. To do so, the following questions must be answered:

1   What does the actor want to achieve with regard to the problem situation?
2   Why do these actors pursue these objectives with regard to the problem situation?
3   What costs and benefits for the actor are related to the problem situation or the suggested directions of solutions?

The systematic method: designing objective–means schemas

In addition, the analyst can work in a more systematic and monitored manner by grounding his argument on objective–means schemas, which he designs on the basis of text and interview analysis per actor (see Chapter 6). In the tree-structure that this technique uses, the means (measures and instruments an actor will use to achieve a goal) and the goals of actors are hierarchically ordered (Kuijpers, 1980).

This technique is often used for designing policy where, based on general goals and via sub-goals, the analyst can logically deduce the means to be used. Here, however, we use the goal-means schema in a different manner: as an analytical instrument. Used in this manner, the goal-means schema is not constructed from general goals, but it is more like putting together a puzzle: what puzzle pieces do we have (i.e. which goals and means do we know?), and how are they related? When putting the puzzle together, we must decide whether a particular piece is a means, a goal or an interest. Next, these pieces must be related to each other: where do they fit in the tree-structure? We place the goals that do not serve higher goals at the top of the tree. These are the interests that serve as the foundation of goals (the so-called 'fundamental objectives'; Keeney, 1992). Working in this manner serves to determine what the goals are and, ultimately, what the actor's interests are.

Remember that many puzzle pieces may be missing. The analyst can guess what these are, but can also leave them open by, for instance, using a question mark.

Comparable and contradictory interests

Although a goal-means scheme invites us to name one (fundamental) goal at the top of the tree-structure, in reality actors will often serve different interests simultaneously. Frequently, these interests may be at odds with each other. Thus, the Ministry of Traffic and Water Management attempts to improve mobility in the Netherlands but also attempts to achieve an effective expenditure of limited public finances. The observation that the Ministry must serve these interests simultaneously is crucial. If one of these interests is removed from the goal-means schema, it will not be clear that the problematic issue in a situation is that *both* interests are simultaneously at stake and that an adequate approach to the problem must contain an answer to this dilemma.

A systematic comparison

Using earlier steps, we can now fill in the following summarizing table (Table 7.3). This summarizing table serves to support a systematic comparison of the initial problem identification with that of other actors. We can see what the similarities and differences are. This knowledge can be used to add to, or redefine, one's own problem analysis. It can also be used to make stakeholders or network managers aware of how other parties view the problem or solution, where potential points of conflict exist, but also of the points where agreement can be achieved.

Table 7.3 Summarizing the problem perceptions

Actor	Problem perceptions				Interests	Goals
	Standard	*Core of the problem*	*Causes*	*Opportunities for influence*		
Actor 1						
Actor 2						
Actor N						

Step 4: Positions of actors: a dependency analysis

After we determine who the most important actors are, and what perceptions, goals and interests are characteristic for these actors, we can take the next step: determining the dependency relations between these actors. The question of the degree of dependence can be answered by looking at these actors' resources and what these resources mean to other actors.

Types of resources

To do this, we must first distinguish types of resources. A variety of resources are distinguished in the literature (Aldrich, 1979; Benson, 1982), but we limit our discussion here to five types:

- *Financial resources*: these are often very important for initiatives to solve complex problems. They not only provide opportunities to truly realize solutions, but also to cover the (extra) organizational costs attached to complex decision making processes for wicked problems.
- *Production resources*: these are necessary for enabling policy initiatives. One can think of, for instance, owning land in an urban restructuring issue. In the same case, one can think of building capacity, etc. In other cases, it might be the capacity of realizing production resources and services such as the number of beds of a hospital, medical equipment, etc. In many cases, production resources concern what actors have previously invested in, and these are often specialized by nature, e.g. the equipment and know-how of a construction company, the specific technology necessary for problem solving, etc. On the one hand, this makes the owners of these resources dependent upon the initiators and decision makers since the owners seek opportunities for using their specialized resources in projects in order to earn a profit on their previous investments (Williamson, 1996). On the other hand, the initiators cannot easily acquire these resources through other actors since they require a substantial investment. We address this issue below.
- *Competencies*: this concerns the formal/juridical authority to make certain decisions. For instance, the authority to decide planning and zoning plans, to issue permits for certain activities, etc. These resources generally rest with a public or semi-public actor (independent regulatory agency, etc.).

- *Knowledge*: this is an important resource for development solutions but also for investigating the nature of the problem. Knowledge can be available in various types of documents, but it can also be implicit (experience knowledge). This last type of knowledge is difficult to transfer to other actors, so it is necessary to activate the actor in order to use his implicit knowledge in the decision making process.
- *Legitimacy*: this is clearly a 'vaguer' resource than the others, but it is certainly not unimportant. Some actors have the ability to give or withhold legitimacy from decisions made to solve difficult problems. One example is, of course, elected political bodies whose support can give extra weight to a project or policy initiative. But also, societal groups can search the media to fulfil such a role. Thus, legitimacy in the network society, where the media has become increasingly important, has also become an important resource.

Degree of dependence

When the resources have been mapped, it is important to determine the degree of dependence. This can be done by means of Scharpf's taxonomy discussed in Chapter 3.

Two issues are important: the importance of a resource and its substitutability (Scharpf, 1978). With the first issue, the question is how important the resource of one actor is to others. With the second issue, the question is whether the resources can be acquired through other actors.

The degree that one organization is dependent upon another organization is measured by the importance of their resource for the realization of objectives as well as the degree to which it is possible to acquire the resource elsewhere (substitutability). An analysis by means of these concepts provides an insight into various dependency relations.

Hence, organizations can be more or less dependent upon another organization. Furthermore, that dependency may or may not be mutual. When an organization (A) finds itself in a position of greater dependence vis-à-vis another organization (B) for the realization of its own goals, and where the other (B) is not at all dependent upon the first organization (A), then the position of that organization (A) is weak. Clearly, there are many more actors in a network and thus many more dependencies. In principle, these can all be analysed according to the model in Table 3.4.

Determine the resource dependency of an actor: who are the critical actors?

In order to determine the resource dependency of a specific actor, we need to find out what resources are crucial given the objectives, and in whose hands these resources are concentrated.

Since every actor possesses a range of means, an extensive overview is not very helpful; what is important is mapping the most relevant resources given the

Table 7.4 Analysing dependencies between actors

Actors	Very important resources	Degree of replaceability	Dependency: low, medium, high	Critical actor? yes/no
Actor 1				
Actor 2				
Actor N				

problem situation. Next, when the degree of substitutability is assessed, we can determine the degree to which the problem owner, depends upon the actor. 'Critical actors' are actors who own resources which are important to the problem owner, or own resources that can be used to hinder the activities of the problem owner (hindrance power).

Determine the involvement of other actors in the problem situation: who are dedicated actors?

The dependency of other parties is not only influenced by the resources they control, but also by their subjective involvement with the problem and their willingness to use their resources. The interest that an actor attaches to a problem or solution can become clear from his problem perception. But that is not always the case. It might be useful to determine whether an actor is faced with clear costs and benefits. If so, he will probably be a dedicated actor or he might become one. When an actor does not perceive clear costs or benefits, or when these offset each other, he will be less inclined to work hard for the solution. It is then likely that we are dealing with a non-dedicated actor.

Similarities and differences between problem perceptions, interests and objectives: potential support and resistance

The earlier analysis of the perceptions, objectives and interests of actors provides information that can be used for taking the next step: determining similarities and differences between actors' problem perceptions, interests and objectives. By filling in the cells of Table 7.5, we acquire an overview of categories of actors in which the problem owner is more or less dependent.

This overview provides an impression of an actor's possible responses to a specific problem formulation and the solution direction that is linked to the response. This can serve as a reason for parties to alter the problem solution, or to cash in potential support by making alliances with especially dedicated and non-dedicated critical actors. We must keep in mind, though, that mustering support does not remedy the problem of dedicated, critical actors who can block. Their status as critical actors gives them veto power over the majorities.

Table 7.5 Dependencies of a specific actor

	Dedicated actors		Non-dedicated actors	
	Critical actors	*Non-critical actors*	*Critical actors*	*Non-critical actors*
Comparable perceptions, interests and goals	Actors who are likely to participate and be potential allies	Actors who are likely to participate and be potential allies	Necessary potential actors who are hard to activate	Actors who will not have to be involved at first
Contradictory perceptions, interests and goals	Potential blockers of (certain) changes (biting dogs)	Potential critics of (certain) changes (barking dogs)	Potential blockers who will not directly act (sleeping dogs)	Actors who do not require attention at first

We also must keep in mind that by reformulating problem formulations and objectives, we can bridge contradictions between parties. In other words, the positions that actors occupy in this diagram are highly determined by the problem perception and the objectives taken as a starting point for the analysis. Changing that can make allies of potential blockers. Thus, this figure also provides suggestions about where one can find a substantive change of the problem formulation.

Conclusion: dynamics in the analysis

Actors and dependencies can change during the game. This can take place because of changes in the problem formulation or in the series of solutions considered attractive by actors. When other solutions come into the picture, other actors with other resources might become important. In the longer term, this may result in changes in the network. Hence, a dependency analysis should be conducted frequently in order to determine if the earlier analysis is still applicable.

7.4 Game analysis: identification and analysis of arenas, progress and stagnation

The analysis of the game is especially focused on two aspects: identifying the arenas where the parties make relevant decisions for the problem and the related solution, and the analysis of stagnation that occurs during the course of the game. The first activity clarifies for parties and network managers where attempts to influence can be placed; the second provides insight into the nature of stagnation that prevents parties from developing a common understanding and action and also provides guidelines for how these can be overcome.

Identify the relevant arenas for the policy game

Policy games take place in arenas, activated parts of a network, or simultaneously in multiple networks. Identifying the arena or arenas where the game is played serves as a first demarcation of the playing field of the interactions. It also provides an overview of the possible locations where actors can employ strategies and what decisions are related to each other, even when actors do not always interact.

We must answer a number of questions in order to identify the most important arenas:

- Who are the most important actors in the policy game and what subsets can be recognized? This step concerns the identification of the central players in the game (Laumann and Knoke, 1987; Bryson and Crosby, 1992). These can be actors who have been identified in previous steps with the problem field. Actors may have interests or power positions, but are not always prominently involved in the game. In the zinc case, it quickly became clear that while a large number of actors was involved, their commitment varied substantially.
- What decisions are made at which locations? By analysing the decisions important to the issue, one gets an idea as to whether these decisions are made in the same places or in very different places. This step must be linked to the previous step in order to determine whether different subsets of actors are involved in certain decisions. These subsets may be possible arenas.
- Where are actors coming from and which issues occupy them? This analysis completes the image of the first two steps. We are concerned here with the background of actors, their interests, substantive interests, etc. An answer to this question will suggest what clusters of actors have the same background, and it provides the opportunity to see whether these actors are part of the same arena. The analysis conducted in Steps 2 and 3 can be helpful here.
- What organizational arrangements exist to structure the interaction of these actors? Are these arrangements linked to each other (for instance, through formalized decision making procedures or by overlapping memberships of actors)? This concerns the concrete arrangements that are important to the game or even specially designed for the game and are, thus, temporary in nature. Arrangements from the network (see the next section) can be important here but it is also possible that the game has complementary arrangements.

This inventory and analysis of arenas makes it clear that there are frequently very different places where subsets of actors make relevant decisions in the problem solving process. This overview can be a starting point for actors in order to determine the arena where they want to focus their attempts to influence the process and what linkages between the arenas they want to make or should avoid. Given their limited capacity and the varying accessibility and importance of various arenas, this information can be an important basis for the strategy formation of these parties and the assessments that they need to make.

Analyse the nature of impasse in the policy game

If parties or network managers want to have more information about the progress of the policy game, an important moment occurs when an impasse caused by a blockade or stagnation emerges. Information about the nature of the impasse can be the starting point for reviewing strategies or reviewing the use of management attempts. Such an analysis may consist of three steps: (1) determining that there is an impasse; (2) substantively analysing the impasse; and (3) conducting an analysis of the social aspects of the impasse.

Determining an impasse

Determining whether there is an impasse in the process is not as straightforward as it might seem. The presence of differences of opinion does not always point to an impasse; each process contains a certain degree of conflict. Furthermore, conflict does not have to be dysfunctional. Nor is length of time a clear indicator: it is difficult to determine whether the amount of time an activity takes is out of proportion. The opinions of actors involved can differ about this. Conflict, duration and the absence of decisions may point to an impasse, but other extra indications must be found. For instance, parties repeat their arguments and strategic moves, the frequency of interaction declines, polarization emerges around a limited number of standpoints and camps, no new viewpoints have been added to the discussion for some time. An important indicator might also be the atmosphere of the interaction process: conflicts may lead to a hostile atmosphere between parties which will make the constructive continuation of the interaction more difficult. Declining interest may be accompanied by cynicism and a lack of trust that it 'will all work out'. Frequently, this is also accompanied by a negative perception between the most important battling parties.

Analysing the impasse should include analysis of the content of the impasse. By mapping the argumentation structure that emerges in the policy game, the substantive cause of the impasse may become clear. While conflicts of interest form the basis of substantive contradictions, it appears that the content of the policy discussion often rests on the substantive statements that do not necessarily coincide with the parties' interests. In addition, parties frequently have insufficient notions about the substantive structure that the discussion seems to be acquiring and, as a result, they do not see opportunities for reaching agreements with other parties. That is how 'dialogues of the deaf' are created – parties battle each other but, in reality, they enter into a pattern of interaction they can no longer understand nor break through. Often, the discussion seems to focus on a contradiction in which the alternative standpoints are excluded and parties simply no longer see any possibilities for approaching other parties. By mapping the argumentation structure (that is the variety and conflicts of perception) and determining the nature of asymmetry, new methods of intervention can be found. The argumentation structure can be mapped through two steps (van Eeten, 1999).

*   First, map the arguments of the parties in the policy process: here, one can use the indications that were determined when the parties' perceptions were

mapped in the actor analysis. When such an analysis is already available and when knowledge about the perceptions and the arguments that parties use in a specific impasse exist, then that analysis can be used.

- Second, the parties' perceptions need to be compared: what are the similarities, what are the differences? This provides an understanding of the structure of the substantive discussion and the nature of the asymmetry of the contradiction. This might be a substantive contradiction; for instance, an economic standpoint that confronts an ecological standpoint. But it may also be the form or the language in which the debate is conducted: perhaps parties use different languages, or an argument is criticized without providing a decent alternative.

Determining a social impasse

These substantive analyses lead to determining the core of the substantive contradiction between the parties and can serve as a starting point for formulating a 'third' position (in terms of substance or form) that can help parties bridge their contradictions.

An impasse does not only consist of a substantive component, but it also consists of a social component; i.e. how parties exchange their substantive standpoints. This social component can also lead to, or strengthen, contradictions. At the same time, contradictions in the social realm may offer additional opportunities for bridging differences (Termeer, 1993; Termeer and Koppenjan, 1997). Mapping the social component of impasses can be done through the following activities:

- Develop an inventory of the various strategies of parties (Chapter 3) and the relations between them. This offers insight into the policy type that developed and may explain the impasse. Conflicting strategies can be the cause of blockades, avoidance strategies or stagnation. Insight into the composition of the strategies used may lead to proposals for adaptation or the introduction of new strategies in order to change the game type.
- Determine the nature and the frequency of interaction between parties in the context of the game. Decreasing or non-existent interactions can be an important cause of impasses and may make the substantive bridging of contradictions more difficult. Where frequent interaction takes place, the hostile climate that characterizes that interaction may provide an important contribution to maintaining the impasse of interactions not of parties.
- Finally, asymmetries may occur in a social sense: for instance, representation from various levels prevents parties from making decisions; laymen have to talk with experts; representatives of different scholarly disciplines or social sectors are gathered; mutual imaging inhibits a constructive discussion between parties; personal antipathies maintain impasses.

Acquiring an understanding of the social backgrounds of impasses provides angles for attempts to break through them.

7.5 The network: analysis of interactions, relations and rules

Traditionally, a network analysis is an inventory of contact patterns between actors (Aldrich and Whetten, 1981; Scott, 1991). In some cases, decisions and issues are also mapped (for a nice example of this, see Laumann and Knoke, 1987). In both cases, the analysis is almost exclusively quantitative. Data are collected through surveys that are then analysed in specially developed programmes (Scott, 1991). We use network analysis in a somewhat broader sense since it not only includes interaction patterns but also other important aspects such as actors' perceptions and strategies and the rules of the network. A network analysis is not necessarily limited to quantitative methods – it can also be conducted qualitatively.

The reason for conducting such an analysis is to clarify the backgrounds of the various actors involved in the game: do they come from the same network or from multiple networks? What rules do they use in the interaction? Are these shared with other actors in the game or do they differ (for instance, because actors in the game come from different networks)?

In the stepwise plan for a network analysis, two steps are distinguished that focus on the analysis of the (institutional) context: an inventory of the interaction patterns between actors and an analysis of the rules of the network. Both determine the relations between actors.

Making an inventory of interactions in the network

After actors have been mapped and their mutual (dependency) positions have been determined, another important question can be answered: what interaction patterns can be found in the network? This offers two important insights that are also relevant for potential attempts to influence the process later on:

- Who are the central actors in the network, or more specifically: which actors occupy a central place in the network interactions?
- What links exist between actors in the network? This translates specifically into such questions as: which actors have substantial contact with one another? Which actors have no contact with each other? And which actors only have indirect contact (through other actors) with each other?

Important concepts for acquiring these insights are the frequency and the variety of interaction. The first concerns knowledge of how often organizations have contact with each other. Interactions between organizations can be manifold but also sporadic. The second concerns an analysis of the variety of interactions of each actor separately and of the network as a whole. For instance, actors can interact frequently with a very limited set of actors in the network, but they can also interact infrequently with a large array of organizations. Analysing the network with these concepts and questions enables the policy analyst to acquire a better understanding of the network and allows the analyst to distinguish between peripheral and central actors. Central actors are those who have many contacts with other actors and/or a varied contact pattern.

Qualitative or quantitative inventory

In principle, the questions posed above can be mapped in a quantitative or qualitative manner. If there are only a few organizations and/or a 'quick scan' is done, then a qualitative impression of interactions will suffice. That impression can be based on the impressions of the policy analyst or upon a limited inventory of opinions of actors involved. The analyst can present his findings in a table which, through qualifications such as 'frequent' or 'rare' (or other qualifications), provides an impression of the interactions. An example is given in Table 7.6. Notice that the relations are symmetric in principle. When the analyst fills in the data, the interactions of actor 1 and 2 must, in principle, be the same as those of 2 with 1. When actors are asked to provide their own opinion or when set frequency categories are provided for the actors to respond to, differences in opinions may occur.

Table 7.6 Interaction frequencies between actors

	Actor 1	Actor 2	Actor 3	Actor 4	Actor N
Actor 1	–	Frequent	Rare	Rare	Frequent
Actor 2	Frequent	–	Frequent	Frequent	Frequent
Actor 3	Rare	Frequent	–	Rare	Frequent
Actor 4	Rare	Frequent	Rare	–	Rare
Actor N	Frequent	Frequent	Frequent	Rare	–

The example in Table 7.6 shows that actor 2 has frequent interactions with other actors in the network, so actor 2 is the central actor. Actor 4 has few interactions with other actors in the network and is, thus, the peripheral actor. Such a quick qualitative inventory provides a first impression of the interaction patterns and the positions of actors in it.

Quantitative analysis of interactions in networks

If the network has a large number of organizations and/or the policy analyst wants to conduct a detailed analysis of interactions, then quantitative methods are necessary. By asking the relevant actors (for instance, through a survey or semi-structured interviews with set frequency categories such as once a week, once a month, etc.) about the frequency and variety of mutual interactions, a quantitative overview can be acquired. This can also be statistically analysed or presented in graph form. Three steps are necessary for this:

- First, the respondent is provided with a list of actors and must then fill in how much contact he has with each actor.
- Second, the policy analyst compiles a cross-tabulation with the list of actors on both axis of the table (such as was done in Table 7.6 for qualitative data),

Table 7.7 Frequency of interactions in discussions about zinc (averages, I = never, 6 = at least one every two weeks)

Actor	Respondents						
	All respondents	Departments/ ministries	Provinces and municipalities	Water boards	(Organization of the) zinc industry	Researchers/ advisers	Building companies/ developers
Ministry of VROM/housing	1.8	1.6	1.4	2.0	1	1.9	2.4
Ministry of VROM (DGM)	3.16	3.3	1.9	2.1	4.3	4.9	22.0
Ministry of T&W (RWS)	2.81	4.7	2.6	1.6	3.8	3.1	1
Ministry of Economic Affairs	2.16	2.3	1	1.4	4.3	3.1	1
Ministry of Agriculture	1.54	1.9	1	1.9	1	2.3	1
Provinces	2.98	4	2.9	4.7	2.6	1.7	1.8
Municipalities	3	2.7	3	4	2.8	1.7	4
Water boards	3.57	4.1	4.9	4.7	3.2	2.3	1.8
Environmental organizations	2.79	4	2.8	2.2	2.8	2.9	1.8
Zinc industry	2.93	3.3	1.8	1.9	5.8	4	1
(Organization) Architects	2.64	1.4	1.4	2	4	1.7	3.4
Association for Durable Building Materials	2.64	2.7	1.7	2	6	2.6	1
RIVM	2.12	2.5	1.3	1.9	2	4	1
RIZA	3.31	4.2	3.6	2.9	4.2	3.6	1
Contractors/project developers	2.6	1.4	1.7	2.3	4.6	1.7	4.6
SEV	1.7	1	1.4	1.4	1.6	1.7	2.6
SBR	1.98	1.6	1	1.7	2.2	2.1	3.2
VEWIN	1.75	1.9	1.6	2.1	1.4	1.9	1.8
FME/VNO	2.37	3.2	1	1	5	2.7	1

after which a qualification of the intensity of interaction between two actors is placed in each cell.

• Finally, a graphic presentation is made. There are several possibilities for graphic presentations. Graphic presentations can be done by means of lines and points, but also by analysing interaction data through multi-dimensional scaling so that the actors can then be placed in a two-dimensional sphere (Scott, 1991). Actors close to each other have more or less the same interaction patterns while actors further removed from each other have very different interaction patterns.

When only the first two steps are completed, the frequency of interactions can be placed in a table where the average figures indicate a degree of frequency. This has been done in Table 7.7 for the actors in the zinc discussion. The analyst must then reconstruct the networks on the basis of these average frequencies.

There are various computer programs available to further analyse the interaction data (see Scott, 1991). The method of multi-dimensional scaling that we mentioned earlier calculates the distances between actors and their mutual relations. Actors are placed in a two-dimensional graph based on the calculated distance from each actor to the other actors and their mutual relations. The distance between the actors then shows how similar the interaction patterns are. Actors who are close to each other have comparable interaction patterns. Actors that are further removed from each other have significantly different interaction patterns. Using this graphic representation, clusters of actors with the same interaction patterns can be recognized. An example of such a technique is given in Box 7.2. This contains an analysis of a number of actors in a local public housing network.

Imaging interactions

While the quantitative methods generally provide a somewhat more reliable image, they are also more labour intensive. The extra precision gained by using the quantitative method must be weighed against the costs.

Quantitative or qualitative analysis of interaction patterns are useful in providing the policy analyst with insight into which actors have frequent and rare contact with each other (the morphology of the network). However, they provide nothing more (but also nothing less) than an image of interaction patterns. They cannot, for instance, explain why interaction patterns are how they are or how they were created. To answer these questions, an inventory of interactions must be linked to an analysis of positions and the analysis of the rules and perceptions. Or, in more concrete terms, it is not unreasonable to expect that actors with great dependence on each other – and thus need for each other – will interact intensively with each other. If not, then this may be the cause for possible impasses, and a network analysis can provide angles for intervention strategies along the way.

Box 7.2 Example of plotting interactions of actors in a network

The figure in this box is a graphic representation of the interaction in a local housing network in the city of Rotterdam, a large city in the western part of the Netherlands (see Klijn, 2001). If we look at the schemes we see that in Rotterdam basically three clusters can be seen. The first cluster of actors in the right of the figure contains mainly housing associations, subsectoral governments and some sections of the department of City Planning and Housing. In this first cluster one can also find the city alderman and a few politicians. In the second cluster most of the tenant organizations and some of the sections of the department of City Planning and Housing are found. In this case, it concerns sections that work in a more decentralized manner than the sections in the first cluster. Compared to the actors in the first cluster these actors have less frequent contact with other actors and a less varied interaction pattern. The third cluster mainly consists of commercial actors (building companies, real estate agencies and project developers). These actors, in general, have few interactions with the other actors compared with the actors in the other clusters.

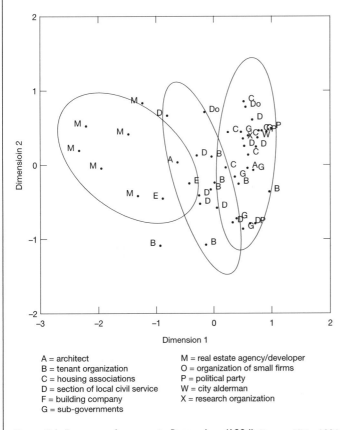

A = architect
B = tenant organization
C = housing associations
D = section of local civil service
F = building company
G = sub-governments

M = real estate agency/developer
O = organization of small firms
P = political party
W = city alderman
X = research organization

Figure 7.1 Patterns of contact in Rotterdam (1994) Source: Klijn, 1996.

The focus on rules: analysis of the institutional context

Interactions between the actors in networks do not operate in a vacuum. While the institutional context ensures that certain interactions are obvious, it can also limit contact with other actors. An analysis of the institutional context can contain many aspects: the distribution of resources – that in the network analysis in this chapter is linked to an actor analysis (Step 3) – the formal structure, informal relations between actors, organizational arrangements, etc.

An important aspect is the analysis of rules. Insofar as the institutional context is captured in formal rules, an analysis is relatively straightforward. An understanding of this part of the institutional context can be acquired by examining:

- *The formal authority of actors*: these include the authority of actors to make decisions, their property rights, etc.
- *The formal institutional characteristics of the interaction*: these concern the legal frameworks for planning and decision making (participation obligations, juridical status of decisions, etc.). These legal frameworks are often important conditions for such issues as when decisions must be made, what the process looks like, which actors have the right to be acknowledged in the process, etc.

The formal institutional context can be reconstructed by looking at the legally defined authorities, the legally framed plan and consultation procedures, etc. The analysis of the informal institutional context, which is comprised of rules that actors have formed during their mutual interaction, is much more difficult and labour intensive. Even though they cannot, or can scarcely, be found in written documents, these rules appear to play an important role in what actors find acceptable

Table 7.8 Types of rules in networks

Description	Aspects	Examples
Interaction rules		
Rules that regulate game interactions (rules that specify what is and what is not allowed in games between actors)	Access to policy game	• Exclusiveness • Selection • Exit opportunities
	Interaction in policy game	• (Non-) intervention • Information provision • Conflict
Arena rules		
Rules that regulate the setting of the game (rules that define the social practices and distinguish important matters from unimportant ones)	Reality	• Identity of actors • Product rules
	Reward	• Status • Evaluation criteria
	Positions	• Status • Competencies

Source: Klijn, 1996, 2001.

and unacceptable in contacts with each other. Thus, informal rules concerning the autonomy of organizations can be highly influential with regard to their willingness to cooperate. In networks where actors place great value on their autonomy and where they are unaccustomed to exchanging information, cooperation is much more difficult to achieve than in networks where there are fewer strict rules demarcating autonomy (Klijn, 1996, 2001).

The reconstruction of informal rules must take place by having respondents reflect on rules of engagement and codes that they consider self-evident. This can be done by asking respondents focused questions about how they select other actors, their habits of information exchange, the standards they use to judge products and outcomes etc. As a guideline, the typology shown in Table 7.8, which was presented in Chapter 4, can be used.

Analysing informal rules requires substantial knowledge about the network in question. Generally, one must consider the following when reconstructing the informal rules shown on p. 158.

Box 7.3 Example of rules in urban renewal

Conflicts and compromises in the Rotterdam urban renewal programme

Avoiding conflict is not an issue in the Rotterdam urban renewal programme. There is a tendency, in fact, to face conflicts head on and fight them. The various council department employees identify strongly with their project group and the neighbourhood. This means that conflicts can arise between the project group and the Planning Department (DROS). In the urban renewal programme 'every project is fought hard for and in every possible way'.

On the other hand, these conflicts are tempered by an attitude of 'working things out together'. This attitude, of course, ties in very well with the 'roll up your sleeves' rule that is also very dominant in this network. 'In the Rotterdam tradition we've always argued in public, made choices and taken decisions based on solid arguments and after that gone and had a pint together in the pub'.

Striving to reach consensus and working it out together depends, in turn, on the rules about the quality of products and the identity of the Rotterdam urban renewal programme. This means there are not only fixed 'standards' for evaluating outcomes but there is also a certain mutual respect and recognition of each other's qualities and positions which underpin the interaction rule 'working it out together'. 'There is also a certain amount of recognition from parties towards each other, they're very knowledgeable, they're carrying the risks, so they can obviously be trusted'.

If after a lengthy battle, however, a decision is finally forced in the project group, then everyone complies with that decision. 'Everyone tries to boost his own position and they make a lot of noise about it, but in the end the no one quibbles about the final results. Everyone puts up with the fact that an acceptable compromise has been reached'.

Source: Klijn, 1996.

- *Repetitiveness*: concerns self-evident issues and procedures that keep repeating. In short, actors must regard something as repetitious and not as something that occurs incidentally. In various situations, the pattern of action occurs and it is not only the consequence of a repetitive strategic choice of actors, but it occurs because actors find this way of acting fitting and self-evident.
- *Generalizability*: rules must hold for all or at least a substantial number of the actors. In short, rules cannot be linked to one actor only (in which case it is something of a decision rule of an actor) but there must be multiple (though not necessarily all) actors in the network that recognize the rule and follow it. This can be investigated by submitting rules previously explicated by respondents to different respondents.

Conclusion: an image of the relations between actors

By developing an analysis of the interaction patterns and the rules that characterize the network, one acquires sound insight into relations as they exist between actors. This knowledge provides something to hold on to when making strategic choices in the game and also when assessing opportunities for certain strategic choices. It also provides insight into possible obstacles that can prove to be important in certain initiatives.

Ultimately, it clarifies divisions that exist between actors and interaction patterns. Thus, it provides an explanation when desired interactions are not realized or when interactions proceed with difficulty.

7.6 Reflection: the opportunities and limitations of a stepwise plan

A number of analytical activities have been described in this chapter which can be conducted in the context of a network approach in order to support the strategic choices of participants in a problem solving process. The analytical methods presented may help map the substantive, strategic and institutional uncertainties that actors confront in their attempts to solve complex problems in network settings.

In principle, each step of the analysis can be linked to concrete questions for management from the actor point of view or from the process as a whole. In this manner, the analysis is a step towards allowing an actor or a process manager to make conscious strategic interventions; in the actor's case to improve his own position and in the process manager's case to improve interactions in the game as a whole. This last perspective, that of management, is further elaborated in the next three chapters. In Table 7.9, we provide an overview of the possible management questions that can be raised in each step of the analysis.

In the next three chapters, we discuss the most important network management strategies that can be used to influence complex processes in networks.

Table 7.9 Analysis of stages and management questions

Analytical step	Management question
Actor analysis	
Formulate the initial problem notion	On what part of the environment is the management focused?
Identify the (important) actors	Which actors must be activated for realizing the initiative?
Reconstruct the perceptions of actors	What differences exist between actors' perceptions and can this cause problems for decision making? Can the differences be overcome, if so, how?
Analyse actor positions	What is the negotiation position of the involved actors and what alternatives are there to get the game going or to keep it going?
Game analysis	
Reconstruct the arenas	Is an actor or the process manager represented in the right decision arenas, if not, do they want to change that?
Analyse impasses	How do interactions evolve and where is stagnation or tension found? What is the nature of the stagnation and where can intervention help to improve the interactions?
Network analysis	
Inventory of interactions in network	Do actors or the process manager have contacts with the right actors in the network and can they reach actors with whom they have little contact through other actors?
Analyse the institutional context	What institutional rules of the game are in play and to what degree do they limit the actor or the process manager? Does an actor or process manager have to accept these rules as given or should they try to change them?

Chapter 8

Managing content

Furthering cross-frame reflection and the creation of negotiated knowledge

8.1 Introduction

In Chapter 2 we argued that complex societal problems are not 'things' that can be objectively ascertained. Whether a societal situation is a problem depends upon the perceptions of the parties involved. These perceptions vary since they are based upon diverging, and sometimes conflicting, interests and frames of reference. As a consequence, parties interpret and evaluate situations, information and proposals for improvement differently. Attempts to reduce uncertainty about content by gathering information, therefore, may be counter-productive; they often contribute to information overload and ambiguity. Research and science cannot overcome differences between stakeholders. Often research results are not perceived as authoritative. This also has to do with the fact that the production of knowledge is always conducted from a specific problem framework: choices with regard to assumptions, questions, techniques, analysis and interpretations are, to some degree, always subjective. In addition to authoritativeness, the conclusiveness of research and science is often a problem too. Given the available knowledge resources and the state of research, answers to questions may simply not be available. But societal conflict might also penetrate the research arena, so that experts are in conflict with one another.

All of this means that the nature and extent of a problem cannot be determined objectively, so there is little point in asking which problem perception is the best one in a field of competing perceptions. Uncertainty about content is not so much a consequence of a lack of information about the real nature of the problem, but of the inability of stakeholders to coordinate their individual interpretations in a particular situation. Furthermore, the intuitive responses of parties to uncertainty (information collection, elaborating their own scientific research tracks, internal strategy formulation before going external) are counter-productive: they enhance differences and uncertainties. As a consequence, cognitive fixations and asymmetric argumentation structures are created that will further inhibit the possibility of overcoming these differences.

Attempts to manage substantive uncertainties must, therefore, not exclusively be focused on clarifying what, exactly, the problem is and which measures will best contribute to solving it. Management of uncertainty, above all, needs to be focused on promoting the ability of the parties to become aware of the existence of various problem perceptions and on the furtherance of favourable conditions for bridging these different perceptions. In the end, the objective is enabling the parties to develop solutions that give just consideration to the variety of perceptions, interests and values involved.

If this occurs, the quality of the joint perceptions and solutions that are developed becomes quite important. The fact that there is no objective, best solution does not diminish the importance of the quality of ideas or measures. A first prerequisite is of course that stakeholders mutually adapt their perceptions and agree upon the selected solution. But that is not enough. If parties achieve consensus about problem formulations and solutions that are at odds with available knowledge and scientific insight, this will lead to disappointment and may result in solutions that will aggravate rather than decrease the problem. This is why managing substantive uncertainty not only focuses on decreasing differences in the perception of problems and solutions between parties but also on furthering the quality of the substantive outcomes that are generated. In this chapter, we therefore address the following questions:

1   When we address wicked problems, how can differences in the perception of the problem situation and solutions be reduced; how can joint image building and cross-frame learning be advanced?
2   How can (scientific) research be organized so that it facilitates the process of joint image building and contributes to the creation of negotiated knowledge?

These questions will be discussed in Sections 8.2 and 8.3.

8.2 Improving frame reflection and cross-frame learning

Building on network theory, in this section we discuss a number of possibilities for managing the substantive uncertainties that play a role in complex societal problems. A network approach to management departs from the usual recommendations of how to deal with uncertainty about content. Rational approaches to policy and policy analysis emphasize the importance of proceeding through the problem solving cycle by first attempting to clarify the problem and the formulation of objectives. These then form the basis for the following steps: generating and assessing alternatives, selecting the optimal solution, which is then further developed, decided upon and implemented.

Even though an awareness of the existence of a multi-actor environment is, by now, almost common, it does not lead to a fundamentally different approach. There is still a search for an optimal problem formulation at the beginning of the process, resulting in the choice of an optimal solution. These activities are now inspired by the wish to do so at a meta-level: integrating the perceptions, objectives and preferences of all relevant stakeholders (Keeney, 1992). This approach, however, is at odds with the erratic and dynamic nature that characterizes complex processes aimed at the resolution of wicked problems. Problem formulations, solutions and participation, under the influence of interactions

Table 8.1 Comparison of traditional and network approaches to managing content

	Traditional approach	*Network approach*
Dealing with uncertainty about problems	*Ex ante* clarification of problem by information gathering and (scientific) research	Avoidance of early fixations; furthering awareness of plurality of perceptions and preferences
Dealing with solutions	Formulation of *ex ante* objectives and criteria for development and selection of optimal solution	Furthering substantive variety and favourable conditions for learning and intermediate adaptations
Reaction to plurality of perceptions and preferences	Searching for a meta-position: a problem formulation of set of objectives that integrates perceptions and values	Joint image building: search for common ground for joint interaction despite recognition of enduring differences

between stakeholders and external developments, are in continuous flux and parties are only gradually able to develop ideas about the nature of the problem and its environment. An early fixation of the problem formulation, objectives and solution does not give appropriate consideration to the fact that parties only learn step by step what opportunities and risks exist in a problem solving process, and that these, in part, depend upon the turns the process takes under the influence of the strategic moves of actors and external developments. An early fixation leads to the exclusion of alternative perceptions, objectives and solutions that would emerge later in the process. Not only would opportunities for learning and enrichment be missed, but also resistance, politicization and turbulence would be created, which inhibit cross-frame learning and the building of a common ground for joint action.

In the network approach, the management of substantive uncertainty is not aimed so much at constructing a (meta-)problem formulation in order to develop solutions that integrate the objectives of all stakeholders. Instead, it is focused on getting some changes in the individual and collective perceptions that motivate parties in order to improve the process of joint image building in such a manner that early fixations, exclusion of learning opportunities and enrichment, and unnecessary politicization are prevented. Thus, joint image building does not imply the creation of a complete consensus about a problem situation or objectives. This would ignore the fact that the different perceptions, objectives and preferences parties hold are institutionally anchored and hard to change. The reality is that parties, despite such differences, must arrive at cooperation. Joint image building and cross-frame learning concerns the creation of a 'common ground' which – despite the existence of varying perceptions, objectives and preferences – enables the mutual adjustment of strategies and joint action.

In the next section, we address the following management strategies that promote the creation of such a common ground:

1   furthering goal intertwinement;
2   creation of substantive variety;

3   breaking through the asymmetric nature of policy debates;
4   preventing early cognitive fixations by starting a process;
5   advancing cognitive reflection;
6   organizing substantive selection.

Furthering goal intertwinement

One characteristic of steering towards goal intertwinement is that the process of problem solving is not focused on achieving a solution for an authoritative problem formulation or set of objectives. Instead, the starting point is that a solution must be found for a problem where a variety of actors with different objectives have different opinions about the issue. The goal is to develop and select solutions that can satisfy the different demands that parties have – given their different perceptions and interests – and to do justice to these differences in such a manner that a situation is created which is an improvement for all parties involved, compared to the existing or expected situation.

The pursuit of such a solution does not necessarily mean that actors develop a common or mutual problem formulation or that they agree about the objectives. If that is their goal, there is a substantial risk that they will engage in conflict: 'if decision makers clarify their values and beliefs, conflict will emerge' (Olsen, 1972: 2). The probability of gaining support for a solution is greater when the parties are willing to accept differences, i.e. room is created for the simultaneous realization of diverging or apparently conflicting objectives. When a solution is able to achieve this, it successfully binds parties together without requiring them to reach substantive agreement on problem definitions or objectives.

This places high demands on the problem solving process since it has to offer sufficient space to allow a solution to be reached. Below, we discuss a number of possibilities for achieving goal intertwinement.

*   *Goal intertwinement through an integrated design.* Occasionally, a technically or substantively clever design is able to integrate the diverging and sometimes conflicting demands of various interested parties. When the construction of a highway through a residential or nature area is perceived as the solution to a traffic problem, the resistance of home owners or of nature and environment organizations will be experienced as irritating, and measures to alleviate the external negative effects will be considered an extra cost. By formulating the problem as a matter of area-development, the interests of other parties in the game can be included, for instance, the objective of local governments to develop an industrial area or the objective of a province to develop a nature area. Thus, a richer design can be made in which various objectives are coordinated and, possibly, various (financial) resources can be brought together. But there are substantive, technical and financial limits to design opportunities: not always can all demands be met simultaneously. However, where the pursuit for intertwinement of all possible objectives is often too ambitious, attempts to combine a selective number of goals may still mean a significant improvement in comparison to more traditional designs.

- *Goal intertwinement through package deals.* When designs for specific problem solutions offer limited opportunities in terms of intertwining objectives, the creation of package deals may be considered. In such cases goal intertwinement does not take place in the framework of one demarcated solution, but through a wider package of measures that considers several problems and their solutions simultaneously (Dery, 1984; Teisman, 1992). By doing this, package deals provide room for exchanging objectives. A solution may be a loss to a certain party, but this can be compensated through the realization of another objective that is also important to that party. Thus, the first loss becomes acceptable and the party will support the package as a whole. Making package deals often means that specific issues, arenas or games are linked to one another so that the scope for solution is enhanced.
- *Goal intertwinement through mitigating measures and compensations.* Sometimes solutions or package deals manage to combine a number of objectives, but not all. In this case, there are still opportunities for taking the latter into account. Actors may be able to limit the disadvantages of solutions to third parties, so that these parties will not resist them even though they will not be better off. When a solution implies a deterioration for certain interests or parties, then those who profit from a solution might consider offering compensation (de Bruijn *et al.*, 2002). This principle is, for instance, used by the European Union regarding the 'Bird Directive' and the 'Habitat Directive'. Activities (such as road construction or the development of business parks) in designated areas are only allowed when the damage to a species or ecosystem is compensated by creating a comparable habitat elsewhere.
- *Goal intertwinement through offering a perspective on future gain.* The principle of compensating loss may be directly linked to achieving a concrete solution in the context of a specific game. The loser gets immediate compensation. But compensation may also consist of offering opportunities for gain in other games or in the future (Axelrod, 1984). Potential losers will not always demand solid agreements regarding compensation. When the procedure and the institutional conditions under which the game is played are well developed and are pluralist in nature, the players know that there is no permanent loser or winner. It then becomes easier to accept a loss since actors know that new opportunities will arise. The greater the trust in the fairness of the rules of the game and the higher the quality of the institutions that generate and guard these rules, the less the need for immediate compensation. We discuss the development of the rules of the game and institutions in Chapters 9 and 10 respectively.

Instruments for goal intertwinement: scope optimization

The opportunity for intertwining objectives and finding compensation measures is related to the available scope for a solution. Linking activities, especially scope optimization, provide an instrument for achieving goal intertwinement. Scope optimization means that the definition of a problem situation provides the room to manoeuvre for finding a solution and for increasing the possibility of an optimal intertwinement of objectives. Often, the demarcation of the problem situation must be enlarged in order to achieve this (Cobb and Elder, 1983; Forester, 1989). In the example mentioned above, while the need for a highway was initially framed as a traffic problem, the problem was eventually redefined as an issue of area-development. This considerably enhanced the room for goal intertwinement. Through enlarging the scope and thus the range of actors involved, various issues and objectives are brought together. New exchange opportunities are created and the process of problem solving is given new momentum.

Enlarging the scope of a problem will not always result in added value, especially when scope enlargement leads to an expanding group of involved actors whose contribution to the solution is unclear. In this case, there is a substantial risk of stagnation. Reduction of scope and decreasing the number of parties to those most involved, may, in some situations, be the right strategy to bring the realization of a satisficing and feasible solution closer.

Instruments for goal intertwinement: statement of multiple objectives

Furtherance of goal intertwinement is not focused on problem and objective specification, as is the case in traditional methods of problem solving, and it is not very helpful for goal intertwinement to develop *ex ante* a coherent and specific programme of demands. Instead, the process of problem solving should be viewed as a search process during which parties become aware of the fact that, in order to achieve their objectives, they must discover trade-offs between their own objectives and ideas and those of others. The most ideal situation is one in which parties find different issues important and manage to reach an exchange of values that leads to an optimal situation for all involved. To facilitate this search process in practice, it may be anchored at the beginning by formulating a 'multiple objective', a listing of objectives that will be simultaneously strived for, even though they may appear contradictory at first sight. For instance, attempting to strengthen the international competitiveness of Schiphol Airport together with improving the safety situation and the quality of life in the environment of the airport. These multiple objectives are more symbolic than instrumental: they are intended to generate search behaviour for solutions that combine the demands from various parties and sectors.

Creation of substantive variety

Furthering substantive variety as a remedy against uncertainty about content is, given the variety of perceptions, opinions and reports that characterize processes aimed at solving a wicked problem, probably not the first thing that comes to mind. However, problem solving processes often display a remarkable lack of choice of solutions. It is precisely the fixation on one single solution that can trigger conflict between parties and disputes on content. These disputes seldom lead to a richer debate that generates multiple options that, in turn, result in a well-reasoned choice. Therefore, the management of substantive uncertainties must be aimed at generating a variety of options and preventing early fixation on specific problem formulations or solutions (Rein and Schön, 1992; Hall, 1993; Termeer and Koppenjan, 1997). The presence of a variety of options offers the parties the prospect of arriving at a solution attractive to them, and it may just provide the starting point for bridging differences.

Given the erratic nature of policy games for wicked problems, it makes little sense to start the process of problem solving by trying to determine the exact nature of the problem, or with the setting of goals that should be realized by the solution still to be developed. After all, these choices will not stand for long. What is more, they are in conflict with the insight that parties will adapt their perceptions and preferences during the process. Instead, these activities must be followed at the same time as searching for and designing the solutions. Only when solutions have been found and elaborated, do the costs and benefits of the various solutions become clear for all parties. It is at this time that other parties can be convinced to participate in the interaction, and to suggest adaptations and alternatives that take their interests into account. In other words, solutions and problem formulations should develop concurrently, according to the principles of the 'garbage can' model of decision making, allowing them to be linked at particular points in time.

Creative competition

One way to generate substantive variety is through 'creative competition'. This means that a problem owner (or group of problem owners) organizes a competition in which various design teams participate. Each of these teams works on the basis of a general description of the problem analysis or programme of demands, and they elaborate a solution (Teisman, 1997).

Traditional methods of problem solving are based on the notion of bounded rationality and assume a trade-off between rational problem solving and efficiency. This leads to a situation where, on the basis of *ex ante* formulated objectives, a preferred option is selected early on in the process, but is then elaborated later in the process. As a result of this early selection, decision makers are entangled in a process dominated by one solution, which can only be amended marginally since alternative options have already been excluded. New insights and changing circumstances are perceived as disturbing and can only be taken into account at great cost. They involve the redefinition of the problem and adaptation of objectives which have, in turn, important consequences for the solution that is considered.

Thus, in 1992, during the parliamentary discussions on the construction of a high-speed railway between Amsterdam and the Belgian border, changes proposed by MPs were so radical, that it was decided that the entire series of earlier steps had to be taken again. Thus, the project ran into several years of delay.

Creative competition implies that options are held open as long as possible during the process and that alternatives are developed simultaneously. This keeps choice opportunities open until close to the end of the process. A second difference from traditional designs is that the selection of alternatives does not take place based on an *ex ante* specified and coherent programme of demands. One can expect such a programme to be outdated by the time the design is completed.

Changing insights, possibly because of changes in the environment or because parties only become aware of the ramifications of their choices during or at the end of the design process, may result in parties adopting new objectives. Creative competition implies the opportunity for comparing the costs and benefits of competing alternatives. Stakeholders can then decide which of the alternatives best addresses the problems at that point in time. These result in *ex post* specifications of objectives which, unlike the *ex ante* formulated programmes of demands, adequately consider the societal problems at hand and the learning experiences of parties during the process. Also, the parties involved are now in a better position to formulate a programme of demands which is more specifically tailored than the general guidelines that the teams started with. In other words: problem and objective specification does not only occur at the beginning of the process of problem solving, but also during and after the process of designing solutions. While the adaptation of objectives in the light of a solution is a mortal sin in the rational model because, in this way, means may determine objectives instead of the other way around, in practice the linear approach appears to limit selection opportunities while creative competition generates alternatives.

After *ex post* problem specification and objective formulation, the next logical step is not just selection: it might be, after all, that parties differ about which option is best, or that they are not content with the existing options. So the next step may very well be another round of design activities. Design teams may be asked to adapt their solutions to the programme of demands. By combining the options of design teams, one can search for solutions that combine the strongest elements of each of the designs.

Just as the 'garbage can' model suggests, problem formulation does not occur before designing a solution. The design process must be regarded as one

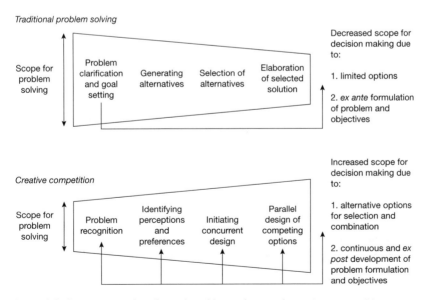

Figure 8.1 Comparison of traditional problem solving and creative competition

which generates solutions for problems that need to be further clarified. And in the process of problem solving, there must be enough room to search for and elaborate solutions and problem formulations that bring parties together. There is no guarantee that this will happen. However, we consider a process a success when a solution has been found that achieves this.

The principle of creative competition implies that parties are willing to invest more than usual in the developments of solutions. This is at odds with continuous complaints about the long duration of decision making processes and the call for firm decisions. However, the idea of creative competition is not entirely impractical. In the private sector, competitive engineering in research and development activities is an accepted design principle (Wheelright and Clark, 1992). In the public sector, the tolerance for high design costs with regard to societal problems is, however, much lower. The huge societal costs of stagnating or blocking decision making, and attempts to 'buy off' resistance against public projects by granting requests for all kinds of additional provisions on the other hand, are relatively easily accepted. Since these costs are often caused by not taking important values into account when designing solutions for societal problems, it makes sense to ask for a shift in investment in problem solving resources towards the earlier design phase.

Breaking through the asymmetric nature of policy debates

Discussions about the solution of complex societal problems easily develop an asymmetric structure. Parties try to convince each other of their own position while in reality they are talking past each other or becoming entangled in a 'dialogue of the deaf' where every effort to break through disagreements only leads to further conflict. The nature of this asymmetry in debates may vary. In the zinc debate between government and the zinc industry, the latter contested the scientific correctness of the eco-toxicity of zinc while the representatives of government did not have the expertise to substantially deal with that issue. They had delegated the answer of the scientific question to their research institutes. Furthermore, governmental policy makers held the position that zinc emissions had to decrease, no matter what. In this case, two types of asymmetry were at stake. Not only did the *problem formulations* of both parties clash; but they also talked in a *different language*: the zinc industry used the language of science that was not understood by the governmental policy makers (van Bueren *et al.*, 2003).

Asymmetry can take different forms. Thus, in his discussion of dike raising around the large rivers in the Netherlands, van Eeten (1999) points to the fact that the interest groups that resisted this were unable to provide a *comparable, fully-fledged alternative* to the option (dike raising) developed by government. Opponents limited themselves to listing objections to various parts of government's proposals. Parties exercised their hindrance powers by making their objections known through hearings and appeal procedures. This resulted in delays and the government taking extra measures to alleviate some of these objections on certain points, but nowhere in the process were serious alternative solutions considered. This pattern can be discerned in other projects as well: for example, processes of problem solving with substantial conflict over one option but with little regard for possible alternatives. One underlying cause is the closed planning by government that takes societal actors by surprise and leaves them little time to develop a comparable alternative. In addition to this, it must be noted that nature and environmental groups, as well as citizens, have limited capacities for developing fully-fledged alternatives that can compete with those of public policy makers.

Attempts to further joint image building can be aimed at reducing asymmetry in debates about problems and their solutions. Following from the notion that there are various types of asymmetry, we consider the following possibilities:

- *Improving frame reflection.* In debates where problem formulations clash and the discussion is focused on the pro and con arguments of a certain solution, one can start by improving frame reflection. The objective is to make actors aware of the fact that they work with different problem formulations or 'problem frames'. Even just this awareness may result in parties changing their strategies. They will search for opportunities to mutually adapt their problem formulations (re-framing). This does not mean that their problem perceptions will become identical. The problem solving process will already be served by decreasing the distance between problem perceptions and encouraging parties to consciously seek points of overlap between their perceptions.

  To break through the pattern of the 'dialogue of the deaf', something in the interaction process needs to be changed: for instance, taking time out so that parties have the opportunity to reflect; substituting individuals so that new representatives of organizations, who are not burdened by the past, become involved and approach each other with fresh viewpoints; or allowing an outsider with a different problem perception, who can confront the parties involved with the limitations of their own approaches, to access the game (Rein and Schön, 1986, 1992; Hall, 1993; Termeer, 1993).

- *Formulating new agendas.* Just because parties in discussion occupy irreconcilable positions, it does not mean that opportunities for goal intertwinement do not exist. When parties dig into previously taken positions, strong polarization may result. The problem is reduced to one dimension in which quarrelling actors occupy extreme positions: for instance the conflict between the economic objectives of realizing an infrastructural service and the values that are jeopardized in the real environment and ecology. The discussion quickly fixes upon whether the project will be realized; other positions are not considered, are suppressed or even forbidden by competing parties (he who is not with us, is against us). Nonetheless, with such an issue there are always more dimensions involved than the dominant economy–ecology dichotomy (see Roe, 1994, 1998). Van Eeten (1999), for instance, showed that in the discussion about airport expansion, the dominant positions – for or against expansion – involved three other issues that were not covered by the conflict between these two positions: these were the importance of a societal acceptance of growing air travel, the significance of the ecological modernization of the airport sector, and the value of sustainable solutions for the growing demand for mobility. Precisely because these arguments did not align with the dominant conflict – for or against expansion – and were adopted by both sides in the debate, they can provide the basis for reformulating the agenda to link opponents and supporters, using these arguments as a starting point for searching for new and mutual solutions.

In the zinc debate, this mechanism emerged when the zinc industry decided to adapt its strategy of disputing the zinc norms and the government measures. The industry proposed to publicize product innovations and thus redefined the problem and introduced a new agenda. No longer was it a discussion about whether government was right or wrong about the eco-toxicity of zinc or of the contribution of building materials to zinc emissions. By investing in product innovations, the industry could secure the market for zinc products and, furthermore, converse with government about the conditions under which these could be achieved. Hence, the zinc industry created new opportunities for the exchange of resources and intertwinement of goals, so that a substantive discussion with the government became meaningful again.

- *Overcoming differences in language.* In the zinc case, the industry's strategy to emphasize the scientific discussion about the eco-toxicity of zinc did not link up with the government's language in the debate. These types of 'language problems' emerge in games especially when laypersons meet with experts, or where experts from different disciplines or sectors must cooperate. An example of an attempt to bridge these language differences is the development of so-called 'water opportunities maps' in the Netherlands.

  Until recently, water management was handled quite autonomously. Given the growing interconnectedness of societal activities, this situation was no longer feasible. Water managers are increasingly confronted with the negative effects of activities in other societal sectors (economic activity, housing, recreation, etc.) on the availability and quality of water. It is impossible for them to maintain water quality when they are positioned at the end of the chain of activities. A pro-active attitude is necessary: water managers must participate in activities at the beginning of the chain. They must convince parties that are engaged in other societal sectors to take the effects upon water management into consideration when they are planning their activities. For instance, water managers need to be more involved in the construction of residential and industrial areas, and especially in the spatial planning processes in which these kinds of land use are decided upon. These decisions are taken in arenas dominated by spatial planning experts, who, by tradition, use visual presentations in the form of plans and maps to communicate their thinking and planning. Hence, the inclination to use maps by the water management sector can be seen as an attempt to become familiar with the language planning experts use and, thus, obtain access to discussions about the use of space usually dominated by the latter.

- *The development of fully-fledged argumentative alternatives.* A fourth way to bridge the asymmetry in debates is to confront the dominant storyline about what the problem is, its causes and what measures must be taken with a fully-fledged and credible 'counter-voice': an alternative vision that does not consist of a casual collection of critiques of parts of the dominant argumentation, but a unique storyline which elaborates and argues a new solution based on an alternative problem formulation (Hajer, 1995; Van Eeten, 1999). This requires a substantial investment of resources and intellectual attention in processes of problem solving that not all parties are able to do. Thus, management strategies can be focused on supporting these parties and thus indirectly furthering the development of a counter-voice. This motive often forms the basis of subsidizing environmental and nature organizations so that they can become more professional. This type of strategy is a form of network constitution, a management strategy that will be discussed more thoroughly in Chapter 10.

The principle of creative competition discussed earlier is one of the ways to pursue the development of competing, fully-fledged argumentative alternatives. The dominance of a single solution in processes of problem solving can be considered as asymmetry in the extreme. Through simultaneously developing comparable alternatives and keeping options open as long as possible, the debate acquires a more symmetric argumentation structure.

Preventing cognitive fixations by starting a process

A characteristic of many problem solving processes is that the discussion is focused on *which* solution should be realized, given an authoritative definition of the problem. Frequently, one solution becomes dominant and parties align for or against it. Thus, it is important to prevent early substantive fixations and postpone selection (de Bruijn *et al.*, 2002).

This may be achieved by initiating an interaction process: proposing that parties talk about conditions that have to be fulfilled and agreements that should be made in order to arrive at joint actions. This proposal will trigger a debate on the organization of the interaction process and will, at the same time, postpone the discussion of the substance of the problem. The logic behind this approach is that discussions about solutions affect actors directly so they will adopt positions and strategies that promote their favoured solutions, which, in turn, will emphasize differences and generate conflict.

Actors engaged in the solution of wicked problems operate in a relatively unstable environment in which they are vulnerable to opportunistic strategies of other parties. As a result, parties will be tense, on the alert and less inclined to cooperate. Starting a process means that difficult and contentious substantive decisions are postponed so that parties can first become acquainted, develop insight into each others' behaviour, motives and ideas, develop rules of the game that will reduce strategic uncertainty and, thus, protect against attacks from others. Decisions about the organization of the process are less risky and easier to make than substantive ones: they have no direct substantive consequences and can more easily be adapted to new situations (see Salisbury, 1968).

In this process of deciding upon the organization of the problem solving process 'defreezing' occurs: parties learn how others view the problem situation and that there are more aspects to the problem and its solution than they initially thought. Thus, they develop a better understanding of the costs and benefits involved and the opportunities for goal intertwinement, compensation and cooperation. So, when substantive decisions are finally addressed, they will now be easier to make, more will be known about the content of the problem, and strategic uncertainty will be reduced by the agreements made in the beginning.

Furthermore, parties have had the opportunity to anticipate the solution and thus limit negative consequences. They will also be more inclined to mitigate their substantive claims since they have been part of a process of joint image building, have become familiar with the dilemmas that are at play and are more aware of their mutual interdependencies.

Making a contested decision to get things started

It is not always possible for parties to postpone a substantive decision. When confronted with serious societal risks, government, in its role as protector of the common good, is forced to take measures even when others contest their necessity and even when uncertainty about content exists. Decisions taken under these circumstances are contestable (Klijn *et al.*, 2000). Their effectiveness is uncertain. They are a form of 'adverse selection': a decision which is made even though it is unclear whether it is a good decision since the available knowledge for making the 'right' decision is lacking (Jensen and Meckling, 1976). Despite that, 'contested decisions' can be legitimate since, if they were not made, risks which are socially and politically unacceptable would be taken.

Nevertheless, a contested decision may harm the interests of actors. When it becomes clear in retrospect that a measure was unnecessary, the situation is worse than before. Given the uncertainty surrounding the contested decision, the extent to which risks will be reduced and interests will be damaged cannot be determined a priori with certainty. We can turn need into a virtue by linking a contested decision to a process in which the parties involved, and especially those who are disadvantaged by a decision, will investigate the effects of the measures that are undertaken. The party taking a contested measure would then have to take the responsibility for organizing such a process and declare itself prepared to adapt the contested decision or alternative solutions on the basis of new information and proposals for improvement. The taking of a contested decision can, thus, be seen as a fallback option that is, at the same time, used to evoke the development of alternative options which are substantively better and enjoy more support.

The contested decision as starting engine

There is yet another reason why a contested decision may fulfil a useful function. The downside to postponing substantive decisions might be that actors become too relaxed; a lack of substance may remove the sense of urgency in the problem solving process and lead to stagnation. In allocating their scarce attention, actors are guided by the choices which are most urgent. They will put energy into games where substantive decisions are likely to be taken. The contested decision creates a sense of urgency: if nothing happens, measures will be taken that may be unfavourable for some stakeholders. This is an incentive for them to invest in the process and to come up with a better alternative. This squares with the insight that parties are only willing to change their behaviour under the threat of hierarchical interventions. The contested decision may fulfil such a function, provided that the decision maker is prepared to accept that a better alternative exists. Without such a prospect, there is no incentive to work constructively on an alternative. All energy will then go into attempts to block the decision and frustrate its implementation.

Advancing cognitive reflection

The substance of the debate about problem solution can be influenced indirectly by changing the social conditions under which the debate occurs. One can attempt to get the involved parties to think about the content of their problem formulation or about the solution they propose by confronting them with the ideas of others. In other words, by creating *social variety* (Levy and Merry, 1986; Termeer, 1993). This may include bringing together representatives from different sectors or networks or inviting the representative of a relatively under-represented opinion or interest to join. It is also conceivable that 'multiple included' parties will become involved: persons or organizations that participate in different networks at the same time, with the expectation that they can help bridge the differences between parties or play the role of 'change agent' in the policy game.

Furthering and guarding social variety can become especially important when parties in a policy game exclude other parties and thus eliminate unwelcome arguments or standpoints (compare Majone, 1986; Dryzek and Ripley, 1988). This behaviour occurs when one actor becomes dominant in a policy game, but also when there are two sides that vie with one another, both of which regard deviant standpoints as hostile or showing a lack of solidarity (Termeer and Koppenjan, 1997).

By consciously introducing new actors and by ensuring that roles such as the devil's advocate, the entrepreneur and the mediator are filled, one can attempt to increase substantive variety and thus, indirectly, advance cognitive reflection.

Organizing substantive selection

How can joint image building and joint action emerge amid a multitude of perceptions, objectives and solutions? As argued earlier, in problem solving processes the selection of problem formulations and solutions are made too early and result in fixations and impasses. Even if problem solving is consciously designed as an interactive process, the selection process is mostly problematic. Often much attention is given to the generation of variety, while the organization of selection is neglected (Klijn and Koppenjan, 2003; Koppenjan, 2003). Especially when it is recognized that there are many differing perceptions and objectives at play and a clear-cut substantive yardstick to assess proposals is missing, selection becomes a difficult job. Nevertheless, at some point in the problem solving process selection of substantive solutions has to take place.

Organizing selection means that parties must make agreements about how they will assess proposals. These agreements may include the criteria used for selection, but also who, and in what capacity, will be involved in the selection, how that selection will be carried out, and when the selection will be made. Each of these elements will be addressed below.

- *Selection criteria.* Agreements about how to assess proposals should not be based on an *ex ante* formulated, detailed and coherent set of criteria. Using such a framework for assessment is at odds with our claim that parties do not always achieve consensus about objectives. Furthermore, it is at odds with the substantive uncertainty at stake so that it is difficult to develop criteria or programmes of demands prior to the process. *Ex ante* criteria will, therefore, have a general and temporary nature. During the design of solutions, these criteria will be amended, adapted and refined under the influence of changing environmental circumstances and learning behaviour.

- *Who selects?* The premise in a complex problem is that multiple parties whose interests, objectives and perceptions are at stake must somehow be involved in the selection. This does not mean that all parties play an equally important role. The nature of the parties' involvement in selection can vary from advising to co-deciding. Furthermore, decision making rules may vary between a majority and unanimity (so that minority parties have veto power). In this context, the possibility of bridging differences between parties by using the principle of joint problem ownership is an interesting one. This principle involves the contracting out of the design of solutions or research activities. In pursuing this as a cooperative effort, actors who provide the contract are implicitly forced to coordinate the demands they have for the design or the formulation of the research question. Given what has been said above about the nature of uncertainty and the necessity of flexibility, this coordination will be of a general nature and not comprise every detail. What is more important is that joint images are developed that lay the basis for a mutual learning process in the future.

- *How is the selection done?* Linked to the question of 'who selects and in what manner' is the question of what avenues are open to parties who do not agree with the selected solution or with the intermediate decision about criteria used. As a result, agreements about decision rules, conflict management mechanisms, and complaint and appeal procedures are also necessary. Clearly, the more that a particular solution takes the variety of interests and objectives into account, the less use will have to be made of these provisions. On the other hand, the mere existence of rules for such instances may help parties to be more relaxed and respond in a more open minded manner to proposals.

- *When is the selection made?* Agreements about when a selection will be made are also important. There must be enough flexibility for a timely consultation with constituencies or parent organizations and for consulting with parties who are not directly involved in the selection process. Building such exchanges between the problem solving process and the formal decision makers in public and private organizations in a manner where the former is not confronted with *faits accomplis* is thus an important challenge. It is also important to prevent premature or belated selection. Premature selection leads to the exclusion of variety and frustration among those who propose variety. Furthermore, there is the risk of selecting the wrong solution. A belated selection leads to declining interest and interaction weariness between participant actors. Selection is not just a question of making *ex ante* agreements but, to a larger extent, a management issue: parties must constantly be on the lookout for signs that suggest premature or belated selection. As long as good and innovative ideas are presented, the moment of selection can be postponed. The presence of conflicts may indicate that parties are not yet content about how their objectives are intertwined. As soon as actors start leaving the process or if they are repeating their earlier moves, the necessity of selection increases (de Bruijn *et al.*, 2002).

8.3 Arranging research activities: the furtherance of negotiated knowledge

In Chapter 2, we argued that in dealing with wicked problems, research rarely leads to a reduction of uncertainty about content. Instead of reducing substantive uncertainty, research and research results frequently become part of the problem. This jeopardizes the authoritativeness of research and may even lead to a departure from rationalism: refraining from research efforts because they fail to provide certainty on the nature of the problem and the effectiveness of solutions. As a consequence, actors may agree to solutions which are untenable in the light of scientific insights, i.e. negotiated nonsense. This risk is increased by the (time) pressure on decision makers to make firm decisions. Initiating research is, then, often viewed as a strategic move: an attempt to avoid responsibility and postpone unpopular decisions (Lovenduski and Outshoorn, 1986). The question we therefore address in the following sections is: how can we organize research in such a manner that its findings correspond to the knowledge needs of stakeholders and contribute to a process of joint image building without becoming part of go-alone strategies of stakeholders and fuelling knowledge conflicts and report wars?

Speaking truth to power or striving for usable knowledge?

The answer to this question includes more than simply reducing the distance between researcher and contractor in search of usable knowledge. While policy focused research may improve the quality of problem perceptions and proposals for solutions, it does not contribute to joint image building and can even strengthen the asymmetry in the policy debate. Nor does the answer lie in anxiously trying to maintain the autonomy of research and science. The idea that research which meets scientific criteria of validity and reliability will lead to 'true' knowledge that eventually will settle knowledge conflicts in problem solving processes is superseded. Such a positivist claim is not in line with the experience of many practitioners that for every opinion, an expert to support it with scientific evidence can be found. This claim also fails to deal with the problem of the non-use of research results which lay at the foundation of critical policy analysis (see Chapter 2). Many research findings, after all, become available at the wrong time, communicate an irrelevant message and are formulated in language that is impossible for outsiders to understand.

Citizens' science as a solution

Another solution for the non-use or advocative use of research lies consists of a plea for citizens' science as, for instance, Wildavsky maintains (1995; see Irwin, 1995). He regards citizens' science as the answer to knowledge conflicts on issues in the areas of health, safety and the environment. He adopts a positivist approach: science produces objective knowledge, but this may be undermined by the strategic use of information by conflicting parties, especially interest groups. Therefore, the citizen must be educated into independently assessing the quality of research and research results. This may lead to the pursuit of certified research and science: researchers must be accountable to citizens, the media and policy makers, by indicating how they have conducted their work according to the elementary rules of science.

Here, too, it is presumed that research and science are conclusive and authoritative. But it is difficult to see how citizens can make sense out of the confusion when researchers fail to convince policy makers and media, and even disagree between themselves about facts, interpretations and the rules that proper scientific research should follow. Obviously, efforts to make citizens better informed and to strengthen their position in the policy arena with the help of scientific research are commendable, but they do not address the issue at stake. The answer to the question how research and science can contribute to bridging diverging perceptions of parties and to the creation of negotiated knowledge should be sought in a different direction.

Arranging research activities in the context of solving wicked problems

In order to contribute constructively to the process of solving complex problems, research activities should be organized in such a way that they decrease the distance between the perceptions of stakeholders and (scientific) researchers regarding a problem, its causes and possible solutions. This not only involves the exchange of knowledge and information *between* stakeholders and researchers, but also *within* each of these groups. It then becomes important that research:

1   is tuned in to the knowledge questions of parties who play a role in the problem solving process;
2   manages to reduce or overcome the differences in substantive insights;
3   fits developments as they emerge during the process of problem solving.

Clearly, research will not be able to provide (definitive) answers to all knowledge questions. What can be expected from research is that it provides an understanding of which insights can be considered tenable given the state of research, and suggests which scientific issues have no hard evidence or information to support them. If knowledge is regarded as relatively 'solid', it can provide the necessary room to manoeuvre for parties to jointly develop solutions; or it can serve as a yardstick to measure the quality of their options. If research is inconclusive, an attempt can be made to formulate tentative and inter-subjective (scientific) insights which – given the available knowledge resources and the state of science at that point in time – is the highest achievable type of knowledge. To make this possible, the organization of research activities within the process of problem solving must meet certain demands (Jasanoff, 1994; de Bruijn et al., 2002), which include:

1 parallel linking of problem solving and research;
2 a facilitating role for research instead of mandated science;
3 the joint commissioning of research activities;
4 boundary work.

Parallel linking of problem solving and research: concurrent research

In traditional policy analysis, research activities are linked to the various phases in the process of problem solving as distinguished in the rational policy model. Hogwood and Gunn (1984) distinguish: issue search, issue filtration, issue definition, forecasting, setting objectives, option analysis, policy implementation, monitoring and control, and evaluation. For each of these steps there is the adage: think first (do research), then act.

When we accept that, in reality, the problem solving process does not develop linearly but rather in a zigzag and jerky fashion, this should have consequences for the place and nature of research activities. Organizing research separately in the chronological steps that, according to the rational decision making model, make up the problem solving process, does not conform with this non-linear model. If research for solutions precedes decision making and solutions, it is likely that the demarcations, assumptions and conditions used in research are already obsolete by the time decisions are made and solutions are elaborated. When research is conducted ex post, then the findings come too late. The solution has already been elaborated and decided upon and research will have a legitimating function at best, and will be destructive at worst: the designed solution cannot be supported and the problem solving process must be repeated (de Bruijn et al., 2002).

If we want research to constructively contribute to the problem solving process, it should not be organized as a separate phase in the process but as a parallel stream: a second arena, a research arena alongside the original arena where the game is played and in constant contact with that arena. Knowledge questions and conflicts emerging in the first arena are brought into the research arena as research questions. The findings are then fed back to the main arena (Van Eeten and Ten

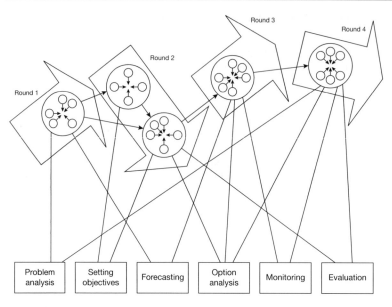

Figure 8.2 **The relationship between research activities and the problem solving process**

Heuvelhof, 1998). They may provide an impulse for joint image building and the development of cooperative strategies in that arena, but they may also lead to new knowledge questions. Thus, the activities in the research arena do not follow the chronological steps of the rational phase model. The knowledge questions that emerge at various points in the game can be very different by nature and may not fit into a chronological order (first issue research, then issue filtration, etc.). Figure 8.2 illustrates this loose coupling between research activities and the problem solving process.

Research that facilitates instead of mandated science

Research will not resolve knowledge conflicts between parties in the policy game. Research does not have that kind of authoritativeness. What is more, research will often not be conclusive either. So when research is, nonetheless, given the role of arbiter, it will become a target of the strategies of actors, that try to influence the formulation of the problem and the solutions considered. Their conflict will trickle into the research arena. In fact, both arenas will merge and the potential contribution of (scientific) research to cross-frame learning and the development of negotiated knowledge will be lost (Salter, 1988; Jasanoff, 1994). So, instead of settling disputes authoritatively, the role of science and research is to facilitate the interaction between stakeholders. This role includes the following:

- Research will not generate ready-made solutions but will indicate which standpoints can be maintained given the state of scientific insights, which issues cannot be conclusively determined, and what, given available knowledge, is the manoeuvre room within which solutions can be found. This, too, is a type of cognitive learning and a contribution to the reduction of substantive uncertainties in the main arena of the policy game in which stakeholders are trying to develop strategies by which the problem can be solved or at least managed.

- By investigating the effects of solutions proposed by parties and demonstrating the degree to which the various preferences of actors may lead to different or comparable outcomes, research can help to understand conflicts and knowledge disputes in the negotiation arena and thus make them easier to overcome.
- Research can generate new insights and knowledge that contribute to the quality of the policy discussion and the problem formulations and solutions that are advanced. It can improve cognitive learning and help enhance the quality, innovativeness and integrative character of solutions.
- In linking up with the negotiation arena, researchers are forced to explain their assumptions, methods and outcomes to the stakeholders. This contributes to both the quality and focus of research activities as well as to communication about them with stakeholders.
- The wish to collaborate in research activities contributes to the convergence of ideas and insights between stakeholders. If stakeholders want to influence joint research activities, they will be forced to consider the research questions that must be addressed and will have to reach agreement about the assumptions and criteria which will serve as the basis for judging the research findings. This negotiation and argumentation process encourages joint image building.
- Research may contribute to a de-politicization of conflicts between parties in the main arena if these conflicts are translated into research questions. Sometimes research will not lead to answers, but it may bring out aspects of a problem that have received little attention, or lead to refining earlier opinions. Research can thus contribute to a situation where parties no longer confront each other but, instead, acquire new insights, experience cognitive learning and see opportunities for new solutions. It is exactly through the loose coupling of research findings and subsequent actions that conflicts over research and research results can be prevented. And, as a result, research can develop substantive answers to the knowledge questions and arguments of both parties so that substantive quality is improved and the divergence of perceptions decreases.

Joint commissioning of research

An important objective of organizing research in the process of problem solving is to prevent research from becoming advocative. This can be done by encouraging stakeholders to jointly commission research activities (van Bueren *et al.*, 2003). Since research is always conducted within a specific problem frame (see Chapter 2) which will influence the choices made with regard to demarcation, assumptions, methods and interpretation of data, each of these issues can become a target of criticism if the parties do not agree with the research results. This is exactly the mechanism that lies behind report wars: commissioned by different interested parties, scholars criticize the choices made on each of these issues. This is not very helpful when the objective is to develop a common understanding in order to arrive at joint action. To achieve convergence, parties ought to negotiate *ex ante* – before they have been confronted with undesirable research results – about what research questions need to be answered, which choices should be made with regard to demarcations, assumptions and methods, and by which criteria findings will be assessed. Parties might not achieve consensus about all these points but, for instance, they may agree to a parallel investigation of assumptions or research questions. It is conceivable that they will have reservations with regard to aspects or sections of the research. Here, too, research questions can help to overcome differences: through a sensitivity analysis, parties may explore the degree to which different assumptions lead to different outcomes. These findings can then be used in the negotiation arena to establish trade-offs. The aim of research is not to arrive at ready-made solutions nor achieve consensus

---

Box 8.1 Joint commissioning of research in the zinc case

One of the few points where cognitive learning occurred in the zinc case was due to the joint commissioning of research. The zinc industry initially fought the scientific foundation of zinc policy. This proved to be ineffective. The research that they initiated as an interested party was viewed as partisan by government actors and not taken seriously. For a number of years, the zinc industry and the RIZA (the research institute of the Department of Transport, Public Works and Water Management concerned with research in the field of water management) disagreed with each other's research findings on the diffusion speed of zinc and zinc building materials into the waterways as a consequence of corrosion. Since the research design, demarcations and assumptions were different, the outcomes were different too – even when the research was done by the same institute. In the end, everyone arrived at a point where a decision was made to have research done on the basis of a jointly formulated research assignment. The outcome of the research that was done on the basis of this assignment, succeeded in convincing both parties. With the RIZA, this led to the acknowledgement that the corrosion speed of zinc was much lower than earlier government figures indicated.

The zinc case also demonstrates that attempts by parties to involve others in their research projects often fail because the way this is done is inappropriate. Thus, government invited the zinc industry to participate in a working group that would think about the design and implementation of research for new norms for zinc. At crucial moments, however, government took unilateral decisions to influence the research, reasoning that, after all, the success of the research was its responsibility. Participating parties allowed this to happen following the same logic: they considered the research to be, first and foremost, an activity of government. This meant that, although they were involved in the research process, they did not really feel responsible for the research. Hence, they also did not feel committed to the outcomes of it (Klijn et al., 2000).

between parties, but to coordinate and share generated knowledge, acquire insight into the nature of the differences, and to support and enrich the negotiation process.

Guarding the borderline between research and negotiation arenas: boundary work

In order to be authoritative, research must not develop an advocacy character. In addition to the parallel linking of the negotiation and research arenas, there should also be provisions that guarantee the autonomy of researchers and establish clear boundaries between both arenas, as well as define the tasks and responsibilities of the actors in these arenas. Jasanoff (1994) calls this 'boundary work': intertwining research with the problem solving process in such a manner that there is intensive interaction between both, without the merging of the two arenas. Researchers must be able to do their research autonomously and not be under pressure by stakeholders to change or ignore findings. Researchers do their work on the basis of rules for qualitatively good and scientifically responsible research. Knowledge questions are provided by practice and the choice that the researchers make with regard to design and implementation of research and the interpretation of findings will be done in consultation with the contractors. All of this will be carried out within the boundaries of acceptable scientific standards.

However, these rules of the scientific game are far from self-evident and uncontested (Nowotny *et al.*, 2001). That is why it is all the more important to be explicit about boundaries, responsibilities and the way in which knowledge problems and disputes will be dealt with. This can be done by negotiating agreements between stakeholders and researchers on these issues and embedding these agreements in, for instance, a contract or covenant. Furthermore, a scientific forum could be appointed, consisting of scholars who are respected and regarded as authoritative by both experts and stakeholders. This forum could be charged with assessing the design, implementation and findings of research activities during various stages of the research from a scientific viewpoint. The judgement of the forum then guarantees the scientific quality and independence of the research. Furthermore, if there is a difference of opinion or conflict about the choices made or about the interpretations of research data, such a forum can advise and, if necessary, mediate or arbitrate. Also, the forum can fulfil the selecting function in tendering processes for hiring researchers or with regard to the results of competitive research tracks. Thus, the opportunities for stakeholders to strategically use research decrease and the autonomy of research is enhanced. Because research will gain authoritativeness, the impact of it on the process will increase, although the coupling between research and process is loose. Figure 8.3 visualizes this loose coupling.

Towards cross-frame reflection and negotiated knowledge

The result of research, organized according to these principles, is not objective knowledge that will erase all of the substantive uncertainties surrounding wicked problems for once and for all. But it does generate inter-subjective knowledge on

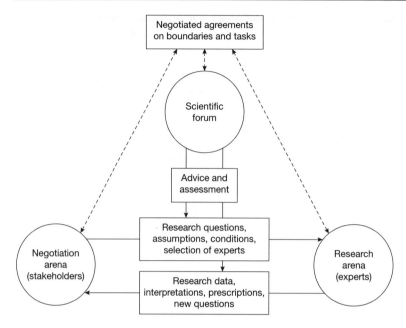

Figure 8.3 Concurrent research: the loose coupling between the arenas of research and negotiation

the basis of scientific insight available at that point in time, and it contributes to the quality of problem solving and the legitimacy of the selected solutions. The role of the scientific forum contributes to guaranteeing the autonomy of research activities and thus to the facilitating role fulfilled by the experts and stakeholders. For stakeholders in the negotiation arena, this type of organizing research has the disadvantage that the findings of researchers are relatively unpredictable. However, they have opportunities to influence research activities, they are certain of the fact that other parties cannot unilaterally manipulate that research and, furthermore, they are not formally bound to the outcomes of research. At the same time there are strong incentives to use these outcomes: the independent nature of the research will lend considerable legitimacy to the outcomes. Also, the discussion in the policy arena between stakeholders will be conducted in terms generated in the research (De Bruijn and Ten Heuvelhof, 2002). Although the research and negotiation arenas are loosely coupled and stakeholders are not formally committed to research outcomes, a proper linking of both arenas will mean that the research arena has a strong steering and disciplining influence on the standpoints taken and strategies employed by actors in the policy game. When parties are able to properly arrange research activities that are undertaken in the context of the problem solving process, the process of joint image building and goal intertwinement will be facilitated and the results and outcomes will be based on available knowledge resources and can be maintained in the light of existing scientific insights.

8.4 Conclusion: conditions for cognitive learning

The management of substantive uncertainty, inspired by the network approach, is not focused on the *ex ante* creation of an authoritative problem and objective formulation that guides the process of problem solving. This approach will lead to early substantive fixation with the risk of excluding alternative perceptions, values and avenues of solution. Chances for learning and enrichment, that manifest themselves during the process, would then be missed. Furthermore, early substantive selection encourages resistance of actors as a result of which conditions for learning will deteriorate.

The objective is not the creation of consensus (although this can sometimes be helpful), but the improvement of joint image building, the use of cross-frame reflection and the development of interesting and appealing solutions that will generate support among actors. Hence, uncertainty management is a search for a 'common ground', a minimal basis for communication that enables further interaction and common learning.

Strategies that can be used include steering towards goal entwinement, improving substantive variety, breaking through asymmetric debates, preventing early substantive fixations, improving cognitive reflection and organizing substantive selection.

Management of substantive uncertainty is also aimed at organizing the input of experts, research and science in such a way that the learning process between stakeholders is supported. This requires the organization of the research process according to the principle of concurrent research: the parallel linking of research and process, providing research with a facilitating role, joint commissioning of research and doing 'boundary work'. The result is the prevention of negotiated nonsense by confronting the outcomes of the interactions between stakeholders with scientific insights. When scientific insights are not conclusive, the efforts should be aimed at organizing a preliminary scientific consensus on the basis of the actual state of scientific insights.

Chapter 9

Managing the game

Selective couplings, rules of the game and process management

9.1 Introduction

As we have seen in Part 1, uncertainty is strongly related to the strategic nature of complex processes of problem solving and decision making. Problem solving takes place in an often hectic and dynamic context where various actors with different perceptions and strategies interact and attempt to influence the problem formulation and the search for solutions. Furthermore, this process of forming and shaping problem formulations and solutions occurs in a fragmented and dynamic environment. Parties make decisions in various arenas that influence the problem situation and contribute to the erratic and unpredictable course of the policy game. Thus, an important challenge in dealing with wicked problems is finding a way of handling strategic uncertainty.

Strategic uncertainties emerge from interdependencies between parties. This requires parties to adapt their strategies on the basis of an initial exploration of their strategic environment (see Chapter 7). Go-alone strategies aimed at problem solving according to one's own perceptions have to be transformed into strategies of searching for common interests and mutual agreements with other parties to make it possible to find a solution that sufficiently considers the range of interests and objectives involved and that can acquire sufficient support. Hence, parties must enter interaction and negotiation processes where couplings frequently have to be made with actors in other arenas, games or networks, which were previously unknown to them.

From go-alone strategies to interaction and concerted action

Actors will not always decide on such a course of action, however. Joint action does have its downside. First, there are decision making costs: investments in terms of money, time and energy which participation in games demands. Second, there are external political costs: the compromises which actors in a game will have to accept. Depending on these transaction costs, actors will have to decide whether to participate in an interaction process (see Hirschman, 1970; Williamson, 1985).

In addition to transaction costs theory, there are theories that suggest that the structure of collective action situations prevent actors from engaging in cooperation on a voluntary basis. The example of the prisoner's dilemma taken from game theory illustrates how the actions of two players, who are out to achieve optimum results for themselves but are unable to communicate with each other, results in a lose–lose game for both players. So, theories about collective action and game theories demonstrate that even though actors have an interest in cooperation, the structure of interaction situations still results in actors clinging to non-cooperative strategies. The reason for this is actors' fear of becoming the victim of the strategic or opportunistic behaviour of the other parties, i.e. premature withdrawal, free-rider behaviour and so forth (Olson 1965; Ostrom, 1990). Furthermore, interaction between actors who pursue their own interest in a rational way, may produce unfavourable outcomes at the collective level. The tragedy of the 'commons', described by Hardin, is an example of this mechanism. He explains the decline of the meadows that were shared in communities in pre-industrial England by the fact that individual shepherds could benefit from the commons, without carrying the costs. This led to overgrazing by their sheep and finally to the destruction of the commons (Hardin and Baden, 1997).

Ostrom (1990) challenges the assumption that actors are unable to voluntarily achieve cooperation. Since actors are allowed to communicate, in contrast to the prisoner's dilemma, they are able to build consensus and agree to the mutual adoption of rules. By committing themselves to collective action, they reduce the strategic uncertainty which prevents them from investing in collective action. Actors commit themselves to agreements in which they promise to abandon opportunistic strategies. This commitment may be established by actors in various arrangements or 'sets of rules', such as cooperative agreements, contracts, joint ventures and so forth.

The need for game management

The question, however, is whether Ostrom might be overestimating the capacity of actors to achieve cooperation by themselves. If actors cannot succeed in achieving cooperation with regard to a concrete problem, how can they conceivably succeed in building consensus on how they are going to organize that cooperation? While given the actors' attitudes, the current game rules and the available social capital, actors might independently reach a consensus on collective action in certain situations, they probably won't in situations of strategic uncertainty. In these cases, an outside impetus is needed. Since actors do not independently achieve cooperation, the game of inter-organizational problem solving must be managed.

This chapter is focused on the issue of what this game management might involve. How can the game that evolves between actors around problem solving be influenced or shaped in such a manner that parties will change their go-alone strategies to cooperative strategies? They will only be willing to do so when they are convinced of their dependency upon other actors for the realization of their objectives, and when the costs of cooperation and risks of opportunistic behaviour by other parties are limited. Given the risk of negative externalities of cooperation (e.g. off-loading the cost to non-represented risk carriers or 'third parties'), an additional question is how parties can be prevented from choosing behaviour by which these are produced.

9.2 Managing the game: general principles

Game management takes the strategic characteristics of processes of problem solving and decision making as its starting point. It considers the institutional characteristics of networks in which these games are played to be given. Attempts to influence the network structure are called institutional design, and we will deal with management strategies aimed at institutional design in the next chapter. A central activity includes the attempts to bring and keep parties together so that they can acquire knowledge of each other's perceptions and discover opportunities for intertwining their objectives and tuning their strategies into these. This is necessary because actors depend on one another and may not achieve favourable outcomes without the effort and input of other actors. 'In short, game management attempts to realize the necessary concerted action so that actors who depend upon each other's resources can achieve interesting outcomes for themselves, without producing unfavourable outcomes for others' (Klijn *et al.*, 1995).

Game characteristics and game management

Attempts to transform go-alone strategies into concerted action are made more difficult because of the characteristics of the game. The game is fragmented and dynamic, there are numerous actors and often there is a lack of institutional provisions that support interaction. Given these characteristics of the game, game management faces the following challenges:

1   The game is characterized by the absence of a hierarchy and the voluntary nature of interaction. This means that incentives for cooperation have to be created by offering and clarifying opportunities for goal intertwinement and mutual benefits.
2   In the game, many actors participate with varying, and sometimes contradictory, perceptions. This implies that interaction does not take place under the umbrella of an *ex ante* problem formulation or solution that is accepted by all. Early substantive fixation must be avoided since it will lead to disinterest or conflict and limit opportunities for goal intertwinement.
3   Since the game is characterized by a high degree of strategic and institutional uncertainty, there is a need to agree upon (temporary) game rules in order to reduce transaction costs and strategic risks without asking for commitment at the start of the process that parties are not yet ready to make.
4   The game is erratic and is played in a dynamic environment. There is need for flexibility through parallel development of problem formulations and solution alternatives.
5   Participants in the game are characterized by bounded rationality and limited resources. This means that they have to be selective when making strategic choices and that interaction is always limited.

Table 9.1 Game characteristics and requirements for game management

Game characteristics	Requirements for 'good' game management
Lack of hierarchy; volunteerism	Incentives for cooperation must be created by seeking and clarifying goal intertwinement opportunities and profit opportunities
Multiple actors, perceptions and objectives	Early substantive selection and fixation must be avoided
Strategic and institutional uncertainty	An agreement to the rules of the game is necessary for reducing transaction costs and strategic risks
Dynamics and erratic nature	Necessity of flexibility through parallel development of problem formulations and solution alternatives; generating substantive variety
Complexity, bounded rationality and resources	Selectivity with regard to content, participation and effort is unavoidable
Risk and unequal representation off-loading	Pay attention to openness, transparency and accountability

6   The dark side of the interaction consists of off-loading risks and costs onto the environment and unequal representation. Therefore, there is a need for guarantees that limit these negative effects: attention to openness, transparency and accountability.

Game characteristics and the consequent requirements for game management are summarized in Table 9.1.

Limitations of game management

Although game management can contribute to reducing strategic uncertainties in the handling of wicked problems, this approach does not resolve everything. Game management has its limitations. First, attempts at achieving interaction are not always meaningful. The interaction must offer the prospect of a solution that represents an improvement on the existing or expected situation for all parties involved and this may not always be the case. Furthermore, parties may lack 'drive' to solve a problem, i.e. because they have other priorities or they don't experience the cost of the problem situation in the short run.

Second, transaction costs limit the opportunities for actors to unconditionally engage in game management activities. That's why game management should not be focused on everything and everyone. It may be aimed at reducing blockages of a limited number of relations. Neither does game management have to stretch out across the entire process of problem solving. Often, it will involve interventions that are limited in time and scope. Even if game management is more comprehensive by nature, it will, nevertheless, be limited to (part of) a game round or at most to some game rounds.

The remainder of this chapter deals with the possible types and activities of game management and builds upon the insights discussed above concerning the demands on, and limitations of, these strategies. We consider:

1   game management as the initiation of new games or game rounds, or the adaptation of existing ones: making couplings and decouplings between actors, arenas and games;
2   game management as the (re-)design of (new) games or game rounds: furthering the creation of ad hoc rules of the game and arrangements (process design);
3   game management as the facilitation of the interaction between parties within games or game rounds (process management).

9.3 Game management as couplings and decouplings of actors, arenas and games

When policy games stagnate because parties use go-alone strategies or become entangled in conflict-inducing or avoidance strategies, game management can take the shape of making selective couplings or decouplings (Friend *et al.*, 1974; Hanf and Scharpf, 1978; Kingdon, 1984). A coupling consists of bringing actors together who are involved in the articulation of a problem situation or the development or promotion of a solution. These activities are undertaken by varying parties at various places. Often, these activities affect each other – even though parties may have no contact with each other or are unaware of this mutual interference. By bringing parties into contact with each other, new opportunities emerge for them to coordinate their activities and achieve a situation that is an improvement for all.

The potentials of couplings

A coupling brings parties together with different perceptions, resources and solution preferences. Couplings are movements when the strategies used by parties in different arenas or games can become intertwined. Through new demarcations of the problem, new intertwinements and exchange opportunities are created (Crozier and Friedberg, 1980):

- New perspectives emerge: new actors with new problem perceptions are involved in the game, which might lead to new discussions or to new points of view. When new dimensions are added to the discussion, earlier deadlocks can be overcome.
- New resources can be brought in so that new exchange opportunities emerge.
- Couplings between games can result in accelerations, if a stagnating game is coupled to a game that makes progress.
- Coupling can result in the possibility of a specific problem or solution no longer being regarded as isolated but, instead, as being related to other societal matters or developments. This improves the embeddedness of the solution in the environment, leads to more integral approaches to problem solving and reduces the chance that unintended or undesired negative effects are produced.

Box 9.1 Couplings in the zinc case

In the zinc case, the employers' organization of VNO-NCW, becoming worried by the negative image effects for the industry of the zinc conflict, wanted to establish a coupling between the activities of the Ministry of VROM and the zinc industry. In the context of a number of other environmental issues, the ministry had made agreements with the industry on a voluntary basis, a formula that the VNO-NCW considered favourable to resolve the conflict regarding the use of zinc in building materials. Through an intensification of contact between the ministry and the zinc industry, new exchange opportunities would be created that could break through the impasse in the zinc discussion. The zinc industry could declare its willingness to invest in product innovations, in exchange for which the ministry would inform lower level government administrations about this in an attempt to mitigate their policies discouraging the use of zinc. This coupling might also have brought new resources into the game: VROM had subsidies available to encourage industries to develop environmental innovations. However, this coupling didn't get off to a good start because both parties – for good reasons or not – were unconvinced that the other's intentions were serious.

Another attempt to create a coupling in the zinc game, concerned the relation between the zinc industry and the sustainable building arena. In this arena companies compiled lists of building materials viewed as sustainable. These lists were made public with the support of the Ministry of VROM. They were quite influential in the circles of lower governments taking decisions on the use of materials in their local building projects. Since the zinc industry was not represented in this arena, it could not influence the content of these lists and was, thus, surprised by both the point at which they came available as well as their content. By accessing the sustainable building arena, the zinc industry attempted both to reduce the uncertainty created by the former's activities and to increase their opportunities to influence the content of the lists.

Source: Klijn *et al.*, 2000.

- When couplings result in making solutions part of a package of measures, the opportunities for package deals are increased. Measures that are unpopular can become part of a package deal and can provide compensating benefits (compare the example in Chapter 3 about the introduction of road pricing in the Netherlands).

Different kinds of couplings: arranging interactions

Couplings can be shaped in various manners. A light coupling can consist of making agreements between parties to serve as a basis for voluntary information exchange. Such an arrangement can have the nature of a gentleman's agreement. A more substantial coupling is created when parties engage in more frequent interaction in the context of handling a problem so that a new arena is created or a new game initiated. Through cooperation agreements, contracts or mutual legal entities, such a coupling, can be organizationally anchored and may even increase

Box 9.2 Couplings in the case of the Venice water problem: the *Comitatone*

An example of a coupling between a large set of actors involved in a complex problem situation is the way the Italian government dealt with the Venice water problem. In 1966 a devastating flood forced awareness of the problem upon the inhabitants of the city, governments and the general public. The entire city was flooded and in some areas the water levels rose by up to a metre. Since then, several high-water events have followed. Causes are the sinking of the ground soil and rising sea levels as a result of climate change. This causes discomfort in the city itself, threatens its cultural heritage, results in economic damage and has a negative effect upon tourism. But the damage is not restricted to the city. The changes in the ecosystem of the lagoon in which Venice is situated, have a deteriorating impact on its unique environmental and ecological qualities. By constructing a dam that closes the lagoon from the Adriatic Sea, the government hopes to safeguard Venice from high-water events. This plan is contested because of the high costs and the negative effects that closing the lagoon could have on the environment, fisheries and shipping. The decision making on this issue is not only difficult because of its substantive complexity, but also because of the wide range of interests involved and the institutional complexity of the political–administrative environment within which a solution must be found. A large number of national, regional and local authorities are somehow involved in this issue.

In an attempt to face this institutional fragmentation, in the 1980s an inter-administrative body was created: the *Comitatone*. Under the leadership of the Prime Minister, it serves to coordinate water policy and the realization of solutions. Represented in the *Comitatone* are the involved ministries, the province of Venice (responsible for the cultural heritage), the region of Veneto (with tasks in the area of water management and environmental protection), the mayors of Venice and of Chioggia, and two representatives of the other local governments that are involved. Their membership of the *Comitatone* gives them the opportunity to articulate their perceptions and objectives in the decision making process and to participate in thinking about necessary solutions. Their participation also contributes to the creation of support for the ultimate solution and is an investment in the cooperation necessary for achieving the solution. The *Comitatone* prepares the policy plan that forms the basis for tackling the water problem. This policy plan is then approved by cabinet and parliament. The implementation is in the hands of a private consortium (*Consorti Venezia Nuova*) regulated by the Venice Water Authority, an implementing body of the Ministry of Infrastructure and Transport. The *Comitatone* is involved in this process as the administrative deliberative body (www.salve.it/banchedati/domande/uk/domande.asp). Figure 9.1 provides a view of this administrative arrangement.

This complex institutional arrangement demonstrates how a coupling can be made in a complex game characterized by a high degree of strategic uncertainty and institutional fragmentation by creating a new arena – in this case an ad hoc consultative structure, whose position and relations with other actors is formally

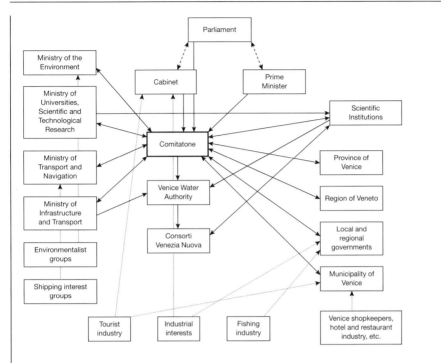

Relations:

⟶ Formal hierarchical relation

⟷ Representation relation

◀----▶ Relation of formal accountability

·········▶ Informal influence relation

Figure 9.1 The arrangement for dealing with the Venice water problem

anchored in a *lex specialis*. In the years that followed, the *Comitatone* evolved into an authoritative consultation platform for the enduring and difficult negotiations between parties concerning the requirements for the dam and additional measures to enhance its effectiveness and to mitigate its negative impacts.

The example of the coupling of actors in the case of the Venice water problem shows that a coupling between parties involved in a problem situation is a condition for interaction, joint image building and concerted action. It is not a guarantee for success though. A vital aspect, for instance, is how interactions are shaped in this new arena. What rules of the game will apply? To what degree will parties have the opportunity to represent their interests and arrive at coordination? In the next paragraph we will address the question of how the interaction of actors, once a coupling has been made, can be shaped by designing rules of the game.

in importance (Rogers and Whetten, 1982). As far as making couplings is concerned, game management consists of bringing parties together by making contacts, giving parties the opportunity to consider the advantages of couplings, and supporting them in seeking the correct design for the coupling. Boxes 9.1 and 9.2 present examples of couplings in, respectively, the zinc case and the case of the Venice water problem.

Decoupling as an option

Couplings are not necessarily fruitful and do not always offer the prospect of opportunities for intertwinement and profit. They can also be dysfunctional, for instance when:

- Parties have an interest in the continuation of the existing problem or when they feel disadvantaged by the desired solution. They might delay or even sabotage the process of problem solving. This is especially the case when initiators of a solution are not willing to rethink their plans or to compensate its negative effects for others.
- Parties are involved in a problem without it leading to new exchange opportunities, representation of interests, or substantive insights. In this case, the costs and risks of cooperation are heightened, without the compensation of substantive enrichment opportunities. This will lead to a deterioration for all parties involved.
- Conflict or stagnation in a certain arena or game to which a problem is coupled inhibits the progress of interaction, while that arena or game is not central to the solution of the problem.

In these cases, decoupling makes sense. This can be done by de-activating actors, by terminating organizational arrangements, or by decreasing interactions between arenas and actors. Instead of being drawn into an impasse or conflict in a parallel process, decoupling may help to give new momentum to the process of problem solving in the current game.

9.4 Game management as furthering the creation of the rules of the game

Interaction between parties will only come about when costs and risks have been reduced to acceptable proportions. This presupposes that the interaction process between parties has acquired a certain degree of organization, in other words that agreement has been reached about the rules of the game that will reduce the strategic uncertainties surrounding the interaction (Ostrom, 1990; Scott-Morgan, 1994). For the game manager, this means that in addition to opportunities for benefits, he has to propose an appropriate way of dealing with the problem or at least to invite participants to discuss the way they are going to organize their interactions. He can do so by providing them with a set of rules of the game about which they can make agreements. We call these agreements about the rules of the game the 'process design': they constitute the course and content of the interaction process (de Bruijn *et al.*, 2002). These agreements can be general and limited in nature, given the form of the coupling and the degree of game management necessary to get parties to cooperate. They can also be a rather comprehensive design of the game with specific and detailed agreements. These rules of the game concern temporary agreements aimed at the game in which, and for which, they are designed. The agreements regard the more enduring relations and institutional rules of networks in which the game is played as given. Changing the institutional context of the game requires institutional design, the subject of Chapter 10.

In this section, we provide an overview of possible agreements from which the game manager can make his own selection depending on specific needs in concrete cases.

Negotiating rules of the game

The set of agreements must ultimately come to life in a concrete game. This means that it is not merely a game manager's blueprint. On the other hand, parties must have some idea about what to expect at the beginning of the interaction. This keeps the game manager from starting the interaction without his own proposals concerning the rules of the game, in the same way that a process without a substantive proposal will probably not 'take off'. Furthermore, the principles that form the foundation of game management must be reflected in the set of agreements: when it concerns flexibility, for instance, there must be enough room provided for multiple perceptions and objectives (Goodin, 1996).

The establishment of the rules of the game is primarily a meta-decision making game between stakeholders: they determine which rules of the game they want to agree to. At best, the game manager can present arguments and ideas in order to feed and enrich the argumentation process in this decision making, in addition to the preferences and ideas that the parties themselves bring in (De Bruijn *et al.*, 2002).

With regard to the content of the problems, actors have to take care not to develop negotiated nonsense in developing their set of rules. For this, it is probably useful to separate the role of game manager, who brings parties together and encourages them to make agreements about rules of the game, and that of process designer who, as an expert, provides ideas about the content of the agreements.

Rules of the game as 'living' constitution

In the end, the process design must become a set of agreements that provides parties with sufficient trust to work together. This set of agreements is not a blueprint for the further progress of the process, but rather a 'living' constitution which evolves from limited, general and voluntary, to comprehensive, specific and more binding, during the process. Ultimately, when parties have developed a mutual manner of working and clarified the solution, the agreements will achieve a more binding nature, for instance through a contract. The danger of the pursuit of binding agreements at the start of interaction, is that it leads to conflict and stagnation. Parties will be scared of the demand of such a commitment because of the uncertainties involved. Instead, the rules of the game should facilitate voluntary and informal forms of interaction. In time, parties will develop the feeling that they cannot entirely withdraw from the interaction process. A certain kind of *social binding* will develop. Informal rules, whether part of the process design or not, will increasingly steer the initially ambiguous interactions. This process also implies that at first, agreements are general by nature and limited in scope: the design must provide enough room for the process to do its work. Gradually, the rules of the game will be discovered, specified, tried, adjusted or replaced as the process evolves.

In this section, we discuss which rules of the game can be agreed upon. We will specify the most important choices that play a role in that decision. Although the categories of rules of the game we use correspond with those of the institutional rules we distinguished in Chapter 4, we present them here in a slightly different way. Furthermore it should be clear in what way they differ from institutional rules. In contrast to institutional rules they have an ad hoc character and are specific to the game in which they are used. When successfully applied in a game and reused in other settings they may evolve to institutional rules, but not all rules do.

Rules about objective, agenda and conditions

At the start of the interaction, there should be no definite problem analysis, solution or objective. There must be opportunities for influencing the content of the process of problem solving. Otherwise there is little reason for potential participants to join the process, and blockades may emerge immediately. Successful cooperation requires parties to agree to a mutually attractive agenda. The game manager's function here is to investigate what parties find attractive – given their perceptions and objectives – and make proposals for an agenda. In this phase, there must be enough space for the various objectives that the different parties are pursuing, even if they appear to be contradictory or difficult to combine. Parties can then distinguish between issues that can be put on the agenda because they want measures on those issues, and issues about which opinions vary or about which substantive uncertainties exist and that should be subject to further study.

In determining the agenda, it is wise to work with the principle of an 'open agenda': this means parties can suggest topics they want to see addressed ensuring they will be included in the consultation process. This should be possible at both the start and in the later rounds of the process. This also means that later on in the process, it should be possible to place new topics on the agenda.

Formulating 'don'ts'

The agreements can specify outcomes that parties want to avoid at all costs. By formulating 'don'ts', parties are able to protect themselves against the risk of investing their resources in an interaction process that ultimately achieves an undesirable or unfavourable solution (de Bruijn *et al.*, 2002). An important 'don't' for companies that participate in interaction is the leaking of sensitive information or innovative ideas to competitors. For governments, the don'ts are usually in the realm of harm to public interests: interaction with the private sector, for instance, should not come at the price of protecting the environmental interest. Also, interaction should not limit the opportunities for government to use their legal public powers. However, governments can make agreements about how they are planning to use these powers.

Not only does the formulation of 'don'ts' create a secure environment that enables actors to access interactions, it also serves an information function: it makes parties sensible to the 'core interest' and vulnerabilities of other parties so that they will moderate their strategies. Furthermore, the game manager can use these insights to refine his intervention attempts.

This inventory of dos and don'ts can help parties acquire insight into each other's expectations and preferences. It helps to make clear which elements of proposals are negotiable and which not. It offers vital information for mutual adjustment of strategies. Thus, clarity emerges about how much room for manoeuvre there is for specifying problems and developing solutions, and about the possible products and their status: will proposals be realized without alteration or will they retain the character of a proposal for the relevant authority to make decisions about?

The dos and don'ts parties formulate at the start of a process can be quite rigid. During the course of the process, when parties have come to know each other, distrust and tension have decreased and a perspective of joint benefits has emerged, parties will become prepared to reconsider their dos and don'ts. So, instead of denying actors the right to take a stand at the start of the process and to formulate dos and don'ts, it is wise to allow them to do so. It helps them to start to interact with each other.

Rules of the game regarding participation, access and exit, and role distribution

The second set of rules of the game concern who can participate (Friend *et al.*, 1974; O'Toole, 1988). The answer greatly depends on the opportunities for profit that parties can envision. There will often be a trade-off between the size of the group of actors and the added value that can be achieved: as the number of players increase, so do the costs and risks of interaction. On the other hand, we must warn against the natural inclination to keep the number of actors small so that crucial resources, interests and insights are excluded. This can unintentionally lead to the organization of hindrance power and resistance during the rest of the process.

Representation of interests

An important question regarding the composition of the group of actors is whether all interests involved are sufficiently represented (Klijn and Koppenjan, 2000, 2000a). Especially for public parties, this can be a reason to confront the process with demands. For instance, by demanding that certain stakeholders must be involved or that their interests are looked after by others, so-called 'accounts' (de Bruijn *et al.*, 2002). This requires agreements about how these 'accounts' are to be held accountable to the stakeholders they represent.

Role distribution

Parties don't have to play the same roles, nor do they have to have an equal say in the interaction. Examples of different roles are: observer, co-designer, adviser, expert, game manager and decision maker (see also Teisman, 1992).

A party that provides an important financial contribution to the process of problem solving will probably want to have an important vote in the selection of a solution. On the other hand, an environmental organization that is afraid that by participating it might compromise itself in the eyes of the constituency, might be content with the status of observer. In this way, they can formally distance themselves from the outcome of the interaction while still providing their ideas about the desired solution.

The demarcation of roles can prevent the development of closed circuits between stakeholders and experts, which could jeopardize the independent input of experts in the process, subjecting their contribution to conflict (see Chapter 8).

Access and exit rules

Not all stakeholders will be willing to participate at the beginning of an interaction process. Often, parties only learn during the process that solutions are being considered that concern their interest. So, during the interaction process, continuously, new participants might want to access the game.

Sometimes interacting parties may fear 'cherry-picking' by newcomers, i.e. selecting the commercially interesting parts of a project and leaving the less interesting parts to others. Access rules can help here: they specify the conditions under which new parties can join interaction. When necessary and justified, certain efforts or contributions can be required from newcomers.

Exit opportunities ease the participation of actors in interaction processes since they give them the opportunity to withdraw if they find that their interests are being harmed. On the other hand, the possibility of exit may make the process vulnerable to hit-and-run strategies by parties: exiting as soon as favourable decisions have been taken or after having learned interesting things. An exit rule might be that the exiting party has to explain his decision to exit. Formally, this does not seem much of a barrier but, in practice, it appears that social pressure or political loss of face can throw up a serious barrier against early exits.

When parties invest large amounts of money in the process of problem solving, they will engage in more juridically binding agreements that sanction exit and that protect intellectual property. In the starting phase of an interaction process, this type of 'heavy equipment' is not appropriate: rather, it is the voluntary nature of the interaction that makes it acceptable to parties to join interaction – the outcome of which will be unclear.

Rules regarding the structuring of activities

Parties can make agreements about structuring their interaction: the creation of 'sub-arenas' that determine a division of labour and prevent a situation where everyone is involved in everything. This contributes to reducing the costs and risks of interaction. In structuring their activities, parties might consider to establish a top-level consultation platform, a steering group and working groups at the operational level.

Given their limited time and full agenda, the involvement of public and private office holders invited to participate in top-level consultations will be limited to being kept informed and making selective decisions at crucial moments in the interaction process. Their involvement is essential for the feedback of ideas presented during the interaction to the various 'parent organizations'. The more commitment power they have vis-à-vis their own organizations and constituencies, the more the interaction process will be connected with its wider environment. The administrative experience of these top-level managers and authorities will have a moderating impact on conflicts. Their authoritativeness contributes to the legitimacy of the game and the willingness of parties to participate.

The coordination of concrete activities often occurs at the level of a steering group, where the game manager occupies an important position. This steering group coordinates the activities undertaken in the context of the interaction process and manages the interface with the consultation platform at the top level and the broader environment.

Concrete activities are taken up by working groups where stakeholders and experts meet. Here, problems are assessed and solutions designed. Activities are divided between specialized working groups in order to tackle them in an efficient and effective way. Of course, provisions for the integration of the findings and the products of the working groups have to be in place.

The choice of representatives in the interaction: preventing social asymmetries

The zinc case revealed the importance of avoiding social asymmetries with regard to which persons should represent involved parties in the diverse sub-arenas of the

---

Box 9.3 A working group on safety in designing a high-speed railway in the Netherlands

How the work division and integration in interaction processes are organized ought to be a matter of great concern. For instance, there is the risk of isolating interest in sub-arenas. During the planning of the high-speed railway between Amsterdam and the Belgian border, a special working group on safety was created. This might indicate that the interests of safety were acknowledged by the project leaders. The creation of this working group certainly offered the various institutions involved in safety issues (Ministry of Traffic, Public Works and Water Management, Ministry of Home Affairs, municipalities, emergency services) the opportunity to coordinate their varying safety concepts and develop an integral approach to safety. However, placing safety experts in a separate working group may, at the same time, prohibit the influence of safety considerations and ideas on the activities in other working groups. It may well be that by doing so the safety interest was marginalized instead of internalized.

interaction process. The representatives of the different stakeholders should be matched. A situation where one party sends managers or administrators while the other sends experts should be prevented. These individuals speak different languages and possess different skills and competencies. As a result, their interaction will probably not be very fruitful. Similarly, when companies send directors while the ministry is represented by 'lower-level' administrators, the interaction will also fail. In addition to this, one should realize that the level of representation of the parties has strong symbolic value. It reveals something about how important they consider the interaction. High-level representation contributes to the trust that parties have in the process and to their willingness to invest in it.

The function of multiple levels of interaction

The structuring of interaction through multiple sub-arenas contributes to the robustness of interaction. Since there is communication at different levels, it is possible to deal more effectively with differences of opinion and conflicts. When at a certain level differences of opinion escalate, blockades and fixations between parties involved will emerge. However, because of the multiple layers of interaction that have been created, this conflict does not necessarily jeopardize further interaction between parties (de Bruijn et al., 2002). In other working groups and at other levels, other representatives of the same parties are still communicating. This prevents conflict from escalating because these representatives have different concerns, being engaged in different activities. They have developed loyalties to their counterparts with whom they interact, making it possible for them to place the conflict in a different perspective or to provide opportunities for new trade-offs.

Agreements with regard to working methods

Within the different working groups, various approaches and methods of working can be used (Susskind and Cruikshank, 1987). So, agreements can also be made with regard to the methods of working, e.g. the type of research that is to be conducted, the information system used, or the approaches used to facilitate interaction between stakeholders. In the zinc case, for instance, the methods used for developing zinc norms and the use of life-cycle analysis to determine environmental effects of zinc and zinc products were quite influential on the way the interaction between parties developed. These methods became part of the controversy themselves. Since it is important that participants in the process have insight and trust in the methods used, it is wise to involve them in the decisions by which the methods are chosen.

Rules regarding information

Parties will often make agreements about how they will use information or information systems and about the accessibility of this information for others.

Different perceptions about the role of information

Regarding information, public parties will emphasize the need for transparency and openness. This is not self-evident to private actors. They may fear that company-sensitive information or innovative ideas will be leaked to competitors. Or that information provided to public parties will be used by them to propose unfavourable regulation or contract conditions.

These different perceptions about information, transparency and openness can inhibit interaction and cooperation, and it is important that parties reach agreements that give adequate consideration to the various positions. When, for instance, parties are working together on a regional or national traffic information system (road managers, police, public transport companies, taxi companies, consumer organizations, governments, media, computer and software companies), some parties will participate because they want to have a commercial product in the marketplace. While governmental organizations view information as a public good that must be available to all, from a market perspective, information has a monetary value. The question is whether agreements can be made that differentiate information types and information streams in such a way that the public interest (providing free information about the traffic situation to the public) and the commercial interests (the commercial use of information for which certain target groups are willing to pay) can be reconciled.

Addressing a wider audience

It is also important for parties to agree on the information that gets communicated to the outside world. Parties involved in a conflict may want to address the media in order to win – or they might use this as a threat in the hope that they will get their way. Of course, this mobilization strategy may jeopardize the relations between parties engaged in the game. It introduces new uncertainties and changes the balance of power that has been developed during the interaction process. Although the inclination may be to forbid this behaviour, one might question whether this is sensible. Instead, it seems wise to develop an agreement about a mutual communication plan – certainly when the transparency of what goes on in the process enhances the external legitimacy and provides third parties the time to respond to proposals of the cooperating parties. A better approach than trying to prevent parties from using public opinion is making an agreement about the condition under which they are allowed to do so. As long as parties do not undermine cooperation through, for instance, frontal attacks on each other's reliability, it is wise to work with a certain tolerance for the fact that parties must blow off steam and occupy strong positions in order to put their constituency at ease.

Rules regarding process steps and time-schedules

Parties can try to reduce uncertainty by making agreements about the steps that will be taken and time-frames connected with them. Often, the first step involves mapping the problem followed by the steps of generating, elaborating and selecting solutions. Usually, parties will want to separate these steps by intervals during which the results of the previous step are communicated to the outside world and formal decisions that set the conditions for the next round of interaction can be taken. Also, they may link these steps to certain times or deadlines in order to assure the progress of the process.

The principle of parallel development

Given the character of complex policy games, it is not very fruitful for parties to opt for a project management approach to the process of problem solving. While there may be an understanding between parties about the content of the next step, there is usually uncertainty about what must happen after that and where the process will end. As we argued earlier, when one tries to acquire consensus about the problem analysis or the direction of the problem solving process at the beginning of the process, conflict may arise and parties may exit. By making loose couplings between the various process steps, by parallel development of problem formulations and solutions, and by postponing selection, substantive variety emerges: various and competing problem formulations, solutions and measures can be seen alongside each other. This will provide decision makers with the opportunity to choose between alternatives and also to combine elements of these alternatives in order to create solutions or packages that realize beneficial trade-offs, bringing about improvements for all, or compensations in the case of losses.

Deadlines

Establishing and manipulating deadlines is a powerful instrument to influence the course of a game. When parties have the idea that 'something is about to happen', their willingness to participate and to invest resources will increase. But deadlines can also have counter-productive effects. Since the content of interaction is not given at the start, it is often difficult to determine how much time will be necessary to attain results. Too much time pressure will jeopardize the quality of the interaction (Bronner, 1982). Hence, the 'blind' use of deadlines, makes little sense and can endanger the quality of the game and its outcomes. A deadline is not an output variable, to which parties can be held accountable, but rather a beacon in an ambiguous interaction process. The time schedule might have to be adjusted after each step when parties have acquired more insight into what the next step will be about.

Actors can use deadlines strategically. When parties use time pressure to force their own favourite solution and prevent substantive discussion, conflict will result (Koppenjan, 2001). On the other hand, parties who do not like the direction of the problem solution may use delaying tactics. When participants or game managers commit to a deadline, they make themselves vulnerable to such delaying tactics.

Finally, an important observation is that parties may use a different time perspective for their activities than others do: generally internal activities are given more time than external activities such as providing feedback to the electorate and constituencies, external advising, and input by third parties (Boniecki, 1980; McGrath, 1988). This jeopardizes external support for the process of problem solving and the quality of the solutions generated in the process.

Rules about decision making

Parties who enter the interaction will want to make agreements about how decisions are made. Since parties often participate voluntarily, in principle, each party has the opportunity to leave the interaction process and a common decision can only be made when all parties are in agreement. However, during the course of the process, parties might want to bind themselves to stricter decision making rules in order to further progress, since they have acquired an interest in realizing a solution.

On decision criteria and the delay of substantive decisions

If efforts to determine criteria for the selection of solutions are made at the beginning of the process, the process will quickly grind to a halt. This premature decision making will invariably fail to consider all parties' perceptions and objectives adequately. Instead, parties may want to make general agreements about the object of the interaction and about the dos and don'ts. Criteria will become clearer during the course of the process. A final understanding about the content of the solutions and the distribution of costs, benefits and the risks involved will only emerge at the end of the process.

This goes along with the notion that the selection of substantive proposals must be conducted as late as possible. An early selection will remove any incentive for parties to contribute their resources and ideas in order to create new profitable opportunities, and learning experiences and opportunities for adaptation to changing environmental influences will be excluded. For some parties, the profit may have already been achieved; they can take it easy. For others there is little gain or there may even be loss. Parties should refrain from an early selection in order to avoid loss of interest, conflict, or attempts to impede the progress of the problem solving.

Conflict regulation

Agreements about how parties will resolve conflicts over knowledge, solutions, direction and methods of working are crucial (Ostrom, 1990; Burton, 1996). Such agreements further the transparency of the process and protect parties against opportunistic behaviour. Furthermore, they contribute to the creation of a level playing field: offering a last resort for weaker parties and for minorities if their arguments are not heard or not taken seriously.

Conflict regulation agreements determine how a conflict will be dealt with before the conflict has arisen and escalating emotions make any agreements unlikely. One agreement might be about procedures for appealing against a decision. When multiple levels of interaction have been created, parties engaged in the conflict will appeal to the next higher level. Ultimately, when conflicts cannot be settled in this manner, mediation or arbitration will be necessary. Agreements on conflict regulation should include rules about how mediation and arbitration will be organized.

Conflict regulation mechanisms also have a strong symbolic meaning: they are, after all, a type of insurance against opportunistic behaviour and thus contribute to the trust that parties – who do not yet know each other very well – have in the interaction process. Thus, they contribute to the emergence of mutual trust and make parties' access to policy games easier.

Rules about communication with the environment

Parties should also agree on how they will communicate the outcomes of their interaction with others in their environment. Primarily, this involves organizing the interface between representatives of organizations in interaction arenas and their constituencies and parent organizations.

The principle of 'loose couplings'

These feedback relations can best be shaped by means of 'loose couplings' (Weick, 1979). This is relevant to both the mandates that officials in parent organizations give their representatives as well as to the degree to which the negotiation results are binding. Tight frameworks and rigid starting points at the outset of the game (or game round) limit opportunities for seeking mutual benefits and hence opportunities for goal entwinement. Rather, they give rise to fixation of content and relations. The end of the process also requires 'loose coupling'. There is 'tight coupling' when parties want the public and private office holders in their parent organizations to accept the outcome of their interaction without alterations. In practice, such an agreement is a guarantee for conflict at the end of the process when the outcomes of interaction do not meet up with the expectations of persons and organizations not actively involved (Klijn and Koppenjan, 2002a and 2003).

It makes much more sense to loosely couple the outcome of the interaction process to the decision making in formal arenas. This means that although interacting parties have no certainty about whether their proposals will get through unchanged, there will be a greater chance that their arguments and solutions will play an important role in further decision making. Instead of trying to eliminate uncertainty by demanding *ex ante* commitments and cartes blanches, it should be possible to *manage* the interface with decision makers in formal institutionalized decision making arenas. The opportunities for influencing formal decision making are greatest when learning processes are not limited to the most direct participants in the game, and when there is continuous communication with the broader environment. Thus, formal decision makers, third parties and the public at large can experience the learning process as well – at least in its main outline.

Table 9.2 Game management as process design: making agreements about the rules of the game

Category of rules	Description of rules
Rules concerning the objective of interaction	Defining the objectives of interaction, the agenda and dos and don'ts where the guiding principle is an open agenda
Rules concerning participation	Indicating participants, their quality, and entry and exit rules
Rules about methods of working	Structuring work activities via sub-arenas, task division, inclusion of research and experts, symmetrical representation, and work forms in which the principle of multiple cross-links is used
Rules about information	Determining between whom, in what manner and under what conditions information is exchanged, internally as well as externally
Rules concerning the steps in the interaction process	Setting the timing and sequence of activities, what deadlines apply and how these are handled. The principle of parallel ordering is used here as much as possible
Rules about decision making	Determining what criteria and decision rules apply, who makes decisions, how the decision making will proceed and what objection or appeal procedures apply
Rules concerning external coordination	Setting the timing, intensity and nature of communication with constituencies, the larger environment, third party interests and the media, using the principle of loose coupling

9.5 Game management as facilitating the game

One of the agreements that parties can make and that has not been mentioned in the previous section is how, and by whom, they will let their interaction be supported. The questions here are what the role of the facilitator or process manager can be, who will perform this role, what means have to be available and who will provide them (O'Toole, 1988; Forester, 1989; Moore, 1986).

When choosing a facilitator or process manager, it is crucial for parties to trust the impartiality of this person or actor. When a party claims process management on the basis of substantive involvement, it may be the signal to others that the room for discussing the content of the solution is limited. Their contribution is then seen in the light of legitimizing a solution that has already been decided, or there is at least the risk that the process manager may confront them with unpleasant surprises in the interaction to come. It is thus important that the facilitator holds a neutral position with regard to the content of the problem and its solutions. He must have the trust of the parties involved, must have sufficient means and competencies, and be perceived as authoritative (Lynn, 1981). This role can be fulfilled by both public and private parties and the function should not be linked to an individual. A temporary bureau can be created in which various individuals with complementary competencies and representing various

Box 9.4 An example of a process design: involving citizens in local community planning

As an example of a process design, we present an experimental project of the Institute for the Public and Politics regarding interactive decision making processes in Dutch municipalities (Klijn and Koppenjan, 2003). This Amsterdam-based institute aims at increasing political and societal participation. The IPP initiated the experimental project with a focus on developing an overview of the various experiences with interactive decision making in municipalities and at other levels of government. The project's objective is to evaluate the potential and limitations of this approach and to further develop the approach. In cooperation with an inter-university research team and a number of municipalities, several experiments have been initiated: two-year projects where an interactive work style – developed according to a process design by the IPP – is attempted and evaluated. Below, we present the content of the general IPP design.

The IPP design

The IPP design for interactive decision making processes is focused on establishing political–administrative commitment, the clear formulation of conditions and coordination between the process design and political and administrative processes. The IPP includes the commitment of the mayor and aldermen and also of the council (by way of committee) in their respective roles as facilitator(s) and commissioners of the process. This commitment is realized through a formal decision about a procedure proposal of the IPP at the end of a consultation and by a decision on the assignments for work projects that develop various solutions.

With regard to *participation* and the relevant roles, the generic process design assumes that citizens will be involved from the start as co-designers of policy. This results in a new set of roles: from the very beginning, citizens and council members are involved in formulating problems and developing potential solutions. The municipal council (or committee) acts as commissioner. It establishes conditions for the creation of variety by formulating assessment criteria for the solutions prior to the process. Meanwhile, the council members express their ideas about problem formulation and solution alternatives. Thus, they actively participate in the interactive process since they become acquainted with the arguments and proposals that are brought to the table. At the end of the process, the council's role changes to that of a decision maker. Decision aspects are initially prepared in mutual consultation with all participants and the council also debates with all participants in one or more public debates during the course of decision making. The Board of mayor and aldermen establishes conditions but has no steering role. Civil servants serve all participants in the project, not only the council members. Together with external experts, they provide citizens with background information and make corrections if unrealistic proposals are brought to the table.

The *structuring of the interaction* in the generic IPP design is as follows. Daily coordination of activities is provided by a core group of municipal representatives together with the IPP. A discussion group chaired by the IPP discusses the most important steps in the process. All parties involved participate in this discussion group. It is thus possible to respond to unexpected circumstances. Hence, decision making and conflict management are regulated within the process.

The process design contains several process steps. In the first *consultancy phase*, meta-decision making occurs: the IPP drafts a procedure proposal or process design after hearing all those involved speak on the topic and method of working. This process design is submitted for approval to the Board of mayor and aldermen and to the council. In the *agenda formation phase*, the problem is defined, partially on the basis of a telephone or written survey. This survey is conducted by council members to the greatest extent possible. During the phase of identifying the problems, inspection can be used, e.g. visiting the problem area. In an introductory public meeting, the initial basis for generating solutions can be determined, which will be confirmed or amended by the Board and council. In the third phase, *the exploration and design of solutions*, citizens formulate solutions in so-called 'workshops', preferably together with politicians. In a public meeting, the intermediate results of the work studios are presented. In the fourth phase, *the Board prepares a draft council decision*. Participants in the work studios will express their opinion about this draft. This is followed by an investigation of the support within the population at large. At a public meeting, the Board states why certain proposals have not been included. Then, the council makes a *final decision*. Prior to phase six, *implementation*, agreements are made about the role of citizens during implementation.

In this presentation of the process, the most important working methods have also been mentioned: the survey, the monitoring, public meetings, workshops and support surveys. Council and Board members are assumed to participate in these activities.

Lessons from the IPP design

Although the IPP design was not a complete failure in the practice of five local projects, it did generate a number of problems. This experience shows that process designs can violate the basic requirements of good game management, as outlined at the start of this chapter. Rules may then prove to be counter-productive and divide parties rather than unite them. The problems with the rules of the game as formulated in the IPP design involved the following issues:

- The design prescribed tight coupling between outcomes of interaction and formal decision making. This resulted in conflicts at the end of the process when it appeared that formal decision makers had only participated in a limited manner in the process – contrary to the general design – and were confronted with outcomes they did not want to be responsible for.
- The design provided an overly idealistic definition of roles for parties. The assumption was that they would interact under Habermasian conditions of power-free dialogue instead of pursuing their own objectives and using strategic behaviour (Habermas, 1981). Even the citizens, who in the design had been placed on a pedestal, approached the process opportunistically. They were not at all concerned with the principle of participation, but simply with the question 'what can be gained?'. The design was naive and, what is worse, by being naive offered participants, and especially citizens, insufficient protection against the opportunistic behaviour of others.

- Structuring participation was done based on a concern for equality and was insufficiently inspired by differences in interests, risks and resources. In one of the experiments, the private parties who were important suppliers of funding for the plans that had to be realized, did not get a separate position in the process because of the notion that all parties should be treated equally. This resulted in a situation where the process design became an immediate subject of conflict and the interaction could only proceed once private parties had strengthened their position.
- To a large degree, the design was an academic and bureaucratic exercise. The design was made in close cooperation between the IPP and municipalities involved. Interested parties were consulted, the outcome of which was set in a written agreement that was also presented before a plenary of the various participants. But, when push came to shove, representatives of interacting parties appeared to be unaware of these agreements or had certainly not internalized them.

Reaching agreement on rules between parties who do not know one another, come from different backgrounds and want to protect themselves against high costs and interaction risks, can help initiate the exchange of ideas and coordination of strategies. Still, this does not mean that any design is better than no design. Rules may prove to be inadequate or even counter-productive. Also, the way the rules are developed and communicated can influence the remainder of the process and could be a source of difficulties or even failure.

organizations cooperate. Furthermore, the nature and content of process management may change during the interaction process.

In addition to who will be the facilitator, parties can reach agreements about what this role must accomplish. Clarity is important in order to prevent the role of facilitator from becoming subject to conflict on the grounds of unclear or mistaken task expectations. What tasks the facilitator fulfils depends upon the rules of the game actors have agreed upon. It is important for the facilitator to mainly fulfil a procedural role. He is neither an entrepreneur nor a project manager. He himself has no direct responsibility for the creation and quality of substantive solutions. Parties will be responsible for progress and content of the process.

Nevertheless, procedural decisions may have substantial influence on the progress of the process and its content and outcomes. For instance the facilitator may have a major impact on the agenda setting process because of the themes he puts up for discussion or the actors he involves. Here, the issue of the hidden power of the facilitator plays a role (Edelenbos and Monnikhof, 2001).

It would be unwise for the facilitator to make such decisions on his own authority. He would be taking on too much responsibility and would risk becoming a party among parties. Instead, he should formulate proposals and leave decisions to the interacting parties. The development of a closed circuit between game manager and the most central parties in the interaction, in which these types of decisions are taken behind the scenes, should be prevented. Decisions about the organization and methods of the process should be made in a transparent manner and in interaction with parties involved. Agreements about process management will, in any case, also include provisions about to whom and in what manner the game manager is accountable.

Activities of the process facilitator

Earlier we indicated that the agreements parties make to shape and support their interaction are not automatically followed, nor do they stay unchanged during the interaction. The creation, implementation and adjustment of the rules of the game is an ongoing process wherein the facilitator or process manager plays an important supporting role (Brown, 1983; Agranoff, 1986; Moore, 1986; Susskind and Cruikshank, 1987; O'Toole, 1988; Forester, 1989; Kickert *et al.*, 1997; de Bruijn *et al.*, 2002). The facilitator:

- Explores and explicates profit opportunities for parties, (de)couples actors, arenas and games, and recruits and motivates parties to participate in inter-action.
- Provides meeting facilities, draws up the agenda, administers the interaction and the necessary information and information systems.
- Invests in the social aspects of cooperation and furthers the creation of a favourable climate in which parties meet.
- Improves interaction by asking for understanding of the core values that parties pursue as well as for their problem perceptions and objectives. He articulates the concerns that parties have and puts them up for discussion before they result in conflict.
- Helps determine process agreements, and to that end explores the expecta-tions and objectives of parties as well as their mutual differences, makes suggestions, and ensures that differences and areas of agreement are raised for discussion. He also ensures that agreements are written down, signals whether they function properly, reports his observations to the parties involved and proposes changes.
- Prevents early substantive standpoints and furthers the creation of substan-tive variety.
- Protects the substantive quality of the discussion by ensuring that expert know-ledge is brought into the process according to principles of disentanglement and boundary work (see Chapter 8). He signals the existence of negotiated nonsense and confronts parties with the perceptions and interests of outsiders.
- Raises questions to clarify discussions, signals misunderstandings, social asym-metries, differences in language and tries to find solutions for these.
- Signals contradictions, fixations, conflicts and impasses, and takes care of mediation: ensuring that relations are maintained; opens up channels or keeps them open; explores standpoints; explores possible solutions through, e.g. 'shuttle diplomacy' and putting out feelers; makes procedural and, on occasion, substantive proposals; makes suggestions for carrying out research, involving legal or technical exports and so forth.

- If necessary, proposes arbitration for the solution of conflicts: appoints a committee of 'wise men' and asks them to come up with solutions for breaking the impasse.
- Signals opportunities and threats in the environment of the interaction process and suggests proposals for using these in order to improve the quality and progress of cooperation.
- Keeps the agenda up to date and attractive to parties by drawing attention to new developments, new insights and new opportunities.
- Protects the external legitimacy and embeddedness of the process by assessing which insights and decisions in the process must be communicated externally with regard to timing, content and type of interaction with the constituents, third parties and the public at large.
- Ensures the creation of a level playing field by signalling information differences, under-representations and capacity limitations among actors; puts these on the agenda and makes proposals to resolve them.

Management strategies of the facilitator in various game rounds

During the interaction process, the nature and content of these activities change. At the beginning of the interaction, the facilitator will make every effort to get the process going and to motivate parties to join. He will identify opportunities for goal entwinement and present these to parties in order to generate their interest. He will also discover whether parties feel a sense of urgency to work together. If this is not the case, he can try to establish a sense of urgency, for instance through finding a party who will exert external pressure or by searching for a possible link with important events, accidents or crises that could serve as a trigger or point to the temporary nature of opportunities for benefit. The facilitator will not demand a commitment from parties to the outcomes of interaction, but will ask parties instead to commit themselves to the process. He will try to moderate claims for unrealistic commitments and demands upon the process. He will also warn against early substantive position taking. Instead, he will organize a platform for discussion about how parties can interact. He will help establish a situation where parties agree on rules of the game and codify these in flexible arrangements. Thus, he takes care of the quality of these agreements by including expert knowledge in the process design. He furthers a match between representatives of parties and a proper role distribution between stakeholders and experts. He furthers the communication about the process design to participants, constituencies and the environment and their acceptation and internalization of it.

During the process, the facilitator endeavours to keep it going. He can do this by keeping the agenda attractive, noticing opportunities, supporting the creation of substantive variety, translating conflict points into research questions, translating research results into design activities, and proposing questions for further investigation. He sees to it that actors' interests do not come under pressure and encourages parties to look for measures acceptable to all. Where parties are not yet in agreement, he will try to postpone selection; where consensus emerges and further discussion will add little to the propositions already there, he can further selection and commitment. Renegotiations, though, continue to be possible. The facilitator notices deviations from agreements and confronts parties with these. In the case of stagnation or conflicts he introduces new ideas and, if necessary, sees to mediation or arbitration. He emphasizes the need for coordination with constituents of the participants (office holders in public and private organizations or political bodies) and for communication with the environment. He tries to prevent the process separating from the environment. He notices new developments, opportunities and threats in the environment and develops proposals for adaptation of the agenda, the group of participants and the rules of the game.

When an interaction process is nearing the end, centrifugal forces will become stronger. Actors want to cash in on profit and loss so that incentives for prudent behaviour decline. Chances for opportunistic behaviour and conflict increase. Parties will try to utilize opportunities; when profit is gained or loss is inevitable, they will try to back out of agreements. The facilitator will point parties to future dependencies and profit opportunities and will actively seek these in order to moderate behaviour and solidify commitment. When parties fail to keep their agreements, the facilitator will make this visible for other parties and the environment in order to use the social and political control mechanisms that may generate moderation. In addition, conflict management and arbitration remain important in this round.

In addition to preventing loss of interest in this phase, the facilitator can make the effort to keep choices open. For instance, by not focusing on a design that everybody must agree to but, instead, holding several alternatives open. Thus, the room for manoeuvre for formal decision makers in the organizations involved – who most likely have not participated directly in the interaction – is enlarged. As a result, they develop an interest in the interaction process, so that the interaction does not limit their room for manoeuvre. This means that a loose coupling exists between interaction and decision making. It is not certain that the products of interaction will be realized and implemented. At the same time, the chance is greater that ideas and learning behaviour in that process will spill over into following rounds of interaction, decision making and implementation. Attempts to reduce uncertainty by committing parties to the outcomes of interaction result in tough confrontations in this round. It is better to invest in intermediate communication so that those involved, their constituencies and the wider environment become receptive to cognitive learning effects, substantive ideas and solutions generated in the interaction process.

Hence, the qualities of the facilitator or process manager are, to a large extent, in the area of empathy, diplomatic skills, tacit knowledge, procedural creativity, motivation and integrity. Affinity with the content of the problem area is necessary in order to identify substantive profitable opportunities and negotiated nonsense. Too great a substantive expertise, however, can be counter-productive: the facilitator should not identify himself with a particular problem formulation or solution direction or act like an expert. If this happens, he will lose the trust parties have in him and thus his authority.

All in all, facilitating games is labour intensive. This is often underestimated by the parties involved. There is a danger that facilitators lack sufficient capacity

Table 9.3 Management strategies for facilitating interaction processes

At the start of interaction	During interaction	At the end of interaction
• Identify and emphasize opportunities for mutual benefits and sense of urgency • Postpone commitments and substantive positions • Create a platform • Further agreement on rules of the game and 'soft' arrangements • Make suggestions for parallel planning and concurrent research • Advance internal and external communication and internalization of rules • Provide organizational and administrative conditions, attend to staffing and division of roles	• Keep the agenda attractive • Challenge parties to look for mutual gains and goal entwinement • Stimulate variety of content • Translate conflict into research questions • Translate research finding into alternatives for action • Look for opportunities for preliminary selection and commitment • Identify and manage impasses and conflicts • Watch over core interests, transparency and representation • Guard communication with parent organizations, third parties and general public • Scan internal and external developments for opportunities and threats and make suggestions to update agenda, participation and rules of the game	• Look for and emphasize opportunities for goal entwinement and compensation • Guard loose couplings and the provision of fully fledged alternatives instead of one 'take it or leave it' solution • Mobilize informal mechanisms and external environment to moderate strategies and to reduce exits • Provide opportunities for mediation and arbitration • Identify and articulate future dependencies and opportunities • Suggest opportunities for further cooperation

and succumb to the created information overload during the interaction process (Lynn, 1981; Susskind and Cruikshank, 1989; de Bruijn *et al.*, 2002).

9.6 Conclusion: conditions for managing strategic uncertainties

In this chapter, we discussed a variety of activities that can be used to bring parties together in complex games around wicked problems. But we must immediately note that while these activities can be considered a condition for the coordination of strategies between parties, they do not offer any guarantees.

For instance, it is far from sure that the game management strategies discussed here will be used in the correct manner. Interventions may be carried out incorrectly, couplings may lack a perspective for profit, agreed rules of the game may be counter-productive, and process managers may make wrong decisions. Added to this is the fact that experiences with game management are rarely documented or systematically evaluated. Thus, it is too early to outline a range of empirically grounded 'good practices'.

The principles of game management, which are formulated on the basis of the network approach, are contrary to the dominant ideas in practice about line and project management. This means that the tolerance for game management is limited: patience and restraint, necessary for interaction processes to come about and produce results, are rare qualities in societal problem solving. This reduces the likelihood that game management will be chosen and that it will be implemented in line with the requirements outlined in this chapter.

A condition for successful game management is that parties are willing to cooperate. When that willingness is present, the ideas formulated in this chapter about managing strategic uncertainties may be helpful in order to prevent spoiling favourable conditions in the interaction by using substantive approaches or principles of line or project management. If this willingness is absent, game management initiatives are often a waste of time or likely to fail.

Finally, despite all activities described in this chapter, one must not hold the illusion that the game around the solution of a wicked problem can be controlled with game management and that all strategic uncertainties can be banished. The best that participants can expect from game management is that there are provisions which make them less vulnerable for opportunistic behaviour and the unpredictability of developments in the game and in its surroundings. The game, however, still has to be played and the challenges it provides still have to be faced.

Chapter 10

Managing the network
Strategies for institutional design

10.1 Introduction: intertwinement or disentanglement?

As argued in Part 1, uncertainty in decision making on wicked problems in networks also has an institutional side. Policy games around wicked problems do not proceed in a vacuum, but in an institutional context where lasting rules, interaction patterns and stable patterns of perceptions can influence the interactions between the involved parties. Attempts at managing uncertainty can stretch into the institutional aspects of networks. We call this *institutional design*: efforts to adapt existing institutional provisions to new circumstances or to develop new provisions. Institutional design is not easy since many institutions cannot be directly influenced and, furthermore, they are embedded in a complicated and difficult-to-oversee entirety of provisions. As a result, an attempt to steer may cause all sorts of unintended consequences. With these strategies, we also touch upon normative and political–ideological themes. These include questions such as what are the core tasks of government, and to what degree and under what conditions may government intervene in societal processes in order to change the positions and authorities of other actors? Yet in practice we see many attempts to change the institutional structure of networks. Before discussing various strategies in the next sections, it is first necessary to outline the normative starting points which form the basis of our ideas about institutional design. We do so by placing the idea of institutional design in context: that is, against the background of the discussions about intertwinement and disentanglement which have been waged in Western countries in the past twenty years.

Intertwinement or disentanglement?

Almost unanimously, political and administrative science opinion about the relations between state and society, government and interest groups, state and societal associations, or whichever other approach is taken, concludes that increasing intertwinement exists (see, for instance, Heisler, 1974; Hanf and Scharpf, 1978; Richardson and Jordan, 1979; Hanf and Toonen, 1985; Ripley and Franklin, 1987). The demarcation between the public and private spheres has diminished substantially, the involvement of private, semi-private or independent public institutions in policy making and implementation has increased markedly, and the complexity of policy processes has increased enormously. These developments have been discussed extensively in this book.

This also applies to attempts to remove this intertwinement. In Chapter 5, we paid attention to the ideas of New Public Management, which advocates the idea of disentanglement, especially through the separation of policy making and implementation. Many reforms in the public sector during the past two decades (see, for instance, Kickert, 1997; Pollitt and Bouckaert, 2000) have also been inspired by the notion of disentanglement. Measures such as establishing greater independence, privatization, new types of contracting out and the discussion about a renewed primacy of politics are all attempts to reduce, or at least change, the institutional intertwinement that emerged in the post-war welfare state.

Almost all management interventions aimed at institutional design concern the discussion about disentanglement and intertwinement. What is interesting in this context is the observation, also mentioned earlier in this book, that disentanglement measures such as greater independence, privatization or innovative types of contracts, simply create intertwinement in another manner. Thus, while innovative contracts do result in a certain degree of disentanglement since private consortiums are made responsible for the integral management of a provision, the long duration of the contract establishes intertwinement in terms of supervisory relations. Increased independence calls for separation and a more autonomous operation of formerly dependent agencies, but it also creates the need for establishing new interfaces to regulate the contacts between the agency and the contracting department (Homburg, 2001; van Thiel, 2002). Other examples are the attempts at intertwinement through horizontal types of steering and network management. Thus, processes of interactive decision making often lead to the explicit intertwinement of the input of citizens and societal groups to policy making, but often at the price of increased disentanglement with other public organizations or interested private organizations.

In the complex network society in which we live, the crucial question appears not to be merely one of intertwinement or disentanglement. Society is complex and the solution for many problems requires such an intricate coordination of knowledge contents, interests and institutions that disentanglement is an illusion. Rather, it involves the question of how to adapt existing types of institutional intertwinement which have become dysfunctional in the light of increasing mutual dependencies between societal activities, problems and sectors. Attempts at disentanglement go hand in hand with furthering and establishing new types of intertwinement (re-intertwinement) that provide a robust and better starting point for tackling various complex and difficult problems.

Institutional design: fundamental and normative intervention?

Institutional design is a fundamental intervention since it is intervention in networks which have evolved over a long period of time under the influence of repeated interactions between a set of actors. Since institutions are gradually created in the context of a series of games – and are sometimes also formally anchored in rules and legislation – the adaptation of institutions is a long-term matter and often, in the light of a solution of a concrete problem, not a viable option. Institutions are not only instruments for tackling problems, but they are multi-purpose vehicles; they are provisions aimed at enabling and supporting societal relations by regulating the mutual interactions in dealing with various problem situations. They fulfil a guaranteed function with regard to the societal interests involved, and especially those interests that are not directly, or are weakly, represented. They are an expression of the modus vivendi which societal parties have established in the past and form the basis for the trust that parties need in uncertain situations when engaging in interaction. Thus, institutional design, much more than game management, concerns changing the delicate balance that has been established between various societal values and opening up for discussion the normative choices that have been made. But there must be good grounds for doing so. The legitimacy for carrying this out does not exist off-hand, all the more since changed interaction patterns and rules cannot be re-established when, in retrospect, the effects appear less positive than expected. After all, institutions can be viewed as institutional capital. In applying institutional design, one must be aware of interfering with an existing field of forces, and that the flip side of the creation of new institutions is the destruction of the old. Opposite the uncertainty about the viability of new institutions is the certainty of the destruction of the old. This means that institutional design must be used carefully and with restraint. Especially when this type of management is inspired by the pursuit to solve a concrete problem or realize a specific solution, one must ask whether such intervention is justified. Often such intervention is considered from a specific objective or value that does not consider the variety of values that might be of interest in the longer term and the perspective of a larger set of problems.

A better motive for institutional design is the observation that certain interests in various policy games are structurally under-represented. Institutional design then concerns the intertwinement of values and interests that are systematically excluded or under-represented by the existing institutions. Thus, it is not inspired by motives of effectiveness or efficiency in the first place. Rather, it concerns breaking through the institutionally anchored cognitive and social fixations upon such criteria as openness, integration and legitimacy.

The structure of this chapter

In this chapter, we discuss the most important strategies in the context of institutional design. Many of these will be elaborated with examples. In Part 1, we examined the content, the game, the interactions and the institutional characteristics of networks. All attempts to deal with the development of interactions through institutional design amount to changing the rules. Attempts to intervene directly in game interactions have been discussed in Chapter 9, so we will not pay separate attention to changing interactions. We call attempts to establish radical changes in the pattern of perception in the network 'reframing'.

In Section 10.2, we discuss strategies for changing rules in the network. In Section 10.3, we address strategies of reframing. In Section 10.4, we examine management strategies for enhancing trust. In Section 10.5, we discuss a proposal for reducing the tensions between the horizontal types of steering and the institution of 'primacy of politics'.

10.2 Changing network rules: tinkering at the foundation of the network

Rules form a sort of social infrastructure for networks. They make interactions and mutual action possible and provide actors with a context and basis for their actions. They are, as stated in Part 1, one of the robust characteristics of networks. But the logical conclusion is that when rules are formed by actors through interactions, they can also be changed by interactions. And when rules change, so do the frameworks and self-evident assumptions that actors use to work with and make and elaborate strategies. In short, changes in network rules will lead to different strategies and interaction patterns and, thus, to different solutions. It is from this logic that frequent attempts are made to change networks by changing the rules.

Types of strategies for changing rules: an overview

Several management strategies for changing rules can be distinguished. These can be classified in three categories:

- Strategies aimed at the *composition of the network*: these strategies are focused on changing or influencing the composition of the network. They aim to enlarge or decrease the number of actors, influence access, etc.
- Strategies aimed at *network outcomes*: these strategies attempt to have sustained influence upon standards or upon the cost-benefit logic so that games in networks develop differently because different strategic assessments are made. This involves efforts at changing the reward structure, changing professional codes and mores, etc.
- Strategies aimed at *network interactions*: these strategies attempt to have sustained influence upon the interactions between actors through, for instance, developing conflict management mechanisms or through creating certain procedures for interaction.

In Table 10.1, the most dominant and prevalent strategies are mentioned along with the types of rules that are influenced through that strategy. We use the same classification of types of rules as in Chapter 4.

Two remarks need to be made. First, in attempts to change rules in the network, more than one strategy is frequently used. Second, the table indicates which types of rules are changed by a certain strategy, but the manner in which this happens can vary greatly. In short, the table provides an analytic overview of the various strategies for changing rules in networks.

Table 10.1 Strategies for influencing and changing rules in networks

Strategy	Arena rules			Interaction rules	
	Identity/ product rules	Reward rules	Position rules	Access rules	Interaction rules
Network composition					
1 Change actor positions			X		
2 Fix actor positions	(X)			X	
3 Add actors			(X)	X	
4 Change access rules for games				X	
5 Influence network formation			(X)		X
6 Enhance self-regulation			(X)		X
7 System changes (e.g. marketization, reorganization)	X	X	(X)	X	X
Network outcomes					
1 Change evaluation criteria	X	(X)			
2 Influence reward structure	(X)	X			
3 Influence professional codes	X	(X)			
Network interactions					
1 Conflict regulation			(X)		X
2 Procedure development for interactions				(X)	X
3 Certification	X				X
4 Changing overview (relations)	(X)			X	X

Changes in network composition: actors, their positions and access rules

Changes in the composition of the network mean that game interactions that occur in that network may develop differently. By tinkering with the number of actors, their positions, the access rules, or other strategies that influence the composition or development of the network, other arenas and game areas are potentially created.

Pushing and pulling actors: solidifying and changing positions

The first two strategies in Table 10.1 accept the composition of the network as a given, but attempt to establish changes in the relations between the existing group of actors in a network. This can be done by changing the positions of certain actors or by explicitly formulating the actor positions. The latter concerns the formalization of domain rules in particular. This can be effective when cooperation is difficult because of domain conflicts and uncertainties. Especially in the case of new initiatives in relatively young networks, domain uncertainty can inhibit

Box 10.1 Creating new actors: PFI in road provision in the UK

One of the objectives of the Private Finance Initiative (PFI) in the UK in the area of road contracting was the creation of a new industry of private actors engaged in the construction, exploitation and financing of road projects. When examining the first eight large road projects that were contracted out in the middle of the 1990s (projects concluded in 1996), we can see that certain new consortiums were created that frequently bid on one of the projects. A total of eleven consortiums were involved in eight DFBO projects. Six of these had the winning bid one or more times. As was clear in Chapter 5, the procedure is to work towards a situation where two bidders remain. When we consider the remaining two consortiums and the winners and losers, it is clear that several consortiums were mentioned as winners and losers several times. Two consortiums won twice. Furthermore, in some cases the organizations of different consortiums were involved. In later negotiations about contracts, these again played an important role. Thus, we see that the intervention to change the rules of the game in the implementation of road provisions led to a substantial shake-up of the network but that after a while, stabilization occurred and a relatively set group of players formed around a policy issue. In short, a (new) process of network formation evolved, especially because the long-term contracts (30 years) involve long-term relations between public and private actors.

Source: Haynes and Roden, 1999; Immers, 2001.

interaction and cooperation either out of uncertainty about the boundaries of each other's domains or out of fear of losing one's own domain. The cooperation between actors from different networks may also lead to conflicts about the distribution of responsibility. Formalizing the competencies and domains of actors in rules can establish certainty from which further work is possible. Informal agreements about domains can be formalized. It is, however, also possible that together, actors design new domain agreements. Covenants and contracts may play a role as agreements made between equal actors. Solidifying positions especially concerns the position rules in the network but often also demands some reflection on the identity of the actors.

Changing the positions of actors in the network is a more sensitive matter than solidifying them. This almost always involves changing the power relations between actors in the network. A classic example of changing actor positions is the internationally famous Rotterdam city redevelopment where resident associations were assisted by external experts. These experts were usually educated in construction and supported residents in working groups on the city's redevelopment where decisions were made about destruction, new construction and improvement. They could present demands on behalf of the residents, translate them into city and architectural plans and, subsequently, assess costs. Thus, the residents' associations became full participants in the discussions about the city's redevelopment.

Changing access opportunities and actors: shaking up the network

Another way to influence the composition of the network is to introduce new actors. In this case, the access rules almost always have to be changed. These two strategies are therefore usually, though not necessarily, linked. Introducing new actors is pursued in order to acquire the participation of actors who are not part of the network. The Private Finance Initiative in the UK, and many other attempts by governments to contract out products or services to private actors, are an attempt to acquire new, in this case private contractors, into the network. As a result, this often involves changes in the access rules of the game. Thus, the PFI initiative in the UK assumed a contract length of 30 years in which, through DBFO (design, build, finance and operate) contracts, private parties were made responsible for road provision over an extended period of time. Not only did this attract new actors to the network, i.e. large consortiums who were truly able to manage the risk of such a large project in the longer term, but also different selection rules were applied and different reward rules were established. The strategy of changing access in the network can be pursued without introducing new actors, but then the strategy mainly appears to be one of changing the positions of the actors (at least in its effect). Thus, in the Netherlands, the geographical limitations of housing associations – which were previously allowed to operate *only* in one city – were made more flexible. In part due to changes in public housing (an increased market orientation and reduced subsidies), this quickly resulted in scale enlargement of housing associations (by means of merging) and in the creation of various associations which had housing stock in several cities. This has significantly changed the local public housing networks. Larger and capital-strong housing associations acquired a stronger position vis-à-vis local government. Another example of changing access rules without adding new actors is that the non-profit health insurers are no longer tied to a particular region but have access to the entire country, which improves competition.

In the PFI examples mentioned, the initiative is taken by public organizations who can change the bidding rules and also change the implementation of road construction and maintenance. One can imagine that actors in a network set these rules together.

Network formation, self-regulation and system change: a silent revolution?

Another way to influence the composition of the network is to improve the process of network formation. This can be done by creating special subsidies (for instance, premiums for an integral approach which can be an incentive for cooperation between actors from different networks). However, network formation can also occur within a network, as is clear, for example, from the use of subsidies for regional knowledge centres for medium and small businesses. It is known that medium and small businesses do not have large research and development units, so the exchange of knowledge between companies and businesses has a network-like character (Nooteboom, 1998). Regional knowledge centres can

Box 10.2 California Bay-Delta: adding actors and other reward rules

In the water management of the California Bay-Delta, the interests of energy provision and the environment (especially the protection of the fish stocks) frequently clash. Each decision has consequences for both systems, which makes water management very complex. Various methods have been developed to improve water management and the required interactions between actors. For example, there was an experiment with 'ecologists in the control room' where ecologists translated policy instructions in operational terms and used ecological information when making real decisions about water supply and electricity. By introducing actors in a game (the concrete implementation level) where they hitherto have not been involved, other assessments and trade-offs can be made and other information can be used in making these decisions.

Another example is the water budget, which concerns changes in the reward systems and assessments (see the subsection about influencing network outcomes). A water budget is a quantity of water which falls under the direct control of nature and environmental authorities. It can be used for specific ecological events (for instance, moving the salmon populations). Actors who consider actions in the context of environmental management can, at a certain moment, relinquish part of the amount of water available to them and 'save it' for when it is needed. The same can be done by actors with an interest in energy. It is an incentive to both parties (environment and energy) to assess the effectiveness of their demands and set priorities. The instrument of the water budget, thus, leads to a strategic response of actors in all games that continue in the future.

Source: van Eeten and Roe, 2002.

improve knowledge exchange. In mentioning knowledge networks and platforms, we have thus brought up an important type of network formation which has become very popular recently. Knowledge networks are both created by actors in networks and initiated by public organizations.

A more interventionist type of strategy is to promote *self-regulation*. This stimulates (sometimes compels) actors to take care of the quality of output themselves. This is done both by changing the reward rules (through specifications of output, performance indicators, etc.) as well as by influencing identity and product rules. A good example is the emergence of international accreditation systems for universities. Departments within universities are monitored less by the inspectors of government departments of education, and more by various sorts of 'peer reviews' where the departments must meet an a priori set of standards which is then assessed by committees of peers from various countries. Universities are then marginally tested by public inspection agencies, and the acquired accreditation and peer review plays an important role at that point.

The most radical changes in network composition are system reform and (large-scale) reorganization. These usually involve all sorts of rules in the network. Reorganization attempts such as the liberalization efforts in the European Union influence both the access and the interaction rules, as well as the position rules and even the identity and reward rules. The position of existing providers and the way in which providers behave (interaction rules) are affected and changed; and which players can access outcomes and products, and why, should also be considered. Thus the liberalization efforts of the EU in the transport sector have had substantial consequences for transport networks in the individual member states. The same holds for the opening up of the electricity market which has meant that, within certain European countries, providers no longer have monopoly positions but must compete nationally and internationally with other providers of electricity services.

Effort and assessment in games: adapting the reward and evaluation rules

Interactions can also be influenced by changing reward rules (for instance, through establishing or abolishing subsidies) or by attempting to change the rules that actors use to evaluate outcomes. The strategy of changing professional codes, as mentioned in Table 10.1, is related to, but more encompassing than, changing evaluation criteria. The last two strategies are certainly effective when inflexible product and identity rules make it difficult to evaluate problems and solutions using other than the accepted standards.

One problem can be that actors apply different evaluation criteria when assessing knowledge about problem solutions or other important matters. These evaluation criteria are solidly anchored to the identity of actors and the (professional) standards that they use. The zinc case demonstrates this. In such a situation, reframing is a strategy often recommended for changing the ideas of actors, but it can be difficult to apply (we discuss this in the next section). When identity and product rules are highly solidified, as was the case with zinc, the opportunities for radical changes in perceptions are limited and the identity and product rules, themselves, must be discussed first. In this case, it is better to work on the development and acceptance of more or less common evaluation criteria. These can then help to solve interaction problems and differences in interpretation about available knowledge in later conflicts.

Professional codes: influencing ways of looking and acting

It is more fundamental when the problem concerns professional codes and product rules of actors in the network, i.e. when the professional codes of actors in the network prohibit the solution of a wicked problem, either because certain solutions cannot yet be discussed or because the problem orientation is highly solidified. In this case, it becomes necessary to change the actors' product rules as well as the reward rules. Although the strategy itself concerns changes of product and reward rules, it is conceivable that the way this is achieved is based upon another change. Thus, subsidy rules that change the reward of games may also influence professional codes about what constitutes a good and desirable product.

During the Rotterdam city renewal in the 1980s, for instance, a strong and shared opinion existed about the end product (the renovated houses). This was inspired in part by the existing subsidy rules. By optimizing these, a product was achieved where the outer walls remained standing, while the renovations took place inside. When the subsidy regulations changed, that product became less attractive in terms of price–quality balance and other standards were developed about what constituted a good renovation project. Over the course of time, for instance, there was more demolition than renovation (see Klijn, 1996 and 2001).

Adapting the reward rules: influencing the pay-off

Here, we arrive at a different strategy that is often used when solving wicked problems: changing the reward rules. The simplest of these is, of course, the well-known instrument of the subsidy, but the example of PFI in the building of roads is also an example. By granting the contract to a consortium for thirty years, different reward rules were created: the consortium had an interest in long-term profit. Note, however, that the consortium also had to maintain a relationship with the public sector for a longer period. Hence, paradoxically, the emphasis upon division of responsibility (contracting and separating policy making from policy implementation) can lead to long-term reciprocal relations between the consortium and the public contracting agency (in this case, the Highways Agency).

Through subsidies, an incentive is created that changes the reward rules for the strategic action of other actors. Note that, in a network perspective, a different view of subsidies, and instruments in general, is used from in other approaches. Within this perspective, subsidies are considered to be one variable among many in the strategic assessment of the actors, providing an important condition, but certainly not the only one. The functioning of subsidies depends greatly upon the other issues (the other rules, the relations between actors, etc.) and the perceptions of the actors. Reward rules are not only of a pecuniary nature. They also include status, or what is regarded in a network as prestigious outcomes. These reward rules are less formal and less easy to trace, and changing them is more a matter of patience and discussion about the value of such outcomes. But the two aspects are often linked. In changing the subsidy rules, the Rotterdam city renewal was transformed, as was the professional appreciation of the resulting homes. The houses built according to the old standards (and within the old subsidy rules) were regarded as efficient but not attractive from an architectural point of view. Thus, the prestige related to certain products changed. No longer was it more important to build good, efficient and (especially) cheap housing, but it became increasingly important to make these houses attractive to a variety of target groups.

Influencing network interactions: regulating conflict and designing procedures for interactions

Finally, strategies can be aimed at influencing and changing interaction patterns between actors in networks for the longer term. As with the other strategies of institutional design we discussed earlier, the intervention here is not in the outcomes but in the interaction context. The strategy is aimed at making interactions easier or at framing the interactions by establishing general rules for them.

Conflict regulation: solving and channelling conflicts

Network games frequently involve conflicts. This is not surprising given the various interests of the actors and the range and complexity of possible solutions and

---

Box 10.3 The zinc case: conflict regulation, designing procedures and monopoly positions in research

One of the problems in the decisions on zinc emissions concerns the role of research institutions such as RIVM, which is related to the Department of Housing, Spatial Planning and the Environment (in Dutch: VROM). RIVM practically holds a monopoly position with regard to scientific research concerning the environment. The policy makers at VROM use their scientific insights blindly and regard them as the domain of RIVM. Furthermore, RIVM uses certain criteria of status and reliability of research. The research done by the zinc industry was simply not considered legitimate. In the eyes of RIVM (and the policy makers at VROM), the research simply did not meet the professional codes for research. Furthermore, the world of environmental research was somewhat closed in that most specialists involved were in the orbit of the RIVM scientific network. The asymmetric discussion was, thus, enhanced by the institutional characteristics of the network with regard to standards of research, the position of research institutions, and the closedness of the scientific sub-network to outsiders. This only changed somewhat after 2000 when representatives of the zinc industry, after substantial critique, became involved in the research discussion.

It is striking that as soon as the discussion moved to the international level, RIVM met with increased opposition. Big international players in the zinc industry, such as the Union Minière, involved other (foreign) scientific institutions in the discussion so that it became much more diverse.

This example not only shows how strict domain demarcations and existing codes can inhibit a substantive discussion, but it also demonstrates that improving variety and competition is good for substantive discussion. In this case, breaking through a closed network by allowing other research institutes in, or by reducing the monopoly position of existing research institutes, is an interesting option for network management. In doing so, the manager uses the strategies described above (see strategies for network composition). But it is also possible to improve variety through conflict regulation and the establishment of procedures. In this case, one can imagine giving the zinc industry a position in the remainder of the procedure in which research and norm setting are conducted. Critique can then enter the process. But also, some kind of conflict regulation strategy, where research results are re-examined by an external research institute (for instance, a foreign one), could play a meaningful role.

problem formulations. It is often difficult to make agreements within the game itself on how to handle conflicts and disagreements. In the first place, at the point when conflicts arise, relations are not usually conducive to reaching good conflict regulations. But more important than that is the fact that actors can more or less assess the effect of possible conflict regulation mechanisms on their conflict. The conflict regulations themselves then become part of the conflict. In short, developing rules will be influenced by the conflict itself.

This means that conflict regulation mechanisms cannot be designed during the conflict but must be arranged by actors prior to the conflict. Given that such designed rules of the game literally regulate many games, this constitutes a case of institutional design (see Klijn, 1996). There are all sorts of conflict regulation mechanisms. For instance, actors can appoint an arbitrator who can make binding decisions when differences arise. They then effectively sacrifice the strategic margin for action during future conflict. There is thus a strong incentive to try very hard to arrive at an acceptable situation. The 'conflict' commissions, which exist in various European countries to determine the outcome of labour conflicts, are an example of such a construction.

Another manner of conflict regulation is regulating the procedure in the case of conflict. This can range from employing a mediator to submitting the conflict to a judicial body. In such a situation, a whole range of procedural steps is agreed, instead of appointing a body that makes binding decisions.

Finally, an important method of conflict regulation is the creation and appointment of official bodies that examine complaints and concerns. The ombudsman, an institution found in many European countries, is one example of an institution to which citizens can submit their complaints about public organizations.

Conflict regulation mechanisms can be regulated in various ways. Cooperating actors in a network can establish contracts or other agreements together and for a longer term. They can also be arranged through public law (either unilaterally by public actors or after consultation). Sometimes, conflict regulation mechanisms are informal in nature and have become self-evident during the course of interaction between actors (see Klijn, 1996, 2001).

Making procedures: creating interaction arenas

In this case, an attempt is made to ensure that interactions in networks take place according to set procedures. The intention is not only to acquire more transparency in the interaction but to provide actors with predictability. Actors in networks then know how interaction and decisions will evolve. An example of this, for instance, is the extensive regulation of decision making on zoning in many European countries. Although the number of procedures and the degree of detail varies, many European countries work with set systems for making zoning plans, for determining the input procedures of citizens and societal actors, and for how other political and public bodies (consider the many levels of government) are involved in the procedure.

Another example of this is, obviously, the set procedures for the PFI initiatives in the UK. Yet another is the obligation to compare the private situation to one where a service or product is provided by a public actor (Public Sector Comparison, PSC). It is interesting that the Dutch Department of Finance has attempted to establish the British PFI rules for contracting out and PSC as the norm for the relations between public and private actors. Thus it tries informally to establish procedures for how contact between public and private actors in networks can be conducted, whether for contracting out or for mutual engagement in public–private relations.

Establishing procedures can be done through formal and informal rules and, in reality, they establish other conditions for interactions between actors and thus create new interaction arenas. Hence, procedures change interaction patterns – at least for a number of activities – in the network and lead to new network formation. Networks, after all, are the result of mutual interaction between actors; hence a different interaction process as a consequence of establishing procedures leads to changes in the network.

Certification: determining quality

In this case, there are standards or judgements that guarantee certain quality. The judgements often concern the characteristics of an actor or his relation to other actors, his internal functioning (often related to the first) or his external behaviour ('good behaviour'). Quality judgements are then related to standards with regard to one or more of these aspects. The standards are sometimes unilaterally defined by public organizations, but they are also often the result of consultation and interactions within networks. In the latter case, the medical codes and norms determined and maintained by professional groups themselves are a well-known example. In the Netherlands, housing corporations are officially allowed (they are known as 'allowed institutions'). They are officially acknowledged by government to be non-profit organizations that build and manage low-income rental homes. This official recognition implies that they must meet certain demands (no profit, certain types of accounting rules, etc.) and must maintain certain types of behaviour, such as allowing tenant participation, meeting certain performance standards, etc. Certification, thus, concerns both the internal characteristics of the actor as well as his behaviour to other actors in the network. In this case, central government sets the certification demands. The corporations themselves, however, have all sorts of informally established codes for their functioning and have their own codes of practice.

The emergence of various citizens' charters in some European countries is another interesting example of certification. Citizens receive certain rights, and sometimes also guarantees, for service delivery and this will, in turn, influence the interactions between citizens and the service-providing institutions. Also, the independence of actors in their relations to other actors in the network can be set as a quality criterion. Thus, the independence of the national central banks and of the central European bank is an essential characteristic of these organizations and it provides them status in the network.

The types of certification determine interaction in the sense that they specify the boundaries of strategic action, and which strategic actions are considered to be high quality, good or poor (independence, too, is considered a quality). In this sense, they influence the strategic interactions between actors in networks in a lasting manner.

Regulating and changing supervision: checks and balances

Finally, through institutional design, the supervision of actors or interactions in networks can be regulated. This can be a supervision regime determined by a public organization or one designed by the actors themselves. The inspectorates of education and health care in many European countries are examples of public units of departments that allow regulation of these institutions. Their creation and authority are regulated by public decision. On the other hand, supervision of the stock exchange is an example of self-regulation. After several stock exchange scandals in various Western countries, however, the call for better supervision has increased significantly.

Like certification, supervision provides a certain legitimacy since it provides guarantees for the quality of the actors and their practice. Furthermore, supervision arrangements, just like certification, provide limits to strategic behaviour. As a result, they reduce uncertainty in interactions between organizations.

Adapting rules: who and how?

One quickly assumes that the adaptation of rules is the exclusive privilege of public actors and, especially, central public actors, departments and political bodies. However, in the modern complex network society, this is seldom the case. First, as we have seen, there is much more self-regulation. And, with the growing attention from the public and the media to the behaviour of public and private organizations in society, this lack of exclusiveness only increases. Sectors reorganize themselves after scandals or if they come under external pressure, as was recently seen with the stock exchange scandals. Guidelines for accounting controls are sharpened and companies propose their own rules of conduct. In short, types of certification and supervision are developed or strengthened and improved by the actors themselves. The increased transparency and (international) visibility of organizations and their strategic behaviour through modern communications and internet technology, on the one hand, and the increasing risk of damage to their good name, on the other hand, certainly play a role here.

Hence, rules are not only adapted by public organizations nor are they adapted only through formal legislation, although these are, of course, still important. Many rule changes in the network are a consequence of mutual interactions, either between public and private actors or between private actors and self-regulation.

We must note, however, that the effects of rule changes in networks do not always coincide with the intentions of the initiator(s). Actors in networks are relatively autonomous and respond strategically to proposed and implemented rule changes. Furthermore, the effects of rule changes only become visible after a period of time, either because the change itself is subject to interactions, or because new rules only gradually win over the old rules. Hence, the effect of rule changes is often ambiguous and only visible in the longer term.

10.3 Robust changes of perceptions: reframing

As indicated in Part 1 and Chapter 9 of this book, actors' perceptions generally change gradually. Perceptions change through the incorporation of new knowledge and experiences. The strategies discussed in the previous chapter all assume relatively small change and incremental change. They concern the creation of space for looking at new solutions and for establishing the fact that actors view problems differently, etc. These are not fundamental changes in actor perceptions that force actors to adjust their perceptions of reality. Sometimes such a change is necessary. It might be that the nature of a problem is such that during the interaction it becomes clear that actors cannot reach a solution because their perceptions of the problem, solutions or other aspects, have become entrenched to such a degree that creative or effective solutions are inhibited. This may be apparent from the fact that interactions between actors come to a standstill since there are no useful solutions available or because the discussions endlessly repeat themselves.

In this case, a more radical change of perception is desirable. In this section we discuss some strategies for radically changing perceptions which we refer to as *reframing*. It is important to note that these strategies, initiated by any one or more of the actors, are only one of the many steering opportunities in a network. They can, just like other strategies, increase confrontation, be interpreted by different actors in different ways, or – because of an unexpected series of strategies, interactions and interpretations – achieve a different effect from that initially desired.

Policy documents as an attempt to reframe

A strategy used often by public actors to influence actors in networks is the preparation and publication of central policy documents. These can be viewed as a collection of policy proposals that give substantial attention to concrete measures and possible plans for implementation. Often, though, policy documents only contain vague indications of proposals and instruments, and more often are texts that develop and elaborate a (policy) vision. These are often explicitly intended to change the minds of other actors in the network, such as local governments and semi-private actors.

This is the case in physical planning, which can only be achieved with a large number of actors. Lower level governments must include the general guidelines of higher level governments in their own (planning) documents and semi-private and private actors must invest according to the ideas of central governments. With the exception of orders and prohibitions which are difficult to uphold and are only of limited use, central governments can only employ the recruiting force of their documents to guide (physical planning) investment and structural decisions (Klijn, 2002a).

In short, one of the most important aspects of the physical planning of central public bodies is to influence the perceptions of other actors in such a manner that, as a consequence of other decisions by these actors, changes occur in physical planning decisions. In short, policy documents and planning documents aim at influencing the ideas in the strategic decisions of other actors. This can be strengthened by involving these actors actively in the preparation phase of such documents. Central ideas in the documents can then be discussed and possible critiques incorporated in the final document. In this manner, introducing new ideas with the aid of large policy documents, combined with certain types of game management, constitutes a reframing process.

'Administrative stories': direction in chaos?

Related to using policy documents to radically change the perceptions of actors in networks, is the use of lofty administrative stories. While these are sometimes linked to one or more policy documents, they are more frequently organized as a type of ongoing discussion in which political and administrative actors prepare the ground for certain changes. A good example is the concept of the 'third way' embraced by Tony Blair and the Labour Party in the UK. With it, Blair and Labour hoped to present a future vision on citizenship, reciprocity and responsibility, justice and the role of government. It was an image of a society somewhere between the individualism of the market, which the Labour Party linked to the period of government of the Conservatives – especially during Margaret Thatcher's terms of office – and the somewhat collectivist and strong-state approach of earlier Labour governments. It would be a society where citizenship and individual responsibility become stronger and government does not draw everything to itself but, rather, creates the conditions and cooperates with other public and private organizations at the central and local levels in order to provide services and products to citizens (Newman, 2003; Pollitt, 2003).

The idea of the third way was intended to give the Labour Party, which had lost successive elections in the UK, a new face and thus make it acceptable and believable for voters in the electoral 'middle'. But the third way was more than that. It was a programme and guideline set against a background of events, ideas, administrative decisions, etc. In short, it was a 'story' and 'narrative' that provided a context for a number of somewhat loose policy measures and ideas about service delivery, cooperation between organizations, etc., and made these more acceptable. It was, thus, an administrative story with the clear intention of changing ideas in various policy networks and preparing the ground for a different approach. Such an idea can also provide legitimacy to separate smaller interventions. Administrative stories, thus, can function as an important aid for changing actor perceptions, for providing legitimacy to sets of ideas and proposals in the perceptions of other actors, and for stimulating the search for other solutions. In this sense, they clearly establish a reframing of perceptions.

Comparable examples of administrative stories used as reframing instruments can be seen in the discussion about stimulating the market function which is conducted in almost all Western European countries, and also in the numerous attempts of political leaders to carry out reforms in the public sector (for an overview, see Pollitt and Bouckaert, 2000). Thus, for instance, a slogan, reminiscent of New Public Management ideas (see Chapter 5), such as that of 'Making a government that works better and costs less', of the Clinton–Gore administration can be regarded as an administrative story (Pollitt and Bouckaert, 2000).

Each of these administrative stories has several different objectives. It must serve as an overarching idea for concrete, substantive proposals; it must provide political office holders with an image; but it must also function – and this is important for this chapter – as a means to convince others of different ideas and thus drastically change the perceptions of these others.

Sensitizing concepts: the steering function of a good idea

In addition to policy documents or administrative stories, individual concepts may fulfil a role in the desired process of reframing. The word 'sensitizing' refers to the fact that it must be a guiding concept which makes actors sensitive to certain developments, problems, solutions, etc. Sensitizing concepts which have drawn much attention in recent administrative practice are: autonomization, agencies, core departments, performance indicators, steering at a distance, horizontal steering, public–private partnerships, etc. A concept such as autonomization leads to reflecting on the selection of administrative and societally relevant developments. The emphasis is on the relations between parts of public organizations (mostly ministries) and executing agencies or non-profit actors and problematizes these (for instance, there is too little distance and separation between policy and execution, there is a responsibility problem, etc.). At the same time, it suggests a solution: by establishing more independence for executing agencies or non-profit organizations, the effectiveness and efficiency of government policy can be improved. Almost all sensitizing concepts have such a function: they point to a problem and focus attention on the one hand, and suggest solutions on the other. They have this in common with the two previous strategies of reframing.

Sensitizing concepts can be part of the administrative stories mentioned above but can also have a life of their own and be used without such a story. Autonomization, in principle, fits the administrative story of 'improving market functioning' but is also used outside that connection.

Sensitizing concepts are introduced to disseminate or realize ideas. The agency concept was disseminated in the Netherlands by the Ministry of Finance to initiate a discussion about different types of organization of national government that fit in the context of budget cuts. Sometimes, concepts are imported from other countries. Ideas for the PPP Knowledge Centre in the Netherlands and about the organization of PPPs in general were imported from the UK where they were introduced under the heading of the Private Finance Initiative (PFI) and Design, Finance, Build and Operate (DFBO) contracts (see Chapter 5). In this manner, many concepts are imported from other countries (see also Pollit and Bouckaert, 2000; de Jong et al., 2002). Such foreign concepts may be received differently in the adopted country than in the originating country. Reception depends on factors such as the network rules and perceptions in the adopting country involved and the strategic choices of the actors.

Crisis situations and big events: using policy windows

Actors can also use crisis situations or 'big events' for reframing purposes. The most dramatic example is the attack on the twin towers of the World Trade Center in New York on 11 September 2001. This had many consequences but one of them was a radical change in the thinking of American politics and the American people about security and the actions required to guarantee that security. Politicians in the US have actively used these events to persuade the population to accept a more active and military-led intervention in global security.

In short, crisis situations and big events may turn regular expectations on their heads and create the opportunities that allow new perceptions to evolve. One could also say, in the terms used in Chapter 3, that these events create a policy window for decisions and changes in perceptions. They establish a sense of urgency among the actors involved since that action is demanded and they also create an atmosphere of agreement.

But it is important to use that moment appropriately since the sense of urgency and willingness to change perceptions will not continue indefinitely. In short, it demands good management and a good sense of timing.

Reframing: everyone interprets

When applying reframing as a management strategy, one must keep in mind that the meaning and effort of the manager can be interpreted differently by other actors. The network manager, by means of the concept of agencies, might desire to create a situation where policy is executed more efficiently and effectively through independent agencies bound by performance demands closely tied to the 'mother department'. But the agencies themselves may regard the greater independence as a means to secure their own domain and protect it from the meddlesome involvement of a higher unit of the department.

In short, whether administrative stories, sensitizing concepts or lengthy memos are involved, the actors who are targeted by the management strategy can and will interpret steering signals in their own way. They do so because ambiguous concepts that can have different meanings are involved, even more so than with steering through network rules.

This means that the effect of reframing, just as we have seen with steering through rules, may have unexpected consequences. Making a number of executing agencies more independent in the Netherlands has had certain desired effects in the original objectives (improving effectiveness and efficiency). One of the side effects, however, has been a growing self-awareness within a number of these agencies. They have now developed numerous external assessment mechanisms where external customers are involved. Based on the idea that they also perform functions for their clients, they carefully try to reduce the importance of ministerial performance indicators to no more than a measurement of performance outcomes. This was unexpected and has resulted in mixed feelings in the monitoring departments (see also van Thiel, 2003). The concepts of agencies and autonomization have been defined anew by the independent agencies themselves, i.e. by holding themselves accountable to their stakeholders, which was not the original intention. Reframing thus has its own dynamic and is formed and changed in the interaction process itself. Here too, it is clear that controlling developments is an illusion and that time and again, network management involves responses to new developments and opportunities.

10.4 Enhancing trust: a matter of patience

Trust, or the lack of it, in networks has far-reaching consequences for the degree to which parties are willing and able to interact and cooperate. That trust is regarded as important in practice is illustrated time and again (see Box 10.4). Many actors involved in cooperative projects mention trust as an important factor for success.

When present, trust can be an important force for action in situations of substantial uncertainty. A high degree of trust provides relative certainty that other actors will not abuse initiatives. Furthermore, trust can provide a 'safe environment' for the search for solutions. In Chapters 8 and 9, we indicated the importance of the development of innovative solutions that encompass differences in values and problem perceptions. Trust in other actors provides an important condition for such a search process in a context where actors know their interests to be protected. Thus trust can help in reducing uncertainties in the strategic behaviour of other actors and in reducing cognitive uncertainties by stimulating the exchange of knowledge.

The institutional characteristics of networks play an important role in the growth and sustainment of trust, but can trust be managed?

Box 10.4 The importance of trust

Practitioners often mention trust as an important factor for the success of public–private projects. On the statement (presented at a large conference in the Netherlands on public–private projects) 'trust is the most important condition for public–private project success' the respondents (n = 207) answered:

	%
very much agree:	53.62
agree:	33.33
no opinion/neutral:	3.86
disagree:	5.31
very much disagree:	3.86

Source: Edelenbos and Klijn, 2003.

Can trust be managed?

Trust between actors in networks emerges gradually (see Chapter 4). Some authors even speak of 'spontaneous trust' to indicate its gradual and unplanned nature

(Fox, 1974). Other authors state that managers are inclined to overestimate their ability to influence trust, and this is demonstrated when other actors recognize the intention to create trust and become suspicious (Sydow, 1998). Difficulties are further exacerbated because trust can easily be damaged. Trust develops only slowly but can disappear rapidly.

Trust emerges gradually in concrete games where parties learn from each other through interaction, learn to tackle problems together and thus gain intermediate victories, all the time supported by strategies of game management. At the same time, such trust is vulnerable. It can easily be jeopardized by go-alone or contentious strategies, opportunistic behaviour, or careless, misunderstood and unsupported management interventions. Often, it is important that the right institutional conditions exist like a good conflict regulation mechanism, or clear but not rigid domain separations, etc.

Strategies aimed at institutional design can have far-reaching effects on trust between involved parties since they often directly affect the positions and core interests of parties and may be seen as threatening as a result. Nothing is as damaging to trust as unexpectedly starting a discussion on the positions of actors or changing other institutional rules that set the context for the game. All the more so when this is done by an actor with a direct substantive interest. The choice to build trust leads to necessary restraint in the application of strategies of institutional design.

Enhancing trust by institutional design

Trust can be enhanced in various ways. The flow of interactions around substance and game of problem solving and the way these interactions are managed can influence the growth (or reduction) of trust. Most of these have been discussed in the previous chapter. In this chapter, we focus on the management strategies of institutional design for promoting trust.

Certification rules which set standards for actors, their internal organization and their behaviour can enhance trust in actors and their actions since they establish a sound basis for the expectation that other actors will behave in a certain way. In short, certification not only enhances the quality of interactions in networks but also contributes to building and maintaining trust. It can even lead to a situation where actors no longer have to make an effort with regard to certain aspects of the decision making but can work with the guarantees offered by certification. Also, the creation of conflict regulation mechanisms will have a positive effect on trust. Since parties know that they can turn to certain mediating bodies in the case of conflict, they will access interaction processes with more confidence and trust relations will be damaged less because of the ability to call on mediation if needed. Changing or creating rules of supervision (such as supervision of certain actors or of certain procedures and professional standards) may also have a positive effect on the interaction patterns between parties; chances for opportunistic behaviour on the part of actors are then reduced. For example, consumers gain more trust in hospitals and medical specialists when they know that an effective supervisory or regulatory regime is in place. Other strategies of institutional design, however, can have a negative effect or appear to counteract the creation and maintenance of trust relations. Clearly, interventions in the institutional structure can also have a negative effect on trust; for instance, because trusted institutional practices are changed, or because new institutions that have not yet earned trust are created.

Conclusion: trust develops only slowly but disappears rapidly

As indicated in Chapter 4, the creation of trust takes time. Strategies of institutional design can contribute to the building of trust (as in the case of certification or conflict regulation mechanisms) if and when applied with restraint. Trust, however, can be lost very quickly. Sudden and abrupt institutional interventions can create substantial unrest. Furthermore, we must realize that institutions provide the basis of trust for fruitful interactions in concrete games. In other words, they are the reflection of years of investment in interaction between parties and the crystallization of an ongoing and lengthy institutional learning process; they must therefore be regarded as types of institutional capital. When the institutional design intervenes in these institutions, it may lead to a loss of trust with serious consequences for the interaction in the involved networks. Re-establishing trust will take time and much effort. This is enough reason to tread carefully with institutional design.

10.5 The role of political bodies: a design proposal

In Chapter 5, we witnessed how frequently tensions emerge between all sorts of horizontal steering and the role and action of politically representative bodies. Changes that can contribute to the solution of problems are often in the sphere of institutional design. They quickly touch upon the heart of the functioning of democracy and its related notions about the primacy of politics. In recent years, lively discussions about innovations in democracy and particularly the relations between government and citizens have taken place (see Hirst, 1997; Daemen and Schaap, 2000; Klijn and Koppenjan, 2000a; McLaverty, 2002). The proposals, formulated to reduce the tensions between the (actions of) political bodies and the characteristics of horizontal types of government, or even the empirical, day-to-day decision making around wicked problems, certainly fit into this discussion.

Before addressing possible strategies for reducing this tension, we first examine the background of the tension between empirical decision making on wicked problems and the role of political bodies. This background has everything to do with the dominant democracy theory, which also provides the backdrop for the primacy of politics, which is, from here on, referred to as the 'instrumental vision of democracy'. This tradition, going back to a rich tradition in political philosophy, can be positioned vis-à-vis ideas about a more substantial democracy, which has an equally rich tradition in political philosophy.

Democratic traditions and the primacy of politics

Generally, thought on democracy has two rivalling traditions (Pateman, 1970; MacPherson, 1979): one emphasizes democracy as a procedure for decision making, and the other considers democracy as a goal in itself. The first tradition will be referred to here as the *instrumental vision of democracy* since democracy is regarded as an efficient means of decision making that, in the longer term, has good results and protects the individual freedom of citizens. The latter is necessary so that individual citizens can pursue economic development. The instrumental view of democracy goes back to the utilitarianism of Bentham and James Mill (Sabine and Thorson, 1973) and is again voiced in the post-war years by such theoreticians as Schumpeter and the pluralists.

The second tradition is referred to here as the *substantive vision of democracy* which regards democracy as a desirable normative idea. It emphasizes democracy not only as a decision making procedure but as a societal ideal: the ideal that we can interact on the basis of equality and equity as verbally capable citizens. This substantive vision of democracy goes back to the early utopian democracy theories of people such as Jefferson and Rousseau and to authors such as John Stuart Mill (MacPherson, 1979). One could also include the work of a theoretician such as Habermas with his emphasis on the interactions between verbally equally equipped citizens who reach agreement about values in a *Herrschafsfreie Diskussion* (discussion between equals), i.e. a more modern phrasing of this second tradition (Habermas, 1989).

The first tradition emphasizes that the democratic state exists because individuals form some kind of contract. Democracy is then an efficient form of governing that helps to express different preferences. Both for theoreticians such as James Mill and Bentham as well as Schumpeter, the essence of democracy is that citizens can overthrow their rulers. A citizen's right to vote is an important means for expressing preferences and ensuring that individuals who assume political office can translate these preferences into actions (Schumpeter, 1943; Sabine and Thorson, 1973; MacPherson, 1979). Schumpeter argues that democracy is a political method, hence an institutional arrangement for achieving political–legislative and administrative decisions and that it can never be a goal in itself (Schumpeter, 1943). In this instrumental vision of democracy, market analogies provide attractive metaphors. Citizens are consumers and politicians are suppliers and both pursue utility maximization (see Downs, 1957). Furthermore, a negative understanding of liberty is emphasized. Democracy is an institutional design to protect the freedom of citizens. With reason, this understanding of democracy is regarded as a liberal market interpretation (Couwenberg, 1979; MacPherson, 1979).

Opposing this instrumental notion of democracy is a more substantive vision. Theoretically, this notion is not as tightly and elegantly defined as the instrumental approach. In part, it only exists as a critique of the instrumental model (Pateman, 1970). In this approach, democracy is a goal in itself and not only a decision making procedure. Democracy is a value, a political system that involves citizens in government policy and stimulates them in activity and verbal participation. In this vision, seen in early democracy theories but also in the work of

Table 10.2 Two democratic traditions

	Instrumental vision	*Substantive vision*
Image of democracy	Representative democracy	Direct democracy
View of democracy	Democracy is a method for making decisions	Democracy is a societal ideal
Image of freedom	Negative image of freedom (emphasis on curtailment of power of state apparatus via right to vote and protection of rights)	Positive image of freedom (emphasis on self-development of citizens)
State and society relationships	The state is an 'executive institution' of citizens and is 'above the parties'	State and society function thanks to one another (political and social democracy are inextricably linked)
Role of government	Executor of citizens' preferences and guarantor of rights to freedom	Active support of democratic society (creation of opportunities for participation and development)
Role of citizens	Passive role; emphasis on citizens as consumers (expression of preferences)	Active role; emphasis on citizen as civic subject (importance of participation in decision making)
Adherents	James Mill, Bentham, Schumpeter, Downs	Rousseau, Jefferson, John Stuart Mill, Habermas

Source: adapted from Klijn, 1996.

theoreticians such as John Stuart Mill, the importance of a democratic society and of social movements is emphasized. Democracy then is the institutionalization of certain values and norms which is never complete and always in flux. In this second approach, democracy is much less linked to the organization of the government apparatus and much more to a system of values and norms that have to be institutionalized in society at large. These two approaches are summarized in Table 10.2.

The role of political bodies in the two democratic traditions

What is the relevance of these two traditions for thinking about the role and responsibilities of actors in networks? Clearly, the first model emphasizes political control and the hierarchy of the administrative apparatus. Only the minister, as 'executor of the will of the people', can control the executive power and the many interests that stand in the way of his plans. It is an idea of democracy that quickly leads to more control and centralization in order to strengthen political steering. This idea is strongly present in the ideas and proposed measures from the New Public Management perspective, as we have seen in Chapter 5. It is also this idea that dominates in the political debate and in the media.

Two doctrines about the role of public actors

It is, however, not the only conceivable way to shape the idea of democracy. The substantive vision of democracy emphasizes much more the democratic quality of societal processes. A democratic system is one where verbally independent societal groups and individuals interact with each other and, time and again, negotiate the proper shaping of democratic ideals. Extrapolating this second vision, one can conclude that nineteenth-century parliamentary democracy as we know it, which is linked to the doctrine of the primacy of politics, is one of the possible manifestations of democracy. In this second vision, the state or government is not a body above parties but one that actively enhances equality of opportunity of individuals and groups (others refer to 'societalization': see also Hirst, 1994 and 1997). Many recent attempts to involve citizens in decision making and in the delivery of public services more or less depart from a substantive vision of democracy. In contrast to the primacy of politics, the role of political bodies is more that of a democratic mediator. In Table 10.3, these two visions about public, and especially political, bodies are contrasted.

Table 10.3 Two doctrines about the role of public actors

	Primacy of politics	Democratic mediation
Image of public actors	Caretaker of common interest above parties	Process mediator between parties and mediator between interests
Role of public bodies	Initiator/executor: • Of (cumulations of) preferences of citizens • Controller of bureaucracy	Referee: • Monitoring the democratic quality of the policy process • Oversight of adequate interest assessment
Public–private relationship	Superiority: • Objectives of public actors prevail over those of private actors • Emphasis on control by politically elected bodies of the environment	Equality: • Emphasis on relation between objectives and variety as condition for democracy • Emphasis on facilitating and supporting role of political elected bodies for democratic processes
Evaluation criteria for the outcome of policy processes	Agreement between outcomes of policy processes and the objectives of elected bodies	Degree to which outcomes reflect different objectives of actors (including those of public actors)
Responsibility	Political responsibility: • Political bodies responsible for content of policy and action of bureaucracies (ministerial responsibility) • Enhancing control over content and execution of policy	Procedural responsibility: • Political bodies responsible for careful assessment • Enhancing cooperation between equal actors

As is clear in Table 10.3, the substantive vision of democracy results in a (normative) perspective about the role of public actors in general and of politically elected bodies specifically, different from the instrumental vision of democracy which emphasizes the primacy of politics. Politically elected bodies no longer appear as the sole determinants of substantive values in society but also as supporters and guardians of the political debate and as referees of the outcomes of that debate. And when the interests of groups in decision making are insufficiently considered, they can serve as a corrective influence.

Institutional clashes: hybrid democracy

In various horizontal forms of governance, and certainly in forms such as interactive decision making processes or the modern local government reforms of the UK Labour Government that are aimed at improving citizens' involvement, various features can be recognized which come from the substantive view of democracy. This applies to the greater emphasis on the direct participation of citizens, their responsibility and active role. But the emphasis on interaction and achieving mutual agreement also fits into this picture. This is not surprising considering that a lot of the horizontal governance forms are meant to more actively involve social groups and citizens (think of ideas of the third way and the attempts at interactive decision making). Many local initiatives, in particular, are taken from the need to narrow 'the gap between government and citizen'.

One can rightly argue that through these horizontal governance forms, an *institutional regime* of roles and rules, based on views of democracy that emphasize direct participation and interaction between government and citizens, is introduced into a system dominated by instrumental democracy in which decision making power is concentrated in elected representatives. This mix of different institutional regimes (Klijn and Koppenjan, 2000a) – one can say hybrid democracy (Edelenbos and Monnikhof, 1995) – is not without problems. There are tensions between the rules of instrumental democracy, with its emphasis on the passive role of citizens and the strong decision making power of elected politicians, and the rules of substantive democracy that are oriented much more towards interaction and communication. All of the rules of representative democracy are aimed at a procedure in which elected political institutions pronounce a final judgement at the end of the decision making process in which they represent the general interest, unhindered and without consultation. On the other hand, many horizontal forms (and practices) of decision making are precisely aimed at settling the question of what the common interest is using interactions between the interested parties. The question is then what can the role of elected politicians still be at the conclusion of a process of policy preparation if in that process there has been broad social participation? Elected politicians rightly fear for the erosion of their political primacy. And if the horizontal governance forms of decision making are also emphatically legitimized as a correction of the gap between citizens and government that is so salient for representative democracy, the competition between both regimes is sharpened: we then have a zero sum game. On the other hand, most of the experiments that involve citizens in decision making are actively promoted by elected politicians themselves. And, if one does not adopt the cynical view that they apply this only in rhetoric, there should be found a common ground where both practices can co-exist together.

Institutional redesign of the role of politicians: a proposal

How can the involvement of politicians in horizontal governance processes take shape? The solution must be sought at the level of institutional design: reconciling the practice of instrumental and substantive democracy by making agreements between the parties involved about rules and roles, which must subsequently be applied in practice (Weimer, 1995; Goodin, 1996).

In any case, the situation we want to avoid is clear. Namely, that in which politicians unilaterally dictate conditions in advance, do not participate in the decision making process for fear of being committed at a later stage, and make their decision with little regard for the outcome of the decision process. But what should also be avoided is that participants in decision making processes expect politicians to adopt their proposals unaltered or that, out of their lack of trust, they formulate only a single policy proposal and thereby confront politicians with a fait accompli.

The role of politicians at the start of the process: politics taking the lead

At the start of complex interaction processes on wicked problems, politicians can play an active role as initiators or by picking up and supporting the initiative of others. This gives them the opportunity to politically direct the social debate around a concrete issue, giving a signal to parties within society that something is actually about to happen. In a political–administrative environment in which attention and time are scarce, this can be a powerful impulse for participating in a decision making process (compare Kingdon, 1984 and 1995).

Politicians and political institutions can establish substantive preconditions for the decision making process: an indication of which direction to look for solutions and/or measures to be taken. These preconditions, however, should leave space for the substantial development of policy proposals: rather, it is a matter of marking the terrain within which involved parties can develop substantive solutions. By indicating these preconditions, political majorities can profile themselves politically. For the participants in the process, they are crucial in order to curtail the strategic uncertainties that surround the interaction process and to align expectations concerning the interaction process between the involved parties. Because only the main lines are sketched, politicians are in a position to further develop their selection criteria during the course of the process and to sharpen or adjust them. The assumption is that the interaction process is a learning process for politicians as well. Through the process, they can gain more insight into the substance of problems and alternatives, which can also lead to the realization that previously proposed preconditions are not realistic or are unnecessarily restrictive.

In addition to substantive directives, political actors can also pose preconditions for the quality of the decision making process. They can restrain the power of the bureaucrats in such processes and introduce game rules that manage the risks identified in these kinds of processes (insufficient openness, under-representation, exclusion and arbitrariness due to procedural vagueness).

The role of politicians during the process: steering and learning

During the process, politicians should stay involved to avoid the risk of failing to assimilate the developed solutions and discussions which take place in the decision making process. Given their limited time, this involvement will usually remain restricted. Politicians could take part in interactive workshops. A promising alternative is to come to some agreement about how frequently they are to be informed of the most important developments in the process and are given the opportunity to influence the process. In fact, some of these arrangements are appearing in complex decision making in urban restructuring in the Netherlands for coping with the evolving character of ideas and plans on the one hand and the need to inform political actors on the other hand. In such a manner, they become standard informal procedures and actually function as extra arrangements in the policy making process.

This also means that in the design of the process, time must be allocated for such a feedback mechanism. This interim involvement enables politicians to familiarize themselves with the process of shared visioning that has taken place in the interaction process, to fine tune their own assumptions and criteria accordingly and to influence the interaction process. These interim opportunities are particularly important when significant changes occur at the political end, for example when new representatives and administrations take office following elections.

The role of politicians at the end of the interactive process: combining and selecting

In the decision making process, what matters is that one knows how to create a variety of directions towards solutions that give adequate consideration to the multi-interpretability and complexity of the problem situation. This occurs through establishing a design process between involved actors and experts that is inspired by the principles of creative competition: solutions elaborated simultaneously by competing design teams (Teisman, 1997). In addition, the design process must allow the strong points of the competing designs to be woven together in an interaction process with politicians and administrators. The task is to create such a mix that a diversity of social preferences is satisfied. For politicians, this can mean that through these decision making procedures, their field of choices at the end of the process can be enlarged. Compared to current practice in which politicians often deal with proposals that have been developed in relatively closed bureaucratic and neo-corporatist circles, alternative solutions can come onto the table. In this way, the decision making can enhance the freedom of choice for politicians and political institutions in relation to the existing practice of policy preparation. In Table 10.4 the role of politicians during the process and the demands that are made on the process itself are summarized.

Table 10.4 Politicians in decision making on wicked problems: roles and requirements

Phase	Role of politicians process	Design requirements for the decision making
Start	• Initiating and legitimizing • Formulating substantive terms of the game • Rules of the game for those involved (access to process) • Support for initiatives, clarifying status in decision making	• Space for political initiative and rules of the game • Commitment to rules of the game • Acceptance of limited commitment of politicians and political institutions • Attune process design to interim involvement of politicians
During	• Actively involved and supportive • Prevent exclusion of actors • Feedback to initial terms • Foster confrontation of different ideas	• Building-in feedback opportunities for administrators and politicians • Accepting possible adjustment of the interactive process • Realizing mobilization of expertise and variety
End	• Reconciling points of view and selecting alternatives • Attempt to forge majorities in favour of proposals • Selection and combination of attractive policy proposals	• Offer competing alternatives • Open up the possibility of combining alternatives

10.6 Conclusions: the possibilities and pitfalls of institutional design

Tampering with the characteristics of networks is not a simple matter. It takes time, the effects cannot always be overseen, and there are considerable normative consequences. Despite this, in the practice of government we see many attempts to change the institutional dimensions of networks. These attempts, which we called institutional design, are aimed at changing the rules or establishing drastic and robust changes in the perceptions of actors in the network. As is clear from the examples, attempts to change the institutional characteristics of networks have a good chance of success. The attempts to achieve privatization and the formation of agencies through the reframing and changing of the rules have most certainly had important effects in many networks, despite the occurrence of un-intended consequences. Provided that the various strategies of institutional design are well coordinated, they have a good chance of success.

At the same time, steering attempts in the area of institutional design are part of the strategic game that is, time and again, played in networks. Initiatives for institutional design are interpreted, bent, opposed, and they confront other institutional barriers. In short, it is and will remain a risky venture, particularly in the light of the normative implications described, which have to be dealt with extremely carefully.

Chapter 11

Managing uncertainties in networks

11.1 Introduction

In the first part of this book we presented a theoretical framework based upon network theory for the analysis, explanation and assessment of uncertainties in dealing with complex societal problems. We addressed the nature and causes of these uncertainties and showed how these influence the process of problem solving. We identified points of intervention for uncertainty management:

- The analysis of substantive uncertainties led to the conclusion that management must focus on joint image building and cross-frame learning and the development of negotiated knowledge.
- The analysis of strategic uncertainties pointed to the characteristics of the policy game as a starting point for uncertainty management, structuring the game in such a manner that mutual adjustment and cooperation are improved without the costs of these efforts devolving to third parties.
- The analysis of institutional uncertainties suggested other strategies beside game management strategies such as furthering the rules of the game's institutional design as an option for uncertainty management.

In Part 2 of this book, we have elaborated on the strategies that address these points of intervention. In this concluding chapter, we summarize the insights of the various chapters and relate them to each other. We reflect upon the nature, the opportunities and the limitations of uncertainty management based on the policy network approach. In Section 11.2, we give a description of what this type of uncertainty management is, by contrasting it with more conventional responses to uncertainty. Section 11.3 provides an overview of the management strategies discussed. In Section 11.4, we address the principles that can guide the choice from this repertoire of management strategies, i.e. when can each strategy be used and how do the various strategies relate to one another? In Section 11.5, we present some reflections on the importance and normative implications of a network approach to uncertainty management in solving complex problems in the contemporary network society.

11.2 Management of uncertainties in networks: disentanglers and entanglers

The underlying notion in this book is that standard responses to uncertainty are inadequate for dealing with complex societal issues in the contemporary network society. This raises the question of how the network strategies we discuss differ from the more conventional management strategies towards uncertainty. We answer this question by contrasting both responses to uncertainty. We define standard responses as the inclination of parties to approach problems substantively and to ignore, or reduce and even eliminate, the uncertainty emerging from the multi-actor nature of network situation (see Chapters 1 and 5). We emphasize that these standard responses are not 'typical responses' which may not actually exist in reality. Quite the contrary, these standard responses outlined below are prominent and influential in the practice of problem solving. The new answers of the New Public Management reforms, which have been discussed in Chapter 5, are a clear example of a new version of the standard answer. These solutions, advocated by 'disentanglers', are quite different from the solutions derived from a network perspective advocated by those we call 'entanglers'.

Management of uncertainty: the perspective of the disentanglers

According to the diagnosis of disentanglers, uncertainty in problem solving – if they have an eye at all for the multi-actor nature of problem solving – emanates from the presence of many parties that inhibit an action-oriented approach to the problem. This line of thought can be found in many public management reforms, especially those which promote privatization, (market) competition and the increase of market incentives (see Pollitt and Bouckaert, 2000; Koppenjan, 2003a, 2004), discussions about New Public Management (Osborne and Gaebler, 1992) and also in the publications of international organizations such as the World Bank (World Bank, 1992).

The main causes of this inertia have been identified as structural and cultural. The structural cause has been referred to as 'institutional sclerosis'. This alludes to the fact that almost every conceivable interest in modern society is protected in law with extensive advising, participation and appeal procedures. This widens the *hindrance power* and seriously inhibits the *realization power* of administrators. This results, among other things, in the Not In My Backyard (NIMBY) syndrome, where parties block the creation of arrangements of collective interest (such as the location decision concerning an industrial site, a road, an asylum centre, etc.) based on their own private interests (Klijn, 2003).

The cultural equivalent of this phenomenon is the preference of authorities for consensus building and the resistance to taking unpopular measures (Richardson and Jordan, 1979; Lovenduski and Outshoorn, 1986; Koppenjan, 2001; Weggeman, 2003). Wherever legal provisions exist to overrule the resistance of, for instance, local governments to projects of national interest, decision makers refrain from doing so because this violates the existing governing culture and because they fear repercussions in other games.

In reality, the diagnosis concerns also (but not only) a critique of the existence of horizontal relations and network-like settings. This type of critique can already be found in the analysis Scharpf (1978) made of the fragmented and intertwined decision making structure in the German Federal Republic. In his view, this prohibited an action oriented (forceful) approach to, for instance, environmental problems.

In line with this diagnosis, the solution proposed by the disentanglers has institutional and process-like dimensions. The institutional remedy consists of 'disentanglement':

* Simplifying procedures by reducing the participation and appeal procedures of local governments, interest organizations and citizens.
* Reducing the intergovernmental dependencies through, for instance, reorganizations, (de)centralization of operations or the abolition of governmental bodies (in order to reduce the administrative density), but also the creation of new organizations (in order to concentrate authority).
* Avoiding and disentangling public and private interdependency through privatization, contracting out, limiting public participation and formalizing contract relations (see especially the publications of the World Bank in the 1990s (World Bank, 1992)).

With regard to the organization of the processes of problem solving, 'disentanglers' recommend:

* limiting the number of actors involved;
* initiating an intellectual design process and using scientific knowledge that culminates in an unambiguous problem analysis with solutions emanating from them;
* formulating objectives and conditions as early on as possible and testing subsequent steps against these;
* selecting a solution on that basis and, subsequently, elaborating and submitting that solution to decision makers;
* ensuring the resources needed for realization are available following authoritative decision making and bringing them together;
* implementing the solution through tight planning, where factors of money, information, manpower, quality and time are controlled (project management).

On the basis of these elements, the disentanglers can also be called 'accelerators'. They search for ways to simplify and accelerate decision making about societal problems and perceive the objections brought against their substantive solutions in terms of resistance. What is noteworthy in this line of reasoning is that the substance of proposed solutions is not problematized. The starting point is that a well-organized process and the involvement of science and experts will help to mitigate substantive uncertainty. In our view, the standpoint of the disentanglers does not fit the nature of the uncertainties involved. Given the nature of these uncertainties, the approach that disentanglers suggest will lead to conflict, impasse and 'garbage can'-like decision making. Even so, disentanglers may succeed in pressing their solutions through. If they do, the result will most probably be sub-optimal: poor solutions that were difficult to achieve and were arrived at through great costs, but only do limited justice to the interests and perceptions involved.

Network management: the diagnosis and remedies of the entanglers

Network management takes the multi-actor and multi-purpose nature of processes of problem solving and decision making as a starting point and thus has a very different orientation from that of the disentanglers. Central is the effort to bring and keep the parties together, so that they are able to become acquainted with each other's perceptions, objectives and resources, discover opportunities, mutually adapt their strategies and intertwine their objectives. Thus, insights and resources are combined to arrive at high-quality solutions that take into account the complexity of contemporary issues. From this follows a completely different way of dealing with uncertainty.

Substantive uncertainty cannot be tamed by initiating an intellectual design process that culminates in a solution whose solution is unclear. The question is, rather, how varying perceptions, information and knowledge scattered over stakeholders and experts can be brought together and how – through a process of mutual learning – these can acquire a common meaning and result in interesting solutions that can be maintained in the light of scientific insights.

At the same time, the question is how this cognitive learning process can be managed in a strategic context: not by excluding actors, but by bringing them together so that they can coordinate their strategies, i.e. through strengthening interaction rather than avoiding and reducing it. At the institutional level, the challenge is not one of reducing dependencies through disentanglement. Instead, the question is how institutional arrangements can support the processes of cognitive learning and strategic interaction. Instead of *disentanglement*, it is *entanglement* that should be pursued. It is conceivable that historically developed arrangements have become dysfunctional and must be rearranged. But even then, institutional strategies are not about disentanglement but about re-entanglement. Table 11.1 summarizes the differences between disentanglers and entanglers in their handling of uncertainty.

11.3 The management of uncertainties in network settings: the repertoire of strategies

Network management is thus focused on handling uncertainty through furthering interaction between the parties involved. It concerns improving learning processes between the parties with regard to substance, process and institutional context. In this section, we summarize the management ideas that have been developed in the preceding chapters of Part 2.

Table 11.1 Disentanglers and entanglers: two perspectives on uncertainty management

Characteristics of the management of uncertainty	Disentanglers: reducing uncertainty	Entanglers: managing uncertainty
Content	• Concentrating on *ex ante* formulated objectives • Focusing on good substantive, scientific problem analysis • Optimizing one solution based on analysis	• Facilitating the search for profit opportunities and goal intertwinement • Postponing substantive attitudes • Promoting mutual cognitive learning, substantive variety and negotiated knowledge
Process	• Focusing on getting proposals accepted; faith in quality substantive solutions and political support • Sequential ordering of steps distinguished from one another by test moments followed by correction • Reducing the number of actors • Involving parties based on expertise and competence • Combining competence and resources in one hand	• Focusing on the investment in cooperation and support by being aware of opportunistic behaviour, fragmentation and dynamics • Using a substantive starting point without a premature fixation • Parallel linking of the design solutions and formulation of problems and objectives • Involving parties based on interests • Supporting interaction through couplings, agreements of game rules and facilitation
Institutions	• Reducing dependencies through simplifying procedures, reducing the number of rules and separating tasks, responsibilities and domains • Furthering firm (political) leadership	• Promoting the creation of institutional links between actors, sectors and domains that support more integral problem solving • Recalibrating dependencies focused on the integral approach to new problems
Core management activities and management capacities	• Managing central factors such as staff, quality, information, budget and time • Ensuring through manager who is strong in content, monitoring and control, and building political support	• Activating and coupling actors, arenas and games; accomplishing concerted action through facilitating activities • Ensuring through a manager with diplomatic skills, who can bring parties together, generate enthusiasm, who is inventive in terms of substance and process, who has no substantive interest

The management of content

The management of substantive uncertainty, inspired by the network approach, is not focused on the *ex ante* creation of an authoritative problem and objective formulation that guides the process of problem solving. This approach will lead to early substantive fixation with the risk of excluding alternative perceptions, values and avenues of solution. The chances for learning and enrichment that manifest themselves during the process would then be missed. Furthermore, early substantive selection encourages the resistance of actors, as a result of which conditions for learning will deteriorate. A network approach implies that the management of uncertainty is focused on mapping the distance between perceptions of the different parties involved and attempting to reduce this distance, or at least achieving a package of objectives and agreements that the critical parties involved can agree upon.

The objective is not the creation of consensus (although this can be helpful sometimes), but improving joint image building, cross-frame reflection and developing interesting and appealing solutions that generate support among actors. Hence, uncertainty management is a search for a 'common ground', a minimal basis for communication that enables further interaction and common learning. Such common ground can be found in relatively elementary things like the development of a common language, agreement about the authoritativeness of a third party, mutual agreement with a certain way of doing things, etc. Strategies that can be used include steering for goal entanglement, improving substantive variety, breaking through asymmetric debates, preventing early substantive fixations, improving cognitive reflection and organizing substantive selection.

The management of substantive uncertainty is also aimed at organizing the input of experts, research and science in such a way that the learning process between stakeholders is supported. The problem of analytical policy contributions is generally that the distance to the process of problem solving is either too great or too small. When research is too far removed from practitioners it will lead to scientifically valid research results that are nonetheless irrelevant or become available at the wrong time. They probably will not be used. On the other hand, too small a distance can result in policy advocacy that most likely will evoke counter-research. Research will be used intensively, but primarily to strengthen one's own standpoint. This is not supportive of mutual learning. For mutual learning, a more satisfactory link needs to be established between the research track and the process of problem solving.

What is necessary is the exchange of information, knowledge and insight between stakeholders and researchers, but also between those in each of these groups (see also Patton, 1997). This requires the organization of the research process according to the principle of concurrent research: the parallel linking of research and process, providing research with a facilitative role, joint commissioning of research and doing 'boundary work'. The result is the prevention of negotiated nonsense by testing the outcomes of the interactions between stakeholders to scientific insights. When scientific insights are not conclusive, the efforts are aimed at organizing a tentative scientific consensus on the basis of the available insights. (See also Table 11.2.)

Table 11.2 Management of content

Strategy	Description
Furtherance of goal intertwinement	Initiating a search for solutions that can unite the diverging objectives of the involved parties, through, for example, integrating subjects, package deals, mitigating and compensating measures, or offering a perspective of future benefits
The promotion of substantive variety	Increasing the scope for seeking goal intertwinement by stimulating the parallel development of competitive solutions and the parallel linking of these activities with the process of problem and objective formulation
Breaking through asymmetrical policy discussions	Bringing the knowledge conflicts and asymmetries into light in the policy discussion and seeking the possibility of reducing these. For example, through the promotion of frame reflection, the formulation of new agendas and the bridging of language differences, the development of fully-fledged counter-voices
Preventing premature cognitive fixations	Ensuring at the beginning of the process that the focus is on the question of how the process should be organized and not on the content of the problem. A substantive decision can be used to jumpstart the process as long as it is open to adjustment
Promoting cognitive reflection	By consciously introducing new actors and roles such as entrepreneurs, brokers and devil's advocates in order to bring up for discussion perceptions that are taken for granted
Organizing substantive selection	The conscious organizing of the process in which substantive selection occurs by making agreements over how solutions will be chosen (by whom, when, in what manner and by which criteria)
Linking of parallel arenas of research and problem solving	Conducting research in a second, parallel arena in addition to the negotiation arena. Research questions and findings are continuously traded back and forth between these two arenas
Facilitating instead of decisive research	Ensuring research that is not focused on settling knowledge conflicts, but on supporting interaction by addressing diverging knowledge issues and demonstrating the consequences of alternatives, showing the bandwidth within which solutions can be generated or to nuance these, suggest new angles, account for and explain research findings and offer the opportunity to reformulate conflicts as knowledge questions
Joint commissioning of research	Coordinating the research efforts of parties by the joint commissioning of research in order to mutually adapt expectations and demands with regard to research questions, assumptions, methods, scope, length and the selection of researchers
Boundary work	Guaranteeing the independence of research by making agreements about boundaries and role assignments between the research and the negotiation arenas. Instituting a scientific forum as a guarantee for scientific quality and to arrive at an inter-subjective, agreed standpoint in the case of inconclusive findings

The management of the game

Conditions for managing strategic uncertainties and improving social learning include engaging in interactions so that parties get to know each other better and find ways to coordinate their strategies and solutions. This often requires new linkages between actors, arenas and games. These linkages bring parties with very different backgrounds, perceptions and objectives together in an environment characterized by a high degree of dynamics. Their interaction will seldom emerge spontaneously nor will it inevitably lead to joint image building and concerted action, but must be initiated and supported. Interaction must get the chance to gradually strengthen and institutionalize. This means that there must be room in the process for different perceptions and substantive preferences. It is, however, also important that the 'core values' of actors are protected against unexpected and possibly unintended attacks from others. Parties must get to know each other on a step-by-step basis, develop tacit rules and build trust. Through this process, they gradually develop conditions for getting down to business: reaching agreements about the nature of the problem and the desired solutions. In doing so, game managers must be aware that the process does not become disconnected from the environment in which formal office holders will take authoritative decisions, that they make the connection with unrepresented or under-represented parties or interests, and that they respond to external threats and opportunities. Table 11.3 summarizes the management strategies focused on managing strategic uncertainties.

The management of institutions

In making process agreements and supporting interaction, the management of strategic uncertainty has already partially considered the institutional uncertainty surrounding problem solving. Parties who interact from different institutional backgrounds and do not share a common frame of reference, who are guided by various institutional reward structures and who act according to different rules, can be facilitated by making agreements about the rules of the game before dealing with the problem at hand.

Strategic and institutional uncertainties, however, can also be managed by influencing factors at the institutional level through, what we call 'institutional design'. This may be necessary when it is clear that the institutional bottlenecks are so systematic that they inhibit interaction and problem solving, especially in the long run. Institutional design involves changing the institutional characteristics of a network: the relation patterns and the institutional rules that support these relations, the (patterns of) opinions that guide strategic behaviour within a network, and the institutional arrangements that shape the relations between parties. This institutional design can also be aimed at enhancing the compatibility of processes within different networks or by establishing institutional cross-linkages.

By adapting institutional arrangements, the nature and stake of concrete games around complex problems can be altered significantly. It might change actor participation or stimulate actors to select different strategies given the changes

Table 11.3 Managing the game

Strategies	Description
Initiating or terminating interactions	*Through coupling or uncoupling of actors, arenas and games*
Coupling actors, arenas and games	Bringing about new interactions through which opportunities for goal intertwinement and learning are created
Uncoupling actors, arenas and games	Terminating dysfunctional interactions
Arranging interactions	Choosing a light or heavy arrangement for the coupling. Varying from informal agreements via cooperative agreements and contracts to joint legal corporations, either public or private
Designing games	*Promoting agreements between stakeholders about the rules of the game*
Agreements about the objective	Formulating the objective of interaction, the agenda of dos and don'ts, guided by the principle of an open agenda
Agreements about participation	Indicating participants, their quality, and entry and exit rules
Agreements about methods of working	Structuring work activities via sub-arenas, task division, inclusion of research and experts, symmetrical representation, and work forms in which the principle of multiple cross-links is used
Agreements about information	Determining between whom, in what manner and under what conditions information is exchanged, internally as well as externally
Agreements about steps in the process	Timing and sequence of activities, what deadlines apply and how these are handled. The principle of parallel ordering is used here as much as possible
Agreements about decision making	Determining what criteria and decision rules apply, who makes decisions, how the decision making will proceed and what objection or appeal procedures apply
Agreements about external coordination	Moments, intensity and nature of communication with constituencies, the larger environment, third party interests and the media, using the principle of loose coupling
Facilitating the game	*Supporting the interactions between stakeholders, in part through promoting the implementation and when necessary the readjustment of the process agreements*
Facilitation at the beginning of the game	Focusing activities on the motivation of parties, the creation of game rules, a balanced composition of the game field, the management of expectations and the promotion of a climate in which parties can get to know one another
Facilitation during the interaction	Attending to the provisions for interaction, maintaining an attractive agenda, promoting substantive variety, signalling assuring communication with the environment, adjusting and preventing fixations, conflict management, process and process agreements to changed circumstances
Facilitation at the end of the game	Signalling the selection opportunities, mediating and regulating conflict, guarding goal intertwinement and negotiated knowledge; preventing destructive strategies in view of the conclusion of the process; pointing to future dependencies and opportunities

in the frames of reference or the reward structure that guide them. It might also be that other arenas are formed or are composed differently, etc. In short, the conditions under which the game is played can change through institutional measures.

However, institutional measures are not easy to achieve because, among other reasons, they only take hold in the long run. Changing formal relations must be accomplished in a game. This involves the recognition that processes can only be controlled to limited extent, so that the effects of attempts at institutional design are uncertain. There are significant risks, too. Institutions are a reflection of institutional learning processes developed in a series of games. Often they have proven their value over a long period of time and gradually gained in authoritativeness. Institutional innovations frequently involve the destruction of existing institutions. When new institutions fail to meet expectations, it is often not possible to fall back upon the old. Furthermore, we must realize that institutions are 'multi-purpose vehicles' whose effectiveness is not related to the fate of a specific process of problem solving. They regulate societal interaction between actors around a number of issues. The fact that they may inhibit the development of a concrete solution says little about their value that, after all, goes beyond a specific issue. These considerations imply that the management of uncertainty is, in the first instance, not focused on institutional factors. However, when institutional factors limit the possibility of dealing with a variety of problems over a long period, or produce systematically undesirable outcomes, there are reasons to consider institutional design.

Strategies aimed at institutional design, discussed in Chapter 10, include the adaptation of network rules, the changing of shared opinions and frames of reference (reframing), the management of trust through the creation or change of institutional arrangements and the redesign of institutions, such as the primacy of politics. Table 11.4 provides an overview.

Management of uncertainties: furthering learning processes

These attempts at managing uncertainty do not automatically lead to problem solving. They are, rather, focused on achieving conditions under which it is possible to deal with wicked problems. They involve enhancing learning processes between parties aimed at substance, process and institutions. They are thus focused on improving cognitive learning processes, on joint image building, enrichment and goal entanglement, and on strategic and institutional learning processes, aimed at establishing and maintaining trust between parties with diverging interests, perceptions and objectives, roles (experts, citizens, users, civil servants, entrepreneurs, politicians) and diverging institutional backgrounds.

11.4 The choice of network management strategies

In the previous section, we outlined the repertoire of management strategies for dealing with uncertainties in network settings. The remaining question is when a certain strategy should be used in dealing with wicked problems. In this section,

Table 11.4 Management of institutional uncertainty

Strategies	Description
Changing network rules focused on network composition	Changing the number of actors within the network, their positions, the entry rules, the process of network formation, the degree of self-regulation and organizations
Changing network rules focused on network outputs	Changing the reward and evaluation rules, setting guidelines for actors' behaviour and influencing professional codes
Changing network rules focused on network interactions	Adjusting the arrangements that regulate the interaction of actors in concrete games such as conflict regulation mechanisms, procedures, certification, standardization and regulatory regimes
Reframing through the launching of major plans	Introducing new ideas or values by drafting strategic policy documents
Reframing through narratives	Presenting authoritative narratives as new frame of reference within which problems and solutions can be regarded in a sector or network
Reframing through sensitizing concepts	The use of sensitizing concepts to bring attention to proposals for a new idea, a new method or organizational form
Reframing through the use of focusing events	Using invasive, striking events in order to introduce and emphasize the urgency of new methods of working or new evaluation frameworks
Managing trust through institutional design	The promotion of trust between parties through institutional regulations such as the introduction of a certification system, conflict regulating institutions and regulators
Redesigning the primacy of politics	Redefining the role of politicians, political bodies and administrators for policy preparation and decision making: from authoritative allocation of values to initiating and guiding interaction processes by which meaning and values are discovered and assessed

we discuss the most important issues at play in the selection of a management strategy.

In addressing this question, we cannot expect much from a search for a fit between management strategies and the objective characteristics of a problem or problem situation (Lowi, 1963; Scharpf *et al.*, 1976; Waddock, 1991). Such a *structural-contingent approach* does not fit the basic premise of this book, i.e. that there is no objective problem. Rather, wicked problems are characterized by the fact that a number of actors are involved who each maintain their own perception about the nature of the problem – and none of the perceptions is authoritative. This means that the effectiveness of management strategies is not determined by the content of the problems. Hence, there are no standard recipes for selecting management strategies. But this does not mean that nothing sensible can be said about the selection of strategies or that 'anything goes'.

We believe that a *strategic-contingent approach* must be applied in the selection of strategies. Management strategies must fit the characteristics of, and the problems in, the processes of problem solving in the light of the perceptions and strategies of the actors involved. The effectiveness of these strategies is limited and influenced by the institutional context in which the network manager operates. To formulate this in a somewhat more complicated manner: management strategies are dependent upon the social constructions which actors involved in the network have created (perceptions and institutions) and upon the process characteristics of the interactions. With this approach we can formulate a number of guidelines for the application of management strategies in dealing with complex societal issues.

We need to point out a reservation. In discussing the selection of strategies, we implicitly assume that this selection is the result of a rational decision. This assumption, however, is only partially correct. Just as with the processes of problem solving, the selection of network strategies occurs within a political–strategic game and the outcome is more frequently the unintended product of routines, negotiations, dominant opinions and power balances. It may be politically impossible to choose the most appropriate management strategy. Just as the problem solving process is a political process in an institutionally fragmented context, so is the choice of management strategies. With the presentation of guidelines that should inform the selection of strategies, we wish to contribute to the quality of this selection process. We are aware of the fact that our guidelines often will not be followed in practice and that other considerations play a role, too. But at least it informs parties about the considerations that, according to us, should be taken into account. And it provides them with the opportunity to put these guidelines up for discussion in the argumentation process on the selection of management strategies. Below, we discuss nine guidelines.

Guideline 1: Analyse perceptions, actors and networks: not only beforehand, but continuously

When we want to direct our game management strategies to the sources of substantive, strategic and institutional uncertainty, we must develop an idea about what these sources in a specific process of problem solving are. Obviously, this must be done prior to the decision about how the problem situation will be managed. But since the process of problem solving is erratic and unpredictable, we also need to evaluate and monitor uncertainties during the process and think their consequences through. This can be done by (repeatedly) executing one or more of the analysis steps discussed in Chapter 7. But even when an explicit analysis is not conducted, the network manager receives continuous information about these issues during the interaction between actors. This information will enable him to track developments in perceptions, interactions and institutional relations and adjust his strategies accordingly. During the process of problem solving, the manager must ensure a continuous alternation between analysis and evaluation on the one hand, and selection, application and adjustment of management strategies on the other.

Guideline 2: Assess starting conditions: look before you leap

The question of which strategy is appropriate is preceded by the question of whether a network management strategy should be chosen in the first place. At any rate, three starting conditions must be considered:

- Is there urgency?
- Is there any chance of cooperation?
- Does the network manager possess the necessary means and capacities?

The first condition concerns the sense of urgency experienced by stakeholders that makes it likely that they are prepared to commit their energy and resources to the process (de Bruijn *et al.*, 2002). Attempts at network management are not always useful. Parties must have a 'drive' to solve a problem. This drive can come from the fact that the cost of the problem situation has grown beyond their means or because they perceive opportunities to arrive at a considerably improved position through cooperation with others. There may also be external pressure, for instance when government threatens to take legal measures that can only be avoided through concerted action. Without this sense of urgency or external pressure, it is questionable whether network management efforts will be meaningful.

Second, we should consider whether the relation between the parties involved offers any outlook for future cooperation. When parties are disinterested, or dislike each other and have a history of deep-rooted hostility and distrust, efforts to improve cooperation might be doomed from the start. Network management also appears to be an 'impossible job' in the case of opposing interests or in the absence of a common interest that might bring the parties together.

The third starting condition concerns whether there are sufficient means and skills available to the party planning to initiate the network management. Network management is a highly intensive activity, requiring a high degree of steering ability and a considerable investment of resources. Not all the actors necessarily possess these requirements and when these intra-organizational conditions are not met, it may be better to refrain from network management. A shortage of means or strategic skills can inhibit network management from channelling the inter-action process in desirable ways. Badly managed processes do more harm than good for the societal problem to which they are applied.

When it is clear that the starting conditions for network management are unfavourable, it is reasonable to refrain from it. Possibly, one can wait for more favourable circumstances, and when activities are embarked upon, they ought to be aimed at improving the starting conditions.

Guideline 3: Focus strategies on preventing or taking away fixations and impasses

Efforts to manage uncertainty in dealing with wicked problems must be aimed at its substantive, strategic and institutional sources. It is obvious to search for a match between the nature of stagnation and conflicts as they manifest themselves in the process of problem solving and the points of intervention on which strategies must focus. Substantive stagnation requires substantive management; social stagnation requires game management; and institutional problems call for managing institutions. In other words, when the process grinds to a halt because of diverging perceptions or knowledge conflicts, strategies can be used to explicate, change or link perceptions. If, on the other hand, there is little contact between actors, the efforts must be focused on intensifying the interaction, for instance, through the creation of temporary organizational arrangements. Important structural institutional limitations to problem solving require institutional measures.

Yet this presentation of the issue is too simple. After all, substance, process and institutional uncertainty are not separate but highly interconnected. Furthermore, there is no watertight separation between substantive, process-like and institutional network strategies. This implies, for instance, that substantive differences of opinion may arise from the power struggle between parties. A social stagnation may arise from parties interacting from different institutional backgrounds. This has a number of consequences for network strategies. First, as has been mentioned already, the choice of strategy must be guided by the nature of the problems under consideration. Second, when it appears that a substantive strategy is insufficient for resolving a substantive difference of opinion, one must consider other types of strategies (game management strategies or strategies of institutional design), in order to get the train moving (Termeer, 1993). Strategies focused on the game, such as agreement on the ad hoc rules of the game, may provide an answer to the lack of a set of institutional rules that would support the relations between stakeholders. Finally, there is the possibility of working with a mix of strategies combining, for instance, a substantive with a process type of management strategy. Figure 11.1 illustrates the interconnections between sources of uncertainty and management strategies.

Guideline 4: Be selective: minimize transaction costs

When managing uncertainty, the complexity and size of the management effort should be as limited as possible. For both the parties involved and the network manager, interactions have high transaction costs. Involved actors must have the feeling that these costs are balanced by real benefits and they also must be able to carry the cost. This is not always the case. Parties are certainly not willing to invest without limit in interaction. In the choice of strategies, the network manager must try to keep the transaction costs as low as possible, both for him and for the other actors. Management efforts must not be focused on everything and everyone at the same time. Given the complexity of policy games, the large group of actors and the specific nature of the relations involved, not every player or interested party will be involved in interaction attempts at the same level of intensity. Transaction costs call for selection. Game management can, for instance, focus on unblocking a limited number of relations instead of on all the relevant relations.

Also, management efforts will not always extend through the entire process of problem solving. The processes of problem solving are complex, take time, and are characterized by an erratic course. It is unlikely that attempts at managing

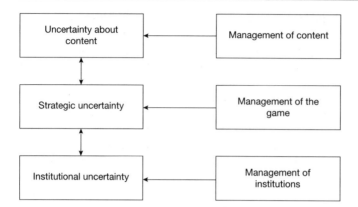

Figure 11.1 Sources of uncertainty and strategies of uncertainty management

uncertainty will be maintained throughout the process, or that the manager is able to maintain his authoritativeness throughout this process. Generally, the management of uncertainty will consist of limited interventions in time and scope. Where management becomes more comprehensive, they may still be limited to (a part of) a game round or – at most – to a number of game rounds.

Guideline 5: Tune strategies into the institutional environment

Earlier in this book we paid extensive attention to the network rules that actors have created in earlier interactions. These rules set boundaries to the strategies to be selected or at least limit the effectiveness of those strategies. Hence, this also concerns network strategies. Thus, in networks characterized by strong domain separations between actors and lack of information exchange, information strategies aimed at altering perceptions are not likely to be effective (Klijn, 2001). Rather, in such networks, a choice must be made for explicating and determining (temporary) conflict management strategies that provide a basis for further interactions. So, institutional factors influence the effectiveness and legitimacy of selected strategies. This is also the reason why it is important to develop an insight into the institutional characteristics of networks and to choose carefully network management strategies that fit, or at least take into account, institutional characteristics.

However, this does not rule out the possibility of choosing ill-fitting strategies. Rules, too, are man-made and can thus be changed. It is possible that the choice of strategies that do not fit the existing rules because of the substantial attention they require may get parties moving, may make them think and may even lead to a change of rules. But this is a risky and conflict sensitive strategy, the success of which cannot be determined beforehand.

Guideline 6: Differentiate according to the progress of the process of problem solving

The timing of strategies is very important in processes around wicked problems. It makes no sense to develop ad hoc conflict arrangements once a conflict has broken out. Such arrangements must be part and parcel of a game design that needs to be agreed upon as much as possible at the start of the interaction process. Hence, there is a link between the progress of the interaction process and the adequacy of a management strategy. At the start of interaction, strategies are necessary that are focused on the selective activation of actors, the creation of discussion platforms, and making agreements about rules of the game. Once a process is on its way for some time, strategies are aimed at supporting interaction, creating substantive variety and the proper use of rules of the game and of arrangements. Conflict management is required in the case of stagnation and conflict. Scope, substance and rules of the game must be closely monitored and reconsidered, just like the role of the manager and the approach used. At the end of the process it is important to intensify process management, because parties are about to cash in on profit and loss in the light of the conclusion of the interaction. This generates centrifugal forces. By pointing out future profit and compensation opportunities, network management can help to keep the interaction on track.

Guideline 7: Take an independent position

The management of uncertainty presumes that the management role is taken by an actor (or more that one actor) who can occupy an independent position. After all, the manager has to earn the trust of the parties involved in order to be authoritative. This independent role is not always easy to realize or to maintain. When, for instance, a problem falls under the formal jurisdiction of a ministry, that ministry will – despite substantive interests and preferences – be required to engage in initiatives of managing uncertainty. A solution, then, is to separate those organizational units that represent the substantive interest from those who will assume network management. Possibly, a ministry may decide to involve an independent third party for this role in order to avoid any semblance of partisanship.

In addition, network managers mobilize parties to deal with a problem situation. This will bring them unavoidably into a partisan position vis-à-vis those who have interests in maintaining the problem situation. In this case, the task of the manager is to bridge the supporters and opponents of change (Forester, 1989). Also, there is a danger that network managers sooner or later will become engaged in conflicts between stakeholders, for instance, because parties feel that they are at the short end of the stick and blame the network manager for it, or because network managers can make mistakes just like anyone else. When managers lose their authoritativeness during a process, it is hardly possible to maintain the management role. In most cases it would be best to transfer their managerial role to other individuals or other organizations.

Guideline 8: Be prudent with institutional strategies

The limitations generated by institutional factors can be regarded as very disruptive by actors involved in complex decision making processes and may lead to a call for adapting institutions. Yet we must warn against the inclination of 'blaming the system'. As we stated in Chapter 10, institutions are multi-purpose vehicles that do not service dealing with specific issues alone. Institutions form the social infrastructure of many interactions and changes may have large, often unintended effects on other interactions (Hood and Jackson, 1991; Goodin, 1996). Besides that, it is very difficult and mostly impossible to return to the old situation if the effects of strategies of institutional design do not meet the expectations.

But besides the normative argument why managers should not be too quick to use strategies of institutional design, there is also the reason of efficiency. Strategies of institutional design take a lot of time and effort to implement and the results are uncertain. They also often encounter a lot of resistance from other actors because strategies of institutional design mostly try to change the 'status quo'. So, from a transaction cost perspective, strategies of institutional design are costly and should only be chosen when potential gains or costs of impasses are high and cannot otherwise be respectively achieved or reduced.

It is for these reasons that we have a preference for substantive and process-like strategies when the situation allows and only advocate the use of institutional design with some reluctance. By improving the influx of new ideas, information and knowledge, the interaction between previously divided parties, and the creation of new rules of the game and of new practices, the management of content and game will contribute in the long run to network formation and institutional innovation. Where the existing institutional relations result in a lack of focus on interests or groups and in the systematic exclusion of certain problems from the arenas of societal problem solving and decision making, it is absolutely necessary to use institutional design and network change. Incidentally, this does not have to involve comprehensive system innovations, but often will include more modest and specific forms of institutional change.

Guideline 9: Continuously evaluate management efforts and adjust when necessary

In the choice and application of network management strategies for reducing uncertainty around wicked problems, all sorts of problems may emerge. Strategies may not realize the desired results, mistakes can be made (for instance, when parties are 'forgotten' or unintentionally insulted). Naturally, one can try to remedy these mistakes. When that does not work, the network manager's reputation may become damaged. Of course, the manager can try to resolve the situation, but if he has lost his credibility and authority, he may well have to reconsider his position.

Other problems concerning the function of network management may be that the efforts required are underestimated and that more capacity has to be made available than initially planned for.

Dealing with the uncertainty of wicked problems is thus not only a continuous learning process for stakeholders about content, process and institutions, but also for the person(s) or organizations that fulfil the role of network manager. Network management, too, is a learning process. This learning results in the continuous evaluation and adjustment of one's own activities. This adjustment may include:

1   the decision to apply or suspend network management;
2   the choice and application of management strategies;
3   the scope of management strategies and efforts;
4   the conditions for network management (capacities, resources, organization, mandate);
5   the staffing of the management function: the choice of the person or organization that will fulfil this role;
6   the decision to end network management activities or to transfer the management role to others.

Management of uncertainties: a condition, but no guarantee for problem solving

Network management does improve the chances for good, interesting results as research shows (Meier and O'Toole, 2001; Agranoff and McGuire, 2003) and the lack of good network management certainly contributes to policy failure (Mandell, 2001; Van Bueren, 2003). We do want to point out, however, that the application of management strategies for dealing with uncertainties around wicked problems does not offer a *guarantee* of success. That would mean that uncertainties could be made manageable at all times. This is not the case. The management strategies we propose are aimed at starting up interaction processes between crucial actors to prevent and break through stagnation in the interactions. Whether this will succeed is not certain since management efforts will not necessarily be executed flawlessly, but also because there are more factors at play than just the activities of the network manager. But even if there is success in this regard, a ready-made solution may not be available. The management of uncertainty contributes to the creation of a favourable starting position for problem solving by bringing parties together. But it is the parties themselves who must use these opportunities to realize satisfactory solutions or measures.

11.5 Some reflections upon the management of uncertainties

Uncertainty is a phenomenon that we find hard to live with in both our private lives as well as in societal interaction. If we could, we would certainly banish uncertainty. We want to control the circumstances that determine our lives and often fool ourselves into believing we can. However, when we do not recognize our dependency upon the environment we live in, and do not try to cope with the uncertainties that follow from that, the price we pay is high: not only because we will be confronted with the limits and implications of our go-alone strategies, but also because we will miss opportunities to realize our ambitions and potential. It sometimes appears, however, as if we would rather take a certain loss than accept the uncertainty of opportunities for profit.

In this book we advocate a management of uncertainty that is not based on denial of the fundamental uncertainties surrounding contemporary societal problems nor on the inclination to eliminate them. Instead, we propose an approach that is focused on exploring and working with the difficulties and opportunities that emanate from that. The management of uncertainty, inspired by network theory, is focused on improving the learning processes that help to map the nature of uncertainties in order to discover appropriate action perspectives.

Our recommendations are focused on enhancing cognitive insights into the nature and effect of problems and solutions by involving different perceptions and ideas in the process of problem solving, and tapping into and using a larger range of research, experts and scientific insights than is usually the case (without returning to a rational synoptic approach): not to find final answers, but to get at better problem formulations, richer solutions and more choices.

By encouraging parties into strategic learning, we hope they will become aware that opportunities for dealing with their problems and achieving their objectives largely depends upon how they respond to uncertainties in their environment. Acknowledging strategic dependencies must lead to the development of new practices of problem solving where they develop skills and invest resources for cooperation and learn to bridge differences and conflict.

Institutional learning, which we strive to enhance, is highly related to the awareness that the existing institutions are often ill-equipped to support these new initiatives. In interaction processes, this insight helps to find an answer to the lack of institutional arrangements, for instance, through developing new rules of the game. Institutional learning may also result in initiatives for institutional design, aimed at developing institutional links or breaking through institutional barriers, or enabling new types of interaction and supporting these in a robust, transparent and fair manner.

A normative position: improving problem solving and decision making in network settings

To avoid any misunderstanding of our normative positions, we would like to explicitly illuminate them at the end of this book. This sketch of the management of uncertainty through enhancing interaction between mutually dependent parties, although based on network theory, is not a plea for the institutionalization of the practices we associate with empirical policy networks. We should not make the mistake of confusing the empirical object of network theory with the normative implications and recommendations this theory suggests.

We subscribe completely to the criticism about closed processes of problem solving and decision making in sheltered institutional settings, which we normally refer to as networks. Much problem solving takes place in closed subsystems, where vested interests attempt to realize solutions on close cooperation with government through the exclusion of non- or weakly represented parties, the blocking of innovative solutions that violate the dominant interests and preferences, and non-transparent processes that lack democratic control and legitimacy. The outcomes are ineffective, inefficient and insufficiently legitimized solutions and decisions that benefit those directly involved in the short run, but are undesirable from a broader perspective.

We want to emphasize that much of this criticism was raised by network theoreticians. Confusion about normative positions emerges when network theoreticians consider mutual dependencies an unavoidable, inherent characteristic of relations in a network society and take these empirical realities as a starting point for formulating recommendations. They differ in this from the 'disentanglers' who believe that dependencies must be reduced and advocate the disentanglement and simplification of institutional structures.

Our attempt to ground the management of uncertainty in network theory – which may be considered as taking a stand as 'entanglers' – is inspired by the wish to find answers to the dysfunctioning of closed networks. It is a plea for improving the quality of the process of societal problem solving and decision making in network settings. This improvement can be achieved through supporting and organizing interaction between societal parties from different sectors, breaking through the boundaries of existing networks and creating linkages between:

- ideas and representatives from different networks;
- vested interests and weak or non-represented interests;
- stakeholders and experts;
- experts (who can also be located in different networks);
- interacting parties and public and private office holders in parent organizations, especially political representatives and public authorities that seek to represent the general interest and preserve the primacy of politics.

From this perspective it is the disentanglers who (in their pursuit to limit interaction, keep arenas manageable, and to cut into institutional provisions meant to guarantee the interests of other sectors and parties with little societal resources) inhibit breaking through closed networks between vested interests and governments. In general our position can be summarized as follows:

- Networks are here to stay and we need concepts and theories to analyse and understand complex processes in networks. This book is a further attempt to develop these necessary conceptual tools.
- Anyone who tries to solve societal problems has to deal with these networks and find ways to initiate and promote interactions between actors to achieve problem solutions. This calls for a special way of looking at management (in which learning and developing interesting solutions that mobilize necessary actors are important) and especially network management strategies. This book provides those kinds of strategies. However, there is more work to do to operationalize and validate these strategies and to identify conditions and pitfalls.
- If networks are here to stay, we must rethink the way we incorporate important concepts like democracy, accountability, general interest and so on.

It is clear that strong tensions exist between the usual institutional features of parliamentary democracy and the empirical reality of decision making in networks. Although we give some suggestions in this book, for instance, to enhance transparency in networks, to incorporate a broader set of actors and interest in problem solving, and to link traditional democratic decision making to horizontal forms of policy making, this is a field where much work still has to be done. It is certainly a field of research for network theory that we consider very important, not only because we think networks represent a more advanced form of democracy (Pollitt, 2003: 65), but also because this could be the way to improve the democratic character of decision making in networks.

The management of uncertainties: wicked problems, difficult challenges

We are aware that our message is not an easy one: our proposals for the management of uncertainty do not lead to the simple and unambiguous solutions, management proposals or organizational models that everyone silently hopes for.

This book does not provide clear-cut recipes for dealing with societal issues and for organizing societal decision making. Although we have systematically and coherently elaborated the scientific and societal added value of theoretical and empirically founded insights of, among other things, the network approach, and have provided prescriptions for dealing with the substantive, strategic and institutional factors that play a role in societal problem solving, the result is not an operational design of uncertainty management of wicked problems. We are aware that, for application in practice, our ideas require further elaboration, that they will not always work in every situation, and that, when applied, many questions will be raised that we have not foreseen. Our work, therefore, is not finished with this book. We see it as an ongoing concern. We hope that the publication of our book will inspire practitioners in governments, private business and civil society, researchers like ourselves, and students to further think through the consistency and implications of our ideas and to further operationalize, test and improve them.

Bibliography

Agranoff, R.I. (1986) *Intergovernmental Management. Human Services Problem-Solving in Six Metropolitan Areas*, Albany, New York: State University of New York Press.

Agranoff, R.I. (2003) *Leveraging Networks: A Guide for Public Managers Working Across Organizations*, Arlington: IBM Endowment for The Business of Government.

Agranoff, R. and M. McGuire (2001) Big questions in public network management research, in: *Journal of Public Administration Research and Theory*, 11: 295–326.

Agranoff, R. and M. McGuire (2003) *Collaborative Public Management; New Strategies for Local Governments*, Washington, DC: Georgetown University Press.

Aiken, M. and J. Hage (1968) Organizational interdependence and intra-organizational structure, in: *American Sociological Review*, 33 (6): 912–930.

Aldrich, H.A. (1979) *Organizations and Environments*, Englewood Cliffs: Prentice-Hall.

Aldrich, H.A. and H.D.A. Whetten (1981) Organization-sets, Action-sets and Networks: Making the most out of Simplicity, in: P.C. Nystrom and W.H. Starbuck (eds) (1981) *Handbook of Organizational Design*, vol. 1, Oxford: Oxford University Press: 385–408.

Allison, G.T. (1971) *Essence of Decision*, Boston: Little, Brown & Company [second edition 1999, co-authored by Ph. Zelikow, New York: Longman].

Alter, C. and J. Hage (1993) *Organizations Working Together*, Newbury Park: Sage.

Anderson, J.E. (1984) *Public Policy Making*, New York: CBS College Publishing.

Arentsen, M., H. Bressers and L. O'Toole (1999) Omgaan met onzekerheid in het milieubeleid: een analyse met illustraties uit de Nederlandse en Amerikaanse beleidsspraktijk, in: *Beleidswetenschap*, 4.

Argyris, C. and M.D. Cohen (1976) Single loop and double loop models in research on decision making, in: *Administrative Science Quarterly*, 21 (3): 363–375.

Argyris, C. and D.A. Schön (1978) *Organizational Learning: a Theory of Action Perspective*, Reading, MA: Addison-Wesley.

Arrow, K.J. (1963) *Social Choice and Individual Values*, second edition, New York: John Wiley.

Axelrod, R. (1984) *The Evolution of Cooperation*, New York: Basic Books.

Bachrach, P. and M.S. Baratz (1962) Two faces of power, in: *American Political Science Review*, 56 (4): 947–952.

Bachrach, P. and M.S. Baratz (1970) *Power and Poverty; Theory and Practice*, New York: Oxford University Press.

Bardach, E. (1977) *The Implementation Game: What Happens After a Bill Becomes Law?* Cambridge, MA: MIT Press.

Barney, J.B. and W. Hesterly (1996) Organisational economics: understanding the relationship between organisations and economic analysis, in: S.R. Clegg, C. Hardy and W.R. Nord (eds) *Handbook of Organisation Studies*, London: Sage.

Barret, S. and C. Fudge (1981) *Policy and Action; Essays on the Implementation of Public Policy*, London: Methuen.

Baumgartner, F.R. and B.D. Jones (1993) *Agendas and Instability in American Politics*, Chicago/London: The University of Chicago Press.

Beck, U. (1992) *Risk Society. Towards a New Modernity*, London/Newbury Park/New Delhi: Sage.

Benson, J.K. (1978) The interorganizational network as a political economy, in: L. Karpik (ed.) (1978) *Organization and Environment*, Deventer: Kluwer: 69–102.

Benson, J.K. (1982) A framework for policy analysis, in: D.L. Rogers and D.A. Whetten (eds) (1982) *Interorganizational Coordination: Theory, Research, and Implementation*, Ames: Iowa State University Press: 137–176.

Berger, L. and T. Luckmann (1966) *The Social Construction of Reality, A Treatise in the Sociology of Knowledge*, Harmondsworth: Penguin Books.

Blau, P.M. (1982) Structural sociology and network analysis: an overview, in: P.V. Marsden and N. Lin (eds) (1982) *Social Structure and Network Analysis*, London: Sage: 273–280.

Blom-Hansen, J. (1997) A new institutional perspective on policy networks, in: *Public Administration*, 75 (winter): 669–693.

Boniecki, G. (1980) What are the limits to man's time and space horizon, in: *Technological Forecasting and Social Change*, vol. 17: 161–175.

Börzel, T.A. (1998) Organising Babylon – on the different conceptions of policy networks, in: *Public Administration*, 76: 253–273.

Bozeman, B. (1987) *All Organisations are Public*, San Francisco: Jossey-Bass.

Bozeman, B. (ed.) (1993) *Public Management: the State of the Art*, San Francisco: Jossey-Bass.

Bradach, J.L. and R.G. Eccles (1989) Price, authority and trust. From ideal types to plural forms, in: *Annual Review of Sociology*, 15: 97–118.

Brandenburger, A. and B. Nalebuff (1996) *Co-opetition*, New York: Doubleday.

Brans, M. (1997) Challenges to the practice and theory of public administration in Europe, in: *Journal of Theoretical Politics*, 9 (3): 389–415.

Braybrooke, D. and C.E. Lindblom (1963) *A Strategy of Decision: Policy Evaluation as a Social Process*, New York: Free Press.

Bressers, J.Th.A., L.J. O'Toole Jr and J. Richardson (1994) Networks as models of analysis: water policy in comparative perspective, in: *Environmental Politics*, 3 (4): 1–23.

Bronner, R. (1982) *Decisionmaking Under Time Pressure*, Lexington, MA: Health.

Brown, J. (ed.) (1989) *Environmental Threats, Perception Management*, London: Belhaven.

Brown, L.D. (1983) *Managing Conflict at Organizational Interfaces*, Reading, MA: Addison-Wesley.

Bruijn, J.A. de and E.F. ten Heuvelhof (2002) Policy analysis and decision making in a network: how to improve the quality of analysis and the impact on decision making, in: *Impact Assessment and Project Appraisal*, 4 (20): 232–242.

Bruijn, J.A. de, E.F. ten Heuvelhof and R.J. in 't Veld (2002) *Process Management. Why Project Management Fails in Complex Decision Making Processes*, Dordrecht: Kluwer Academic Publishers.

Bryson, J.M. and B. Crosby (1992) *Leadership for the Common Good; Tackling Public Problems in a Shared Power World*, San Francisco: Jossey-Bass.

Bueren, E. van, E.H. Klijn and J.F.M. Koppenjan (2003) Dealing with wicked problems in networks: analysing an environmental debate from a network perspective, in: *Journal of Public Administration Research and Theory*, 13: 193–212.

Burns, T.R. and H. Flam (1987) *The Shaping of Social Organization; Social Rule System Theory with Application*, London: Sage.

Burton, J.W. (1996) *Conflict Resolution. Its Language and Processes*, London: Scarecrow Press.

Buuren, M.W. van (2002) *Productschap, Quo Vadis? Vechten en volgen in een dynamisch netwerk. Afstudeerscriptie*, Erasmus Universiteit Rotterdam.

Buuren, M.W. van and E.H. Klijn (2004) *Kapitein in de storm; een instutionele analyse van de rol van het productschap vis in een veranderend zeevisserijnetwerk*, Bestuurswetenschappen, forthcoming.

Castells, M. (1997) *The Power of Identity*, Oxford: Blackwell Publishers.

Castells, M. (2000, first edition 1996) *The Rise of the Network Society: Economy, Society and Culture*, Cambridge: Blackwell Publishers.

Cawson, A. (1986) *Corporatism and Political Theory*, Oxford: Blackwell.

Chandler, A. (1962) *Strategy and Structure: Chapters in the History of Industrial Enterprise*, Cambridge, MA: MIT Press.

Chandler A.D. Jr, (1977) *The Visible Hand. The Managerial Revolution in American Business*, Cambridge: Harvard University Press.

Child, J. (1998) Trust and international strategic alliances: the case of sino-foreign joint ventures, in: C. Lane and R. Bachman (eds) *Trust Within and Between Organizations. Conceptual Issues and Empirical Applications*, Oxford: Oxford University Press: 241–272.

Cobb, R.W. and C.D. Elder (1983, first edition 1972) *Participation in American Politics: The Dynamics of Agenda-building*, Baltimore: Johns Hopkins University Press.

Cohen, I.J. (1989) *Structuration Theory: Anthony Giddens and the Constitution of Social Life*, London: St Martin's Press.

Cohen, M.D., J.G. March and J.P. Olsen (1972) A garbage can model of organizational choice, in: *Administrative Science Quarterly*, 17 (1): 1–25.

Cohen, M.D., J.G. March and J.P. Olsen (1976) People, problems and solutions and the ambiguity of relevance, in: J.G. March and J.P. Olsen (1976) *Ambiguity and Choice in Organizations*, Bergen: Universitetsforlaget: 24–37.

Coleman, J.S. (1990) *The Foundations of Social Theory*, Cambridge, MA: Belknap Press of Harvard University Press.

Cook, K.S. (1977) Exchange and power in networks of interorganizational relations, in: *The Sociological Quarterly*, 18 (1): 62–82.

Couwenberg, S.W. (1979) *Modern constitutioneel recht en emancipatie van de mens*, deel 1 en 2, Assen: Van Gorcum.

Crozier, M. (1964) *The Bureaucratic Phenomenon*, Chicago: University of Chicago Press.

Crozier, M. and E. Friedberg (1980) *Actors and Systems: The Politics of Collective Action*, Chicago: University of Chicago Press.

Daemen, H.H.F.M. and L. Schaap (eds) (2000) *Citizen and City: Developments in Fifteen Local Democracies in Europe*, Delft: Eburon.

Dahl, R.A. (1961) *Who Governs? Democracy and Power in an American City*, New Haven: Yale University Press.

Dahl, R.A. (ed.) (1966) *Political Opposition in Western Democracies*, New Haven: Yale University Press.

Dahl, R.A. (1970) *After the Revolution? Authority in a Good Society*, New Haven: Yale University Press.

Dahl, R.A. and C.E. Lindblom (1953) *Politics, Economics and Welfare: Planning and Politico-economic Systems, Resolved into Basic Processes*, New York: Harper and Brothers.

Deakin, S. and J. Michie (eds) (1997) *Contract, Co-operation, and competition; studies in economics, Management and Law*, Oxford: Oxford University Press.

Deakin, S. and F. Wilkinson (1998) Contract law and the economics of interorganisational trust, in: C. Lane and R. Bachman (eds) (1998) *Trust Within and Between Organizations; Conceptual Issues and Empirical Applications*, Oxford: Oxford University Press.

DeLeon, P. (1988) *Advise and Consent. The Development of the Policy Sciences*, New York: Russel Sage Foundation.

Denters, B., O. van Heffen, J. Huisman and P.J. Klok (eds) (2003) *The Rise of Interactive Governance and Quasi Markets*, The Hague: Kluwer Academic Publishers.

Dery, D. (1984) *Problem Definition in Policy Analsysis*, Kansas: University Press of Kansas.

Dimaggio, P. and W. Powell (1983) The iron cage revisited: institutional isomorphism and collective rationality in organizational fields, in: *American Sociological Review*, 48: 147–160.

Donaldson, G. and J.W. Lorsch (1983) *Decision Making at the Top: the Shaping of Strategic Direction*, New York: Basic Books.

Douglas, M. and A. Wildavsky (1982) *Risk and Culture. An Essay on the Selection of Technological and Environmental Dangers*, Berkeley/Los Angeles/London: University of California Press.

Dowding, K. (1995) Model or metaphor? A critical review of the policy network approach, in: *Political Studies*, XLIII: 136–158.

Downs, A. (1957) *An Economic Theory of Democracy*, New York: Harper.

Dryzek, J.S. (1990) *Discursive Democracy: Politics, Policy and Political Science*, Cambridge: Cambridge University Press.

Dryzek, J.S. (1997) *The Politics of the Earth. Environmental Discourses*, Oxford: Oxford University Press.

Dryzek, J.S. and B. Ripley (1988) The ambition of policy design, in: *Policy Studies Review*, 7 (4): 705–719.

Duintjer, O.D. (1977) *Rondom Regels: Wijsgerige Gedachten omtrent Regel-geleid gedrag*, Meppel: Boom.

Dunn, W.N. (1981) *Public Policy Analysis: an Introduction*, Englewood Cliffs: Prentice-Hall.

Dunsire, A. (1993) Modes of governance, in: J. Kooiman (ed.) (1993) *Modern Governance. New Government-Society Interactions*, Newbury Park: Sage: 21–35.

Easton, D. (1965) *A Systems Analysis of Political Life*, New York: Wiley.

Edelenbos, J. (2000) *Proces in vorm; procesbegeleiding van interactieve beleidsvorming over locale ruimtelijke projecten*, Utrecht: Lemma.

Edelenbos, J. and E.H. Klijn (2003) *Trust in Complex Inter-organisational Cooperation*, Paper for The British Academy of Management, Knowledge into Practice, 15–17 September 2003, track: Inter Organisational relations.

Edelenbos, J. and R.A.H. Monnikhof (eds) (1998) *Spanning in interactie; een analyse van ninteractief beleid in lokale democratie*, Amsterdam: Instituut voor Publiek en Politiek.

Edelenbos, J. and R.A.H. Monnikhof (1998a) Naar een hybride democratie, in: J. Edelenbos and R.A.H. Monninkhof (red.) (1988a) *Spanning in interactie*, Amsterdam: Instituut voor Publiek en Politiek.

Edelenbos, J. and R.A.H. Monnikhof (eds) (2001) *Lokale interactieve beleidsvorming*, Utrecht: Lemma.

Edelman, M. (1971) *The Symbolic Uses of Politics: Mass Arousal and Quiescence*, Chicago: Markham Publishers.

Edelman, M. (1977) *Political Language: Words That Succeed and Policies That Fail*, New York: Academic Press.

Eemeren, F.H. van and W.K.B. Koning (red.) (1981) *Studies over taalhandelingen*, Amsterdam: Boom.

Eeten, M. van (1999) *Dialogues of the Deaf: Defining New Agendas for Environmental Deadlocks*, Delft: Eburon.

Eeten, M. van and E.F. ten Heuvelhof (1998) Servable Truth: de procescontingente inzet van wetenschappelijke expertise, in: R. Hoppe and M. Peterse (eds) (1998) *Bouwstenen voor Argumentatieve Beleidsanalyse*, 's-Gravenhage: Elsevier: 161–173.

Eeten, M. van and E. Roe (2002) *Ecology, Engineering and Management: Reconciling Ecosystems Rehabilitation and Service Reliability*, Oxford: Oxford University Press.

Eijk, C. van der and W.J.P. Kok (1975) Nondecisions reconsidered, in: *Acta Politica*, 10 (3): 277–301.

Elmore, R.F. (1979) Backward mapping: implementation research and policy decisions, in: *Political Science Quarterly*, 94 (4): 601–616.

Elster, J. (1986) Introduction, in: J. Elster, *Rational Choice*, Oxford: Blackwell.

Emerson, R.M. (1962) Power-dependence relations, in: *American Sociological Review*, 27: 31–40.

Emery, F.E. and E.L. Trist (1965) The causal texture of organizational environments, in: *Human Relations*, 18 (1): 21–32.

Erickson, B.H. (1982) Networks, ideologies and belief systems, in: P.V. Marsden and N. Lin (eds) (1982) *Social Structure and Network Analysis*, London: Sage: 159–172.

Esselbrugge, M. (2003) *Openheid en geslotenheid: een kwestie van combineren; een onderzoek naar de betekenis van openheid en geslotenheid voor het managen van meervoudige besluitvorming over ruimtelijke investeringen*, Delft: Eburon.

Etzioni, A. (1968) *The Active Society: A Theory of Societal and Political processes*, London: Collier-Macmillan.

Falconer, P.K. and K. McLaughlin (2000) Public–private partnerships and the 'New Labour' Government in Britain, in: S. Osborne (ed.) *Public Private Partnerships; Theory and Practice in International Perspective*, London: Routledge.

Faulkner, D. (1995) *International Strategic Alliances*, London: McGraw Hill.

Fischer, F. and J. Forester (eds) (1993) *The Argumentative Turn in Policy Analysis and Planning*, Durham, NC: Duke University Press.

Fisher, R. and W. Ury (1981) *Getting to Yes: Negotiating Agreement without Giving in*, Boston: Houghton Mifflin.

Freeman, J.L. (1965) *The Political Process*, New York: Random House.

Freeman, J.L. and J.P. Parrish Stevens (1987) A theoretical and conceptual re-examination of subsystem politics, in: *Public Policy and Administration*, 2 (1): 9–24.

Friend, J.K., J.M. Power and C.J.L. Yewlett (1974) *Public Planning: The Inter-corporate Dimension*, London: Tavistock.

Forester, J. (1989) *Planning in the Face of Power*, Berkeley: University of California Press.

Fox, A. (1974) *Beyond Contract; Work, Power and Trust Relations*, Oxford: Blackwell.

Fox, C.J. and H.T. Miller (1995) *Post-modern Public Administration; Towards Discourse*, London: Sage.

Fukuyama, F. (1995) *Trust, the Social Virtues and the Creation of Prosperity*, New York: The Free Press.

Gage, R.W. and M.P. Mandell (eds) (1990) *Strategies for Managing Intergovernmental Policies and Networks*, New York: Praeger.

Gambetta, D. (1988) *Trust: Making and Breaking of Cooperative Relations*, Oxford: Blackwell.

Gambetta, D. (1988a) Can we trust trust?, in: D. Gambetta (ed.) *Trust: Making and Breaking of Cooperative Relations*, Oxford: Blackwell.

Gibbons, M., C. Limonges, H. Nowotny, S. Scott and M. Trow (1994) *The New Production of Knowledge: The Dynamics of Science and Research in Contemporary Societies*, London: Sage.

Giddens, A. (1979) *Central Problems in Social Theory*, London: Macmillan.

Giddens, A. (1984) *The Constitution of Society: Outline of the Theory of Structuration*, London: Macmillan.

Glasbergen, P. (ed.) (1995) *Managing Environmental Disputes, Network Management as an Alternative*, Dordrecht: Kluwer.

Godfroy, A.J.A. (1981) *Netwerken van Organisaties: Strategieën, Spelen, Structuren*, 's-Gravenhage: Vuga.

Goodin, R.E. (ed.) (1996) *The Theory of Institutional Design*, Cambridge: Cambridge University Press.

Goodsell, C.T. (1983) *The Case for Bureaucracy*, New Jersey: Chatham.

Graeber, G. (1993) *The Embedded Firm; Understanding Networks: Actors, Resources and Processes in Interfirm Cooperation*, London: Routledge.

Grant, W.P., W. Paterson and C. Whitson (1988) *Government and the Chemical Industry*, Oxford: Clarendon Press.

Guba, E.G. (ed.) (1990) *The Paradigm Dialog*, Newbury Park, CA: Sage.

Guba, E.G. and Y.S. Lincoln (1987) *Fourth Generation Evaluation*, Beverly Hills: Sage Publications.

Guehenno, J.M. (1994) *Het einde van de democratie*, Tielt: Lannoo.

Gunsteren, H.R. van (1976) *The Quest for Control*, London: John Wiley.

Habermas, J. (1981) *Theorie des Kommunikativen Handeln*, Frankfurt am Main: Suhrkamp.

Habermas, J. (1989) *De nieuwe onoverzichtelijkheid en andere opstellen*, Meppel/Amsterdam: Boom.

Hajer, M. (1995) *The Politics of Environmental Discourse: Ecological Modernization and the Policy Process*, Oxford: Clarendon.

Hajer, M. and Wagenaar, H. (eds) (2003) *Deliberative Policy Analysis; Understanding Governance in the Network Society*, Cambridge: Cambridge University Press.

Hakansson, H. and J. Johansson (1993) The network as a governance structure; interfirm cooperation beyond markets and hierarchies, in: G. Grabher (ed.) (1993) *The Embedded Firm*, London: Routledge: 35–51.

Hall, P. (1993) Policy paradigms, social learning and the state, in: *Comparative Politics*, (25) 3: 275–296.

Ham, H. van der and J.F.M. Koppenjan (2002) *Publiek-private samenwerking bij infrastructuur; wenkend of wijkend perspectief*, Utrecht: Lemma.

Hanf, K.I. and F.W. Scharpf (eds) (1978) *Interorganizational Policy Making: Limits to Coordination and Central Control*, London: Sage.

Hanf, K.I. and Th.A.J. Toonen (eds) (1985) *Policy Implementation in Federal and Unitary Systems*, Dordrecht: Nijhoff.

Hanf, K.I., B. Hjern and D. Porter (1978) Local networks of manpower training in the Federal Republic of Germany and Sweden, in: K.I. Hanf and F.W. Scharpf (eds) (1978) *Interorganizational Policy Making: Limits to Coordination and Central Control*, London: Sage: 303–344.

Hardin, G. and J. Baden (1977) *Managing the Commons*, San Francisco: Freeman.

Hart, P. 't (1990) *Groupthink in Government. A Study of Small Groups and Policy Failure*, Amsterdam: Swetz en Zeitlinger.

Haynes, L. and N. Roden (1999) Commercialising the management and maintenance of trunk roads in the United Kingdom, in: *Transportation*, 26.

Hazeu, C.A. (2000) *Institutionele economie; een optiek op organisatie en sturingsvraagstukken*, Bussem: Uitgeverij Coutinho.

Heclo, H. (1978) Issue networks and the executive establishment in: A. King (ed.) *The New American Political System*, American Enterprise Institute for Public Policy Research, Washington, DC: 87–124.

Heclo, H. and A. Wildavsky (1974) *The Private Government of Public Money*, London: Macmillan.

Hedberg, B. (1981) How organizations learn and unlearn, in: P.C. Nystrom and W.H. Starbuck (eds) (1981) *Handbook of Organizational Design*, vol. 1, Oxford: Oxford University Press: 3–27.

Heffen, O. van, W.J.M. Kickert and J.J.A. Thomassen (eds) (2000) *Governance in Modern Society; Effects, Change and Formation of Government Institutions*, Dordrecht: Kluwer Academic Publishers.

Heinrich, C.J. and L. Lynn (2000) *Governance and performance: New Perspectives*, Washington, DC: Georgetown University Press.

Heisler, M.O. (1974) Patterns of European politics: the European 'Polity' model, in: M.O. Heisler (ed.) *Politics in Structure: Structures and Processes in Some Post-industrial Democracies*, New York: David McKay: 27–89.

Heuvelhof, E.F. ten (1993) *Gedragsnormen voor overheden in horizontale structuren: het alterneren van eenzijdige en meerzijdige vormen van sturing bij de toepassing van het principe 'de vervuiler betaalt'*, 's-Gravenhage: Vuga.

Hindmoor, A. (1998) The importance of being trusted: transaction costs and policy network theory, in: *Public Administration*, 76 (spring): 25–43.

Hirschman, A.O. (1970) *Exit, Voice and Loyalty. Responses to Decline in Firms, Organizations and States*, Cambridge, MA: Harvard University Press.

Hirst, P. (1990) *Representative Democracy and Its Limits*, Cambridge: Polity Press.

Hirst, P. (1994) *Associative Democracy*, Cambridge: Polity Press.

Hirst, P. (1997) *From Statism to Pluralism; Democracy, Civil Society and Global Politics*, London: UCL Press.

Hisschemöller, M. and R. Hoppe (1996) Coping with untractable controversies. The case for problem structuring in policy design and analysis, in: *Knowledge and Policy. The International Journal of Knowledge Transfer and Utilization* 4 (8): 40–60.

Hjern, B. and D.O. Porter (1981) Implementation structures: a new unit for administrative analysis, in: *Organizational Studies*, 3: 211–237.

Hogwood, B.W. and L.A. Gunn (1984) *Policy Analysis for the Real World*, Oxford: Oxford University Press.

Holland, P.W. and S. Leinhart (1979) *Perspectives of Social Network Research*, New York: Academic Press.

Homburg, V.M.F. (2001) Politics and property rights in information exchange, in: *Knowledge, Technology and Policy*, 13 (3) (Fall): 49–66.

Hood, C.C. (1983) *The Tools of Government*, London: Macmillan.

Hood, C.C. (1991) A public management for all seasons, in: *Public Administration*, 69 (1): 3–19.

Hood, C.C. and M. Jackson (1991) *Administrative Argument*, Dartmouth: Aldershot.

Hood, C.C., H. Rothenstein and R. Baldwin (2001) *The Government of Risk; Understanding Risk Regulation Regimes*, Oxford: Oxford University Press.

Hoppe, R. (1989) *Het beleidsprobleem geproblematiseerd*, Muiderberg: Continho.

Hoppe, R. (1999) Policy Analysis, Science and Politics, from 'Speaking Truth to Power' to 'Making Sense Together', in: *Science and Public Policy*, (26) 3: 201–210.

Hoppe, R. and A. Edwards (1985) Beleidsvorming: benaderingen in soorten en maten, in: R. Hoppe (ed.) *Trends in beleidsvormingstheorieën en ontwerpleer*, Amsterdam: VU Uitgeverij: 27–62.

Hoppe, R. and M. Peterse (1998) *Bouwstenen voor Argumentatieve Beleidsanalyse*, s'-Gravenhage: Elsevier.

Hufen, J.A.M. and A.B. Ringeling (eds) (1990) *Beleidsnetwerken: Overheids-, semi-overheids- en particuliere Organisaties in Wisselwerking*, 's-Gravenhage: Vuga.

Hult, K. and Ch. Walcott (1990) *Governing Public Organizations*, Brooks/Cole, Pacific Grove.

Hunt, J.W. (1972) *The Restless Organization*, Sydney: Wiley.

Huxham, C. (2000) The challenge of collaborative government, in: *Public Management Review*, 2: 337–357.

Huxham, C. and S. Vangen (2000) What makes partnerships work?, in: S. Osborne (ed.) *Public–Private Partnerships; Theory and Practice in International Perspective*, London: Routledge.

Immers, W. (2002) *PFI, een goede weg naar wegen*, doctoraalscriptie, Rotterdam.

Irwin, A. (1995) *Citizen Science: A Study of People, Expertise and Sunstainable Development*, London: Routledge.

Jacobs, J. (1992) *Systems of Survival, a Dialogue on Moral Foundations of Commerce and Politics*, New York: Random House.

Janis, I.L. (1982) *Groupthink. Psychological Studies of Policy Decisions and Fiascoes*, Boston: Houghton Mifflin.

Jasanoff, S. (1994) *The Fifth Branche. Science Advisers as Policy Makers*, Cambridge, MA/ London: Harvard University Press.

Jasanoff, S. (1996) Science and norms in global environmental regions, in: O. Hampson and J. Reppy (eds) *Earthly Goods: Environmental Change and Social Justice*, London/Ithaca, NY: Cornell University Press: 173–179.

Jenkins, W.I. (1978) *Policy Analysis. A Political and Organizational Perspective*, London: Martin Robertson.

Jensen, M.C. and W.H. Meckling (1976) The theory of the firm: managerial behaviour, agency costs and ownership structure, in: *Journal of Financial Economics*: 305–360, reprinted in: P.J. Buckley and J. Michie (eds) *Firms, Organizations and Contracts; a Reader in Industrial Organization*, Oxford: Oxford University Press: 103–167.

Jong, M. de, K. Lalenis and V. Mamadouth (2002) *The Theory and Practice of Institutional Transplantation; Experiences with the Transfer of Policy Institutions*, Dordrecht: Kluwer Academic Publishers.

Jordan, G. (1990) Sub-governments, policy communities and networks: refilling the old bottles?, in: *Journal of Theoretical Politics*, 2 (3): 319–338.

Kalma, P. (1982) *De illusie van de democratische staat*, Deventer: Kluwer.

Karpik, L. (ed.) (1978) *Organization and Environment*, London: Sage.

Kaufmann, F.X., G. Majone and V. Ostrom (eds) (1986) *Guidance, Control and Evaluation in the Public Sector: The Bielefeld Interdisciplinary Project*, Berlin: Walter de Gruyter.

Keeney, R.I. (1992) *Value-focused Thinking. A Path to Creative Decision Making*, Cambridge, MA/London: Harvard University Press.

Kelman, S. (1987) *Making Public Policy: a Hopeful View of American Government*, New York: Basic Books.

Kenniscentrum (1998) Eindrapport Meer Waarde door Samen Werken, 's-Gravenhage. Ministry of Finance Projectbureau PPS.

Kenniscentrum (1999) Ministerie van Financiën (1999) Kenniscentrum Publiek-Private Samenwerking, Voortgangsrapportage PPS, April 1999, 's-Gravenhage.

Kettl, D.F. (1988) *Government by Proxy*, Washington, DC: Congressional Quarterly Inc.

Kettl, D.F. (2000) *The Global Public Management Revolution; a Report on the Transformation of Governance*, Washington, DC: Brookings Institution Press.

Kickert, W.J.M. (ed.) (1997) *Public Management and Administrative Reform in Western Europe*, Cheltenham: Edward Elgar Publishers.

Kickert, W.J.M., E.H. Klijn and J.F.M. Koppenjan (eds) (1997) *Managing Complex Networks; Strategies for the Public Sector*, London: Sage.

Kingdon, J.W. (1984) *Agendas, Alternatives and Public Policies*, Boston: Little, Brown & Company [second edition 1995, New York: Harper Collins College Publishers].

Kiser, L. and V. Ostrom (1982) The three worlds of action: a meta-theoretical synthesis of institutional approaches, in: E. Ostrom (ed.) *Strategies of Political Inquiry*, Beverly Hills: Sage: 197–222.

Klijn, E.H. (1996) *Regels en sturing in netwerken. De invloed van netwerkregels op de herstructurering van naoorlogse wijken*, Delft: Eburon.

Klijn, E.H. (1996a) Analysing and managing policy processes in complex networks, in: *Administration and Society*, 28 (1): 90–119.

Klijn, E.H. (1997) Policy networks: an overview, in: W.J.M. Kickert, E.H. Klijn and J.F.M. Koppenjan (eds) (1997) *Managing Complex Networks; Strategies for the Public Sector*, London: Sage: 14–34.

Klijn, E.H. (2001) Rules as institutional context for decision making in networks; the approach to post-war housing districts in two cities, in: *Administration and Society*, 33 (3) (May): 133–164.

Klijn, E.H. (2002) Governing networks in the hollow state; contracting out, process management or a combination of the two, in: *Public Management Review*, 4: 149–165.

Klijn, E.H. (2002a) Ruimtelijk beleid voor bestaand stedelijk gebied, in: *Beleidswetenschap*, 15: 444–460.

Klijn, E.H. (2003) Does interactive policy making work?; expanding Rotterdam port, in: B. Denters, O. van Heffen, J. Huisman and P.J. Klok *The Rise of Interactive Governance and Quasi Markets*, Den Haag: Kluwer Academic Publishers: 15–42.

Klijn, E.H. and J.F.M. Koppenjan (2000) Public management and policy networks; foundations of a network approach to governance, in: *Public Management*, 2 (2): 135–158.

Klijn, E.H. and J.F.M. Koppenjan (2000a) Politicians and interactive decision making: institutional spoilsports or playmakers, in: *Public Administration*, (78) 2: 365–387.

Klijn, E.H. and J.F.M. Koppenjan (2003) Rediscovering the citizen: new roles for politicians in interactive policy making, in: P. McLaverty (ed.) *Public Participation and Innovations in Community Governance*, Aldershot: Ashgate: 141–164.

Klijn, E.H. and G.R. Teisman (2000) Governing public–private partnerships; analysing and managing the processes and institutional characteristics of public–private partnerships, in: S. Osborne (ed.) (2000) *Public–Private Partnerships; Theory and Practice in International Perspective*, London: Routledge.

Klijn, E.H. and G.R. Tiesman (2003) Institutional and strategic barriers to public–private partnerships: an analysis of Dutch cases, in: *Public Money and Management*, 23 (3): 137–146.

Klijn, E.H., E. van Bueren and J.F.M. Koppenjan (2000) *Spelen met onzekerheid; over diffuse besluitvorming in beleidsnetwerken en de mogelijkheden voor management*, Delft: Eburon.

Klijn, E.H., J.F.M. Koppenjan and C.J.A.M. Termeer (1995) Managing networks in the public sector: a theoretical study of management strategies in policy networks, in: *Public Administration*, 73 (3): 437–454.

Kooiman, J. (ed.) (1993) *Modern Governance. New Government-Society Interactions*, Newbury Park: Sage.

Kooiman, J. and K.A. Eliassen (1987) *Managing Public Organizations: Lessons from Contemporary European Experience*, London: Sage.

Koppenjan, J.F.M. (1993) *Management van de Beleidsvorming: Een Studie naar de Totstandkoming van Beleid op het Terrein van het Binnenlands Bestuur*, 's-Gravenhage: Vuga.

Koppenjan, J.F.M. (2001) Reorganizing government. institutional sclerosis and polder politics, in: F. Hendriks and Th.A.J. Toonen (eds) *Polder Politics. The re-invention of Consensus Democracy in The Netherlands*, Ashgate: Aldershot: 163–172.

Koppenjan, J.F.M. (2003) Interactive policy making as institutional design for local democracy, in: B. Denkers *et al.* (2003) *The Rise of Interactive Governance and Quasi-Markets*, Dordrecht/Boston/London: Kluwer Academic Publishers: 69–90.

Koppenjan, J.F.M. (2003a) Building Public Private Partnerships: Towards a Logic of Connection, in: P. Hibbert (ed) *Co-creating Emergent Insight. Multi Organizational Partnerships, Alliances and Networks*, Glasgow: University of Strathclyde: 297–303.

Koppenjan, J.F.M. (2004) The Formation of Public Private Partnerships: Lessons from Nine Transport Infrastructure Problems in the Netherlands, in *Public Administration*, forthcoming.

Koppenjan, J.F.M., A.B. Ringeling and R.H.A. te Velde (eds) (1987) *Beleidsvorming in Nederland*, 's-Gravenhage: Vuga.

Kramer, R.M. and T.R. Tyler (eds) (1996) *Trust in Organizations; Frontiers of Theory and Research*, Thousand Oaks: Sage.

Labohm, H.H.J. and D. Toenes (2001) Opwarmingstheorie is kwestie van politieke correctheid, NRC-Handelsblad, 31 July 2001.

Lane, C. and R. Bachman (eds) (1998) *Trust Within and Between Organizations; Conceptual Issues and Empirical Applications*, Oxford: Oxford University Press.

Lane, J.E. (2000) *New Public Management*, London: Routledge.

Lasswell, H.D. (1958) *Politics: Who gets What, When, How?*, Cleveland, Ohio: Meridian Books [first edition 1936].

Laumann, E.O. and D. Knoke (1987) *The Organizational State: Social Choice in National Policy Domains*, Wisconsin: University of Wisconsin Press.

Laumann, E.O. and F.U. Pappi (1976) *Networks of Collective Action: A Perspective on Community Influence System*, New York: Academic Press.

Lawrence, P.R. and J.W. Lorsch (1967) *Organization and Environment*, Boston: Harvard University Press.

Lehmbruch, G. and P.C. Schmitter (eds) (1982) *Patterns of Corporatist Policy-making*, London: Sage.

Levine, S. and P.E. White (1961) Exchange as a conceptual framework for the study of interorganizational relationships, in: *Administrative Science Quarterly*, 5: 583–601.

Levy, A. and U. Merry (1986) *Organizational Transformation. Approaches, Strategies, Theories*, New York: Praeger.

Lijphart, A. (1975) *Politics of Accommodation, Pluralism and Democracy in the Netherlands*, Berkeley: University of California Press.

Lindblom, C.E. (1959) The science of muddling through, in: *Public Administration*, 19: 79–88.

Lindblom, C.E. (1965) *The Intelligence of Democracy*, New York: Free Press.

Lindblom, C.E. (1979) Still muddling not yet through, in: *Public Administration Review*, 39 (6): 517–523.

Lindblom, C.E. and D.K. Cohen (1979) *Usable Knowledge: Social Science and Social Problem Solving*, New Haven: Yale University Press.

Lipsky, M. (1980) *Street-level Bureaucracy: Dilemmas of Individuals in Public Service*, New York: Russell Sage.

Litwak, E. and L.F. Hylton (1962) Interorganizational Analysis: a Hypothesis on Co-ordinating Agencies, in: *Administrative Science Quarterly*, 6 (4): 395–420.

Lorenz, E.H. (1988) Neither friends nor strangers. Informal networks of subcontracting in French industry, in: D. Gambetta (ed.) *Trust. Making and Breaking Cooperative Relations*, Oxford: 194–210.

Lorsch, J.W. (1975) Environment, Organization and the Individual, in: A.R. Negandhi (ed.) (1975): 77–89.

Lovenduski, J. and J. Outshoorn (eds) (1986) *The New Politics of Abortion*, London: Sage.

Lowi, T.J. (1963) American business, public policy, case studies and political theory, in: *World Politics*, 16: 677–715.

Lowndes, V. and C. Skelcher (1998) The dynamics of multi-organisational partnerships: an analysis of changing modes of governance, in: *Public Administration*, 76 (2): 313–334.

Lowndes, V., L. Pratchett and G. Stoker (2001) Trends in public participation: part 1 local government perspectives, in: *Public Administration*, 79 (1): 205–222.

Lundvall, B.A. (1993) Explaining interfirm cooperation; limits of the transaction-cost approach, in: Graeber (ed.) (1993) *The Embedded Firm; Understanding Networks: Actors, Resources and Processes in Interfirm Cooperation*, London: Routledge.

Lynn, L.E. (1981) *Managing the Public's Business, The Job of the Government Executive*, New York: Basic Books.

Lynn, L.E. Jr (1993) Policy achievement as a collective good: a strategic perspective on managing social programs, in: B. Bozeman (ed.) (1993) *Public Management: the State of the Art*, San Francisco: Jossey-Bass: 108–133.

Lyons, B. and J. Metha (1997) Private sector business contracts: the text between the lines, in: S. Deakin and J. Michie (eds) *Contract Cooperation and Competition; Studies in Economics, Management and Law*, Oxford: Oxford University Press: 43–66.

McGrath, J.E. (1988) Time and social psychology, in: J.E. McGrath (ed.) *The Social Psychology of Time*, Beverly Hills/London: New Perspectives: 255–268.

McLaverty, P. (2002) (ed.) *Public Participation and Innovations in Community Governance*, Aldershot: Ashgate.

MacPherson, C.B. (1979) *The Life and Times of Liberal Democracy*, Oxford: Clarendon Press.

Majone, G. (1986) Mutual adjustment by debate and persuasion, in: F.X. Kaufmann, G. Majone and V. Ostrom (eds) (1986) *Guidance, Control and Evaluation in the Public Sector: The Bielefeld Interdisciplinary Project*, Berlin: Walter de Gruyter: 445–458.

Mandell, M.P. (1990) Network management: strategic behavior in the public sector, in: R.W. Gage and M.P. Mandell (eds) (1990) *Strategies for Managing Intergovernmental Policies and Networks*, New York: Praeger: 20–53.

Mandell, M.P. (ed.) (2001) *Getting Results Through Collaboration; Networks and Network Structures for Public Policy and Management*, Westport: Quorum Books.

March, J.G. (1962) The business firm as a political coalition, in: *Journal of Politics*, 24: 662–678.

March, J.G. (1978) Bounded rationality, ambiguity, and the engineering of choice, in: *The Bell Journal of Economics*, 9 (2): 587–608.

March, J.G. (1988) The technology of foolishness, in: J.G. March (ed.) *Decisions and Organisations*, Oxford: Basil Blackwell: 253–265.

March, J.G. (1989) *Decisions and Organizations*, Oxford: Basil Blackwell.

March, J.G. and J.P. Olsen (1976) *Ambiguity and Choice in Organizations*, Bergen: Universitets-forlaget.

March, J.G. and J.P. Olsen (1976a) Attention and the Ambiguity of Self Interest, in: J.G. March and J.P. Olsen (1976) *Ambiguity and Choice in Organizations*, Bergen: Universitets-forlaget: 38–53.

March, J.G. and J.P. Olsen (1983) Organizing political life: what administrative reorganization tells us about government, in: *American Political Science Review*, 77: 281–296.

March, J.G. and J.P. Olsen (1989) *Rediscovering Institutions: The Organizational Basis of Politics*, New York: Free Press.

Marin, B. and R. Mayntz (eds) (1991) *Policy Networks: Empirical Evidence and Theoretical Considerations*, Colorado: Westview Press.

Marsden, P.V. and N. Lin (eds) (1982) *Social Structure and Network Analysis*, London: Sage.

Marsh, D. (ed.) (2002) *Comparing Policy Networks in British Government*, Oxford: Clarendon Press.

Marsh, D. and R.A.W. Rhodes (eds) (1992) *Policy Networks in British Government*, Oxford: Clarendon Press.

Mason, R.O. and I.I. Mitroff (1981) *Challenging Strategic Planning Assumptions: Theory, Cases and Techniques*, New York: Wiley.

Mayntz, R. (1993) Governing failures and the problem of governability: some comments on a theoretical paradigm, in: J. Kooiman (ed.) (1993) *Modern Governance. New Government-Society Interactions*, Newbury Park: Sage: 9–20.

Meier, K.J. and L.J. O'Toole (2001) Managerial strategies and behaviour in networks: a model with evidence from U.S. public education, in: *Journal of Public Administration and Theory*, (11) 3: 271–293.

Miles, R.E. and C.C. Snow (1986) Organization: new concepts for new forms, in: *California Management review*, 28 (3).

Milward H.B. and K.G. Provan (2000) Governing the hollow state, in: *Journal of Public Administration Research and Theory*, 10 (2): 359–379.

Milward, H.B. and G.L. Wamsley (1985) Policy subsystems, networks and the tools of public management, in: K.I. Hanf and Th.A.J. Toonen (eds) (1985) *Policy Implementation in Federal and Unitary Systems*, Dordrecht: Nijhoff: 105–130.

Mintzberg, H. (1979) *The Structuring of Organizations*, Englewood Cliffs: Prentice Hall.

Moore, C.W. (1986) *The Mediation Process. Practical Strategies for Resolving Conflict*, San Francisco: Jossey-Bass.

Morgan, G. (1986) *Images of Organizations*, London: Sage.

Mulford, C.L. and D.L. Rogers (1982) definitions and models, in: D.L. Rogers and D.A. Whetten (eds) (1982) *Interorganizational Coordination: Theory, Research, and Implementation*, Ames: Iowa State University Press: 9–31.

Negandhi, A.R. (ed.) (1975) *Interorganization Theory*, Kansas City: Kansas University Press.

Nelkin, D. (1977) *Controversy: The Politics of Technical Decisions*, London: Sage.

Nelson, B. (1984) *Making an Issue of Child Abuse*, Chicago/London: University of Chicago Press.

Nestle, M. (2002) *Food Politics. How the Food Industry Influences Nutrition and Health*, Berkeley and Los Angeles: University of California Press.

Newman, J. (2003) New Labour and the politics of governance, in: A. Salminen (*et al.*) *Governance in Networks*, Amsterdam: IOS Press.

Noordergraaf, M. (2000) *Attention! Work and Behaviour of Public Managers Amidst Ambiguity*, Delft: Eburon.

Nooteboom, B. (1997) *Inter-firm Alliances; International Analysis and Design*, London: Routledge.

Nooteboom, B. (2000) *Management van Partnerships*, Schoonhoven: Academic Service.

Nooteboom, B. (2002) *Trust: Forms, Foundations, Functions, Failures and Figures*, Cheltenham: Edward Elgar Publishing.

Nooteboom, B., H. Berger and N. Noorderhaven (1997) Effects of trust and governance on relational risk, in: *Academy of Management Journal*, 40 (2): 308–338.

Nowotny, H.P. Scott and M. Gibbons (2001) *Rethinking Science. Knowledge and the Public in an Age of Uncertainty*, Cambridge: Polity Press.

Nystrom, P.C. and W.H. Starbuck (eds) (1981) *Handbook of Organizational Design*, vol. 1, Oxford: Oxford University Press.

Olsen, J.P. (1972) Public policy making and theories of organizational choice, in: *Scandinavian Political Studies*: 45–62.

Olson, M. (1965) *The Logic of Collective Action. Public Goods and the Theory of Groups*, Cambridge, MA: Harvard University Press.

Osborne, D. and T. Gaebler (1992) *Reinventing Government. How the Entrepreneurial Spirit is Transforming the Public Sector*, Reading, MA: Addison-Wesley.

Osborne, S.P. (ed.) (2000) *Public–Private Partnerships; Theory and Practice in International Perspective*, London: Routledge.

Ostrom, E. (1986) A method for institutional analysis, in: F.X. Kaufmann, G. Majone and V. Ostrom (eds) (1986) *Guidance, Control and Evaluation in the Public Sector: The Bielefeld Interdisciplinary Project*, Berlin: Walter de Gruyter: 459–479.

Ostrom, E. (1990) *Governing the Commons. The Evolution of Institutions for Collective Action*, Cambridge: Cambridge University Press.

Ostrom, E., R. Gardner and J. Walker (1994) *Rules, Games and Common Pool Resources*, Ann Arbor: University of Michigan Press.

O'Toole, L.J. (1986) Policy recommendations for multi-actor implementation: an assessment of the field, in: *Journal of Public Policy*, 6 (2): 181–210.

O'Toole, L.J. (1988) Strategies for intergovernmental management: implementing programs in interorganizational networks, in: *Journal of Public Administration*, 11 (4): 417–441.

O'Toole, L.J. (1997) Treating networks seriously: practical and research-based agendas in Public Administration, in: *Public Administration Review*, 57 (1): 45–52.

O'Toole, L.J. and R.S. Montjoy (1984) Interorganizational policy implementation, in: *Public Administration Review*, 44: 491–503.

Parker, D. and K. Vaidya (2001) An economic perspective on innovation networks, in: O. Jones, S. Conway and F. Steward (eds) *Social Interaction and Organisational Change; Actor Perspectives on Innovation Networks*, London: Imperial College Press.

Parsons, W. (1995) *Public Policy. An Introduction to the Theory and Practice of Policy Analysis*, Chetterham/Lyme: Edward Elgar.

Pateman, C. (1970) *Participation and Democratic Theory*, Cambridge: Cambridge University Press.

Patton, M. (1987) *Utilization-focused Evaluation*, London: Sage [third edition].

Pauly, S. (2001) *Ambiguïteit in het spel. De casus PolyVinylChloride*, Delft: Eburon.

Perry, J.L. and H.G. Rainey (1988) The public–private distinction in organization theory, in: *Academy of Management Review*, 13 (2): 182–201.

Peters, T.J. and R.H. Waterman (1982) *In Search of Excellence*, New York: Harper & Row.

Pfeffer, J. (1981) *Power in Organizations*, Boston: Pitman.

Pollitt, C. (1990), *Managerialism and the Public Services: the Anglo-American Experience*, Oxford: Basil Blackwell.

Pollitt, C. (1993) *Managerialism and the Public Services. Cuts or Cultural Change in the 1990's*, Oxford: Blackwell.

Pollitt, C. (2003) *The Essential Manager*, Maidenhead: Open University Press.

Pollitt, C. (2003a) Joined-up government: a survey, in: *Political Studies Review*, 1: 34–49.

Pollit, C. and G. Bouckaert (2000) *Public Management reform; a comparative analysis*, Oxford: Oxford University Press.

Pollitt, C. K. Bathgate, J. Caulfield, A. Smullen and C. Talbot (2001) Agency fever: analysis of an international policy fashion, in: *Journal of Comparative Policy Analysis*, Spring issue.

Powell, M. and P. DiMaggio (eds) (1991) *The New Institutionalism in Organizational Analysis*, Chicago, IL: University of Chicago Press.

Pressman, J.L. and A. Wildavsky (1983; first edition 1973) *Implementation: How Great Expectations in Washington Are Dashed in Oakland*, Berkeley: University of California Press.

Pröpper, I.M.A.M. (1996) Succes en falen van sturing in beleidsnetwerken, *Beleidswetenschap*, 10: 345–365.

Provan, K.G. and H.B. Milward (1995) A preliminary theory of interorganisational network effectiveness: a comparative study of four community mental health systems, in: *Administration Science Quarterly*, 40: 1–33.

Putnam, R.D. (1993) (with R. Leonardi and R.Y. Nanetti) *Making Democracy Work; Civic Traditions in Modern Italy*, Princeton: Princeton University Press.

Putnam, R.D. (1995) Tuning in, tuning out: the strange disappearance of social capital in America, in: *Political Science and Politics* (1995/XII): 664–683.

Quade, E.S. (1989) *Analysis for Public Decisions*, New York: North-Holland.

Radford, K.J. (1977) *Complex Decision Problems. An Integrated Strategy for Resolution*, Verginia: Reston Publishers.

Rainey, H.G. (1991) *Understanding and Managing Public Organizations*, San Francisco: Jossey-Bass.

Rein, M. and D.A. Schön (1986) Frame-reflective policy discourse, in: *Beleidsanalyse*, 15 (4): 4–18.

Rein, M. and D.A. Schön (1992) Reframing policy discourse, in: F. Fischer and J. Forester (eds) *The Argumentative Turn in Policy Analysis and Planning*, Durham, NC: Duke University Press: 145–166.

Rhodes, R.A.W. (1981) *Control and Power in Central and Local Relations*, Farnborough: Gower.

Rhodes, R.A.W. (1988) *Beyond Westminster and Whitehall: The Sub-central Goverments of Britain*, London: Unwin Hyman.

Rhodes, R.A.W. (1990) Policy networks: a British perspective, in: *Journal of Theoretical Politics*, 2 (3): 293–317.

Rhodes, R.A.W. (1996) The New Governance: governing without government, in: *Political Studies Association*: 651–667.

Rhodes, R.A.W. (1997) *Understanding Governance*, Buckingham: Open University Press.

Rice, T. and P. Owen (1999) *Decommissioning the Brent Spar*, London/New York: Routledge.

Richardson, J.J. (ed.) (1982) *Policy Styles in Western Europe*, London: Allen & Unwin.

Richardson, J.J. and A.G. Jordan (1979) *Governing under Pressure. The Policy Process in a Post-Parliamentary Democracy*, Oxford: Martin Robertson.

Riet, O. van de (2003) *Policy Analysis in Multi-actor Policy Settings*, Delft: Eburon.

Ring, P.S. and A. van der Ven (1992) Structuring cooperative relations between organizations, in: *Strategic Management Journal*, 13: 483–498.

Ring, P.S. and A.H. van der Ven (1994) Developmental processes of cooperative inter-organizational relationships, in: *Academy of Management Review*, 19: 90–118.

Ringeling, A.B. (1993) *Het imago van de overheid*, 's-Gravenhage: Vuga.

Ripley, R.B. and G. Franklin (1987) *Congress, the Bureaucracy and Public Policy*, Homewood, IL: Dorsey.

Rittel, H.J.W. and Webber, M.M. (1973) Dilemmas in a general theory of planning, in: *Policy Sciences*, 4: 155–169.

Robbins, S.P. (1980) *The Administrative Process*, Englewood Cliffs: Prentice Hall.

Roe, E.M. (1994) *Narrative Policy Analysis: Theory and Practice*, Durham/London: Duke University Press.

Roe, E.M. (1998) *Taking Complexity Seriously: Policy Analysis, Triangulation, and Sustainable Development*, Boston/Dordrecht/London: Kluwer.

Rogers, D.L. and C.L. Mulford (1982) Consequences, in: D.L. Rogers and D.A. Whetten (eds) (1982) *Interorganizational Coordination: Theory, Research, and Implementation*, Ames: Iowa State University Press: 32–54.

Rogers, D.L. and D.A. Whetten (eds) (1982) *Interorganizational Coordination: Theory, Research, and Implementation*, Ames: Iowa State University Press.

Rosenau, J.N. (1993) Environmental Challanges in a Global Context, in: S. Kamiencki (ed.) *Environmental Politics in the International Arena*, New York: State University of New York Press: 257–274.

Rosenthal, U., P. 't Hart and A. Kouzmin (1991), The bureaupolitics of crisis management, in: *Public Administration*, 69: 211–233.

Rousseau, D., S.B. Sitkin, R.S. Burt and C. Camerer (1998), Not so different after all: a cross discipline view of trust, in: *Academy of Management Review*, 23 (3): 393–404.

Sabatier, P.A. (1986) Top-down and bottom-up approaches to implementation research, in: *Journal of Public Policy*, 6 (1): 21–48.

Sabatier, P.A. (1988) An advocacy coalition framework of policy change and the role of policy oriented learning therein, in: *Policy Sciences*, 21: 129–168.

Sabatier, P.A. (1999) *Theories of the Policy Process. Theoretical Lenses on Public Policy*, Boulder/Oxford: Westview Press.

Sabatier, P.A. and K.I. Hanf (1985) *Strategic interaction, learning and policy evolution: a synthetic model*, in: K.I. Hanf and Th.A.J. Toonen (eds) (1985) *Policy Implementation in Federal and Unitary Systems*, Dordrecht: Nijhoff: 301–334.

Sabatier, P.A. and H.C. Jenkins-Smith (1993) *Policy Change and Learning. An Advocacy Coalition Approach*, Boulder, CO: Westview Press.

Sabine, G.H. and T.L. Thorson (1973) *A History of Political Theory*, Hinsdale, Ill.: Dryden Press.

Sako, M. (1998) Does trust improve business performance?, in: C. Lane and R. Bachman (eds) (1998) *Trust Within and Between Organizations; Conceptual Issues and Empirical Applications*, Oxford: Oxford University Press: 88–117.

Salisbury, R.H. (1968) The analysis of public policy: a search for theories and roles, in: A. Ranney (ed.) *Political Science and Public Policy*, Chicago, IL: Markheim: 151–75.

Salminen, A. (with W. van de Donk and E.H. Klijn) (eds) *Governing Networks*, Amsterdam: IOS Press.

Salter, L. (1988) *Mandated Science*, Boston: Kluwer Academic Publishers.

Schaap, L. and M.J.W. van Twist (1997), The dynamics of closedness in networks, in: W.J.M. Kickert, E.H. Klijn and J.F.M. Koppenjan (eds) *Managing Complex Networks*, London: Sage: 62–78.

Scharpf, F.W. (1978) interorganizational policy studies: issues, concepts and perspectives, in: K.I. Hanf and F.W. Scharpf (eds) (1978) *Interorganizational Policy Making: Limits to Coordination and Central Control*, London: Sage: 345–370.

Scharpf, F.W. (1997) *Games Real Actors Play. Actor-centered Institutionalism in Policy Research*, Boulder, CO: Westview Press.

Scharpf, F.W. (ed.) (1993) *Games in Hierarchies and Networks: Analytical and Empirical Approaches to the Study of Governmental Institutions*, Boulder, CO: Westview Press.

Scharpf, F.W., B. Reissert and F. Schnabel (1976) *Politikverflechtung: Theorie und Empirie des kooperativen Federalismus in der Bundesrepublik*, Kronberg: Scriptor.

Scharpf, F.W., B. Reissert and F. Schnabel (1978) Policy effectiveness and conflict avoidance in intergovernmental policy formation, in: K.I. Hanf and F.W. Scharpf (eds) (1978) *Interorganizational Policy Making: Limits to Coordination and Central Control*, London: Sage: 57–114.

Schattschneider, E.E. (1960) *The Semisovereign People: a Realist's View of Democracy in America*, New York: Holt, Rinehart and Winston.

Schein, E.H. (1985) *Organizational Culture and Leadership*, San Francisco: Jossey Bass.

Schmitter, P.C. and G. Lehmbruch (ed.) (1979) *Trends Toward Corporatist Intermediation*, London: Sage.

Schon, D.A. and M. Rein (1994) *Frame Reflection: Toward the Resolution of Intractable Policy Controversies*, New York: Basic Books.

Schumpeter, G.A. (1943) *Capitalism, Socialism and Democracy*, London: George Allen & Unwin.

Scientific Group on Decommissioning Offshore Structures (1998) *Second Report, A Report by the National Environment Research Council for the Department of Trade and Industry*.

Scott, J. (1991) *Social Network Analysis*, London: Sage.

Scott, W.R. (1995) *Institutions and Organizations*, Thousand Oaks: Sage.

Scott-Morgan, P. (1994) *The Unwritten Rules of the Game*, New York: McGraw Hill.

Searle, J.R. (1971) *The Philosophy of Language*, London: Oxford University Press.

Simon, H.A. (1957) *Administrative Behaviour: A Study of Decision Making Processes in Administrative Organization*, New York: MacMillan.

Simon, M. (1990) *De strategische functietypologie*, 's-Gravenhage: SDU.

Sociaal Cultureel Planbureau (2000) *Sociaal Cultureel Rapport; Nederland in Europa*, 's-Gravenhage: Sociaal Cultureel Planbureau.

Steunenberg, B. (2001) *Institutionele verandering; naar een bestuurskunde bewegend tussen 'vloeibare' en 'gestolde' voorkeuren*, Bussum: Uitgeverij Coutinho.

Stoker, R.P. (1991) *Reluctant Partners: Implementing Federal Policy*, Pittsburgh: University of Pittsburgh Press.

Streeck, W. and P.C. Schmitter (eds) (1985) *Private Interest Government: Beyond Market and State*, London: Sage.

Susskind, L. and J. Cruikshank (1987) *Breaking the Impasse, Consensual Approaches to Resolving Public Disputes*, New York: Basic Books.

Sydow, J. (1998) Understanding the constitution of interorganisational trust, in: C. Lane and R. Bachmann (eds) *Trust Within and Between Organizations; Conceptual Issues and Empirical Applications*, Oxford: Oxford University Press: 31–63.

Taylor, M. (1987) *The Possibility of Co-operation*, Cambridge: Cambridge University Press.

Teisman, G.R. (1992) *Complexe Besluitvorming: Een Pluricentrisch Perspectief op Besluitvorming over Ruimtelijke Investeringen*, 's-Gravenhage: Vuga.

Teisman, G.R. (1997) *Sturen via creatieve concurrentie*, Nijmegen: Katholieke Universiteit Nijmegen.

Teisman, G.R. (2000) Models for research into decision making processes: on phases, streams and decision making rounds, in: *Public Administration*, 78: 937–956.

Teisman G.R. and Klijn, E.H. (2002) Partnership arrangements: governmental rhetoric or governance scheme?, in: *Public Administration Review*, 62: 197–205.

Termeer, C.J.A.M. (1993) *Dynamiek en Inertie rondom Mestbeleid: Een Studie naar Veranderings-processen in het Varkenshouderijnetwerk*, 's-Gravenhage: Vuga.

Termeer, C.J.A.M. and J.F.M. Koppenjan (1997) Managing perceptions in networks, in: W.J.M. Kickert, E.H Klijn and J.F.M Koppenjan (eds) (1997) *Managing Complex Networks; Strategies for the Public Sector*, London: Sage: 79–98.

Thiel, S. van (2003) Sturen op afstand; over de aansturing van verzelfstandigde organisaties door kerndepartementen, in: *Management in Overheidsorganisaties*, 19 (mei) A5215: 1–25.

Thomas, W.I. (1966) *On Social Organization and Social Personality*, Chicago, IL: University of Chicago Press.

Thompson, G.J., Frances, R. Levacic and J. Mitchell (eds) (1991) *Markets, Hierarchies and Networks*, London: Sage.

Thompson, J.D. (1967) *Organizations in Action*, New York: McGraw-Hill.

Truman, D. (1964) *The Governmental Process*, New York: Knopf.

Tsebelis, G. (1990) *Nested Games: Rational Choice in Comparative Politics*, Berkeley: University of California Press.

Twist, M.J.W. van and C.J.A.M. Termeer (1991) Introduction to configuration approach: a process theory for societal steering, in: R.J. in 't Veld, L. Schaap, C.J.A.M. Termeer and M.J.W. van Twist (eds) (1991) *Autopoiesis and Configuration Theory: New Approaches to Societal Steering*, Dordrecht: Kluwer: 19–30.

Veld, R.J. in 't (1997) *Noorderlicht; over scheiding en samenballing*, 's-Gravenhage: Vuga.

Veld, R.J. in 't (ed.) (2000) *Willens en Wetens. De rollen van kennis over milieu en natuur in beleids-processen*, Utrecht: Lemma.

Veld, R.J. in 't, L. Schaap, C.J.A.M. Termeer and M.J.W. van Twist (eds) (1991) *Autopoiesis and Configuration Theory: New Approaches to Societal Steering*, Dordrecht: Kluwer.

Voogt, A.A. (1991) Managing of social cognitive configurations in a multiple context, in: R.J. in 't Veld, L. Schaap, C.J.A.M. Termeer and M.J.W. van Twist (eds) (1991) *Autopoiesis and Configuration Theory: New Approaches to Societal Steering*, Dordrecht: Kluwer: 67–79.

Waddock, S.A. (1991) A typology of social partnerships, in: *Administration and Society*, 22: 481–406.

Walker, W.E. (2000) *Uncertainty: the Challenge for Policy Analysis in the 21st Century*, Delft: Delft University of Technology.

Wamsley, G.L. (1985) Policy subsystems as a unit of analysis in implementation studies: a struggle for theoretical synthesis, in: K.I. Hanf and Th.A.J. Toonen (eds) (1985) *Policy Implementation in Federal and Unitary Systems*, Dordrecht: Nijhoff: 71–96.

Wamsley, G.L. (1990) *Refounding Public Administration*, Newbury Park: Sage.

Weggeman, J. (2003) *Controversiele besluitvorming; opkomst en functioneren van groen polderoverleg*, Utrecht: Lemma.

Weick, K.E. (1979) *The Social Psychology of Organizing*, New York: Random House.

Weimer, D. (1995) *Institutional Design*, Boston/Dordrecht: Kluwer Academic Publishers.

Weiss, C. (1977) *Using Social Research in Public Policy Making*, Lexington, MA: Lexington-Health.

Weterings, R.A.P.M. (1992) *Strategisch gebruik van risico-informatie*, Utrecht: University of Utrecht.

Wheelwright, S.C. and K.B. Clark (1992) *Revolutionizing Product Development*, New York: The Free Press.

White, H.C. (1992) *Identity and Control. A Structural Theory of Social Action*, Princeton: Princeton University Press.

Wildavsky, A. (1987) *Speaking Truth to Power: The Art and Craft of Policy Analysis*, Brunswick, NJ: Transaction Publishers.

Wildavsky, A. (1991) *Searching for Safety*, New Brunswick/Oxford: Transaction Publishers.

Wildavsky, A. (1995) *But is it True? A Citizen's Guide to Environmental Health and Safety Issues*, Cambridge, MA/London: Harvard University Press.

Wildavsky, A. and E. Tenenbaum (1981) *The Politics of Mistrust, Estimating American Oil and Gas Resources*, Beverly Hills: Sage.

Wilks, S. and M. Wright (1987) *Comparative Government Industry Relations*, Oxford: Clarendon Press.

Williamson, O.E. (1985) *The Economic Institutions of Capitalism*, New York: The Free Press.

Williamson, O.E. (1996) *The Mechanisms of Governance*, Oxford: Oxford University Press.

Williamson, P.J. (1989) *Corporatism in Perspective*, London: Sage.

Wilson, J.Q. (1973) *Political Organizations*, New York: Basic Books.

Wynne, B. (1982) Rationality and ritual, the Windscale inquiry and nuclear decisions in Britain, in: *Society for the History of Science*, Chalfont St Giles: Buckinghamshire.

Wynne, B. (1989) Frameworks of rationality in risk management. towards the testing of naïve sociology, in: J. Brown (ed.) (1989) *Environmental Threats, Perception Management*, London: Belhaven: 33–45.

Wynne, B. (1989a) Building public concern into risk management, in: J. Brown (ed.) (1989) *Environmental Threats, Perception Management*, London: Belhaven: 119–132.

Wynne, B. (1991) Risico en reflexiviteit, in: N. Hulst (ed.) *Sturing in de risico maatschappij*, Zwolle: W.E.J. Tjeenk Willink: 93–114.

Zijderveld, A.C. (1974) *Institutionalisering; een studie over het methodologische dilemma der sociale wetenschappen*, Meppel: Boom.

Zucker, L. (1986) Production of trust: institutional sources of economic structure, 1840–1920, in: *Research in Organisational Behavior*, 8: 53–111.

www.salve.it/banchedati/Domande/uk/Domande.asp
www.save.it/uk/sezioni/itermose/mosenews/mosenews.html
www.salve.it/uk/news/news.htm

Index

content uncertainty example **20–2**, **24**; couplings example **189**; evolution and outcome **122**, *123*; as example of rounds in policy games **62**; formulating new agendas 170; fragmented policy games example **56**; frequency of actors' interactions *153*; institutional

complexity/fragmentation 66–8; joint commissioning of research **180**; language difficulties 170; perceptions of actors **140**, *141*, 142; standard reaction example **96**; and strategy games 39, **40–1**, 51; working method agreements 198